SOCIAL BONDS
IN
LATER LIFE

DEDICATION

To Cheryl Allyn Miller

SOCIAL BONDS IN LATER LIFE
Aging and Interdependence

EDITORS
WARREN A. PETERSON
AND
JILL QUADAGNO

Published in cooperation with the
Midwest Council for Social Research in Aging

SAGE PUBLICATIONS Beverly Hills London New Delhi

Copyright © 1985 by Sage Publications, Inc.

All rights reserved. No part of this book may be reproduced or utilized in any form or by any means, electronic or mechanical, including photocopying, recording, or by any information storage and retrieval system, without permission in writing from the publisher.

For information address:

SAGE Publications, Inc.
275 South Beverly Drive
Beverly Hills, California 90212

SAGE Publications India Pvt. Ltd.
M-32 Market
Greater Kailash I
New Delhi 110 048 India

SAGE Publications Ltd
28 Banner Street
London EC1Y 8QE
England

Printed in the United States of America

Library of Congress Cataloging in Publication Data

Main entry under title:

Social bonds in later life.

   1. Aged—United States—Social conditions—Addresses, essays, lectures. 2. Aged—United States—Family relationships—Addresses, essays, lectures. 3. Aged—United States—Psychology—Addresses, essays, lectures. 4. Dependency (Psychology)—Addresses, essays, lectures. 5. Aged—Services for—United States—Addresses, essays, lectures. 6. Aged—United States—Care and hygiene—Addresses, essays, lectures. I. Peterson, Warren A., 1922-   II. Quadagno, Jill S.
HQ1064.U5S594   1985   305.2′6′0973   85-1830
ISBN 0-8039-2237-X
ISBN 0-8039-2238-8 (pbk.)

FIRST PRINTING

SOCIAL BONDS
IN
LATER LIFE

CONTENTS

Preface
    WARREN A. PETERSON   9

Introduction
    JILL QUADAGNO   13

PART I: INTERDEPENDENCE IN INTIMATE RELATIONSHIPS

1. Responsibility for Household Tasks: A Look at Golden Anniversary Couples Aged 75 Years and Older
   TIMOTHY H. BRUBAKER   27

2. Equity, Role Strains, and Depression Among Middle-Aged and Older Men and Women
   PATRICIA M. KEITH and ROBERT B. SCHAFER   37

3. Marriage, Gender, and Social Relations in Late Life
   KAREN ALTERGOTT   51

4. Marital Status and Life Satisfaction: A Study of Older Men
   NANCY F. MOUSER, EDWARD A. POWERS, PATRICIA M. KEITH, and WILLIS J. GOUDY   71

5. Family Relations of the Older Widow: Their Location and Importance for Her Social Life
   JEANNE M. GIBBS   91

6. Elderly Parents and the Caregiving Role: An Asymmetrical Transition
   LUCY ROSE FISCHER   105

7. Dating and Courtship in Late Life: An Exploratory Study
   KRIS BULCROFT and RICHARD BULCROFT   115

PART II: INTERDEPENDENCE IN SOCIAL SUPPORT SYSTEMS

8. Affectivity and the Interweave of Social Circles: Life Course Transitions
   JAMES C. CREECH and NICHOLAS BABCHUK   129

9. Network Analysis of Mid-Life Transitions: A Hypothesis on Phases of Change in Microstructures
   JOHN E. O'BRIEN   143

10. Interdependence in Informal Support Systems: The Case of Elderly, Urban Widows
   GLORIA D. HEINEMANN 165
11. The Mediating Role of Social Networks in the Housing Decisions of the Elderly
   ADRIAN RUTH WALTER 187
12. Who Helps the Elderly Person: A Discussion of Informal and Formal Care
   NEENA L. CHAPPELL and BETTY HAVENS 211
13. Service Needs and Support Networks of Elderly Native Americans: Family, Friends, and Social Service Agencies
   ROBERT JOHN 229

PART III: INTERDEPENDENCE IN HEALTH AND SOCIAL SERVICES

14. The Older Volunteer: The Case for Interdependence
   BARBARA PAYNE and C. NEIL BULL 251
15. The Voluntary Organization as a Support System in the Aging Process
   LINDA M. BREYTSPRAAK, BURTON P. HALPERT, and PHILIP G. OLSON 273
16. Interpersonal Support and Health of Older People
   MARSHALL J. GRANEY 287
17. Social Support and Chronic Disease: A Propositional Inventory
   SIDNEY M. STAHL and MARILYN K. POTTS 305
18. Chronic Illness and Care Provision: A Study of Alzheimer's Disease
   RACHEL FILINSON 325
19. Alzheimer's Disease as Biographical Work
   JABER F. GUBRIUM and ROBERT J. LYNOTT 349
20. Hospice: Interdependence of the Dying with Their Community
   HARRY S. SHANIS 369
21. Social Factors in Institutional Living
   EVA KAHANA, BOAZ KAHANA, and ROSALIE F. YOUNG 389

References 419

PREFACE

In this volume, we report some recent research on social bonds of older people, research conducted by predoctoral fellows, postdoctoral fellows, and faculty associated with the Midwest Council for Social Research on Aging, an interuniversity program devoted to research and research training in social gerontology. Here in the preface to the volume, I shall comment on the evolution of the Midwest Council and the development of some of the ideas upon which this research is based.

On one level, this research concerns fundamental problems in social science: What is the role of group life? What kinds of social bonds do people have and what are the consequences? How do (or can) people adjust or adapt to losses and other changes in social bonds or networks or support systems?

When such questions are applied to people in later life, there are additional, compounding issues. As people age, the physiological and social-structural conditions that favor, enable, or support interaction in social groups—conditions that support the person's social supports—change or wither or crumble. How do (or can) "supports for social supports" come to be retained or restructured?

That increasing numbers and proportions of older people live into advanced age assures that the social conditions of the older population will change, will be problematic, will be questioned. The dramatic and unprecedented shift in age composition that has occurred in this century leads to changes in norms and values and in the structures of institutions, neighborhoods, communities, and the larger society.

Part of the role of social science research in gerontology is to document, interpret, and evaluate such changes. Another role—potentially a very significant one—has to do with identifying the processes and potentials of "adding life to years" through the maintenance and reconstruction of social bonds. We can advance the proposition that the essence of meaning and fulfillment in later life (the opposite of loneliness and anomie) lies in belonging and participating in family, community, peer groups, reference groups, and other forms of group life. This leads to an associated proposition: A full and abundant social life affects mental and physical health positively; when social life is lacking or unsatisfactory, mental and physical health are adversely affected. Conversely, when mental and/or physical health falter, participation in group life declines or changes.

In social gerontology, such sentiments are likely to be identified as an expression of "activity theory," as articulated in *Personal Adjustment in Old Age,* by Ruth Cavan et al. (1949). Their central finding, based on research in a small city in Illinois, was that personal adjustment is positively associated with continued activity, social interaction, and participation in institutional life.

In the early 1950s, I found myself conducting applied research on aging in Kansas City and in need of a dissertation to fulfill the requirements for a Ph.D. in Sociology at the University of Chicago. In discussing dissertation possibilities with members of the Chicago faculty, I found that Robert Havighurst had received a grant from Carnegie to do a study of middle age and aging in an American city—a solid or typical American city, one less complex than Chicago. In part because Kansas City is reasonably typical, and because there were receptive hosts (the Kansas City Association of Trusts and Foundations and Community Studies, Inc.), the Kansas City Study of Adult Life came about.

The Kansas City Study of Adult Life had a special impact on the emerging field of social gerontology. From the study, Cumming and Henry in *Growing Old* (1961) advanced the double-barreled propositions of "disengagement theory": Societies, because of functional needs, normally and naturally encourage elders to disengage; coincidently, aging individuals receive a psychogenic message to disengage with content and resignation. From the same study and with some of the same data, Havighurst, Neugarten and associates further articulated "activity theory" and otherwise pursued issues pertaining to social interaction and social activities of older people, as reported, for example, in *Middle Age and Aging,* edited by Bernice Neugarten (1968).

A number of sociologists in the Midwest collaborated in conducting statewide surveys of the needs of the elderly in advance of the 1961 White House Conference on Aging and with the encouragement of the Regional Office of the Department of Health, Education, and Welfare. In Washington during the White House Conference, plans were made for the organization that became the Midwest Council for Social Research in Aging. To enable faculty in the region to conduct research development seminars, Arnold Rose, then at the University of Minnesota, secured a small grant from the Hill Family Foundation of St. Paul, which was matched by a grant that I secured from the Kansas City Association of Trusts and Foundations. The first seminar of the Midwest Council for Social Research on Aging was conducted in St. Paul in June of 1961. We estimate that there have been about seventy seminars since that time.

In retrospect, it appears that the Midwest Council for Social Research on Aging was born in a crest of interest and concern in social gerontology: the activity-disengagement controversy on the academic front and the 1961 White House Conference on the policy front. The 1961 Conference established aging as significant on the agenda of the liberal-welfare state. About that time aging started to become legitimate on the research agenda of sociology, psychology, and other disciplines.

The Midwest Council began with faculty research development seminars. Some of the products were brought together in *Older People and Their Social World*, edited by Arnold Rose and Warren Peterson (1965). Let me mention some highlights from that volume, published twenty years ago.

"The subculture of aging," conceptualized and discussed at some length in the faculty development seminars, was articulated in the volume by Arnold Rose. It is, in our opinion, a theorem rather than a theory or hypothesis. When a segment of people is separated or segregated from others, in-group interaction will intensify, resulting in the development of a separate identity, an "aging group consciousness," a separate set of values, a "subculture of aging." In another chapter Arnold Rose gave the interactionist's critique of disengagement theory. Pihlblad and McNamara reported from a study of the elderly in small towns that social adjustment in aging is positively correlated with high levels of social participation, good health, and higher income.

In *Older People*, Edwin A. Christ reported on the social world of stamp collectors, a world in which aging members can continue to function into advanced age. If one is embedded in the stamp collector's world, one need not participate in the subculture of aging.

Several chapters in *Older People and Their Social World* concerned the effect of formal support systems on the elderly. In this conceptualization, contradictory processes in modern aging are identified. On the one hand, informal or primary support systems seem to support and sustain morale and adjustment in aging. On the other hand, although necessary for physical maintenance, formal support systems (institutionalization, in particular) often and under some conditions have a demoralizing, depersonalizing effect.

Soon after the publication of *Older People and Their Social World*, the Midwest Council received the first of a series of training grants from the aging division of the National Institute of Child Health and Human Development and, subsequently, from the National Institute on Aging. Through 1984, over 100 predoctoral fellows and 40 postdoctoral fellows have gone through the program. They have been trained and encouraged to apply sociology and social psychology to aging in a fundamental sense. Inasmuch as social interaction, social participation, and social conditions affect, influence, and sustain people in diverse ways, the need of and potential for research seems greater than ever.

—Warren A. Peterson
Kansas City, MO

INTRODUCTION

This book focuses on the ties that hold people together and yet allow them to function with a maximum amount of self-sufficiency. Called social support systems by some, social networks by others, the terminology is less significant than the issue of how older people interact with others and establish meaningful social ties.

A core assumption that informs this book is that older people do not engage in relationships on the basis of a one-sided dependency; rather, relationships tend to be reciprocal, or, in the terminology of Maggie Kuhn, interdependent. All of the chapters examine, in one sense or another, how and the extent to which interdependence is maintained in relationships in later life. Whereas some authors find more dependence at work, others find more reciprocity; each of these forces us to recall the extent to which we are social beings, gaining meaning and purpose in life through interaction with others.

PART I: INTERDEPENDENCE IN INTIMATE RELATIONSHIPS

We begin the book with a group of articles that discuss primary relationships in later life—between parents and children, spouses and intimate others. The first article by Timothy H. Brubaker analyzes how couples who have been married for at least 50 years divide household tasks. Brubaker examines both expectations regarding work within the home and the actual division of responsibility. Some literature suggests that older couples may be more traditional in terms of the division of labor than younger couples, with males performing chores more typically defined as masculine and females doing so-called feminine work. Other research, however, has indicated that as people grow older, they become less differentiated on the basis of gender. In interviews with 32 couples in which one partner was at least 75 years old, Brubaker finds that although both husbands and wives expect some traditional division of labor, there are many activities they share. Husbands expect to be responsible for all "masculine" tasks such as doing yardwork, maintaining the car, or doing household repairs, but with the exception of cooking meals and washing dishes, they also expect to participate in many traditionally feminine tasks, such as cleaning house, shopping, and arranging family social events. Wives' perceptions are similar to those of their husbands. In general spouses' expectations were similar to their actual division of labor. Husbands generally took responsibility for all of the masculine chores, whereas wives performed several of the most basic feminine tasks. Yet they shared responsibility for earning money, planning family social events, and making family decisions. Interdependence in these relationships was manifested if, for example, a wife became ill and her husband took over more "feminine" chores. Long-term marital relationships, Brubaker concludes, are not based solely on traditional role expectations but are sufficiently flexible to meet the changing needs of the individuals.

Pat M. Keith and Robert B. Schafer are also interested in exploring the division of tasks within the family unit. Their chapter focuses on the impact various arrangements have on psychological well-being. According to concepts derived from equity theory, people determine what they feel they deserve in relationships through comparisons with others. The sense of contributing either too much or too little can lead to stress. Research has also shown that persistent role strain over the life course may have more negative consequences for mental health than a crisis such as divorce. In later life a number of readjustments in family roles occur: children leave home, women enter the labor force, and men and women retire. Keith and Schafer interviewed a sample of middle-aged and older couples to determine how they perceived their own and their spouses' efforts in performing family roles and activities. They analyzed housekeeping, cooking, companionship, and provider roles, asking respondents if they or their spouses should increase or decrease their activity in each area. The authors found that inequity and role strain were sources of stress and that women in inequitable roles were more likely to be dissatisfied than men. However, equity theory was only partially supported, and the authors conclude that the well-being of others may be given greater consideration than equity in intimate relationships and that inequities may not be important in relationships that are long-term and permanent.

Marriage affects many aspects of life, not only interactions between individuals within the household, but also their relationships to others in society. The central question asked by Karen Altergott in the next chapter concerns how marital status affects social interaction. The literature indicates that marriage enhances well-being and mental health, but findings are conflicting in terms of explaining why. One theory suggests that married people are more likely than single or widowed individuals to be more integrated into other social relationships. Other research suggests the widowed compensate for the loss of a spouse by establishing new social relationships. According to this theory, the nonmarried should be more socially involved and interact at higher levels with alternative social partners. Using a time budget analysis in which a sample of older people recorded details regarding activity, social companions, and the location and duration of events over four days—two weekdays and a Saturday and a Sunday—Altergott found that married men and women spent less time in solitude than single people. The findings changed, however, when the time spent with a spouse was eliminated. Marriage was more integrating for women, more privatizing for men. Married men were likely to spend more of their social time with spouses, whereas married women had many other social contacts. In contrast, widowed women were more likely to be socially isolated, whereas widowed men were more socially involved, usually with other relatives and with friends. Thus marriage is not the most important factor in predicting levels of social interaction; gender differences must also be taken into account.

The chapter by Nancy F. Mouser, Edward A. Powers, Patricia M. Keith and Willis J. Goudy also focuses on marital status. The authors compare the life satisfaction of married and widowed men and find that it is lower for the widowed. This in itself is not surprising. When other factors are taken into account, however, the significance of marital status disappears. What other factors contribute to increased well-being in later life? Most important is having a single confidante who provides emotional closeness. Being affiliated with voluntary organizations also raises subjective well-being as does having good health and adequate personal resources. Although children were shown to provide important aid and services, having children nearby and seeing them often had no impact on life satisfaction.

Jeanne M. Gibbs is concerned with the importance of the children and siblings for a widow after the initial period of grief is over. Using an in-depth standardized questionnaire, she examined the family support systems of forty older widows residing in two nonmetropolitan communities. Gibbs found that the widows who had family members living in the community and who interacted with them frequently experienced the greatest emotional benefits. The study concludes that rather than the net size of the family, it is the number of family members immediately available and the quality of their social interaction with the widow that is more likely to predict the importance of family relations for her.

According to Lucy Rose Fischer, children provide substantial care and support in times of crisis. Although most older people prefer to remain independent, many children, mostly daughters, provide care for their aged parents in their own homes during some period in their lives. Fischer examines the impact of a parent's health crisis on the parent-child relationship, focusing on the nature of the role transitions that occur as children assume the caretaking position. In caring for parents who had recently been released from the hospital, all of the children interviewed described their relationship to the ailing parent in terms of role reversal. None of the parents, however, defined the relationship in this way, either because they did not perceive a relational change or because they were uncomfortable with such a reversal. Because the health crisis brought about significant losses in functioning, all of the parents were depressed and experiencing frustration over their changed status and sense of helplessness. The children expressed concern for their parents' depression, as well as their accompanying personality changes, but they did not feel burdened. Many had already had a long-term history of high contact and involvement and willingly assumed increased responsibilities in giving care. In times of stress, the parent-child relationship becomes asymmetrical. Interdependence is still present, however, as a part of a long-term commitment by children to aid parents who had supported them earlier in their lives.

Although widowhood may be associated with decreased life satisfaction, this decline in sense of well-being does not occur, as we have seen, when the widowed individual is able to become a part of a social network. Particularly important is the ability to establish close emotional ties with one significant other. The chapter by Kris and Richard Bulcroft examines the quality of heterosexual dating among a group of men and women over age 60 who were members of a singles club. The authors find that the couples tended to maintain traditional role expectations; the women never asked the men for dates. However, their expectations in terms of the sexual aspect of the relationship were similar to those of younger couples. Sex was expected on the fourth or fifth date, and those who were cohabiting still maintained their own residences. Although mate selection was an important part of the dating process, some women expressed reluctance to give up their new-found freedom. Because the women generally had close friends among other women, the men were more likely to view their dating partner as a confidante.

PART II: INTERDEPENDENCE IN SOCIAL SUPPORT SYSTEMS

In this section we move beyond those relationships based largely within family networks or circles of intimate others to include a broader range of individuals who are part of support systems. These chapters focus on such issues as how social networks change over the life cycle, the ways in which informal and formal support systems provide varying kinds of help, how reciprocity affects the nature of a support network, and how formal and informal support networks interact.

James C. Creech and Nicholas Babchuk analyze how relationships change over the life course. Young adulthood tends to be characterized by low levels of involvement with others because people at this life stage are usually engaging in high levels of career and residential mobility. In the next phase, which extends into early middle age, activities with both nuclear and extended kin increase; "family-home localism" comes to dominate social involvement. In late middle age, many forms of social participation, such as the expansion of participation in voluntary associations, reach their peak. As mobility declines in old age, family and neighbors become more central. Using data from the Northern California Community Study, Creech and Babchuk mapped the social circles of dyads to determine the extent of overlap in their social relationships. The authors found that the stage in the life cycle did affect both the number and type of social networks and that the most important social circles were formed through kin ties, particularly in old age. Contrary to expectations, few of the dyads they studied had more than two social circles in common. These findings emphasize how segmented relations are in our society.

The life course is also the focus of the chapter by John O'Brien, who uses semi-structured interviews to assess the impact of a major life change—marriage, parenthood, divorce, an empty nest, residential relocation, job change, retirement, widowhood, or entry into a nursng home—on the individual personally and on his or her social network. O'Brien finds that the transitions all involve four common phases. Initially, the individual is in a condition of relative equilibrium, enacting some role in a relatively well-defined social position and supported by a social network. During the transition process, people move through four standard phases of change: (1) assessment, (2) search, (3) encounter, and (4) establishment of a new (relative) equilibrium. At the end of the transition, the individual was enacting a new role in a different social position supported by a different social network. The O'Brien chapter, then, describes both the process and the end point of major transitions in individuals and their social networks over the life course.

Although numerous transitions may occur over the life course, one common to most women is widowhood. One of the consequences of widowhood is the disruption of the informal support system. The chapter by Gloria D. Heinemann attempts to discern the relationship between the family and friendship support system, interdependent and complementary in nature and yet also unique so as to merit independent investigation. Family support systems, according to Heinemann, tend to be heterogeneous, whereas friend support groups are homogeneous; each provides different kinds of supports. The family support system, in general, is more flexible, supporting more vulnerable kin and providing them with a sense of security. The friendship support system is less flexible, requiring more from the individual

Introduction

and supporting vulnerability only when it applies to the aged cohort as a whole. This support system also fosters a sense of self-worth and accomplishment in the individual because it requires more assertiveness and reciprocal exchanges.

The chapter by Adrian Ruth Walters examines how social networks mediate housing decisions of older people. Noting that social networks are contained within the physical dimensions of home and neighborhood, Walters asks what kinds of services family and friends provide that affect housing choices. Her study was based on the analysis of data from a study conducted by the U.S. Department of Housing and Urban Development. The study was conducted to determine whether direct cash grants to families to allow them to make their own housing decisions might provide a better alternative than increases in fixed-location public housing projects. Walters found that families were a mediating structure in housing decisions, and that stage of the family life cycle was a major correlate of residential mobility. Bound by social ties, older people are willing to remain in substandard housing rather than sever meaningful relationships. Younger people, in contrast, were much more willing to move when offered a cash subsidy. Even among those older families who did choose to move, social networks played an important role. Friends and family members often helped them locate, repair, and move into new housing.

Neena Chappell and Betty Havens analyze the relationship between informal and formal care received by noninstitutionalized elderly respondents living in Winnipeg, Manitoba, Canada. Individuals were asked questions regarding their own social networks and their assistance networks. The authors compared those receiving formal assistance from community services with those who were not. In general, nonusers of formal services received less assistance and provided more assistance to others than did users. Those who received formal assistance also received a substantial amount of informal assistance. This does not mean that informal assistance can replace formal assistance; rather, they are complementary.

Robert John is also concerned with the relationship between formal and informal service utilization. John compares informal and formal service use among urban and rural Native Americans, examining how the extended family network provides direct assistance to elderly family members and how it facilitates formal service use. Using data from a 1980 nationwide study of Indian elders, John finds that reservation Indians have greater service needs than those living in urban settings, and that these needs are more likely to be filled by family members. Although urban Indians tend to rely more heavily on formal services, in both groups the family network is a primary source of aid, with children providing the most important care-giving services. That urban Indians rely more heavily on formal services may be because family members are less likely to be available to provide informal services than they are on reservations. For both groups, however, the resources available are inadequate, and many needs go unmet.

PART III: INTERDEPENDENCE IN HEALTH AND SOCIAL SERVICES

Many theories of aging tend to focus on the dependence of older people, ignoring how mutually supportive interdependent social networks temper the impact of stress. Further, by concentrating on help received, they often obscure the significant contributions older people make to these networks. In the first chapter in this section, Barbara Payne and C. Neil Bull argue that volunteering represents a unique case for studying the phenomenon of interdependence. In this study of three volunteer programs that used substantial proportions of older citizens, Payne and Bull studied how the role skills of the aged could be restructured into new peer volunteer roles. They found that the process of helping others maintain autonomy gave the volunteers increased power and independence. As the study progressed, some of those who had initially volunteered in the program found themselves in the role of recipient. Whereas research has demonstrated that the sense of reciprocity is often lost when crisis strikes an older family member, interdependence was maintained in this situation of peer helping peer.

The next chapter, by Linda M. Breytspraak, Burton Halpert, and Philip Olson, is also concerned with the significance of peer support. Focusing on informal support networks, this study compares the relative strengths of intergenerational versus peer relations in supporting women who encounter transitions of aging in themselves and among close family members and friends. The data come from a study of sixteen homemaker clubs and include group interviews with the whole club and individual interviews with club members. The authors address two interrelated issues: First, how important is the voluntary organization in lending support, and second, is the age structure of the organization a factor in its ability to provide instrumental and expressive support to individuals. Breytspraak, Halpert, and Olson conclude that the clubs were able to function as support systems and that the age structure was a determining factor in the type of support provided. Clubs with an aging membership were more likely to provide emotional support, whereas those of mixed ages provided both instrumental and expressive support.

As numerous articles have demonstrated, intimacy and strong social support networks enhance psychological well-being by making people feel needed and wanted and by allowing them to give as well as receive. Support networks also provide tremendous amounts of instrumental care, both in times of crisis and on a long-term basis. Marshall Graney, in the next chapter, examines how interpersonal supports have an impact on health. There is evidence that the presence of a positive support system can relieve stress and have an ameliorative impact on health. However, Graney advises caution in interpreting these findings too strongly because support networks may generate as well as relieve stress. Overall, it is helpful to remember that support systems may not only alleviate conditions of illness but may also contribute to wellness—an individual's capacity to manifest high levels of vigor.

A similar theme is pursued in the next chapter by Sidney M. Stahl and Marilyn Potts, who review the evolution of social support theory in relation to health, illness, and disease. Stahl and Potts point out that research has shown that family influence is important in helping an older person adhere to a medical regime, such as taking medication properly. However, like Graney, they note that family support may also have adverse consequences, as in instances when family members are overprotective and thus impede full recovery of an individual after a stroke or heart attack. In addition to informal sources of support, formal support groups that are made up of peers and health professionals may have a positive impact on an individual's ability to cope with illness. The authors integrate these different perspectives on social support through a typology of its sources, scope, and content. What is unique is their application of the theory to the chronically ill, a salient topic considering the high rates of chronic illness among the aging.

Although older people suffer from a greater variety of chronic ailments than younger people, treatment protocols have been derived from models of acute illnesses. Chronic illnesses often require care outside of a medical setting, a mode of care that impinges heavily on formal and informal support networks. However, many formal services have custodial rather than rehabilitative objectives, and it is often impossible for any single profession to provide all of the care that is necessary. Long-term assistance becomes, by default, the responsibility of the informal support group. We can observe this dilemma operating in the case of Alzheimer's disease. In her participant-observation study of an Alzheimer's support group, Rachel Filinson finds that the disease, which has no clearly identifiable etiology, is defined through a process of negotiation by the layman. Disease, in this context, is viewed more as a personal trouble rather than a health issue, and with no cure in sight, treatment is individualized. The problem is that the support group, though useful, is limited in its ability to help family caretakers cope with the practical aspects of the disease.

Jaber F. Gubrium and Robert Lynott argue even more strongly that Alzheimer's disease is a social construction, a code to render meaningful age-related troubles. They point out that Alzheimer's is both organic and behavioral with a highly variable character that hinders diagnosis. Further, no one is certain whether Alzheimer's is, in fact, a disease or if its characteristics are a part of the aging process. Because people cannot decide if Alzheimer's is a disease or not, they elaborate the definition so that the symptoms come to identify the illness. Alzheimer's becomes a reality because of the interpretive conditions and practices of those concerned.

The next chapter pursues the issue of how support networks are affected by stress, this time through an investigation of the interdependence between hospice teams, the social network of the individual, and the dying patient. According to Harry S. Shanis, the success or failure of a hospice depends at least partly on physician referrals. Because physicians are often reluctant to define patients as terminal until the last days of their lives, hospices frequently do not have the opportunity to render their supportive services properly, if the patient enters at all. Shanis's analysis of hospice care demonstrates that research must include a discussion of the patient's social network. The experience of dying in a hospital tends to exclude family and friends, whereas one of the goals of hospice care is to keep the patient's network intact. Thus a satisfactory understanding of the success of hospice care can only be reached by taking into account the relationship between the medical care-givers, family and friends, and the individual who is the recipient of care.

The final chapter in this section deals with the impact of institutionalization on self-esteem. Eva Kahana, Boaz Kahana, and Rosalie Young argue that although institutions are usually portrayed in a negative fashion, some people are less isolated after they enter an institution. Thus there may be potential for positive growth. The reasons that most studies have not found institutionalization to have positive effects is because they have not focused on the emotional gratification derived from interpersonal interactions. Using data from a four-wave longitudinal study of elderly adaptation to institutionalization, the authors compare older people who moved to an apartment complex with those who moved into nursing homes. They found that those in an institutional setting generally found life no worse than they expected and, in many instances, better. Their morale remained at moderate levels or increased during their first year of institutionalization. Kahana, Kahana, and Young believe that one explanation for the comparatively high scores on self-esteem relates to the living situation of the institutionalized elderly prior to the move. One-fourth reported having no confidantes, and the majority had only one other person to whom they spoke regularly. Thus social isolation, which was an important factor in institutional placements, may have been lessened by entry into the institution.

The chapters in this volume cover a wide range of topics from dating in later life, marital relationships, widowhood, and peer bonds to the complex network of associations that make up support systems. The theme that unites them is that of interdependence in social relationships. Some authors find a high degree of interdependence; others find that relationships become less reciprocal as people grow older. Conclusions often depend on the phase of the life cycle and the type of relationship studied. Relationships with children do appear to become more one-sided, as children fulfill a variety of service needs for elderly parents. Friendship networks, however, remain much more balanced, and it is the knowledge of interdependence that maintains them.

The findings from these chapters indicate some of the directions future research should take. Many emphasize the importance of the informal support network in providing both instrumental and emotional support. Yet it seems likely that in the future there will be fewer couples who have been married for many years, and fewer children available. One consequence will be an increase in the importance of peer bonds. The shrinking of informal support networks is also likely to increase reliance upon formal support systems, making long-term care increasingly impersonal. Thus one of the more important issues for the next century will be how to meet the instrumental and emotional needs of the aged in a manner that is not dehumanized. In a world that seems to be increasingly dominated by impersonal bureaucratic structures, it is worthwhile to consider the human side of aging and to focus on the ways social bonds render life meaningful.

—Jill Quadagno
The University of Kansas

Part I

Interdependence in Intimate Relationships

1
RESPONSIBILITY FOR HOUSEHOLD TASKS:
A Look at Golden Anniversary Couples Aged 75 Years and Older

TIMOTHY H. BRUBAKER
Associate Professor,
Home Economics and Consumer Sciences
Miami University of Ohio

The celebration of 50 years of marriage marks an accomplishment that many individuals admire in our society. While attention has been focused on the current divorce rate, few have considered the individuals who remain in their marital relationships. Although there is no precise manner of determining how many couples achieve such long-term marriages, it is estimated that no more than 3% of all marriages celebrate 50 years together (Parron and Troll, 1978). Another estimate of long-term marriages suggested that approximately 1 in 5 first marriages will remain intact for 50 or more years (Glick and Norton, 1977). Golden anniversary wives characterize a small portion of older women. For example, census data (U.S. Department of Commerce, 1983) indicate that only 1 in 5 women aged 75 years and older is married. Couples who have marked 50 years of marriage are a unique group of survivors in our society. They have survived a long-term marital relationship, and usually, have lived into their seventh decade. They provide a rare opportunity to study the interdependency of marital relationships.

This chapter examines the ways in which golden anniversary couples divide the responsibility for household tasks within their

Author's Note: *I express appreciation to Beth Kinsel for her involvement in the collection of the data and to the Family and Child Studies Center for support of this project. Also, I acknowledge Miami University's assigned research appointments, which enabled the writing of this chapter.*

marriages. Specifically, the expected and actual divisions of responsibility are considered. The following questions will be addressed: What do golden anniversary husbands expect their wives to do? What do their wives actually do? What do golden anniversary wives expect their husbands to do and what do they actually do? The divisions of household responsibility provide a glimpse of interdependency within long-term marriages. Within any marriage, there are tasks that need to be accomplished and the divisions of labor may differ. In some marriages, role differentiation is based on gender. Husbands are responsible for "masculine"-oriented tasks (e.g., taking out trash, car maintenance) while wives are responsible for "feminine"-oriented tasks (e.g., cooking, cleaning). In other marriages, the couples may divide the responsibility based on individual preference or expertise.

Although there are a few studies based on golden anniversary couples (Parron and Troll, 1978; Sporakowski and Hughston, 1978; Roberts, 1979-1980), data on the division of household tasks within these marriages have not been reported. Older couples might be expected to have differentiated household tasks on the basis of gender because they have a more traditional view of marriage than younger couples (Klemmack and Roff, 1980). On the other hand, the distinctions between "masculinity" and "femininity" may become less defined in later life (Guttman, 1977, 1975; Livson, 1983; Brim, 1976), and there may be less gender-specific division of responsibility. Also, it is important to consider the marital history of the couple. Patterns of responsibility may have been developed in earlier years of marriage and continued into the golden anniversary years. Studies of the division of household tasks within marriage will be reviewed before the data from a sample of 32 golden anniversary couples are examined.

REVIEW OF LITERATURE

The sex role literature suggests that older persons become less gender-differentiated and definitions of masculinity and femininity tend to become more similar. For example, Guttman (1977, 1975) portrayed older women as more aggressive and independent and men as less interested in instrumental tasks. It is suggested that men "recapture their femininity" in later life. Similarly, Brim (1976) theorized that there is an equalization of sex role definitions so that the differences between masculinity and femininity become blurred. More recently, Livson (1983) argued that men and women mature to a life stage in which androgyny characterizes definitions of sex roles. These theorists suggested that the differentiations based on gender become less important to older persons. Consequently, husbands are not as oriented toward instrumental activities and wives become more aggressive and independent.

Research on sex role orientations of older persons is inconclusive. Cameron (1968, 1976) and Minnigerode and Lee (1978) reported that older men and women were less gender-differentiated in their definitions of masculinity and femininity. Dobson (1983) found that expressive qualities were more important than instrumental qualities for both older husbands and wives. However, two studies (Puglisi, 1983; Puglisi and Jackson, 1980-1981) indicated that gender differentiation is characteristic of older men and women. Further, it was reported that older men are masculine-oriented. It is clear that the sex roles research does not conclusively support the theories about the definitions of masculinity and femininity in later life. If there is any relationship between husbands' and wives' definitions of sex roles and the ways in which they divide household tasks, the theoretical and research literatures provide little direction.

Older couples' divisions of household responsibility have been explored in several other studies. Keating and Cole (1980) queried 400 retired teachers and their wives to determine if retirement altered the manner in which they divide household tasks. Little change was found in the patterns established before retirement. Most of these couples had traditional divisions of household responsibility. Similarly, Szinovacz (1980) found traditional divisions of labor as well as little change after retirement in her study of 24 retired women. The wives were responsible for "feminine" activities and the husbands performed "masculine" tasks. The absence of change after husbands or wives retire was further supported in a study by Brubaker and Hennon (1982). Dual-retired (N = 62) and dual-earner (N = 145) women were questioned about their expected and actual divisions of household responsibility. Dual-retired and dual-earner women expectred more sharing of responsibility after retirement. However, when the dual-retired wives stated the ways in which the responsibility was actually divided, there was little change after retirement. These wives reported divisions of household responsibility based on gender.

The continuation of patterns established in the middle years and a decrease in the gender-differentiated tasks were found by Dobson (1983). These data were from a sample of 441 persons who were middle-aged and older. In another study of 1193 men aged 60 years and older, Keith et al. (1981) found that retired husbands performed more feminine tasks than did employed husbands. Also, husbands with working wives participated in household activities more than husbands who had wives who were not employed outside the home. Another analysis of these data (Keith et al., 1981) indicated that husbands' involvement in feminine household tasks had little effect on their self-esteem.

Although the findings concerning older couples' divisions of household responsibility are conflicting, there appears to be a tendency for couples to continue patterns into later life. If husbands increase their participation in household activities, the increase is usually in masculine-oriented activities (Keith and Brubaker, 1979). None of these focused on couples married 50 years or more. One study of 22 golden anniversary couples (Parron and Troll, 1978) reported sharing of household activities. However, Parron and Troll did not report the manner in which these couples divided household responsibility for specific tasks.

Are golden anniversary couples' divisions of household responsibility unique? Do they expect to share household responsibility? Do they actually share household responsibility within their marriages? This study explores the ways in which golden anniversary couples divide the responsibility for household tasks.

SAMPLE

Couples married 50 years or more and who include a partner who is 75 years or older are included in this analysis. Data were collected from golden anniversary couples who were listed in senior center memberships, newspaper announcements, and referrals by golden anniversary couples and knowledgeable community persons. Consequently, this is a nonprobability, purposive sample. All couples resided in small- to medium-sized communities. The same represents professional, business, farming, and, most often, factory occupations. The majority of the couples stated that they were retired.

The couples have been married an average of 56 years. The range of years married is 50 to 71. Most (56%) of the couples have an annual income above $10,000. Reported income was between $8,000-9,999 for 28%, $6,000-7,999 for 13%, and $4,000-5,999 for 3%. The only significant difference (t-value = 2.39, p = .02) between the spouses is their age. The husbands' average age is 80.5 years with a range of 75-91 years, whereas the wives' average age is 77.4 years with a range of 68-90 years. The wives' average years of education is 11.3; the husbands' is 11.0. The majority of both spouses rate their health fair or good and few consider themselves in either poor or excellent health. The husbands (X = 124.3) and wives (X = 127.1) are satisfied with their marriages as measured by Spanier's (1976) Dyadic Adjustment Scale. There are no significant differences between the husbands and wives on education, health ratings, and satisfaction with their marital relationship. These golden anniversary couples can be characterized as low to moderate income level, reasonably healthy, and satisfied with their marriages.

MEASURE OF HOUSEHOLD RESPONSIBILITY

The division of responsibility for household tasks was measured with a modified version of an index of household responsibility used in several other studies (Brubaker and Hennon, 1982; Keith and Brubaker, 1980, 1977). Husbands and wives were asked who should have and who actually has primary responsibility for a number of household tasks. The tasks were selected to represent "feminine" (e.g., cooking meals, washing dishes, washing clothes, writing letters, scheduling family social events, cleaning house, shopping) and "masculine" (e.g., doing yardwork, maintaining the car, earning money, doing household repairs, making family decisions) household tasks. Each spouse was asked to indicate whether the husband, wife, or both should or does have responsibility for each task. Responses were coded "1" if a spouse gave a traditional assignment to the task (feminine task to the wife, masculine task to the husband), "2" if the responsibility is shared, and "3" if the assignment is opposite of the traditional expectations (feminine task to the husband, masculine task to the wife). The theoretical range is 12-36 for the expected and actual portions of the divisions household responsibility measures. Traditional orientations are indicated by the lower scores and a nontraditional tendency is indicated by the higher score.

RESULTS

EXPECTED AND ACTUAL
DIVISIONS OF RESPONSIBILITY

The couples' expected division of household responsibility is presented in Table 1.1. These data indicate that both husbands and

TABLE 1.1
Percentage of Expected Division of Responsibility for Household
Tasks by Golden Wedding Husbands and Wives (N = 32)

Tasks	Husbands			Wives		
	Husband	Wife	Shared	Husband	Wife	Shared
Cooking meals	—	88	12	—	88	12
Washing dishes	13	41	56	3	66	31
Yardwork	72	—	28	63	—	37
Washing clothes	—	81	19	3	91	6
Car maintenance	84	—	16	91	3	6
Writing letters	—	50	50	—	56	44
Family social events	—	22	78	—	31	69
Earning money	72	—	28	63	—	37
Cleaning house	—	25	75	—	47	53
Shopping	—	41	59	3	38	59
House repairs	94	—	6	84	3	13
Family decisions	—	3	97	3	3	94

wives expect some traditional divisions of household tasks but there are many activities for which they expected to share. For example, the majority of husbands expected to share the tasks of washing dishes, planning family social events, cleaning the house, shopping, and making family decisions. With the exception of making family decisions, all of these activities were defined as feminine tasks. They expected their wives to be primarily responsible for cooking meals and washing clothes. Half assigned responsibility for writing letters to their wives and the other half expected it to be shared. For the most part, the golden anniversary wives had expectations similar to their husbands. For example, the majority of the wives expected to share the primary responsibility for arranging family social events, cleaning house, shopping, and making family decisions. Washing dishes and writing letters were the only two tasks that the wives expected themselves to be responsible for whereas the men were more likely to expect to share the responsibility.

Are the husbands' and wives' expectations similar? The tasks were combined into an Expected Household Responsibility index similar to the analysis reported by Brubaker and Hennon (1982). The average husbands' score on the expected index was 17.38; the wives' average score was 17.00. These are not significantly different (t-value = .62). Thus the husbands' and wives' expectations for the divisions of household tasks are similar.

TABLE 1.2
Percentage of Actual Division of Responsibility for Household Tasks by Golden Wedding Husbands and Wives (N = 32)

	Husbands			Wives		
Tasks	Husband	Wife	Shared	Husband	Wife	Shared
Cooking meals	9	87	3	3	91	6
Washing dishes	16	50	34	12	69	19
Yardwork	60	12	28	66	9	25
Washing clothes	16	68	16	13	78	9
Car maintenance	87	3	10	97	—	3
Writing letters	6	53	41	9	63	28
Family social events	—	22	78	6	31	63
Earning money	50	—	50	44	—	56
Cleaning house	59	38	3	50	44	6
Shopping	9	38	53	12	47	41
House repairs	88	9	3	82	9	9
Family decisions	3	3	94	3	3	94

Although some tasks are shared, the actual divisions of household responsibility approximate the traditional assignment of tasks (see Table 1.2). For example, the majority of husbands stated that they actually were responsible for all of the masculine activities and their wives were responsible for four (cooking meals, washing dishes, washing clothes, and writing letters) of the seven feminine tasks. Planning family social events and shopping were shared by the couples according to the husbands. Cleaning house was the only feminine task for which husbands stated that they had primary responsibility. The wives' responses of actual divisions of household responsibility were similar. The majority of the wives stated that they were responsible for cooking the meals, washing the dishes, washing the clothes, and writing letters while they shared responsibility for planning family social events and making family decisions. Also, a majority of the wives stated that they shared responsibility for earning money for the couple. They reported that their husbands were primarily responsible for yardwork, car maintenance, cleaning the house, and making household repairs.

The similarity between the husbands' and wives' actual divisions of household tasks was measured by the scores on the Actual Household Responsibility index. The husbands' average score was 18.86; the wives' score was 17.93 (t-value = 1.30). There is no significant difference between the husbands' and wives' actual divisions of household tasks.

Brubaker and Hennon's (1982) study indicated that individuals' expected and actual divisions of household responsibility differ. Is there a difference between the golden anniversary husbands' expectations and actual divisions of responsibility? Likewise, is there a difference between the wives' expected and actual divisions? Both the husbands' expected and actual scores ($r = .51$, $p = .002$) and the wives' expected and actual scores ($r = .55$, $p = .001$) were similar. For these golden anniversary couples, there was an agreement between their expectations and actual divisions of household responsibility.

FACTORS RELATED TO THE DIVISIONS OF RESPONSIBILITY

There is some indication that age and education may be related to the division of household tasks. For example, Albrecht et al. (1979) reported that younger women expect more sharing from their husbands. Ericksen et al. (1979) and Farkas (1976) found that education is related to the division of household labor. Also, marital satisfaction may be related to expected and actual division. Because this sample included older people who have been married 50 or more years, the length of marriage and health status may be 2 additional factors to consider.

Age, number of years married, education, income, health status, and marital satisfaction were correlated with the expected and actual division of household responsibility. For the husbands, the expected division of responsibility was significantly related to the number of years married ($r = -.32$, $p = .04$). The longer the husbands were married, the less traditional their expectations for responsibility. However, there was no significant relationship between the number of years married and the husband's actual division of responsibility. Also, there was a relationship between husbands' marital satisfaction scores and their scores on the expected and actual divisions. The less traditional the husband's expectations ($r = .30$, $p = .05$) and actual ($r = .31$, $p = .05$) divisions of household responsibility, the higher their marital satisfaction scores.

The wives' expected and actual divisions of responsibility were associated with health and marital satisfaction. The lower the wives' self-ratings of health, the less traditional their expected ($r = -.35$, $p = .03$) and actual ($r = -.48$, $p = .004$) divisions of household responsibility. Similar to their husbands, the wives' marital satisfaction scores were positively related to their expected (r = .35, p = .03) and actual (r = .34, p = .04) divisions of responsibility.

DISCUSSION AND CONCLUSION

This analysis of the expected and actual divisions of household tasks of golden anniversary couples reveals several unique findings. First, the golden anniversary spouses expected husbands to share activities that may be defined as feminine-oriented. It is important to note that the husbands were not expected to be responsible for these activities. Rather, they were expected to share the responsibility with their wives. The responsibility was divided with the husband. There is no complete crossover between expectations for the feminine and masculine tasks. Consequently, the responsibility for these feminine tasks was not transferred to or traded with the husband. Second, both husbands and wives reported considerable sharing of feminine tasks. Thus the spouses' expectations are similar to their actual division of household tasks. This is not found in other studies (Brubaker and Hennon, 1982; Keith and Brubaker, 1980, 1977). It is more likely to find a discrepancy between what couples expect and what they actually do. These golden anniversary spouses are actually dividing their household tasks as they expected.

A third finding was that the golden anniversary couples expect husbands to be, and report that they actually are, responsible for most of the masculine tasks. This suggests that the golden anniversary couples are more likely to share feminine tasks while masculine tasks are assigned to the husband. There is no crossover of sex roles in the masculine tasks nor is there much sharing of responsibility. Generally, the findings concerning the golden anniversary couples are similar to Dobson's (1983) study. There is some tendency to assign responsibility to husbands but there is also a tendency to follow the traditional divisions of household tasks. The striking finding with this sample was the amount of expected and actual sharing of feminine household tasks.

The relationship between health status and the wives' expected and actual divisions of household tasks suggests that the less healthy golden anniversary wives assign more feminine tasks to their husbands. The following statements by a traditionally oriented, golden anniversary husband illustrate the relationship between household tasks and health problems:

Question: How do you view husbands and wives sharing within the household?

Husband: I include the basement as my territory along with the outside—there's always repairing and stuff to be done. She has her place and I kinda got mine.

Question: You have things pretty well divided up?

Husband: Yeah, you could put it that way.

Question: How about sharing the household tasks?

Husband: I see these guys doing the dishes, doing half the cooking, changing diapers, and stuff like that. It don't seem to me like that's the thing for them to be doing.

Question: Does that make them less of a man to do that?

Husband: I don't know. I was raised that that is the woman's job. If there's illness or something, then that's different.

This is similar to Szinovacz's (1980) finding that household tasks are more likely to be altered if the wife's health becomes problematic. The husband is expected to, and in many instances actually does, assume the responsibility for feminine household tasks when his wife can no longer complete the tasks.

The interdependence of these golden anniversary spouses is evident in the amount of sharing of masculine tasks and the husbands' assumption of responsibility of feminine tasks when his wife has health difficulties. These long married couples have developed relationships in which they support the traditional divisions of household tasks and, at the same time, share many activities. These husbands and wives agree to the divisions of household tasks and they actually do what they expect. Golden anniversary couples provide an opportunity to examine the complexity of interdependence in the completion of household tasks.

Future research needs to examine the continuity of the divisions of household tasks. These data do not provide a longitudinal picture of the ways in which the golden anniversary couples divide household responsibility throughout their marriages. It is likely that the husbands and wives who shared activities in their middle years also shared activities in their golden years. Likewise, the couples who adhered to gender-differentiated patterns in their middle years probably continue the same patterns into later life. Longitudinal data are needed to assess the continuity of the division of household responsibility.

2

EQUITY, ROLE STRAINS, AND DEPRESSION AMONG MIDDLE-AGED AND OLDER MEN AND WOMEN

PATRICIA M. KEITH
Professor, Sociology

ROBERT B. SCHAFER
Professor, Sociology
Iowa State University

The objective of this research was to examine the influence of equity in an intimate relationship and role strain on depression among 163 married couples aged 45 to 91. Research on equity often has not included older men and women. Yet principles of equity should operate in middle and later life as well as in youth and young adulthood. Furthermore, although previous research on equity has examined intimate relationships, it rarely has focused on presumably long-term relationships such as marriage.

EQUITY AND WELL-BEING

Perceptions of deprivation or advantage are derived from comparisons with others in a process whereby individuals evaluate the adequacy of their own relationships relative to those they believe are experienced by others (Thibaut and Kelley, 1959). According to equity theory, social comparison with a referent or comparison other is the only way in which persons determine what they deserve and on which they base subsequent judgments about fairness (Crosby, 1982). Comparisons, then, are important in determining outcomes that individuals believe they deserve based on their contributions to a specific relationship or situation.

Although some persons may regard intimate relationships as unique and not subject to calculations of input, output, or gain, research has shown that both close and casual friends consider evaluations of fairness in their associations (Walster et al., 1978). Comparisons, then, shape notions of equity in intimate relationships as well as in more formal exchanges between individuals.

As a result of assessments of their contributions and outcomes compared with those of others, individuals may feel either over- or underbenefited. The underbenefited get less than they feel they deserve whereas the overbenefited obtain more from a relationship than they believe their efforts warrant. Thus both the over- and underbenefited experience inequity. But what are the consequences of inequity in an intimate relationship?

Equity theory specifies linkages between inequity and well-being by predicting that persons who are participating in inequitable relationships become distressed. The greater the inequity, the more distress individuals will feel (Walster et al., 1978). Both the overbenefited, who get more than they estimate they deserve, and their counterparts, who obtain less from a relationship than they believe they should, experience greater distress than persons who perceive equity in a relationship.

In a close relationship, the overbenefited may experience guilt at having taken advantage of an intimate. And the underbenefited may be demoralized by receiving unfair treatment from one to whose welfare they feel they have contributed more than their fair share. Moreover, receiving unfair treatment in an intimate relationship may have the potential to hurt more than perceived injustice in less personal circumstances (Traupmann and Hatfield, 1981). Not only then may individuals suffer the discomfort of inequity and feel deprived; the consequences may extend to other aspects of well-being. It was anticipated that inequity would be associated with depression among middle-aged and older couples. Furthermore, inequity in an intimate relationship may engender other role strains.

ROLE STRAINS AND WELL-BEING

House and Robbins (1983) identified some of the relatively durable problems, frustrations, and conflicts that are built into the daily roles of individuals as "role strains." Examples of role strains are stress at work and persistent marital conflict. Frustration or dissatisfaction with daily roles and disagreement between spouses would seem to qualify as role strains. Furthermore, these two types of role strains—disagreement between spouses and dissatisfaction with performing daily roles—may be fostered by inequity in an intimate relationship. Efforts to restore equity in marriage may lead to disagreement and conflict between spouses (Walster et al., 1978). Resentments over the perceived unfairness, attempts to obtain a more equitable relationship, or the inability to do so may foster conflict between spouses and enhance dissatisfaction with carrying out roles or activities that are seen, in part, as a source of the difficulty.

House and Robbins (1983) observed that individuals experience more chronic role strains than major life changes. Persistent life strains may be neglected in research on older persons when greater emphasis is given to more dramatic life transitions. Illustrating the significance of less dramatic difficulties, however, House and Robbins (1983) indicated that persistent marital strain had more negative effects on mental health than did divorce. If life strains are persistent, they may foster negative self-appraisals and demoralization. Indeed, it has been posited that depression is the end product of interactional problems and misunderstandings in a marriage in which the resources of the interpersonal system cannot deal with the role problems or role strains (Hinchcliffe et al., 1978). Disagreement between spouses and dissatisfaction with daily roles are role problems that may evoke depression as hypothesized by Hinchcliffe et al. Although evaluations of roles reflected in satisfaction or dissatisfaction have been considered in relation to marital adjustment, they have been examined less often in relation to a condition as severe as depression. Following Hinchcliffe et al., we expected that role strains reflected in disagreement and dissatisfaction would be associated with depression among middle-aged and older men and women.

It was unclear how the relationship between role strains and well-being would vary by age. There are, however, typically occurring events in the life stages of middle-aged and older couples that might raise questions of equity and foster disagreement between spouses. For the middle-aged couple, some readjustment in family roles may occur when the children leave home or if the wife reenters or enters the labor force for the first time. For older couples, retirement may be a factor in realigning activities in the home (Crawford, 1971; Keating and Cole, 1980) or result in changes in activities that may affect evaluations of fairness that in turn may lead to distress.

Little evidence is available to suggest whether perceptions of equity/inequity, disagreement, or other role strains would influence the psychological well-being of men and women differently. The greater protective function that marriage seems to provide for the physical and mental health of men than for women has been documented (Roberts and O'Keefe, 1981), and there is no evidence that this diminishes with age. Geerken and Gove (1983), however, observed that marital status per se is more important to the mental health of men whereas the affective quality of marriage is more important for women. They suggested that men obtain more instrumental benefits from marriage whereas women make more emotional investments in marriage. This implies that an unfair relationship or one characterized by conflict and resentment might be more distressing to women than to men. However, given the limited evidence, no formal hypotheses were stated about sex differences in the relationship between inequity and distress.

HYPOTHESES

Based on equity theory and the work of Hinchcliffe et al. (1978) on depression, some general hypotheses are derived to assist in assessing the relative importance of equity/inequity and role strains for depression among middle-aged and older husbands and wives. Three hypotheses were formulated: (1) Perceptions of inequity will be associated with higher levels of depression for both men and women; (2) perceptions of inequity will be correlated with higher levels of disagreement between spouses and higher levels of dissatisfaction with roles for both men and women; and (3) higher levels of disagreement between spouses and higher levels of dissatisfaction with roles will be associated with greater depression for both men and women. Because only limited data were available on potential age and sex differences in the relationship among inequity, role strain, and distress, no formal hypotheses were stated about the differential effects of age and sex.

PROCEDURES

SAMPLE

Data were analyzed from a sample of 163 middle-aged and older couples who lived in Iowa. Both spouses were interviewed as part of a study of nutrition, work, and family life. The married couples were selected in a random area sample based upon population concentration. Households with no children living at home and in which the wife was between 45 and 59 years of age, and childless households in which the wife was age 60 or over were included. There was an attempt to obtain, as nearly as possible, equal sample sizes for the groups and to exclude all households that did not fall into these groups. Therefore, the population was subsampled using sampling rates that would reflect the proportions of each group in the state of Iowa. This procedure resulted in a sample in which 81 men and 81 women were interviewed from households in which the wife was between 45 and 59 years of age; 82 men and 82 women were interviewed from households in which the wife was 60 years of age or older. The sampling and screening procedures were designed by the Statistical Laboratory at Iowa State University. A structured interview schedule, which included questions on background, work and family roles, and indices of psychological well-being was administered by trained interviewers.

The sample was Caucasian. The median age was 62 years for men and 60 years for women. About one-third of the men and one-fourth of the women had less than a high school education. Over one-fourth of both sexes had completed some college; 16 percent of the men and 11 percent of the women were college graduates or had done graduate work.

Family income was coded into 13 categories ranging from zero to $50,000 or more. About one-fourth (27 percent) had family incomes below $12,000; 25 percent reported incomes of $12,000 to $20,000. A total of 35 percent had incomes of $20,000-$40,000 and 10 percent reported incomes of $40,000 or more. A total of 60 percent of the men and 36 percent of the women were employed (employment status was coded not employed, 0, employed, 1).

MEASURES

Equity/Inequity

This research considered married couples' perceptions of their own and their spouses' efforts in performing selected family roles and activities. For this investigation, roles central to the functioning of the family unit and frequently performed tasks were selected for the examination of perceptions of equity. Roles that are necessary to the daily maintenance of the family should be salient to partners, thus making it possible to elicit perceptions of equity. To represent routine tasks in a family, the household activities of housekeeping and cooking were included.

Another role, companion to spouse, focused on interpersonal skills within the family; the provider role involved the maintenance of ties and interaction with individuals and organizations outside of the immediate family, as well as producing income. Although a greater variety of roles would have been desirable, those considered involved both routine maintenance tasks as well as the use of interpersonal skills.

To measure perceptions of equity and inequity in the marital relationship, respondents evaluated their own and their spouses' levels of effort in the 4 roles: housekeeping, cooking, provider, and companion. They were first asked about their individual performances: "Do you feel you should either increase or decrease your own efforts in the following to make the marriage relationship more fair for both of you?" There were 5 response categories: decrease effort a great deal (1); decrease effort somewhat; present effort is fair, increase effort somewhat; increase effort a great deal (5). To measure perceptions of their spouses' level of effort, respondents were asked: "Do you feel your husband/wife should either increase or decrease his/her efforts in the following tasks to make the marriage relationship more fair for both of you?" Response categories ranged from decrease effort a great deal (1) to increase effort a great deal (5).

The equity score for each respondent was determined by taking the difference in scores of self-evaluation and evaluation of spouse for each of the 4 roles. This resulted in a 9-point scale, -4 to $+4$. The negative scores represented inequity that was unfavorable whereas the positive scores indicated inequity that was favorable.

For the purposes of this multivariate analysis, scores were recoded from 1 to 5 with the higher scores indicating greater equity and lower scores reflecting greater inequity.

Depression

Depression was selected as a measure of psychological distress because it is regarded as a common condition of life (Silverman, 1968) and, therefore, a fairly sensitive indicator of life stress. A scale used by Pearlin and Johnson (1977) was selected in which respondents were asked to indicate the frequency (1 = never to 5 = very often) with which they experienced 11 symptoms. Examples included the following: lack enthusiasm for doing anything, have a poor appetite, feel bored or have little interest in things, have trouble getting to sleep or staying asleep, cry easily or feel like crying, feel hopeless about the future, have thoughts of possibly ending your life, and feel lonely. Data were coded so that a high score reflected higher depression. The coefficient of reliability for the 11 items was .79 (alpha).

Role Strains

Disagreement over family roles was measured by asking respondents how often, if ever, they and their spouse disagreed about each of the following activities: cooking, housekeeping, earning income, and being a companion or friend to your spouse. The 5 response categories ranged from never (1) to very frequently (5). The score for disagreement over roles was based on the combined responses to the 4 roles with a higher score indicating greater disagreement.

Role dissatisfaction was determined by respondents' indicating how dissatisfied they were with performing each of the 4 roles listed above. Categories ranged from very satisfied (1) to very dissatisfied (4). A high score from combined responses to the 4 items represented high dissatisfaction.

ANALYSES

Separate hierarchical multiple regression analyses were conducted for husbands and wives. Status and background characteristics (age, employment status of self and spouse, education, and income)[1] were treated as control variables and were entered as the first block. Measures of equity/inequity formed the second block. Following the theorizing of Walster et al. (1978) that inequity may lead to discontentment in an intimate relationship, disagreement with spouse and dissatisfaction with roles were considered as a third and final block.

RESULTS

Corroborating other literature (Roberts and O'Keefe, 1981), women reported greater depression than did men ($t = 5.21$, $p < .001$) whereas men experienced greater dissatisfaction in performing roles ($t = 3.07$, $p. < 01$). Husbands and wives did not differ in their assessments of the amount of disagreement with their spouse ($t = .88$). Husbands reported feeling greater inequity on 2 of the 4 measures of equity—housekeeping ($t = 3.24$; $p < .001$) and companion to spouse ($t = 2.27$; $p < .05$). In these family roles, men who felt inequity tended to feel overbenefited more often than their wives. However, the theory predicts that persons who perceive inequity, whether favorable or unfavorable, will experience greater distress than will persons who perceive equity. A preliminary analysis indicated that persons who experienced inequity, either favorable or unfavorable, did not differ significantly on depression. For the purposes of this multivariate analysis, both favorable and unfavorable inequity were coded as inequity with scores ranging from greatest inequity to equity.

INEQUITY AND DEPRESSION

Zero order correlations indicated some support for hypothesis one, which stated that feelings of inequity would be linked with greater psychological distress. Most of the relationships between inequity and depression were in the predicted direction for both husbands and wives; however, in general they were not strong (see Table 2.1).

A multiple regression analysis indicated that perceptions of inequity explained a significant amount of variance (7 percent) in depression of men after social status characteristics were controlled (Table 2.1). Inequity in companionship and to a lesser extent

TABLE 2.1
Hierarchical Multiple Regression Analyses of Status Characteristics,
Equity, Role Strain, and Depression for Men and Women

| | Depression | | | | | |
| | Men | | | Women | | |
	r	B	Beta	r	B	Beta
Level 1: Status Characteristics						
Age	−.11	−.08	−.20	.02	00	−.03
Education	−.03	.05	.02	.03	−.02	−.06
Family income	−.07	−.03	−.14	−.14	.01	.05
Employment status/own	−.04	−.07	−.08	−.11	−.06	−.09
Employment status/spouse	.07	.04	.07	−.07	−.06	−.07
		$R^2 = .041$			$R^2 = .016$	
Level 2: Inequity in Roles						
Housekeeping	−.22	−.08	−.12	−.11	.02	.02
Cooking	−.19	−.02	−.02	−.24	−.19	−.20**
Provider	−.18	−.05	−.05	−.04	−.02	−.02
Companion	−.16	−.12	−.14*	−.14	−.08	−.07
Increase in R^2		$R^2 = .066$			$R^2 = .085$	
Level 3: Role Strain						
Dissatisfaction	.19	.19	.21**	.21	.31	.28**
Disagreement between spouses	.16	.11	.11	.18	.09	.10
Increase in R^2		$R^2 = .060$			$R^2 = .094$	
Total R^2		$R^2 = .167$			$R^2 = .195$	

*p < .10
**p < .05

housekeeping contributed most to depression among husbands. Wives who felt inequity especially in cooking and to a much lesser extent in companionship were more depressed. Assessments of equity/inequity accounted for 8 percent of the variance in depression of wives. Social status and personal characteristics had little direct influence on depression although they were somewhat more important to men than to women. Neither age nor employment status were related to depression.

EQUITY AND ROLE STRAIN

Equity theory suggests that persons who experience equity in a relationship will be happier and more contented (Walster et al., 1978). Hypothesis two, which says that assessments of inequity

TABLE 2.2
Zero Order Correlations Between Inequity and Role Strain for Men and Women

Type of Inequity	Type of Role Strain			
	Disagreement Between Spouses		Dissatisfaction	
	Men	Women	Men	Women
Housekeeping	−.19**	−.01	−.08	−.10*
Cooking	−.11*	−.06	−.07	−.19**
Provider	−.16**	−.07	.06	.07
Companion	−.11*	−.22**	.10	−.13**

*$p < .10$
**$p < .05$

would be positively associated with disagreement between spouses and dissatisfaction with roles, received some support (see Table 2.2). Among men, inequity in all areas was related to perceptions of greater disagreement with their spouses, although none of the relationships was strong. Perceived inequity in the housekeeping and provider roles was most highly linked with disagreement. However, feelings of inequity were not associated with dissatisfaction with roles among men.

Among women, only perceived inequity in the role of companion was related to disagreement between spouses. However, inequity in cooking, housekeeping, and companionship for women was correlated with greater dissatisfaction with roles (Table 2.2). In summary, husbands who felt inequity tended to report more disagreements between themselves and their spouses, whereas feelings of inequity by women were more often reflected in dissatisfaction in performing roles.

ROLE STRAINS AND DEPRESSION

Hypothesis three was that role strains (disagreement between spouses and dissatisfaction with roles) would contribute to greater depression. Greater disagreement and dissatisfaction were correlated at the zero order level with higher depression among both men and women (Table 2.1). However, in the multivariate analysis, dissatisfaction was more salient in fostering depression than was disagreement for both men and women (Table 2.1). In fact, dissatisfaction with roles and inequity were about equal in accounting for variance in depression for both husbands and wives.

DISCUSSION AND CONCLUSIONS

This research found that inequity and persistent role strains that were not outcomes of major life transitions were sources of distress. The strains considered here represented continuous and undramatic difficulties that may be part of daily roles and, as such, were aspects of ordinary, but required, pursuits in maintaining a marital and family relationship.

There is considerable evidence that a supportive marriage increases the ability to manage stressful events and avoid psychosomatic symptoms (see Traupmann and Hatfield, 1981 for a review). Our research suggests that equity may be a component of support in a relationship that can provide some protection from distress and promote mental health in middle and old age.

Furthermore, the investigation demonstrated that the appraisal of inequity in an intimate relationship were not restricted to younger adults. Marriages that survive into middle and old age may be selectively different in some way from those that ended earlier. Nevertheless, even in the more continuous marriages studied here, persons were sensitive to inequity in their relationships and had role strain that was reflected in a response as severe as depression.

As the theory predicted, middle-aged and older persons were distressed by inequity even in situations in which they were overbenefited. For example, although husbands believed that they received more benefits than they deserved based on their efforts in the areas of companionship and housework, inequity was more demoralizing than a relationship characterized by equity. Other research has found that persons who got more from a relationship than they deserved were uncomfortable, less happy, and less content (Walster et al., 1978). Furthermore, our research showed that inequity in a family relationship contributed to symptoms more severe than mild discontentment. Overbenefited individuals may experience guilt that they obtain rewards that exceed their contributions to the relationship whereas the underbenefited may feel resentment because of their disproportionate inputs.

One objective of the research was to examine how equity/inequity was associated with role strains reflected in disagreement between spouses and dissatisfaction. Because equity theory predicts that persons will be content when they are engaged in equitable relationships, it might be expected that those experiencing inequity in work and family roles would be less content and less satisfied wih them. There was only partial support for this. Women, but not men, who were in inequitable relationships tended to be dissatisfied with their roles. Women who were underbenefited especially in some of the more routine maintenance tasks, for example, housekeepng and cooking, may have been resentful and unhappy with carrying them out. However, dissatisfaction with roles was a significant factor in both men's and women's depression.

Individuals in an inequitable relationship will try to restore equity. Experimental research suggests than when intimates do try to restore equity, they attempt to do so in ways that will not damage the relationship (Walster et al., 1978). However, it is plausible that attempts to restore equity and redistribute effort may result in conflict between intimates.

For men, inequity in all areas was linked with disagreement with their spouses. The fact that men tended to be overbenefited in some roles may have led to attempts to rearrange the division of labor resulting in conflict.

Men were especially distressed by inequity in companionship. Because they tended to be overbenefited in this area, their distress may have been due to guilt or stress associated with not being better companions to their wives. This may be a source of stress between husbands and wives because women seem to place greater value on affective aspects of the marital relationship (Geerken and Gove, 1983) and derive satisfaction from them. But men may be less able to provide for these needs (Wills et al., 1974). Our research also showed that women who experienced inequity in companionship reported more disagreements with their spouses.

Presumably, companionship would involve mutual support and help in the marital relationship. Burke and Weir (1982), however, found that older couples exhibited less helping activity between one another and had a decrease in communication about tensions and problems compared to younger couples. They observed that the first preference of older wives was to seek help with difficulties from someone other than their husbands. Perhaps, as our data indicated, requesting a change in effort in the role of companion was seen by women as increasing conflict and disagreement between spouses. The literature generally suggests, however, that women are more successful in establishing and maintaining confidant relationships outside marriage than are men, who are more likely than women to seek their spouse as a confidant (Powers and Bultena, 1976). Even so, although husbands may seem to be advantaged by their wives' interpersonal and affectional skills, benefiting from their wives' expertise was not without cost to the men we studied.

That inequity in all roles did not have a consistently strong influence on depression may be explained in part by the nature of comparisons in long-term intimate relationships compared with those in more formal associations. Assessments of equity in long-term relationships have an interpersonal history as an aspect of the context in which the calculation of fairness occurs and may be buffered by affection. Therefore, in close relationships comparisons may be somewhat less self-serving or they may take welfare of others into more careful consideration. Furthermore, permanency in a relationship may tend to result in downgrading differences in effort. Inequity in the present may be less distressing because there is the possibility that contributions may be negotiated and made more equitable at a future time.

Finally, although retirement is often viewed as a major transition, employment status did not affect depression among these middle-aged and older couples. Furthermore, in contrast to suggestions in the literature that wives may be distressed by their husbands' retirement into the family (Crawford, 1971), there was not evidence that disagreements between spouses or dissatisfaction with roles were associated with the employment status of either spouse. Of course, it may be that consideration of dimensions of well-being (e.g., morale or life satisfaction) focusing on responses less severe than depression might have revealed different outcomes from spouses' employment status. This research considered equity and role strains in only a limited number of areas. Future research on older men and women should include assessments of additional roles as well as a wider range of measures of well-being.

NOTE

1. Length of marriage was not significantly related to psychological well-being and was not included in the analysis.

3

MARRIAGE, GENDER, AND SOCIAL RELATIONS IN LATE LIFE

KAREN ALTERGOTT
Assistant Professor,
Child Development and Family Studies
Purdue University

THE PROBLEM

The central question of this chapter is as follows: How does marital status in late life influence social interaction in daily life? A review of existing research literature and an empirical analysis of the daily lives of married and widowed men and women will be presented. Approximately half of the people 65 years and older are married. Marriage is generally expected to modify the social experiences of an individual. The incidence of marriage, singlehood, widowhood, and divorced statuses in an age stratum is therefore likely to alter the social life of that stratum. The effect of marital role structure of a stratum on social integration cannot be surmised without examining the differential experiences of individuals.

Table 3.1 contains the distribution of marital statuses by age and gender for 1980. Being unmarried is much more typical for women than for men in late life. Arraying marital status and gender categories by their relative frequency in the population 65 years of age and older, we find married men are numerically most frequent (7,590,000), followed by widowed women (7,121,000), married women (5,546,000), widowed men (1,333,000) never-married women (824,000), never-married men (499,000), divorced women (468,000), and divorced men (361,000; U.S. Senate, 1982). There are more widowed people than never-married and more never-married than divorced at the present time. Increased incidence of

TABLE 3.1
Percentage Distribution of Marital Status
of Men and Women Aged 65-74 and 75+ (1980)

	Aged 65-74		Aged 75+	
	Women	Men	Women	Men
Married	50	81	23	70
Widowed	40	9	68	24
Divorced	4	4	2	2
Never married	6	6	6	4

SOURCE: U. S. Senate (1982).

divorce, slower rates of remarriage, and continued increases in the proportion of never-married may led to a preponderance of non-married older people in the future in spite of the fairly stable proportion of widowed elders (Cargan, 1982).

Marriage enhances well-being and mental health (Kessler and Essex, 1982; Gove, 1972). In a society that treats marriage as central to adult life, the married individual is advantaged due to involvement in one central relationship. Some predict that it is this closeness and intensity of connectedness to one person that enhances the well-being of the individual. The married individual may be more likely than the unmarried to be integrated into social life through other relationships that are centrally or tangentially connected to the marital role. Involvement in these role-generated relationships (Kahn and Antonucci, 1981) may provide the causal link between marital status and mental health (Weiss, 1973; Thoits, 1983).

LITERATURE REVIEW

What is already known about the impact of marital status on interaction with others? Although the earliest studies assessed both qualitative and quantitative shifts in the social involvements of older people, the systematic examination of the marital relationship and how its presence or absence influences the social life of men and women in old age was not a central topic. Rather, isolation and loneliness among the aged was the focus of much research. Older people were soon found to be, in general, *not* extremely isolated and *not* very lonely even if they spent a great deal of time alone (e.g., Townsend, 1978; Shanas et al., 1968).

Studies of marital status and social involvement in late life have been conducted. Bock (1972), using both death certificates and information from a representative sample of older individuals, was able to examine differences in suicide rates for married and widowed individuals. He discovered that the widowed, especially men, were more likely than the married, other things being equal, to commit suicide. He also considered other forms of social connectedness and found that marriage was protective but only in combination with other social resources. "Elderly spouses who depended solely on their marriages appeared to be more likely to commit suicide than did the widowed who were engaged in a network of kin and other types of community interaction" (Bock, 1972). The suicide rate was higher for males who were married but who lacked relatives and organizational ties than it was for men who were widowed but had relatives nearby and belonged to organizations. In fact, Bock found that organizational membership had a greater impact than marital status on the suicide rate. The married seem to be protected in part because they are more likely to have other social relationships.

Gubrium (1975a, 1975b) studied older people in the Detroit area. Married and single people in late life experience continuity. Although the single people are often alone, they are not likely to have a negative evaluation of their everyday lives. Those in the marital statuses representing loss (divorced and widowed) are much more likely to experience desolation. That this is due to discontinuity is confirmed by the finding that the widowed who have spent more time in that marital status have less negative evaluations of everyday life (see also Goldstein, 1979). The development of role-generated relationships and the disruption in these relationships at the time of role-change, in addition to the loss of a central other, could account for Gubrium's finding.

In a small study of retired women of two different occupational backgrounds (teachers and clerical workers), Atchley and colleagues (1979) analyzed the relationships with people outside of the household for never-married, married, and widowed women. The researchers found that the widowed interact more with friends than single and married, although the differences were not significant for former teachers. Married women, especially clerical retirees, are least active in friendships. Patterns of interaction with parents, sibs, and children are similar whether or not differential availability of kin by marital status is taken into account. For professional retirees, the widowed were most involved with these close kin. Never-married were lower and married women were lowest. For clerical retirees, the same pattern exists but the differences between marital status, especially the differences between married and never married, are less dramatic. More distant kin were considered as well (grandchildren, cousins, in-laws, and so on). For professional retirees, widows interact least with these kin; married and never married are similar to each other in their somewhat higher level of interaction. Among clerical retirees, however, married women interact more with kin than widowed and especially more than never-married. Widows are not isolated, nor are married women restricted to interacting only with their husbands. Women are selectively involved in social relationships outside of the household, and marital status differentiates the extent and pattern of involvement (Atchley et al., 1979).

Petrowsky (1976) examined the frequency of interaction with kin and friends and the degree of involvement in religious organization for married and widowed men and women. There was no difference by marital status in interaction with kin. For whites, there was no difference in interaction with friends, although for blacks, widowed people see friends more than their married counterparts do. Controlling for gender yields no significant differences in interaction with friends. No difference by marital status was found for religious participation, but women are more likely to participate than are men (Petrowsky, 1976).

Ward (1979) found similarities in the religious or voluntary organization participation rates of never-married and married men and women; however, widowed and divorced people were least likely to belong to a voluntary organization. Married men saw their neighbors less often than the men in other marital categories. Married men and women saw friends for a social evening less frequently than people in other marital statuses. On the other hand, never-married were least likely to see relatives on a daily or weekly basis; married and divorced were similar and moderate, and widowed were the most likely to see their relatives at that high frequency.

Babchuk (1978) examined the availability of close (primary) and very close (confidant) relatives and friends to adults in later life. He found that never-married were most likely to lack primary and confidant relatives, followed by widowed, divorced, and married. That is, the married were most likely to have this interactional resource. For friendship, different rankings emerge. Those least likely to have a primary friend are the divorced and widowed.

Those least likely to have a confidant friend are the never married. The married were found to be generally advantaged in the availability of confidants.

Cantor (1970) examined the social ties of urban elders living in poverty. Living alone or with someone, rather than marital status, is the independent variable used in her study. People living alone (most likely to be never married, widowed, and divorced) have more functional friends than people living with a spouse or with others. People who live alone also know more neighbors. No differences in the number of functional children, siblings, and relatives were found based on marital status. Whereas other studies have been based on small samples, Cantor's large (though class- and area-limited) sample allowed these relationships to be examined in a multivariate analysis. Those living alone seem somewhat advantaged in terms of functional relationships.

"The married had more viable support systems in terms of quality as well as quantity," according to Longino and Lipman (1981) who studied older people in retirement communities. These people are of more advantaged class backgrounds and reside in a different context than the respondents in Cantor's study. Nevertheless it is striking that the findings are so discrepant. The rank order of social, emotional, and instrumental support received via relationships is as follows: married women, who receive more than nonmarried women, who receive slightly more than married men, who receive more than nonmarried men. Although the nonmarried had more secondary relationships, the number of primary relationships was lower for the spouseless, especially for men (Longino and Lipman, 1981).

In terms of emotional support, earlier work (Blau, 1973) showed that men are more likely than women to be reliant on their spouses as confidants. In Strain and Chappell's (1982) more recent study, 81 percent of wives and 85 percent of husbands choose their spouse as confidant. No significant differences by gender or marital status were found for most other types of confidant relationships; the exceptions were that the widowed are more likely than single, divorced, and separated people to have other relatives as a confidant, and single, divorced, and separated were twice as likely to have a friend as confidant than married or widowed individuals. Somewhat greater reliance of married people on spouses, of widowed on other relatives, and of singles on friends is the image that emerges.

Ferraro and Barresi (1982) used a short-term longitudinal study of 4,373 older people with low incomes to examine the impact of marital status and duration in a marital status on interactions with neighbors, friends, relatives, and children. Immediately upon widowhood, there was some reduction in frequency of interaction with friends but no change in the other relationships studied. People who had been widowed one to four years had somewhat more interaction with neighbors, relatives, and children than did married people, but there was no difference between short-term widowed and long-term married in interactions with friends. Those people who were widowed for four or more years (and remained widowed rather than remarrying) had lower interaction with children and other relatives than did married people, whereas interactions with neighbors and friends were similar (Ferraro and Barresi, 1982). These relationships between marital status and interaction exist after the effects of age, sex, education, race, and perceived health are taken into account. According to Ferraro and Barresi (1982: 242), men, rather than women, reported increases in neighbor and friend interactions during widowhood.

In another longitudinal study based on secondary analysis of a large national data set conducted by Wan and Odell (1983), researchers were able to examine the impact of marital status on social involvement for a large sample of men. Decrements of health, other "deteriorative life changes," participation level at an earlier point in time, kin network size, social economic status, and number and types of role loss (widowhood and retirement) were also taken into account. Wan and Odell found that the multivariate model they examined explained little of the variance in informal social interaction rates (with children, siblings, parents, in-laws, relatives, and friends). Their model did explain participation in formal roles. In particular, it was found that loss of work role was more important than loss of spouse for formal social participation. Other things being equal, widowhood was not significantly related to informal participation. However, for those recently widowed, participation in parent, child, and friend relationships was somewhat greater whereas those widowed two or more years had the lowest level of informal participation overall and lower levels of participation with children. Most interactional careers (with siblings, other relatives, and so on) showed no dramatic change with widowhood (Wan and Odell, 1983).

Other recent studies touch directly or tangentially on the effects of marital status and gender on relationships. With a small sample,

Kohen (1983) assesses the frequency of contact and confiding for married and widowed men and women, controlling for health and income. Married people (especially women) are likely to turn to family when worried, whereas the widowed are more likely to turn to their friends. Men and women have similar numbers of confidants but women are more likely to discuss problems with these confidants. Women seek, according to Kohen, more support from their children and friends than men do and, according to other studies, they are given more support as well. Although the widowed have no clear disadvantage vis-à-vis married, the trend of women being more socially advantaged than men is noted. Hoyt and Babchuk (1983) also found that women have more confidants. Quinn (1983: 67) found that married persons have higher filial expectations and are "less participatory in non-family association." Uhlenberg and Myers (1981) considered the satisfaction with friends and with family of married, widowed, single, and divorced people. The married were most satisfied with family life, with over 90 percent expressing high satisfaction. Widowed and single people experienced less satisfaction, and divorced or separated (especially men, with only 42 percent expressing high satisfaction) experiencing the least. However, the married were also most likely to be highly satisfied with their friendships; widowed, single, and divorced men and women expressed less satisfaction.

Previous studies have established that variations exist both within and between marital status categories in the extent and nature of social connections. Such variation is important to understand because both individual well-being (satisfaction, mental health, support available, and support received) and age-related characteristics of society (degree of integration of the aged, role structure in late life) are influenced by these social connections.

These studies have typically used so-called behavioral measures (Lowenthal and Robinson, 1976). The "behavioral measures of social involvement" used by Arling (1976a, 1976b) provide examples of the limited scope of most studies of involvement. Questions concerning the frequency of contact with children and others as well as the number of neighbors and others one feels close to are standard indicators of involvement, to the neglect of duration of contact or activity while together or other behavioral qualities. Self-reported retrospective measures of frequency of interaction using an ordinal scale of measurement and a one-year frame of reference represent only one operationalization of social involvement. A few researchers (Cantor, 1979; Atchley et al., 1979) have attempted to transcend this limited form of measurement. Thus comparing the actual social experiences of married and widowed men and women has just begun.

THE RESEARCH

When comparing the social involvements of the predominant marital statuses—married and widowed—the findings of previous studies provide a complex and sometimes contradictory picture. Obviously married men and women experience more interaction in the intimate, life-sharing, central relationship with a spouse. This seems to lead to different patterns of involvement with others as well. Married people seem to be more involved with relatives and perhaps organizational members, and widowed seem to be more involved with friends and neighbors. Women seem to be more socially active than men. It is not clear from existing research whether marriage is in some sense privatizing, enclosing marital partners in a dyadic social world, or integrating, connecting the married individual to additional social actors.

The research question to be addressed through this analysis, then, is what differences in pattern and extent of social involvement exist for married and widowed men and women in late life? An alternative measure of involvement is used in this study in order to reflect more closely the behavior of people and to add a new perspective to the literature. An aggregate analysis of duration of social contact with various social partners will be presented. Multivariate analyses will also be conducted to determine whether marital status and gender have an impact when other individual characteristics are held constant.

A number of alternative predictions can be drawn from the available literature on marital status, gender, and social involvement in late life. The structural theories (Blau, 1977) suggest that the predominance of particular gender-marital status combinations would favorably affect the opportunity structure for interaction for people in that social position. Therefore, married men and widowed women would have higher levels of social involvement than widowed men or married women. Gender has also been linked to differential socialization, and opportunities and resources for sociability, which provides an alternative prediction: Married and widowed women would be more highly involved than widowed or married men. The "marriage as a central and integrative role-relationship" hypothesis would lead to the prediction that married men and women would be more highly involved in various social relations than nonmarried people, while the "role loss compensation" and the "marriage as a privatizing relationship" hypotheses suggest that nonmarried people, especially widowed and divorced, would interact at higher levels with alternative social partners. Finally, it may be that patterns of interaction across different types of relationship (e.g., friend, organizational member, and so on) vary by marital status. A more complex explanation may need to be developed in order to understand the impact of marital status on social involvements.

METHODS

These predictions are examined for married and widowed men and women 65 years old and older. This study is based on a secondary analysis of a national time-use survey conducted in 1975-1976 (Juster et al., 1977). The sample for the original study was based on multilevel random sampling procedures designed to represent households in the United States. Respondents 65 to 88 years old were selected for this analysis (N = 129). The four social statuses that are to be given greatest attention in the analysis to follow are those of married woman, married man, widowed man, and widowed woman. Each position carries its own social meaning, in part due to demographic distribution and in part due to the differential life course events that bring men and women to old age.

Respondents were interviewed on four occasions; each time they were asked to give a report of their activities for a single day. The questions "What were you doing?" "Where were you?" "Who were you with?" and "Were you doing anything else at the same time?" allowed interviewers to construct a detailed sequential record of behavior. Each respondent in this analysis provided four such records—one each for a Saturday, a Sunday, and two weekdays. This has been found to be a useful sample of time to identify patterns for aggregates and has also been used to discover patterns in behavior at the individual level of an analysis. This behavior record is used to construct measures of interaction. Each respondent would cite several role partners for each activity. A person could be, for example, alone while eating breakfast, with a neighbor while walking to a Senior Citizen Center, and with a neighbor and several organization co-members while at the center.

There were 10 separate measures of involvement created. Time spent in solitude, with one's spouse or fiance(e), with one's children living in the same household, with other household adults, with friends and relatives, with colleagues, with organization members, with neighbors, with service providers, and with strangers and acquaintances can all be examined separately in this study. Each measure was based on the sum of time with a particular type of partner in all 4 days, divided by 4 to produce a daily mean. Because being with 2 different partners at once was counted as time in each type of interaction, summing all types of interaction, solitude while awake, and sleep time may exceed 24 hours.

Two strategies of analyses are undertaken. First, at the aggregate level, the average time spent in particular role relationships and in interaction in general is presented. Because not all people in a given gender-marital status category participated in each type of involvement, the percentage of participants and the daily average amount of time spent by participants is also presented for married men, married women, widowed men, and widowed women. Second, multiple regression provides some indication of the effect of marital status and gender, while controlling for health and propensity to interact (as measured by education and enjoyment), on the social involvements of individuals are introduced (see Table 3.2).

FINDINGS

AGGREGATE ANALYSIS

Every person spent some waking time in solitude. It is clear that widowed men and women spend much more time in solitude than their married counterparts. There is a differential effect of marital status for men and women, with married women being somewhat less protected than men are from solitude.

Married individuals in this study who spent time with their spouse and unmarried persons who spent time with an intimate other (e.g., fiance[e] were treated in a similar manner for the aggregate analysis. Of course, married people spent a great deal more time with their spouse than the unmarried did with their intimates. Married men and women have similar daily mean amounts of marital interaction time. When the percentage of participants is examined, all married men and most married women (96 percent) had marital interaction during the 4-day period of time. Of the widowed men in this admittedly small aggregate, one-third have

TABLE 3.2
Time Spent with Others: Daily Means,
Participation Rates, and Daily Means for
Participants by Marital Status and Gender

	Married Men	Married Women	Widowed Men	Widowed Women	Significance
N	(43)	(25)	(7)	(54)	(12.9)
Solitude					
Time	3:48	4:18	9:33	8:04	.00
% participants	100	100	100	100	
Time/participant	—	—	—	—	
Spouse/Fiancé(e)					
Time	7:37	7:42	:02	:08	.00
% participants	100	96	29	6	
Time/participant	7:37	8:01	:06	2:29	
Child in Household					
Time	:31	:03	:45	:10	NS
% participants	21	12	29	15	
Time/participant	2:28	:23	2:38	1:11	
Household Adult					
Time	:21	:22	1:25	1:00	NS
% participants	14	12	71	22	
Time/participant	2:27	3:05	1:59	4:29	
Friend/Relative					
Time	1:41	2:14	2:25	3:13	.01
% participants	79	84	100	96	
Time/participant	2:08	2:40	2:25	3:20	
Colleague					
Time	:14	:09	—	:17	NS
% participants	19	20	14	15	
Time/participant	1:12	:46	:04	1:56	
Organization Member					
Time	:10	:07	:12	:09	NS
% participants	21	16	14	20	
Time/participant	:46	:45	1:22	:45	
Neighbor					
Time	:05	:02	—	:12	.03
% participants	26	8	14	37	
Time/participant	:20	:28	:04	:32	
Service Provider					
Time	:03	:07	:13	:08	NS
% participants	23	28	57	37	
Time/participant	:12	:22	:23	:22	
Strangers and Acquaintances					
Time	:21	:36	:30	:22	NS
% participants	44	52	71	56	
Time/participant	:48	1:09	:42	:39	
Total Social Time*	11:03	11:22	5:32	5:39	

*Double counts time spent with two types of social partner.

interaction with a significant other whereas only 6 percent of the more numerous widowed women have interaction with such a partner. The few widowed women who did interact with an intimate spent 2 hours, 29 minutes (2:29) on average with this partner.

Comparing daily mean amounts of time for the gender-marital status aggregates, there are no significant differences in the time spent with one's own children in the same household. However, examining the percentages of participants in this type of interaction, one can see the impact of differential availability of such children. Compared to their same sex counterparts, the widowed are more likely than the married to participate in this relationship. Older men, regardless of marital status, are more likely than women to be participants in this type of interaction. Furthermore, when the mean amount of time spent by participants in this relationship is examined, men are clearly spending more time interacting with their children who share a household (2:28 for married; 2:38 for widowed) than their female counterparts (23 minutes for married; 1:11 for widowed). The different durations indicate a qualitatively different relationship for elderly fathers and mothers who share a household with an offspring.

Although no pattern for gender-marital status aggregates emerges for daily time with other household adults, examining the incidence of participation in such relationships again shows that the widowed are more likely to be involved in such relationships. For those spending some time with an adult (other than a spouse or offspring) living in the same household, women spend more time in this relationship (3:05 for married; 4:29 for widowed) than men (2:27 for married; 1:59 for widowed).

Interaction with friends and relatives was coded into the same category by the original researchers and cannot be examined separately here. Because findings have frequently suggested that marital status affects interaction with friends differently than it affects interaction with relatives, the strength of the relationship between marital status and interaction may be masked in this analysis. Nevertheless, there are significant differences between aggregates in the daily time allocated to friends and relatives. Overall, women spend more time than men of similar marital status in interaction with friends and relatives. But also, widowed men and women spend more time than their married counterparts in these relationships. The proportion of widowed men (100 percent) and women (96 percent) who interacted with friends and relatives is greater than the proportion for married men (79 percent) and women (84 percent). For these active participants, the pattern of women spending more time than men and the widowed spending more time than the married is maintained. It is worth noting the high incidence of kin or friend contact across 4 days.

There are no significant differences in terms of overall daily averages or percentages of participants for interaction with colleagues. The fact that married men and widowed women engage in interaction with colleagues for somewhat longer durations than others may reflect longer work hours.

No significant pattern emerges for average interaction time with organization members. Similar percentages participate for each gender-marital status aggregate, with only a slightly higher incidence for married men and widowed women. When the amount of daily time for participants in interaction with organization members is examined, however, widowed men spend more time than others in this type of interaction.

Widowed women, as an aggregate, are more likely to spend time with neighbors (37 percent) and spend a greater amount of time with them for both the overall average duration (12 minutes) and the duration for participants (32 minutes). This is a significant difference when all 4 groups are compared. Widowed men are less likely to see neighbors than married men; married women are least likely to see neighbors, but when they do contact neighbors, they spend almost as much time with them as widowed women do.

Although there is no significant difference for aggregates in the daily mean time spent with service providers, it is clear that widowed men and women are more likely to spend some time with service providers. For those who do contact service providers, an average of about 80 minutes distributed in some manner across the 4 days was observed for married women and widowed men and women. Married men spent the least time with service providers.

Strangers and acquaintances make up the final category of social actor to consider. How do gender and marital status influence these public encounters, fleeting contacts, and perfunctory interactions? Although no significant differences exist in overall durations, widowed men are most likely to interact with someone in this category (71 percent), followed by widowed women and married women (56 percent and 52 percent), and married men (44 percent). For married women who participate in this interaction, the time devoted to it is somewhat more extensive than it is for people in other categories.

A final way to examine social connectedness of members of different social positions based on gender and marital status is to examine the total amount of interaction time. It is clear that married people are advantaged: Adding together all their separate interactions yields over eleven hours of social time per day for married men and women. Of course, some of these interactions are overlapping, such as when a relative visits a couple and each member of the couple is simultaneously with a spouse and a relative. Also, the greatest portion of this social time is time spent in the company of one's marital partner.

A most interesting difference emerges when marital interaction is subtracted from the total social time. We find that married men and women have, on the average, about two hours less social interaction per day with people other than their spouses (children, household adults, friends, relatives, colleagues, organization members, neighbors, service providers, and others) than do widowed men and women. It seems that being married in late life is a somewhat privatizing experience for both men and women rather than an experience that enhances social involvements with others.

In summary, the married seem advantaged only in that they have more extensive interaction with an opposite sex intimate. This condition of social advantage does not extend to friends and relatives, neighbors, service providers, strangers and acquaintances, or even other household members whether offspring or other adults. Widowed men and women have more extensive connections to those other role partners. Gender and marital status sometimes have a more complex impact on duration of interaction, such as for organization- and occupation-related contacts. Married men and widowed women are similar to each other in these involvements.

INDIVIDUAL LEVEL ANALYSIS

To examine the impact of marital status and gender in the context of other individual characteristics, additional analyses were conducted. Bivariate correlations between interaction and other individual characteristics are presented in Table 3.3. The multivariate analyses provide an important check on whether a particular variable is important, other things being equal. In the multivariate analyses, time spent interacting with a spouse becomes an independent variable and replaces the simple measure of marital status used above. This presumes that marriage influences social involvements by competing with the other involvements or by a necessary concurrence of marital and other types of interaction. A separate equation was calculated for each behavioral measure of interaction: time spent with an offspring in the same household, other household adults, friends or relatives, colleagues, organization members, neighbors, service providers and others, as well as time spent in solitude. Besides the independent variables of gender and time spent with marital partner (defined as no time for the widowed men and women), subjective health compared to others who are one's own age, educational attainment, household income, and level of enjoyment of social activities were entered as control variables as suggested by previous research (Arling, 1976b; Lopata, 1973a). Each of these variables is discussed in greater detail elsewhere (Altergott, 1980). The possibility of statistical interaction for gender and marital status is also considered because the aggregate descriptions suggest that marital status may have a differential impact on the social involvements of men and women.

The correlation coefficients for time spent with spouse and time in all other interactions are negative. Considering the strongest bivariate relationships, marital interaction reduces interaction with friends and relatives, household adults, neighbors, and service providers. The strongest inverse relationship is, however, with solitude ($r = -.66$). Integration into wider social circles seems to be sacrificed for intimacy in the realm of daily life by married persons.

Regarding gender, a negative correlation indicates that men spend more time in a particular social involvement. Men spend more time, according to the bivariate analysis, with offspring in the household, whereas women spend more time with friends or relatives, neighbors, and service providers. Being female is also associated with experiencing greater amounts of solitude.

Considering the impact of marital status and gender while controlling for these other variables is the next step in the analyses (see Table 3.4). Although the regression analyses are not presented in detail, the several significant findings of the multivariate analysis can be summarized. In this multivariate context, marital status is the most important (and only significant) predictor of time spent in solitude. Each hour spent with one's spouse reduces solitude by 32 minutes. It seems then that marital status and the differential marital statuses of men and women in old age are important factors in understanding solitude in late life.

TABLE 3.3
Bivariate Correlation Matrix for Time Spent with Others and Select Individual Characteristics (N = 123)

	Interaction with Spouse	Gender (0 = male)	Subjective Health	Education	Income	Enjoys Social Activities
Time Spent with:						
No one	−.66	.31	.02	−.06	−.17	−.10
Own child/shared household	−.07	−.23	−.09	.03	.09	−.24
Household adults other than spouse or child	−.19	.09	.18	.04	.01	.05
Friends or relative(s)	−.28	.25	.18	.02	.06	.22
Colleague(s)	−.08	.02	.14	.24	.25	−.07
Organization member(s)	−.02	−.01	.00	.17	.05	.16
Neighbor(s)	−.16	.14	−.11	.01	−.13	−.06
Service provider(s)	−.16	.12	.05	.20	.07	.08
Strangers and acquaintances	−.05	.07	.06	.11	.26	.05

TABLE 3.4
Significance and Direction of Gender, Marital Interaction Time,
and Interaction[a] Effects on Solitude and Social Involvement
Controlling for Health, Income, Education, and Enjoyment[b]

	Gender	Marital Interaction	Gender X Marital Interaction
Time Spent With:			
No one	NS	−.53***	NS
Children	−253***	−.10**	NS
Other household adults	NS	NS	NS
Friends or relatives	NS	NS	NS
Colleagues	NS	NS	NS
Organization members	NS	NS	NS
Neighbors	NS	NS	NS
Service providers	NS	−.02**	47*
Strangesrs and acquaintences	NS	−.05**	161**

a. Gender X marital interaction.
b. Based on regression analyses.
*p < .05; **p < .01; ***p < .001.

Marital status also affects interaction with offspring of the household in the multivariate analysis, as does gender. Each hour with one's spouse reduces time with offspring in the household by 6 minutes. Women spend less time than men in this form of involvement, other things being equal.

There are no significant relationships between marital interaction or gender and the duration of social interaction with other household adults, friends or relatives, colleagues, organization members, and neighbors in the multivariate context.

Involvement with service providers, strangers, and acquaintances is affected by marital interaction and the effects are different for men and women. Marital interaction tends to reduce interaction with service providers, and the time spent with service providers is significantly lower for married men than for married women. Likewise, interaction with strangers and acquaintances is lower for married people, and is especially low for married men.

Some of the findings of the bivariate and multivariate analyses suggest directions for future inquiry into social involvement. Of the other bivariate relationships portrayed in Table 3.3, health, education, income, and enjoyment of social activities are related to some but not all types of social involvement. Higher subjective health is associated with more interaction with household adults, friends, and relatives and with less interaction with neighbors.

Higher amounts of education are associated with more involvement with colleagues and organizational members. Higher income is associated with more time with colleagues and others as well as less time with neighbors and in solitude. Enjoyment of social activities is related to less involvement with offspring and more time with friends, relatives, and organization members.

In the multivariate analysis, enjoyment of social activities has an impact on interaction with friends, relatives, and organization members, but there is no longer a significant impact on interaction with offspring, other things being equal. Higher income is associated with greater amounts of time with colleagues, strangers, and acquaintances, but controlling for other variables, income no longer affects time with neighbors. And a significant positive relationship still exists between educational level and involvement with organizational members, all else being equal.

In summary, multivariate analysis shows that time spent with a spouse reduces interaction with very close and very distant others—offspring, service providers, strangers, and acquaintances. And, although the aggregate analysis suggests that married people are likely to spend shorter amounts of time with various partners, the multivariate analysis suggests that being married does not have this effect through absorbing an individual's interactional time. Marital interaction, which is zero for all of the widowed individuals by definition, does not significantly reduce or increase most of the nonhousehold involvements examined. If marital status makes a difference, it is through some other mechanism than competitive time allocation for most relationships. Being female neither greatly enhances nor reduces interaction with others (except offspring in the household) in the individual level analysis.

DISCUSSION

Looking at the various patterns identified in this analysis and comparing them to original predictions can shape a theoretical framework for future research.

Gender and marital status combine to explain differential involvement with service providers in a way that is consistent with a gender-role interpretation. Women care for other family members and yet receive more care themselves from professional service providers. Men are cared for by spouses; only widowed men are highly involved in this type of interaction.

Widowed men and women in late life do have social connections that are qualitatively different than those of married men and women, but the differences are complex and sometimes subtle. Although being married provides an intimate relationship that contributes in many ways to individual well-being, it also somehow limits an older adult's involvement with others. In some cases, this may reflect additional advantages such as when married people, especially men, spend less time with service providers. No doubt, caring tasks received from a spouse reduce the perceived amount of care required by professionals. Other interactional deficits of married persons identified in the aggregate analysis may actually be disadvantageous or, at least, privatizing for the married couple. Widowed women and especially men interact more with children and other household adults when these partners are available; widowed men and especially women interact more with friends and relatives.

However, this privatization of married people, in comparison to their widowed counterparts, does not result from married individuals' absorption in conjugal roles. The multivariate analysis shows that only in a few cases does marital interaction directly reduce other interaction. For most involvements, there is some other aspect of being married or being widowed that results in the relative privatization of married women and especially men.

Women do not have, however, the frequently reported advantage in social involvement. Marital status is more critical than gender in determining interactional components of daily life, which leads to the possibility that it is the predominance of widowhood among older women, rather than a gender-specific style of involvement, that leads researchers to conclude that older women are more socially active than older men.

Relatively numerous married men and widowed women were advantaged in terms of collegial, organizational, and neighboring relationships, as Blau's (1981) theory of social structure would suggest. Paying attention to the "objective positions and relations rather than beliefs or mental constructs" of people, we find that the more common social positions are more highly involved in these community relationships. Relationships can be seen as resources differentially available depending upon one's objective social position, and as important regardless of whether or not one is satisfied with such social contact. Based on this theoretical perspective and the findings reported here, people in the common social positions in late life are readily absorbed into public life.

Widowed men and women are numerical minorities and may be less readily recruited into community involvement as a result.

Marriage does seem in general to be a central relationship shaping other involvements, but not in the way predicted by those who suggest marriage is a requisite to involvement in other relationships. Marriage reduces the duration of nonhousehold interaction. Widowed men and women expand involvement in nonhousehold interactions. The compensation hypothesis requires elaboration. Not only do widowed men and women compensate the loss of their spouse through involvement with others; a barrier to interaction with others is removed. That barrier is not the spouse or marital interaction per se, as is clear from the multivariate analysis. Rather, the social position of married older persons changes the opportunities and propensities to become involved in social life.

This complex pattern of findings and the mixed support for alternative hypotheses suggests that more elaborate theoretical understanding of marital status in late life is required in order to understand older people in our present era and to imagine the status of the aged in the future.

First, we should recognize the power of numbers. The dominant groups' members seem to predominate in public roles. That is, those social positions with the highest frequency in the population may have advantages in social life. The mechanism may be more readily available peers, greater social acceptability, or the responsiveness of opportunity structures to the more numerous social categories. Numbers of individuals in gender-marital status categories are also important as compositional characteristics of an age stratum. Whether married or single men or women make up increasing or decreasing proportions of the older cohort is likely to influence the interactional structure for that cohort.

Second, although there seems to be some evidence of gender role continuity in caring roles, there is only a small and doubtful gender-related social advantage in social life. In the multivariate context, this advantage disappears. We have yet to understand why men and women act differently in late life because we have not yet documented how they act differently.

Third, the analysis presented here suggests that an intricate opportunity structure and a complex set of propensities result in differential social involvements in late life. Marital status seems important; the next theoretical advance in this area will be to discover how and why marriage alters daily life in late life.

4

MARITAL STATUS AND LIFE SATISFACTION: A Study of Older Men

NANCY F. MOUSER
Member, Department of Sociology, Anthropology
University of Wisconsin—La Crosse

EDWARD A. POWERS
Professor, Sociology

PATRICIA M. KEITH
Professor, Sociology

WILLIS J. GOUDY
Professor, Sociology
Iowa State University

Role, activity, and stress models predict that widowhood decreases life satisfaction. In contrast, network and exchange theories assume that status transitions such as widowhood modify opportunities, costs, and rewards for gratifying relationships. This chapter investigates whether widowerhood diminishes life satisfaction after a number of intervening network characteristics, network ties, and personal resources are considered. To accomplish that objective, the study design compares small town and rural Iowa men in three status categories—married, widowed, and those formerly widowed but now remarried.

Authors' Note: *We wish to thank Dr. Fred Lorenz of Iowa State University for serving as statistical consultant. Appreciation goes to the Midwest Council for Social Research in Aging for its support of the first author as a predoctoral trainee when the analyses of widower data started.*

LITERATURE REVIEW AND DEVELOPMENT OF HYPOTHESES

MARITAL STATUS

Role, activity, and stress models suggest that widowhood diminishes adjustment and life satisfaction, but each model stresses a different causal chain. Role theory defines widowhood as a role loss typical of old age. Losing a role and relationship disrupts established patterns of behavior, produces differential treatment from others, and modifies one's self-identity. Phillips (1957) found widowed persons more likely than married persons to identify themselves as old, to think that others treated them differently because of their age, and to be maladjusted.

Activity theory predicts that role loss lessens total activity, which reduces opportunities for others to validate one's specific role identities and one's general self-concept. As a result, positive self-concept wanes and decreases contentment with life in general (Lemon et al., 1972). In short, both role and activity theories predict that role loss decreases life satisfaction.

Elwell and Maltbie-Crannell's (1981) stress model treats unpleasant and overwhelming role loss as a stressor that directly reduces the subjective state of life satisfaction. At the same time, role losses of old age erode coping resources such as income, health, and social support and indirectly weaken life satisfaction. On the whole, these three approaches hypothesize declines in life satisfaction.

Network exchange theory, in contrast, assumes that status transitions such as widowhood modify individual opportunities, costs, rewards, and interests that subsequently influence lifestyle and contentment (Dowd, 1980; Fischer et al., 1977). This approach does not assume that old age will be one of despair or despondency. Instead, it predicts that resources and the ability to negotiate rewarding exchanges will determine what life is like in old age (Dowd, 1980). On the whole, role, activity, stress, and network exchange theories all predict that widowhood may prompt changes in contentment, but each approach mediates the relationship in a different way.

Research on widowhood generally reports lower life satisfaction for widowed than for married persons (Elwell and Maltbie-Crannell, 1981; Hoyt et al., 1980; Larson, 1978; Lee and Ellithorpe, 1982; Morgan, 1976; Pihlblad and Adams, 1972). Over half (56 percent) of the widowers in a sample of rural Missouri elderly, for example, ranked low in life satisfaction, and married men were twice as likely as widowed men to have high scores (Pihlblad et al., 1976). Data from five nations also demonstrate that widowed persons have more negative feelings than married people, and this association persists with age and income controlled (Harvey and Bahr, 1974). After reviewing 30 years of research on subjective well-being, Larson (1978) concluded that marital status explains from 1 percent to 4 percent of the variance in life satisfaction.

Widowhood consequences appear more pronounced among men than women (Elwell and Maltbie-Crannell, 1981; Larson, 1978; Lee and Ellithorpe, 1982; Pihlblad et al., 1976). To illustrate, Elwell and Maltbie-Crannell (1981) found significant direct effects of role loss on life satisfaction only among men, and its impact was second only to that of subjective health, outweighing income, informal participation, and formal group memberships.

MEDIATING VARIABLES

Atlhough widowed persons report lower life satisfaction than married persons, role, activity, stress, and exchange network approaches suggest a number of other factors that may mediate between marital status and life satisfaction. For example, Larson (1978) concluded that differences in life satisfaction between widowed and married persons are due more to socioeconomic factors, health, and age than to marital status per se. At the same time, Larson (1978) warns that such studies include more widows than widowers and that death of a spouse potentially reduces life satisfaction for men more than for women. To ascertain the relative consequences of widowerhood on life satisfaction, this study of older men considers and controls a variety of mediating variables. Potential intervening factors are categorized into three blocks—social network characteristics, ties with social networks, and personal resources such as health and socioeconomic status.

Network Characteristics

A central idea in the exchange network approach is that social networks influence individual behavior, attitudes, and values as well as interpersonal relationships. Network characteristics, in addition to personal ties, shape opportunities and constraints (Fischer et al., 1977). Tolsdorf (1976) empirically demonstrated that social networks can mediate the effects of stress on adjustment and coping behavior. When Tolsdorf compared psychiatric and nonpsychiatric male patients, he noted the two groups had different types of networks. Nonpsychiatric patients had larger networks, which included both kin and nonkin, whereas psychiatric patients had smaller networks dominated by relatives. If this research is applicable to older men, it implies that large networks, including both kin and nonkin, may be effective in mediating effects of widowhood on adjustment and subjective well-being.

Network Ties

In addition to network differences, social involvement with networks can support individuals, enhance their coping with stress, and subsequently influence subjective well-being. Tolsdorf (1976) found that nonpsychiatric patients, in contrast to psychiatric patients, had more contact and intimate relationships with network members, and they turned to social networks for support, advice, and feedback in times of stress.

Closely related is the central proposition of activity theory that frequency and intimacy of activity are positively related to life satisfaction. Several authors (Conner et al., 1979; Larson, 1978; Lemon et al., 1972), suggest that the amount of social involvement enhances subjective well-being and stress the importance of informal activity especially with intimate friends and a need to consider type and quality of interaction. With these caveats in mind, social involvement is distinguished by type of network—child, friend, voluntary association, and work. Confidant ties add a qualitative dimension.

Child Interaction

Shanas (1979, 1980) considers family as a "safe harbor" and a "basis for security" in old age. She supports this claim with evidence that relatives, especially children, live nearby, visit regularly, help with chores, and maintain emotional bonds with aging parents. Activity and stress theories also consider family interaction an important source of social support and predict that informal interaction with kin elevates life satisfaction (Elwell and Maltbie-Crannell, 1981; Lemon et al., 1972).

Nevertheless, Dowd (1980), using exchange theory, warns that extensive child contact is sometimes not rewarding. When older men undergo status changes such as retirement and presumably widowhood, resources such as energy, health, and income dwindle and decrease opportunities to renegotiate rewarding exchanges. Family interaction is modified as children note parental declines and, "in behalf of the parent," assume more responsibility for care and decision making. New interaction patterns emphasize a power shift or even dependence. Exchanges with children may be less enjoyable so that extensive child contact depresses morale (Dowd, 1980).

Friend Interaction

Same-age peers, in contrast to children, are candidates for rewarding and balanced exchanges because they share similar interests, life experiences, and resources (Dowd, 1980). Research consistently confirms the importance of voluntary friend interaction, which contributes more than kin interaction to enjoyment, contentment, and life satisfaction (Elwell and Maltbie-Crannell, 1981; Lemon et al., 1972; Pihlblad and Adams, 1972; Powers et al., 1979). Edwards and Klemmack (1973) claim that friend interaction, along with health and socioeconomic status, is one of the three best predictors of life satisfaction.

Confidants

Quantitative measures of friend interaction, however, neglect qualitative dimensions of friend exchanges (Conner et al., 1979; Larson, 1978; Lemon et al., 1972). Emotional closeness, mutual sharing trust, and support of friends are more critical than amount of friend contact to adjustment and morale (Liang et al., 1980). Authors frequently cite the impressive finding from Lowenthal and Haven's (1968) research that having a single confidant is more effective than a variety of acquaintances for buffering the negative effects of retirement and widowhood and for promoting subjective well-being and mental health. More recently, emotional bondedness with a most trusted confidant was observed to predict both life satisfaction and self-rating of physical health (Snow and Crapo, 1982).

VOLUNTARY ORGANIZATIONAL MEMBERSHIPS

According to exchange theory (Dowd, 1980), individuals preserve satisfying exchanges and attempt to avoid unpleasant ones. Because organizational affiliations are not compulsory, old people probably continue those that provide net rewards such as interesting activities, sociability, esteem, and support (Cutler, 1972). Perhaps these rewards account for Pihlblad and Adams's

(1972) finding that organizational involvement contributes more to life satisfaction than family and friends. Additional research confirms that organizational affiliation and participation heighten life satisfaction (Cutler, 1973; Edwards and Klemmack, 1973; Elwell and Maltbie-Crannell, 1981; Hoyt et al., 1980; Pihlblad and McNamara, 1965).

Employment Status

Stress, role, and activity theories predict that role loss diminishes life satisfaction. Empirically, retirement has been associated with anomie (Leonard, 1977), low morale (Morgan, 1976), lowered general happiness with the present (Beck, 1982), and reduced life satisfaction (Larson, 1978). In contrast, exchange theory declares that effects of a lost role vary with resources, freedom, and abilities to negotiate rewarding options. Life satisfaction may be less dependent on employment and more a consequence of remaining resources such as financial assets, health, capabilities, and supportive relationships (Dowd, 1980; Fischer, 1977a, 1977b; Jackson et al., 1977; Stueve and Gerson, 1977). Retirement research indicates that most negative effects are due, not to loss of the work role per se, but to poor health, low income, lack of retirement preparation, involuntary retirement, retiring earlier than expected, lack of retirement activities, and low morale earlier in life (Beck, 1982; Edwards and Klemmack, 1973; George and Maddox, 1977; Larson, 1978; Morgan, 1976). Beck (1982) concludes that when these crucial variables are taken into consideration, retirees and workers have equivalent chances for happiness.

Personal Resources

Exchange theory explains that effects of role loss vary with opportunities to renegotiate satisfying exchanges. Limited assets diminish opportunities to meet a variety of exchange partners and reduce leverage so that others control the negotiations to meet their own needs and objectives. Those with relatively few resources settle for less than satisfying exchanges, and morale declines (Dowd, 1980). Resources considered in this study are age, health, dependence, net worth, education, and occupational ranking.

Age. Dowd (1980) claims that old age as a devalued master status weakens the bargaining position of older people and forces them to prove that other assets such as intelligence and productivity have not declined. This discounting process decreases the probabilities of negotiating profitable exchanges; consequently, subjective well-being may suffer. Some empirical research supports this idea (Back and Bourque, 1970; Harvey and Bahr, 1974; Morgan, 1976). Other research indicates either no linear relationship between age and subjective well-being or relationships that are insignificant when other variables are controlled (Hoyt et al., 1980; Snow and Crapo, 1982; Spreitzer and Snyder, 1974). In his review article, Larson (1978) claims that an inverse age-satisfaction relationship disappears when health, financial resources, widowhood, and activity are controlled. Because of potential direct and indirect effects, it is prudent to include age as a mediating variable.

Health. In later life, chronic conditions are prevalent, and although most people continue to live independently, functioning is often impaired (George, 1980). Health consistently emerges as one of the best predictors of subjective well-being (Edwards and Klemmack, 1973; Larson, 1978;[1] Markides and Martin, 1979; Sauer and Warland, 1982; Snow and Crapo, 1982), sometimes explaining more variance than any other variable including widowhood (Morgan, 1976), socioeconomic factors (Lee and Ellithorpe, 1982; Liang et al., 1980), and confidant ties (Lowenthal and Haven, 1968). Poor health has negative consequences for morale that even confidants cannot ameliorate.

Dependency. Dependence even on family members can lower morale according to exchange theory. Family members with resources have greater control over renegotiations, and older family members may find new exchanges costly in terms of deference, prestige, and self-worth. Lacking independence, they cannot withdraw but must accept less rewarding relationships that diminish satisfaction and morale (Dowd, 1980; Jackson et al., 1977).

Available research substantiates that quality suffers in child relationships when the aged parent has poor health and inadequate income (Johnson and Bursk, 1977; Mindel and Wright, 1982; Robinson and Thurnher, 1979; Ward, 1978). Robinson and Thurnher (1979), for instance, observed children describing their parents using predominantly negative terms—cold, uncharitable, self-indulgent, disinterested—when parents were inactive or in poor health. This tendency was pronounced when children perceived themselves as tied down to meet parental needs. Caring for a dependent parent appears to reduce life satisfaction (Mindel and Wright, 1982) and to increase burdens, friction, and socioemotional costs (Ward, 1978).

Socioeconomic resources. Along with health and independence, socioeconomic status is a major index of opportunities to negotiate rewarding exchanges that alleviate stress and facilitate adjustment (Dowd, 1980; George, 1980; Elwell and Maltbie-Crannell, 1981). Consequently, it is ranked as one of the three best predictors of long-term subjective well-being (Edwards and Klemmack, 1973; Larson, 1978; Leonard, 1977).

As a multidimensional concept, socioeconomic status may be measured using education, occupation, or financial resources. The first, economic resources, can influence subjective well-being by increasing financial security and opportunities for leisure activities and social involvement (Lee, 1979; Liang et al., 1980; Lopata, 1973b; Spreitzer and Snyder, 1974). While research affirms a relationship between income and subjective well-being, this study examines net worth as an economic predictor of life satisfaction.

A second dimension of socioeconomic resources is education, which also increases opportunities for adjustment and well-being by contributing to social and problem-solving skills (George, 1980; Lopata, 1973b). In addition, education widens exposure to leisure activities, which can be shared and used as a basis for developing friendships. Formal schooling of widows is related to development of friends outside the kin group, number of friends, amount of friend interaction, and participation in voluntary organizations (Lopata, 1973b).

Occupational ranking is a third socioeconomic resource used in negotiating profitable exchanges (Dowd, 1980). Although people retire, past occupations—especially high ranking ones—may continue to provide respect and recognition (O'Rand, 1982). Not only is occupational prestige associated with subjective well-being (Edwards and Klemmack, 1973; Hoyt et al., 1980; Hurst and Guldin, 1981; Leonard, 1977), but it is especially important after age 65 (Spreitzer and Snyder, 1974).

METHODS

SAMPLE

Data for this study come from interviews with 1,332 men aged 60 and over in 1974. These interviews were part of a longitudinal study of small town and rural Iowa men who, in 1964, were fully employed in five categories—farmers, blue-collar workers, small businessmen, salaried professionals, and self-employed professionals. The 1,332 men reinterviewed in 1974 represent 91 percent of those who survived the decade. Among the 1,332 continuing participants were 1,113 married, 84 widowed, and 87 formerly widowed but now remarried men to total 1,284. The remaining 48 men belonged to other marital status categories, including never married, divorced, and separated.

ANALYSIS

Multiple regression procedures are used to analyze the data. First, life satisfaction is regressed on marital status. Second, the dependent variable is regressed separately on each block of intervening variables—network characteristics, network ties, and personal resources—thus requiring three additional standard regressions. Results provide the relative contribution of each variable within its set and the effects of each block on life satisfaction. Next, hierarchical regression is used to assess the unique contribution each set of variables makes after the effects of the other two blocks are considered. In this procedure, two blocks of variables are entered in step one; after their contributions are determined, a third set of variables is entered in step two. The R^2 change between steps one and two is calculated to evaluate the unique variance explained by the third block after effects of the other two have been considered. Assessing the unique contribution for each of three sets requires using the hierarchical procedure three times. Finally, an additional hierarchical regression is used to determine whether marital status increases the explained variance for life satisfaction after three blocks of variables—network characteristics, network ties, and personal resources—have been taken into account. This is accomplished by entering the three blocks of variables in step one, and by adding marital status in step two.

OPERATIONAL DEFINITIONS AND MEASURES

The dependent variable, life satisfaction, is measured using Wood and associates' (1969) Life Satisfaction Index Z (LSI-Z). This 13-item form, 7 items shorter than the Life Satisfaction Index A (LSI-A) developed by Neugarten and associates (1961), correlates highly—.941 and .952—with the LSI-A version and with Adams's (1968) revision, respectively (Lohmann, 1977). In addition to being shorter, LSI-Z is particularly well-suited for use with rural aged (Wood et al., 1969).[2] For this Iowa sample, scores ranged from 26 to

64 with a mean of 47.01, median of 47.73, and standard deviation of 5.12.

The first block of independent variables—network characteristics—consists of size of child network, distance of child network, and size of friend network. Size or number of children in the network was figured by summing first names of living children reported by each father. Distance was operationalized by asking where each child lived and assigning scores that ranged from 1 for those in the same neighborhood to 11 for those in another county. Scores were summed and divided by number of children to yield a mean distance for the network. Mean distance scores ranged from 1 to 11 with a mean of 5.26, median of 5.01, and mode of 5.00. Scores of 6 and below indicate Iowa residences.

Friend network in this study refers to the personal social network of most frequently seen people, or the "effective network" (Cubbitt, 1973). To operationalize this variable, respondents were asked to name any relatives, close friends, or neighbors with whom they visit every day or nearly every day. Children, grandchildren, siblings, and household members were excluded. Following this list of daily contacts, respondents were requested to name others with whom they visit regularly each week but not daily. Size of friend network was determined by summing the number of people listed as daily and weekly contacts. Asking for first names helps to minimize distortion that can occur by expecting respondents to generalize how many friends they have or visit with regularly. Distorting size of friend networks may be especially problematic in small towns where, as Pihlblad and associates (1976) found, some old peole may claim "everyone in this town is my friend."

Network ties, the second block of variables, include amount of child interaction, amount of friend interaction, presence of a confidant relationship, number of voluntary association memberships, and employment status. Child interaction reflects a man's total yearly face-to-face contact with all members of his child network. To arrive at this score, each father was asked, after naming his living children, to indicate the frequency of face-to-face contacts with each child. Daily contact was scored as 365, weekly visits as 52, monthly as 12, several times a year as 7, less often than that as 3, and never as 0. Values were summed for all children in a network, producing a yearly child interaction score for each father. Scores ranged from 0 to 4.015. The variable appeared to be neither normally distributed nor homoscedastic; thus violating two assumptions required for multiple regression. Consequently, logarithmic transformation was used to normalize the variable, stabilize the variance, and thereby render the variable tractable and appropriate for use in multiple regression (Weisberg, 1980). The natural log of zero is a minus number and the log of no child interaction consequently would be a negative value. Because the natural log of one is zero, adding one to each total child interaction score gives those with no child interaction a log score of zero. The measure of yearly child interaction used in regression procedures is, therefore, $LN(X + 1)$.

Friend interaction is calculated using the lists of people named as daily and weekly contacts. Weekly friend interaction equals the number of daily contacts multiplied by seven plus the number of weekly contacts, (Number of daily interactions $X7$) + (Number of weekly interactions). Total weekly friend interaction scores range from 0 to 80 with a mean of 12.81, a median of 4.75, and mode of 0. Lack of congruence between the mean, median, and mode suggests that the variable is neither normally distributed nor homoscedastic. Again, logarithmic transformation was used to normalize the variable and stabilize the variance. Weekly friend interaction scores used in regression procedures were $LN(X + 1)$.

The qualitative tie to a confidant was assessed by asking each respondent whether there was anyone with whom he felt particularly close—someone in whom he confided. If the respondent answered the query positively, he received a score of one; if the answer was negative, a score of zero was recorded. This produced a dummy coding that is appropriate for including qualitative variables in multiple regression procedures (Kerlinger and Pedhazur, 1973).

Remaining network ties are those with voluntary associations and employment. To operationalize ties with voluntary organizations, respondents were asked to name organizations to which they belonged. Those were summed to measure voluntary association memberships. Employment ties were measured by self-reports of whether one is working full time for pay or profit, part time, or retired. This variable was dummy coded to render it appropriate for use in regression analysis. Dummy coding with three categories creates two variables. The third category is excluded and served as a reference for judging and interpreting effects. Retirement is the variable excluded so that the first dummy variable considers effects of full-time employment as compared to retirement, and the second dummy variable determines the consequence of part-time employment as compared to retirement. Effects of both dummy codes are taken into account simultaneously so that only one regression run is required. A single F-ratio is calculated so that results are interpreted collectively as the pooled effect of one variable.

The third block of independent variables consists of six personal resources—age, health, dependency, and three socioeconomic resources. Age refers to chronological age measured in years. Health scores are based on subjective health ratings using 5 response categories ranging from poor to excellent. To determine dependency, interviewers asked whether respondents received or needed help with any of 9 activities—cooking meals, cleaning house, getting enough money to pay daily bills, shoveling snow, climbing stairs, getting in and out of bed, taking baths, dressing or putting on shoes, and getting around in the community. Degree of dependency was measured by summing the number of times the respondent reported either receiving or needing help with these 9 chores. Theoretically, scores could vary from 0 to 9, but scores for this sample ranged from 0 to 6 with over half reporting no need for help. The mean, median, and mode were .73, .47, and .00 respectively.

The 3 socioeconomic resources are net worth, education, and Duncan's Socioeconomic Index of Occupations. Economic assets were evaluated by asking each respondent which category of figures most closely identified his net worth. There were 10 response categories ranging from "under $5,000" to "$200,000 or more" provided, and net worth values were coded from 1 to 10. Education reflects a self-report of highest year of formal education completed. Duncan's SEI was developed using three criteria that represent the occupation as a unit of analysis. Those criteria are occupational prestige, education, and income levels of those in the occupation as a whole, not the education and income of an individual respondent (O'Rand, 1982). As a result, Duncan SEI reflects occupational ranking and complements individual status characteristics—net worth and individual educational achievement—used in this study. Theoretical score limits of SEI are 0 to 100; scores in this sample ranged from 3 to 96.

Marital status was ascertained by inquiring about each respondent's present marital status and, if presently married, whether he had ever been widowed. Because this is a nominal-scale variable, two dummy variables were needed to ascertain the effects of three marital statuses—married, widowed, and formerly widowed but now remarried. The first variable assesses the consequence of being married as compared to widowed, and the second notes effects of being remarried as opposed to widowed. Although two dummy variables are created, both are read in one regression run and a single F-ratio is calculated to assess the combined effects of marital status.

FINDINGS

The findings are divided into four segments: the influence that marital status has on life satisfaction; the contribution each independent variable makes within its block of variables and the effect of each set of variables; the unique contributions made by each set of independent variables after the other two blocks have been considered, and an appraisal of significance of marital status to life satisfaction after three blocks of variables—network characteristics, network ties, and personal resources—are taken into account.

MARITAL STATUS

The effect of marital status on life satisfaction is significant (see Table 4.1): widowers ($\bar{X}$ = 44.54) have lower morale than married ($\bar{X}$ = 47.22) and remarried ($\bar{X}$ = 46.67) men. This finding is consistent with previous studies. Unlike other research, however, this study includes remarried persons as a comparative group and indicates that life satisfaction level of remarried men is between that of marrieds and widowers. Marital status explains 1.7 percent of variance in life satisfaction for this sample, a level consistent with the 1 percent to 4 percent range Larson (1978) found in his review. Over 98 percent of the variance remains unexplained, however, leaving much opportunity for network characteristics, network ties, and personal resources to contribute significantly.

MEDIATING VARIABLES

Network Characteristics

Each network characteristic is significantly related to life satisfaction (see Table 4.1). Large nearby networks of children depress life satisfaction. Both child network size and proximity may reflect socioeconomic status, in which case the effects will diminish when resources are controlled in the hierarchical procedure. The third network characteristic, size of friend network, is positively related to life satisfaction. Network characteristics as a block of variables

TABLE 4.1
Regression of Life Satisfaction with Marital Status, Network Characteristics, Network Ties, and Personal Resources for Older Men

Independent Variables	Standardized Regression Coefficients (Beta)	F	R^2 Change	Simple r
Marital Status		11.106**	.01730	.13152
Married vs. widowed	.17901			
Remarried vs. widowed	.10515			
Network Characteristics (Block 1)				
Size of child network	−.08761	8.093**	.00939	−.09691
Mean distance of children	.11315	13.469**	.01410	.12282
Size of friend network	.08279	7.204**	.00680	.09551
Block of variables		10.695**	.03029	.17405
Network Ties (Block 2)				
Child interaction	−.06006	4.098*	.01107	−.10520
Friend interaction	.04668	2.489	.00426	.07611
Confidant relationship	.09288	10.033**	.00844	.12415
Voluntary association memberships	.26262	74.549**	.09058	.31802
Employment status		14.512**	.02441	
Full-time vs. retired	.17761			.17776
Part-time vs. retired	.10400			.02180
Block of variables		27.497**	.13876	.37250
Personal Resources (Block 3)				
Age	−.05961	5.118*	.01039	−.10194
Health	.38005	195.257**	.24627	.49912
Dependency	−.14208	27.095**	.00783	−.19563
Net worth	.15081	29.490**	.02457	.32353
Education	.09946	7.683**	.04851	.32987
Duncan SEI	.12826	12.127**	.00774	.31305
Block of variables		90.191**	.34531	.58763

*p < .05
**p < .01

reach statistical significance and explain about 3 percent of the variance in life satisfaction, that is, about twice as much as marital status explains.

Network Ties

Network ties were hypothesized as important to life satisfaction. Child interaction depresses life satisfaction significantly and accounts for almost (1.1 percent) as much variance as marital status (Table 4.1). This finding counters activity and stress models that predict that child interaction successfully provides social support. If this negative influence is due to declining power within the family and an increased dependence on children, child interaction effects should dwindle when personal resources are controlled in the hierarchical procedure.

Friend interaction or amount of weekly contact is unrelated to life satisfaction but a confidant relationship is significant. Even a single confidant raises life satisfaction more than an array of acquaintances seen regularly. These results affirm the need to consider qualitative dimensions in friend interaction.

Remaining network ties include voluntary association memberships and employment status; both have positive and significant consequences for life satisfaction, explaining about 9 percent of life satisfaction variance. The significance of affiliations may reflect either socioeconomic status, which is controlled in subsequent hierarchical regression analysis, or rewarding exchanges with people who have similar interests, experiences, and resources. Employment status also appears to contribute to subjective well-being. Full-time employees have the highest life satisfaction, followed by part-time employees, and then by retirees. If this relationship is caused by declines in physical and financial resources, the relationship will diminish when resources are controlled in the hierarchical procedure. All network ties except friend interaction help predict subjective well-being. As a block of variables, involvement with social networks explains almost 14 percent of the variance in life satisfaction.

Personal Resources

Personal resources are crucial for negotiating the rewarding exchanges important to morale and contentment. Each resource considered reaches statistical significance in predicting life satisfaction (Table 4.1). Advanced years occur with decreases in life satisfaction. In standard or simultaneous regressions used for Table 4.1, each variable is handled as if it entered the regression last (Kim and Kohout, 1975); this means that age has a significant impact even after health, dependence, and socioeconomic resources are considered. As expected, poor health and dependency diminish subjective well-being. Health ratings explain much more life satisfaction variance than dependency—almost 25 percent versus less than 1 percent. Health problems even with independent living clearly decrease life satisfaction. Limited variance in the dependency measure may explain why its contribution is no greater.

All three socioeconomic resources reach statistical significance. Collectively, the three variables explain over 8 percent of the variance in life satisfaction, with education contributing the most and Duncan Socioeconomic Index of Occupations adding the least. In past research, income explained more variance than other SES variables. For this project, net worth was chosen instead of income because accumulated wealth was expected to be a superior index of status, consumption, and life changes in old age (Henretta and Campbell, 1976; O'Rand, 1981). No research report located for the above literature review investigated the net worth relationship to life satisfaction, and this single finding of less than 2 percent explained variance raises the question of whether net worth is a better predictor of life satisfaction than is income. In the block of resource variables, economic assets are no more important than education, which contributes to social skills, problem-solving techniques, and knowledge of alternatives. Apparently, education enhances life satisfaction for this sample of men. Duncan SEI also reaches statistical significance implying that rank, prestige, and recognition assist one in developing a satisfying lifestyle, but it explains less than 1 percent of the variance.

As a block of variables, personal resources explain almost 35 percent of life satisfaction variance. Health accounts for almost 25 percent, socioeconomic variables add about 8 percent, and age and dependency each contribute about 1 percent. Comparing blocks of variables, personal resources have the most explanatory power, network ties rank second, and network characteristics have the least.

HIERARCHICAL REGRESSION

If variance explained by each of these blocks of variables were unrelated, they would account for over 51 percent of the variance in

TABLE 4.2
Regression of Life Satisfaction Among Older Men with
Network Characteristics, Network Ties, and Personal Resources
After the Other Blocks of Variables Have Been Entered[a]

Independent Variables	Standardized Partial Regression Coefficients (Beta)	F	Percentage of Unique Variance Explained
Network Characteristics (Block 1/Blocks 2 and 3)			
Size of child network	.01419	.212	.030
Mean distance of children	.01780	.235	.014
Size of friend network	.00440	.010	.001
Block 1/Blocks 2 and 3		.240	.045
Network Ties (Block 2/Blocks 1 and 3)			
Child interaction	.01182	.088	.010
Friend interaction	.04821	1.203	.067
Confidant relationship	.08683	11.543**	.795
Voluntary assoc. memberships	.08530	7.052**	.497
Employment status		.583	.073
Full-time vs. retired	.02785		
Part-time vs. retired	.02862		
Block 2/Blocks 1 and 3		3.840**	1.442
Personal Resources (Block 3/Blocks 1 and 2)			
Age	−.04274	2.123	.252
Health	.36510	174.891**	16.635
Dependency	−.15147	30.205**	1.630
Net worth	.12396	18.639**	1.372
Education	.08002	4.563*	1.669
Duncan SEI	.10786	8.051**	.504
Block 3/Blocks 1 and 2		58.758**	22.062
Marital Status			
(Block 4/Blocks 1, 2, and 3)		2.178	.272

a. Total R^2 = .36629.
*$p < .05$.
**$p < .01$.

life satisfaction. A correlation matrix, not included in this chapter, demonstrates that some of these variables are interrelated highly; therefore, it is necessary to ascertain the variance each block contributes after other blocks have been taken into account. As shown in Table 4.2, all network characteristics fail to contribute significantly to life satisfaction after network ties and personal resources are considered. Not only size and proximity of child networks but also child interaction cease to be important after personal resources are controlled. This indicates that children per se—their number, their proximity, their face-to-face contacts—have no significant influence on fathers' life satisfaction. Once resources are controlled, size of friend network also ceases to be significant; therefore, size and amount of contact with the "effective network" of regularly-seen people is also irrelevant to life satisfaction. Furthermore, employment status drops to insignificance.

Only two network ties—confidants and affiliations with associations—continue to be significant when resource effects are eliminated. Both these variables seem to represent qualitative, rewarding exchanges. Confidants provide closeness, trust, and intimacy in relationships. Voluntary associations may not provide such intimate bonds; however, they can provide rewards of shared interests, experiences, and concerns among peers. Although ties to confidants and voluntary associations reach statistical significance, each explains less than 1 percent of the variance in life satisfaction, suggesting that they have little substantive importance. While the F-ratio for the block of network ties is significant, collectively the 5 types of involvement explain 1.44 percent of the variance.

Personal resources as a block continue to be significant and explain over 22 percent of life satisfaction variance when the blocks of network characteristics and network ties are entered first. Each resource except for age continues to make a statistically important contribution to predicting the dependent variable. Health remains the single best predictor, accounting for almost 17 percent of the variance in life satisfaction. Dependency adds 1.6 percent Socioeconomic resources collectively contribute an additional 3.5 percent, with education the most important and Duncan SEI the least. Comparing unique contributions made by these 3 blocks, personal resources remain crucial both statistically and substantively, network ties make a minor contribution, and network characteristics are relatively worthless.

MARITAL STATUS VERSUS OTHER VARIABLES

The remaining question is whether marital status has long-term consequences for life satisfaction once these other variables are considered. The answer is no. Marital status is statistically insignificant at that point and adds .00272 to the R^2 value. In essence, other variables and especially personal resources intervene so that widowhood per se has no long-lasting direct consequences for life satisfaction.[3]

CONCLUSIONS

In this research, widowers as a category appear to have lower life satisfaction than married men. Although this sounds commonplace, it comes from research that compared widowed and married men, not widowed and married persons nor married versus nonmarried men as occurs when widowers are categorized with never married, separated, and divorced males. Furthermore, formerly widowed but now remarried men, a third category in this study, have higher levels of life satisfaction than widowers but not as high as married men. On the one hand, this suggests that future research should distinguish carefully among marital statuses and not include remarrieds in the married category. On the other hand, marital status per se makes no important contribution to life satisfaction after other variables are considered. Can it be that widowhood in old age changes life less than gerontologists have expected?

Potential mediating variables included network characteristics, network ties, and personal resources. The number of children, proximity of children, and child interaction had no effect on life satisfaction once other variables—particularly personal resources—were considered. This finding helps refute the myth among laypersons that adult children are critical to life satisfaction of older persons. Admittedly, children are important for providing aid and services especially to widowers; however, children seem irrelevant to life satisfaction.

In addition to children, employment status, size of friend network, and amount of friend interaction fail to contribute to an explanation of life satisfaction. Instead presence of a single confidant who provides emotional closeness does more for life satisfaction than any amount of friend contact. This finding affirms that quality of interaction is more important than quantity. Future research on quality of closest ties should use Snow and Crapo's (1982) interval level emotional bondedness instrument. Additional instruments are needed to explore quality of interaction and ties with friends other than most trusted confidant.

A second network tie—affiliation with voluntary organizations— also raises subjective well-being. Perhaps such involvement provides opportunities for rewarding exchanges with others possessing similar interests, concerns, and resources. However, membership is too gross a measure to indicate rewards and costs of exchanges; these variables need to be measured to pursue an exchange perspective.

Resources, especially health, were the major contributors to life satisfaction among these rural men. This research also added dependency to the analyses. Although significant to life satisfaction, variance in the dependency measure was limited among this sample of relatively independent men. It would be useful for future research among other populations to measure dependency directly and to assess its effect relative to health conditions.

In general, personal resources were crucial to life satisfaction. The combined effects of resources and network ties suggest that the best way to promote life satisfaction in later life is to promote good health. In planning for old age, one should also maintain independence, get a good education, accumulate assets, develop at least one close relationship, and consider joining others with similar interests in formal organizations. These relational and personal resources mediate the effects of marital status for men and promote subjective well-being. Such resources, however, may not be distributed evenly across marital statuses. Additional analyses are needed to ascertain whether married, widowed, and formerly widowed but now remarried men have similar or different social network ties and personal resources.

NOTES

1. Larson's (1978) article was published before Snow and Crapo's (1982) report that self-rated health explained 28 percent of the variance in Life Satisfaction Index A scores among their sample of 205 older male outpatients at a Veterans Administration Medical Center.

2. For a more complete discussion of life satisfaction instruments, consult Sauer and Warland (1982).

3. One might argue that variables between blocks are interrelated highly and that these potentially create a problem with multicollinearity. To control for the possibility of multicollinearity, additional regressions were run after moving 3 variables—mean distance of children, size of friend network, and Duncan SEI. Regressions run in this manner used only variables that had bivariate correlations under .50. When these 3 variables were excluded, regression results differed little from those reported in Table 4.2. The total R^2 value declined by .00515. Only 1 variable appreciably changed in percent of unique variance explained; that variable was health, which increased by 1.49 percent. The 2 sets of regressions yielded similar findings. In both instances, the total R^2 exceeded .36 and marital status explained less than 0.3 percent of the variance in life satisfaction.

5

FAMILY RELATIONS OF THE OLDER WIDOW:
Their Location and Importance for Her Social Life

JEANNE M. GIBBS
Former Predoctoral Trainee
Midwest Council for Social Research on Aging;
Former Postdoctoral Trainee
The University of Michigan

Before 1965, the literature was virtually devoid of knowledge about family relations of the widowed, a deficiency that was especially marked in the case of the older widow. Discussion focused primarily on the psyche of the widowed person, offering psychiatric and psychological explanations for the reactions and adjustments involved in the process of returning to "normality" after the death of the spouse. There was seemingly little interest in the nature of social relations after the initial year of widowhood.

Research concerning distinctions between types of communities and their implications for social relations in widowhood has likewise received minimal attention. With certain exceptions (Kivett, 1978; Arling, 1976a, 1976b; Pihlblad and Adams, 1972; Berardo, 1967), there has been little research specifically on the nonmetropolitan and rural widow's support including her family relations.

With Lopata's (1979, 1973a, 1973b, 1970a, 1970b) work it was recognized that widows as a social group had specific needs and problems that were protracted well beyond the initial period of crisis. It was found that widowed persons turned more often to

Author's Note: *Research was funded by a grant from the National Institute on Aging awarded to the Midwest Council for Social Research in Aging. I wish to thank Eva Kahana, Tom Hickey, and Ruth Gladstone for helpful criticism of earlier drafts. Responsibility for content, however, remains solely with me.*

their relatives than to friends—especially after the initial period of grief and bereavement—in seeking solutions to their problems (Glick et al., 1974; Lopata, 1973a). The present study verifies the perceived and actual importance of the family, especially children and siblings, for the widow after the initial period of grief.

Early research in this area found that the degree of relatedness of kin influenced the amount of interaction. Burr (1973) proposed further that degree of relatedness of kinship groups not only influenced the amount of interaction among them but also resulted in positive relationships. This is particularly true in the case of the older widow who, because of the loss of her husband as a social companion, will oftentimes substitute interactions with children and siblings, thus renewing or increasing her family interactions (Gibbs, 1978).

This study addresses the perceived and actual importance of family relations of the nonmetropolitan older widow after one year or more of widowhood. Although it was anticipated that rural versus urban nonmetropolitan community structure would affect the nature of social support between the two communities, no formal hypotheses regarding community differences were made due to the exploratory nature of the study. Demographic characteristics of the widow's children and sibling groups are presented as well as the nature and frequency of social interactions of each group with the widow. The relationships between the frequency of specific social interactions and the older widow's feelings of emotional closeness for her children and siblings are analyzed. Further, a distinction is made regarding the importance of physical proximity for social relations.

METHOD

STUDY DESIGN

The family support systems and networks of forty older widows residing in two nonmetropolitan communities were examined. The older widow's primary family support members proved to be her children and siblings. These immediate primary family networks are examined.

The data were collected in 2 nonmetropolitan Kansas communities during 1978. "Urbantown" was a nonmetropolitan community with a population of approximately 34,000. "Ruralville" was a much smaller nonmetropolitan community with a population of less than 1,000. In-depth standardized interviews were administered personally to a nonrandom sample of 20 older widowed women living in each community.

In both communities, lists of widows were compiled with the aid of knowledgeable community informants, for example, women's club officers, county extension agent, and older adult club leaders. Respondents who agreed to participate in the project were interviewed for general background information, basic demographic and life cycle data, housing and living arrangements, health status and history, educational and work history, information about family interaction, and perceptions of emotional closeness to family members. A second interview sought to determine the relative significance of activities, the perceived nature of her family relationships, and the importance of these social relationships.

SAMPLE CHARACTERISTICS

The respondents were Caucasian, 50 years old or older, widowed at least 1 year or more, and not yet remarried. Age range of the Urbantown sample was from 55 to 94 years with a mean age of 74.7. Age range of the Ruralville sample was from 60 to 90 years (mean age was 75.75). The widows were all in relatively good health: 17 rated their health as excellent, 15 as good, and 8 as fair. None of the women rated their health as poor.

Education. Level of educational attainment was considerably higher for the Urbantown respondents: The range of years completed in school was from 11 to 18. Years of completed schooling for the women in Ruralville ranged from 4 to 15. Almost half the sample in the rural community had an eighth grade education or less, whereas all of the women in Urbantown had at least 11 years or more of education.

Income. Besides the difference in educational attainment, there was considerable difference in current annual income between the two groups. The median for the Urbantown sample was $8,500 whereas the median current annual income for the Ruralville women was $4,500.

Length of residence. Length of residence in Urbantown ranged from 3 to 67 years in the community (mean: 39.05 years). Length of residence for the Ruralville sample ranged from 6 to 80 years (mean: 32.65 years).

Length of widowhood. Length of widowhood for the Urbantown respondents ranged from 1 to 42 years, with a mean of 14.25 years. In Ruralville, length of widowhood ranged from 3 to 30 years with a mean of 11.9 years.

DATA ANALYSES

As part of a larger survey, the widows were asked for demographic and interactional information about their children and siblings. Demographic information included age, sex, marital status, and residential location of each child and sibling.

The dependent variables included frequency of social contacts and perceived emotional closeness between the widow and each of these family members. On a 6-point scale, respondents were asked how often they visited, talked on the telephone, and wrote each child and sibling. Responses ranged from: (1) "every day" to (6) "never." Additionally, respondents were asked how emotionally close they felt toward each child and sibling. Based on a 5-point ordinal scale, responses ranged from: (1) "very close" to (5) "very distant."

Pearson (product-moment) correlations, chi-square values, and univariate frequencies were computed. Community comparisons between Urbantown and Ruralville were made using the results of these measures. The acceptable level of significance selected was $p \leq .05$.

RESULTS

LIVING CHILDREN

The widows in Urbantown reported a total of 49 living children at the time of the interviews in 1978 (24 female, 25 male). The ages of the daughters ranged from 25 to 71 and for the sons from 18 to 61. In Ruralville, the number of living children reported by the widows at the time of the interviews in 1978 was 71 (37 female, 34 male). The age range of the daughters was from 26 to 61 and for the sons was 30 to 67.

RESIDENCE OF CHILDREN

A total of 8 Urbantown widows had 12 children living in the community. There were 3 children (all sons) who were reported as living in the same household as the respondents. In 2 cases the widow was the head of household and, in the other case, the son was. There were no minor children residing at home. One child, a daughter, was reported as living in the same neighborhood and 8 children—4 daughters and 4 sons—resided in the Urbantown community but in other neighborhoods. Five children lived in other communities in the state. A total of 32 children of the Urbantown respondents lived outside the state.

In Ruralville, 14 widows had 24 children living in the community. There were 2 children, both sons, who resided in the same household as the respondent. In one case, the son was considered the head of household and in the other case, he was not. Like Urbantown, there were no minor children residing at home in Ruralville. A total of 22 children resided in other neighborhoods of the same community, including 14 sons and 8 daughters. There were 26 children who resided in other communities in Kansas, and 21 who lived outside the state.

Of the total number of 49 living children of the Urbantown widows, 12 resided in the same community as their mothers, while—double this number—24 of the 71 children of the Ruralville widows resided in the same community—offering a far higher degree of physical proximity.

SOCIAL INTERACTION

Table 5.1 displays the frequencies and percent frequencies of specific social interactions with children correlated with the widows' feelings of emotional closeness toward them. The Urbantown women, as indicated, appear to have felt emotionally closer to their children than the Ruralville women. In terms of actual contact, however, the Ruralville widows saw their children and talked with them on the telephone more often whereas the Urbantown widows and their children corresponded more often. Chi-square values for each frequency of interaction ("see," $\chi^2 = 14.04$; "phone," $\chi^2 = 13.07$; "write," $\chi^2 = 9.61$) between the communities were all significant (all p's $\leq .01$).

TABLE 5.1

Frequency and Percentage Frequency of Social Interactions Correlated with Feelings of Emotional Closeness of Urbantown and Ruralville Widows for Children[a]

Type, Frequency of Social Interactions	URBANTOWN (n = 49) Feeling of Emotional Closeness								RURALVILLE (n = 71) Feeling of Emotional Closeness							
	Close		Average		Distant		Totals		Close		Average		Distant		Totals	
	F	%	F	%	F	%	F	%	F	%	F	%	F	%	F	%
See: H	10	20.4	2	4.1	0		12	24.5	17	23.9	8	11.3	0		25	35.2
M	14	28.6	1	2.0	0		15	30.6	26	35.6	9	12.7	1	1.4	36	50.7
L	16	32.7	3	6.1	3	6.1	22	44.9	4	5.6	6	8.5	0		10	14.1
Totals:	40	81.6	6	12.2	3	6.1	49	100.0	47	66.2	23	32.4	1	1.4	71	100.0
Phone: H	17	34.7	1	2.0	0		18	36.7	21	29.6	6	8.5	0		27	38.0
M	18	36.7	3	6.1	0		21	42.9	26	36.6	16	22.5	1	1.4	43	60.6
L	5	10.2	2	4.1	3	6.1	10	20.4	0		1	1.4	0		1	1.4
Totals:	40	81.6	6	12.2	3	6.1	49	100.0	47	66.2	23	32.4	1	1.4	71	100.0
Write: H	10	20.4	2	4.1	0		12	24.5	4	5.6	0		0		4	5.6
M	8	16.3	1	2.0	0		9	18.4	10	14.1	10	14.1	1	1.4	21	20.6
L	22	44.9	3	6.1	3	6.1	28	57.1	33	46.5	13	18.3	0		46	64.8
Totals:	40	81.6	6	12.2	3	6.1	49	100.0	47	66.2	23	32.4	1	1.4	71	100.0

a. Feelings of emotional closeness and frequency of interaction scores are based on ordinal response scales.

Although the Urbantown widows had higher reported feelings of closeness to their children, correlations were not significant, suggesting that the greater reported closeness of the Urbantown women to their children cannot be explained as a function of the smaller number of children.

No significant correlation is evident between the frequency of seeing or writing their children and the widows' feelings of emotional closeness toward them ("see," $r = .207$ in Urbantown and $r = .136$ in Ruralville; "write," $r = .134$ in Urbantown and $r = -.083$ in Ruralville). However, there is a significant correlation in both groups between the frequency of talking on the telephone with their children and the widows' feelings of emotional closeness toward them ($r = .446$, $p \leq .001$ in Urbantown; $r = .226$, $p \leq .05$ in Ruralville).

These results suggest that the quantitative dimension of interaction through "seeing" and "writing" is not central to the quality of the relationships as measured by the widow's feelings of emotional closeness toward the child. However, in the case of telephone calling, especially in Urbantown, the quantity of social interaction is related to the reported emotional quality of the widow-child relationship. This delineates a complex situation. Emotional closeness may be a facet of the relationship developed early in the child's life, and those who are emotionally close may leave the community, making frequent visiting difficult. In these cases, the telephone is a medium of personal contact that allows a familiar interchange that may be the best available substitute for a direct presence. In addition, frequently seeing the child may imply dependency of the widow on that child for money or care, whereas frequent phone calls may be more apt to be related to a desire to share experiences and less apt to imply that the child is taking care of a dependent parent. Letter writing appears to be a lost art as a medium of contact between those emotionally close, though there may be both educational and socioemotional factors involved here in addition to the personal quality of the telephone as compared to the letter.

In any case, the data suggest that feelings of emotional closeness are not contingent on quantities of specific social interactions, except for talking on the telephone. Nor does the quality of the widow-child relationship seem to hinge on the number of children the widow has or the frequency of interaction per se. Rather, it has to do with the nature of the social relationship and the perceived quality of interaction with the child or children. A large quantity of functional interactions may in fact be unrelated to feelings of emotional closeness and can, indeed, lead instead to a lack of emotional closeness (Arling, 1976b; Homans, 1961).

LIVING SIBLINGS

Urbantown respondents reported having 47 living siblings, whereas the Ruralville women had 42. The average age of living siblings of the Urbantown widows was 64.61 for females and 68.87 for males, compared to 71.36 and 70.76 for the Ruralville group. Thus the rural widows had fewer but, on the average, older living siblings.

RESIDENCE OF SIBLINGS

The present residence of the living siblings of the Urbantown respondents shows few in close proximity. One sister resided in the same household as the respondent. Another respondent had a sister residing in the same neighborhood. Other than these 2 cases, the rest of the siblings of the Urbantown respondents lived outside Urbantown, 19 in the state of Kansas and 26 outside the state.

In Ruralville, one respondent's brother resided in the same house. None of the respondents reported a sibling living in the same neighborhood, but 13 lived in the Ruralville community. Of these, 8 are brothers and 5 sisters. In all, 21 siblings of the Ruralville respondents lived in Kansas; another 7 lived outside the state.

There were 9 widows in Ruralville and 2 in Urbantown who had a sibling(s) residing in the same community. The number of siblings of the rural respondents who resided in Ruralville far outnumbered the siblings of the Urbantown widows who resided in Urbantown. A total of 14 siblings (9 brothers and 5 sisters) resided in Ruralville in contrast to only 2 sisters in Urbantown.

SOCIAL INTERACTION

Table 5.2 gives the frequency and percent frequency of specific social interactions correlated with the feelings of emotional closeness of the Urbantown and Ruralville widows to their siblings. As shown in Table 5.2, the Ruralville widows see ($\chi^2 = 27.79$, $p \leq .005$) and speak on the phone ($\chi^2 = 22.04$, $p \leq .005$) to their brothers and

TABLE 5.2
Frequency and Percentage Frequency of Social interactions Correlated with Feelings of Emotional Closeness of Urbantown and Ruralville Widows for Siblings[a]

Type Frequency of Social Interactions		URBANTOWN (n = 47) Feeling of Emotional Closeness								RURALVILLE (n = 42) Feeling of Emotional Closeness							
		Close		Average		Distant		Totals		Close		Average		Distant		Totals	
		F	%	F	%	F	%	F	%	F	%	F	%	F	%	F	%
See:	H	1	2.1	0		1	2.1	2	4.2	14	33.3	4	9.5	0		18	42.9
	M	12	25.5	1	2.1	0		13	27.6	10	23.8	6	14.3	0		16	38.1
	L	20	42.6	7	14.9	5	10.7	32	68.1	4	9.5	1	2.4	3	7.1	8	19.0
Totals:		33	70.2	8	17.0	6	12.8	47	100.0	28	66.7	11	26.2	3	7.1	42	100.0
Phone:	H	4	8.6	0		1	2.1	5	10.7	13	31.0	0		0		13	31.0
	M	10	21.3	1	2.1	0		11	23.4	12	28.6	10	23.8	0		22	52.4
	L	19	40.3	7	14.9	5	10.7	31	65.9	3	7.1	1	2.4	3	7.1	7	16.7
Totals:		33	70.2	8	17.0	6	12.8	47	100.0	28	66.7	11	26.2	3	7.1	42	100.0
Write:	H	3	6.4	0		0		3	6.4	2	4.8	0		0		2	4.8
	M	15	31.9	6	12.8	0		21	44.7	6	14.3	3	7.1	1	2.4	10	23.8
	L	15	31.9	2	4.2	6	12.8	23	48.9	20	47.6	8	19.0	2	4.8	30	71.4
Totals:		33	70.2	8	17.0	6	12.8	47	100.0	28	66.7	11	26.2	3	7.1	42	100.0

a. Feelings of emotional closeness and frequency of interaction scores are based on ordinal response scales.

sisters much more than do the Urbantown widows, but there is no difference in the felt closeness to siblings. Further, the most likely explanation of the greater numbers of social interactions reported by the rural widows with siblings is the larger number of siblings who resided in Ruralville. The widows in Urbantown reported a higher degree of interaction with siblings with respect to "writing." The social interaction of seeing siblings and feelings of closeness was not significantly correlated for the Urbantown sample ($r = .129$) as it was for the Ruralville sample ($r = .361$, $p \leq .01$).

The correlation for the Urbantown sample for "talking on the telephone" with siblings in relation to feelings of emotional closeness toward siblings was not significant ($r = .184$). In Ruralville, this correlation was significant ($r = .536$, $p \leq .0001$).

The correlation for the Urbantown sample for "writing" siblings in relation to feelings of emotional closeness toward siblings was significant ($r = .287$, $p \leq .05$), whereas in the rural sample it was not significant ($r = .045$).

The Pearson r correlations of both community samples regarding number of siblings in relation to the widows' feelings of emotional closeness toward them were not significant for either community sample ($r = .090$ in Urbantown and $r = .140$ in Ruralville).

These findings tend to imply that, as in the case of the Pearson r computations with children, the size of the sibling group is not as important for the widow's feelings of emotional closeness as is the quality of her continued social interactions.

In the case of siblings, for both samples, feelings of emotional closeness seem to be related to the kinds of social interaction most appropriate for their physical proximity: seeing and talking on the phone in Ruralville and writing in Urbantown. Unlike the case of interaction with children, some relationship between type of interaction and feelings of closeness seems most apparent among the rural widows: The highest frequencies of seeing or talking on the phone are with those siblings living in the same community, and they constitute almost half of the siblings to whom the widows feel emotionally close.

DISCUSSION

It should be noted that older American widowed women residing in a specific Midwestern locale were included in the study. Thus the reader is cautioned about the generalizability of the findings because of the limited and specific nature of the sample.

Although the findings on the widows' immediate family groups were presented in terms of their demographic and social interactional characteristics, it should be emphasized that the social support networks of the widow do not operate in a formal fashion, but from day to day, in a fluid process, and, many times, conjointly with one another.

Size of the widow's familial groups were correlated with her feelings of emotional closeness toward each group. Because none of the Pearson correlations for either community were significant, size of family support may not be as important as other factors in determining the salience of the widow's social relationships. However, the size of the family support network that resides in the community itself may be more important than the total numbers of family members as such. The rural widows reported greater numbers of family in close geographical proximity than the Urbantown widows and, correspondingly, definitely heavier reliance on their families living in Ruralville.[1] In addition, the rural women had greater numbers of social interactions with family on a day-to-day basis. It may be concluded that it is not the number of persons in one's social support groups that is of greater moment in explaining the perceived salience (emotional benefits) of social relations in widowhood, but rather that the people in the social support groups be available and frequently engaged in social interactions with the widow. In this connection, this research supports Shanas's (1979b) earlier conclusion that the older person's (in this case the older widow) family, primarily children and siblings, through face-to-face contacts are a major tie of the older adult to the community. A large number of visitors is not necessary. It is much more important that there be regular and concerned visitors (Shanas, 1979b).

When considering the importance of physical proximity for social relations, a distinction must be made. The content of social relations must be viewed along at least two dimensions: functional requirements and socioemotional components. Physical proximity is important in fulfilling the functional requirements of a relationship, especially for the rural widow who has more social than economic resources immediately available and whose community lacks formal service supports. However, physical proximity in regard to the socioemotional requirements of a relationship may not be as important and, indeed, can in some cases be detrimental to the family relationship. Arling (1976b: 766), similarly, has made the point that family contact is not necessarily always "emotionally satisfying to the elderly."

Certainly, future research should look at the question of the nature and degree of dependency between the widow and her various family members and how the quality of their relationships is affected because of it. Further investigation of various types of social interaction (e.g., face-to-face visits, telephone calls, writing) and their effects on social relations is needed. For instance, professional caregivers as well as concerned family members may do well to understand that telephoning the older widow may be much more meaningful for her than writing, and that visiting her in person is even better.

Future inquiries in widowhood, and social gerontology in general, should include in their designs a stratification and comparative component along several interrelated dimensions: age, socioeconomic, and community characteristics. The structure and content of social relations, as indicated in the present research, differs as any, or all, these dimensions vary.

The widow's age at the time she becomes widowed, for instance, and at various junctures afterward, is a major factor affecting the impact of the community's institutional opportunity structure for reconstructing social life because age serves as an eligibility criteria for participation in, or exclusion from, various social institutions within the community. Almost universally, you must be a specific age to join certain social clubs, retire from paid employment and draw a pension, and be eligible to receive certain social security benefits.

In addition to formal eligibility requirements, age serves in a number of nonformalized ways to define normative expectations and behaviors. The average age of widows in the United States is 55.6 years (Lopata, 1973a; Gibbs, 1978). For women, age 55 is not considered sexually and romantically attractive in this country. This makes dating, courtship, and remarriage difficult. Lopata (1973a: 17), in fact, claims that

> life styles for American widows are generally built upon the assumption either that they are young and can soon remarry or that they are very old and removed from the realm of active involvement. The trouble is that most widows are neither, but society has not taken sufficient cognizance of this fact to modify the facilities and roles available to them.

In the present research the average ages of the respondents were considerably higher than the national average for widows. In Urbantown the average age of the widows was 74.7 years whereas in Ruralville it was 75.75 years. Earlier research has it that younger widows appear to "gravitate to urban areas" (Lopata, 1973a, p. 25) and that it is the older women who remain in the rural setting. There is, thus, every reason to conclude that for rural, nonmetropolitan areas, pockets of elderly population composed primarily of older widows create special problems and needs that neither their age nor social position can help to alleviate but that public policy could address.

Socioeconomic status and resources are especially important for the reconstruction of social life for the widow insofar as they enable her to use existing resources or to develop new resources to aid this reconstruction (Gibbs, 1978; Lopata, 1973).

Elderly people belonging to a lower socioeconomic stratum are seen as more likely to lose contact with distant family members than those in other social classes (Lopata, 1973a, 1970a). Other factors can compound the problems caused by lack of socioeconomic resources. Barriers such as poor health and long distances between widows and their children, along with the lack of economic resources, can diminish social contact (Lopata, 1970a; Shanas et al., 1968).

The present study, though it did not concentrate on socioeconomic differences, concludes that social class and the socioeconomic resources available make considerable differences in the widow's processes of social reconstruction. The socioeconomic differences between the Urbantown and Ruralville widows certainly account for many disparities in the general lifestyles of the two groups.

Further, although older women are closer to their families (Clark and Anderson, 1967; Rosow, 1967), they are paradoxically more isolated than men, and have a greater need for services due to lesser financial and technical resources.

The present research has demonstrated that there are important community differences even within what are considered to be similar categories of communities. (Despite the large difference in their sizes, both of the study communities are technically designated as nonmetropolitan.) Studies of similar and contrasting community types, as well as regional variations of location of communities, would be most helpful in the future. The use of "social systems" and "interactional" methods would be useful in analyzing communities as units of social organization. It would also be useful and important to conduct future widowhood research with minority widows (and widowers) in various community contexts.

Finally, widowhood is more generally a woman's experience, not a man's. In fact, should average life expectancies continue to increase, especially for women, the reality of intergenerational widowhood for women becoming more and more common is certainly a possibility. Certainly intergenerational relations among those widowed across generations within families will pose special implications and problems for professionals and family members alike.

NOTE

1. Continuity of farm ownership within the family and ability to secure farm loans more easily in the Ruralville area were major factors in accounting for the greater numbers of Ruralville family members remaining in the area.

6

ELDERLY PARENTS AND THE CAREGIVING ROLE:
An Asymmetrical Transition

LUCY ROSE FISCHER
Assistant Professor, Sociology
University of Minnesota

Numerous studies have shown that adult children, particularly daughters, often provide long-term health care for their elderly parents (see Shanas, 1979a, 1979b). Care provided by adult children can prevent or postpone institutionalization (Dunlop, 1980). While spouses are the most "dependable" caregivers, daughters are especially likely to provide care for widowed elderly parents (Fischer, with Hoffman, forthcoming). Surveys have found that elderly people in our society prefer not to live with their children and, at any one time, only a small percentage of elderly live with adult children in the same household. However, adult children often provide at least temporary care in their homes when their parents are very ill. Several studies have indicated that possibly a third or more of middle-aged daughters and sons spend some time caring for an elderly parent in the children's homes (Robinson and Thurnher, 1979; Johnson and Bursk, 1977). The 1976 Survey of Institutionalized Persons (Current Population Report, 1978: 196) shows that nursing home residents and elderly institutionalized individuals are nearly as likely to have lived with children as with spouses in their last residence.

Although there is much evidence that adult children serve as caregivers, several studies also have indicated that impaired health

Author's Note: *I would like to express my gratitude to Carol Hoffman, who assisted with the interviewing and data analysis for this chapter, and to the other research assistants, the hospital staff, and the subjects who participated in this project. This research was supported by a grant from the All-University Council on Aging/CURA, University of Minnesota.*

strains family interactions and that the caregiving role appears to have a negative impact on the intergenerational relationship (see Lee, 1979; Johnson and Bursk, 1977; Robinson and Thurnher, 1979). Studies comparing children and spouses as caregivers indicate that both experience similar kinds of stress—particularly when children, like spouses, are alone with the disabled person (Danis and Silverstone, 1981).

If the adult son or daughter becomes a parent-caregiver, this means that the health crisis of an elderly parent produces a transition in the intergenerational relationship. By definition, the transition is more "relational" for the son or daughter than for the parent: The parent has undergone an individual crisis; the adult child has experienced a "counter-transition"—having become a caregiver only because of the parent's primary transition.

This study examines the impact of the parent's health crisis on four dimensions of relationships: (1) role perspectives—that is, how do the role partners view each other and interpret the nature of their relationship; (2) emotional attachment—the direction and intensity of emotional involvement; (3) interdependency—what the role partners do for each other; and (4) power—who exercises decision-making control, and under what circumstances. This research asks the following: What is the nature of this transition from the role positions of the elderly parent and the caregiving daughter or son?

THE STUDY

This research examines a time of transition—that is, families undergoing a health crisis, operationally defined as a recent hospitalization. The data reported here are part of a hospital study. This chapter is based on 14 case studies entailing in-depth interviews with 15 caregivers (including 2 sisters) and 11 of their parents. Another paper (Fischer, with Hoffman, forthcoming) has discussed other data from this study—including case surveys and interviews with hospital staff.

The cases in this study constitute a specialized sample, selected according to the following criteria: The patient was over 65, widowed, recently discharged from the hospital, required some kind of posthospital care, had a local son or daughter, and was designated as able to give "informed consent." The subjects were obtained from the caseloads of three social workers in a suburban hospital in the Minneapolis area. The social workers made the initial contact and obtained permission to release names and addresses to the researchers. The adult children in the sample were designated as those who maintained contact with the social workers and included 11 daughters, 2 sons, and 2 daughters-in-law (all of whom were the prime caregivers). The sample of parents was made up of 9 mothers and 2 fathers (with 3 parents who were not interviewed).

The mean age of the parents is 80; for the sons and daughters, it is 47. The adult children were mostly both daughters and youngest children—with the exceptions being cases where there was no daughter and/or no youngest child residing locally.

ROLE PERSPECTIVES: CAREGIVING AS ROLE REVERSAL

An elderly person who begins to have serious functional disabilities will experience a new kind of dependency—needing to depend either on family members or on others to provide assistance with the basic functions of daily living, such as, feeding, toileting, dressing, and mobility. When the caregiver is an adult son or daughter, the parent's dependency might be viewed as a kind of role reversal. The subjects in this study were not asked explicitly whether or not they were experiencing a "role reversal" in the parent-child relationship (a question that might be "leading" and ethically problematic). Nonetheless, in all of the cases, the adult child either described a protective relationship vis-à-vis the parent and/or explicitly labeled this relationship as a "role reversal." Explicit statements about role reversal were made in about two-thirds of the son/daughter interviews. A number of the daughters, in particular, made statements more or less similar to this: "I think now the roles have been reversed. I think she's the child and I'm the parent." In another case, a son indicated that he is trying to renegotiate their intergenerational role positions:

> I don't think she accepts the fact that we are grown up, we're adult, we have families, we make our own decisions now and sometimes maybe know a little bit what's better for her. My sister has gone through quite a bit of medical training. . . . She's not a doctor by any means but yet she knows some things that are good and what's not so good for my mom. My mom does not accept the fact, hey, we

might know what might be good for her now as compared to when we were growing up . . . so she has trouble, I think accepting that, and that creates conflicts because we're looking out for her better and she doesn't accept that fact.

In this case, the ambiguity of status positions of mother versus child is reminiscent of the relationship between adolescent and parent. Just as the parent and adolescent child are likely to disagree about whether or not the adolescent has achieved adult status (see Turner, 1970; Fischer, 1981), there may be intergenerational disagreement on the "postadulthood" of the elderly parent.

It is striking that none of the elderly parents described this process of reversal and almost none expressed a sense of their children's protectiveness toward them. That sons and daughters are conscious of a process of reversal may reflect their normative assumptions about relationships with older parents. But the fact that the elderly parents do not mention this process suggests either that they do not think they are experiencing this type of relational change or that they feel uncomfortable with such a reversal. In any case, the health crisis of the elderly parent and the caregiving role constitute an asymmetrical transition in that the transformation of the relationship is perceived differentially by the two generations.

ASYMMETRY IN THE EMOTIONAL RELATIONSHIP

The elderly parents in this sample were confronted with major life crises: Many of them were experiencing large losses in functional health; for some there was the possibility of imminent death. Therefore, it is not surprising that in this sample, all of the parents appeared to be either depressed[1] and/or to be going through some process of denial to deal with depression. One woman, for instance, lives with her daughter who works all day and with her son-in-law who is retired but who never sits and talks with her. She talked about her frustration about not being able to walk: "It's really depressing. And I can't go out now with the bees, they're terrible, so that I have to stay in, which I don't like . . . I get lonely during the day . . . I'm not able to do things I feel I should." Another man, who has had a second stroke and is in a nursing home (it is not clear for how long; he himself refers to the facility as a "hospital"), complained about the "routine of my life" being "changed drastically." This man suffers from uncontrollable crying fits—probably produced by the stroke—and is both embarrassed and angry that he has lost control over his physical and emotional life. He resents the nursing home where "somebody else is structuring" his life "and they don't know how. I'm the only person who could structure my own life." What is described here, then, is a process of mourning for her or his past life. In interpreting these and the other cases, we can note that for the elderly parents, the crisis is intensely personal.

Conversely, for the daughters and sons, the emotional content of the crisis is both personal and relational—that is, they are dealing with their own grief as well as with their parents' reactions. About half of the adult children expressed concern about their parents' depression. In a number of cases, the adult children reported that their parents told them that they were just waiting to die. The daughters and sons who mentioned such statements indicated that they responded with a sense of frustration and exasperation: They refused to allow their parents to just "give up."

For most of the sons and daughters, the most salient aspect of the health crisis appeared to be not so much their parents' depression but rather their parents' personality change—including forgetfulness and confusion. To a large extent, it was the personality change that created a need for a role reversal. For instance, in one case a mother's "hallucinations" undermined the mother's credibility for her son—and convinced him that he had to make decisions for her. A daughter noted: "One of the things that kind of bothered me is that she doesn't want to take a newspaper anymore." The transformation of the parent's personality means that the parent is lost—as he or she once was (see Coser, 1966). One of the daughters talked about how her father's "personality just switched" when he became paralyzed:

> It sounds terrible to say, I guess, but I could have better handled the fact that he was in pain, because you can control pain with medication, than I handled the fact that he wasn't himself. He wasn't the person that I remembered him being—the caring, lovable person that he was. That was harder for me to adjust to than the fact that he had cancer and was probably going to die soon.

Almost none of the parents themselves suggested that they were aware of a personality change (the only exception being the man who could not control his crying episodes). Thus, although both generations are undergoing a process of mourning, they actually are experiencing different kinds of losses. The parent has lost physical control over his or her life. For the sons and daughters, the crisis is social and interpersonal because their interactions with their parents are transformed.

Both confusion and depression can lead to greater emotional dependence on the son or daughter. For instance, one of the mothers, who is suffering from some degree of mental confusion, needs to be reminded continually of necessary dates, and so on. The daughter noted:

> If there are plans that she's going someplace—there's a wedding or this or that—I tell her the date and everything. She gets very nervous that she's not going to remember it, even if I write it down. So I try not to tell her the day before, because she gets very nervous about it, although she wants to attend everything, but she doesn't want it on her mind.

This daughter is, apparently, protective of her mother's anxiety about being forgetful. The daughter did not want her mother to be interviewed for this study because she believed that her mother would feel distressed if she were not able to remember answers to simple questions.

Depression tends to entail a process of disengagement. With the health crisis, the parent may begin to withdraw emotionally from the relationship, partly in response to pain, partly from despair about the loss of functional abilities. But there is a paradox in this disengagement process: The parent's disengagement leads the son or daughter to become increasingly involved and active in the relationship—both instrumentally and emotionally, as the daughter or son becomes depended upon for services and takes on an emotionally protective role vis-à-vis the parent.

INTERDEPENDENCY: THE BURDENS OF CAREGIVING

The caregiving role increases instrumental involvement by the adult children: Nearly three-fourths of the daughters and sons mentioned that there was an increase in contact. In almost all the other cases, there already had been a long-term history of high contact and involvement. The interview data showed that the daughters, sons, and daughters-in-law assumed heavy responsibilities in caregiving. During the peak of the crisis, almost all of them had daily responsibilities and for many the daily involvement persisted long after the hospitalization. The care provided to the parents tended to be sandwiched into their other responsibilities—to children, spouses, work, and time for their own leisure. The interviews were done during the late summer and early fall and a number of the sons and daughters mentioned that they and/or siblings had given up or postponed vacations because of the parents' illness.

The adult children described a variety of services, which appear to translate to large numbers of hours. One daughter described bringing food to her mother daily before her mother went to the nursing home and mentioned that she continues to attend to various of her mother's instrumental and emotional needs—although her mother's daily routine and medical care are done by health care professionals. In the case of another family, one daughter said that she coordinates the care and six sisters and brothers share responsibility for visiting; they have a schedule so that the father receives a visit from at least one child a day. This daughter said that she herself visits her father about four or five times a week. In this case, the father's nursing home is at least a half hour drive from her home and she reported spending at least an hour during each visit. This daughter has two preschool children, a full-time job, and also has a serious health problem (she was about to have her second operation for cancer).

But despite the high amount of instrumental involvement in caregiving, the sons and daughters do not necessarily portray themselves as burdened. The first daughter mentioned above stated that it was not a lot of work to bring meals to her mother: "I would send food over there all the time because she really couldn't do any cooking. . . . She did not want the meals-on-wheels. I felt she did need it. So I was the meals-on-wheels . . . I did not mind." The second daughter described above suggested that the caregiving has helped to take her mind off her own health problems:

> Sometimes I think Dad's stroke at this time was a godsend for me, or maybe I would be a basket case. Because it's been a long wait between May and now, getting this second surgery scheduled.

One conclusion that we can make, then, is that the objective amount of caregiving responsibility does not necessarily predict the subjective perception of burden. In both cases described above, the daughters apparently have obtained intrinsic rewards from their caregiving role—that is, the provision of the service is its own reward, irrespective of any other motivation. In the case of the woman with cancer, the caregiving role seems to be far more desirable than the patient role. The daughter who didn't mind bringing daily meals to her mother conveys a common attitude expressed by the daughters and sons in this sample—that their responsibilities toward their disabled parents were taken for granted among their interpersonal obligations. LaRossa (1981) suggests that "role strain" is a relative concept—that is, the amount of strain is related to expectations. Thus if we want to understand to what extent the adult children are "burdened" by their caregiving role, we need to ask, compared to what? For instance, "worry" might also be a "burden," so that a daughter or son who is not providing needed care might be subjectively more stressed than the one who is assured that appropriate care is provided by his or her own hands-on assistance.

Nonetheless, the adult children were more likely to describe caregiving "burdens" than were their parents. About two-thirds of the sons and daughters did indicate feeling at least somewhat burdened. Less than half of parents indicated that they thought that their adult children had heavy responsibilities in caregiving. Moreover, the increase in contact with the children was mentioned by only two of the mothers, suggesting, at the very least, that the parents may not focus as much on the new instrumental responsibilities of their sons and daughters.

If the perception of burden is not clearly correlated with the objective amount of work, it may be difficult both to measure levels of "burden" and to assess predictors of stress in the caregiving role. However, there is one indicator of stress that does appear to be correlated with the circumstances of the caregiver role. The sons and daughters were asked: "During the past 6 months—how often have time pressures made you feel anxious?" The sample of adult children can be divided into adult children who report frequently feeling "anxious" (6 cases) and those who say that they are sometimes or never "anxious" (9 individuals, representing 8 family cases). An examination of the caregiving situations suggests that there are striking differences between these 2 groups. For the group of adult children who indicate that they have not felt particularly anxious about time pressures, the elderly parents are all in relatively settled situations—either having a permanent placement in a nursing home (5 cases) or having returned to a long-term living arrangement with the daughter (2 cases). In contrast, in the "frequently anxious" group, the parents all appear to be in transitional caregiving situations—with the parents in some kind of temporary situation for which future health care arrangements are uncertain. Of the 6 "more anxious" children, 3 of the parents are in a nursing home temporarily; 1 mother is temporarily in the daughter's home; 1 mother is in her own home (while the daughter worries); and 1 father has just entered a nursing home—after more than 6 months of negotiating arrangements. This measure of "anxiety" suggests that the caregiver role may be difficult not simply from the amount of work but perhaps even more so from the uncertainty about health care options and outcomes and from the tension of making the arrangements.

CONTROL OVER HEALTH CARE DECISIONS

The data from this study suggest that the "patient" role provides a framework for surrender of decision-making control. In all but one of the cases, decisions about posthospital care were made by the sons and daughters. The patients themselves often have been "out of it" while in the hospital. Thus both the work of arranging for care and the decision-making control tend to fall in the domain of their adult children.

To a large extent, the adult children exercise control for the sake of the parents. The adult children provide information to the staff about the idiosyncratic needs of their parents and they also give salience to the needs and wishes of their family members. This is particularly important when the patient is unconscious or otherwise unable to speak for him- or herself. In two extreme cases, the children fought on the patient's behalf—criticizing the staff for not providing proper care. In one of these cases, the mother remembers almost none of the battling with staff that was done on her behalf. This daughter has little good to say about the care her mother received at the hospital from doctors, nurses, or social workers. She describes the mother being left on a bedpan for long periods of time—with the staff seemingly forgetting that it had been placed there—and a number of other such incidents. The mother, however, says she recalls only one "mean" nurse who flopped her down on her bed uncomfortably and asserts that almost everybody else at the hospital was "very kind." It is not possible here to determine the "reality" of the health care situation in this case. What is clear, however, is that the sons and daughters often see themselves as the allies of their parents in the sense that they speak on their parents' behalf. Anger against the staff is only one manifestation of this alliance.

But despite the existence of this patient-family alliance, the controlling alliances are much more likely to be between the son or daughter and the health care professionals. In 9 of the cases there was some conflict over posthospital care plans. In the majority of such cases (5 out of 9), the adult children "won"—that is, the plans were implemented according to their own and not their parents' direct wishes. In only one case was the parent the "winner" (with the 3 remaining cases having unclear or temporary outcomes). Often, parents appeared to comply with a decision for nursing home placement because of the force of this alliance. The hospital survey data and the staff interviews also indicated that when the hospital social workers and other staff play an explicitly intermediary role, they tend to take the point of view of the son or daughter. Furthermore, our analysis showed that staff mediation greatly increases the probability of institutionalization (see Fischer, with Hoffman, forthcoming).

CONCLUSION

The findings from this exploratory study suggest that the health crises of elderly parents lead to an asymmetrical transition in several senses: First, there is asymmetry in their role relational perspectives—with the son or daughter but not the parent perceiving a role reversal. Second, the health crisis helps to create a psychological gap between parent and adult child so that the son or daughter becomes increasingly "engaged" in the relationship while the parent becomes more "disengaged." Finally, the transition of parent to patient helps to establish a relational hierarchy—with the parent gaining nurturance while losing decision-making control.

NOTE

1. The researchers did not make a clinical assessment of depression.

7
DATING AND COURTSHIP IN LATE LIFE:
An Exploratory Study

KRIS BULCROFT
Assistant Professor, Sociology
St. Olaf College

RICHARD BULCROFT
Ph.D. Candidate, Sociology
University of Minnesota

The extent to which family and friend networks have been important factors in the overall life satisfaction of older persons has been an area of empirical and theoretical concern to social gerontologists for some time. Most of the literature has focused on the quantity of social exchanges between the older person and his or her network, with social exchanges typically being measured along the dimensions of services, aid, or support. As a means of quantifying such exchanges, we tend to count the number of times visited/visiting, amount of aid exchanged, size or extensiveness of the social network, and so on. Little is known, however, about the quality of social relationships in later life. Although attempts have been made to study the quality of family relationships (Fischer, 1981; Baruch and Barnett, 1983) and marital satisfaction in later life (Rollins and Feldman, 1970; Spanier et al., 1975), few studies have explored the content and quality of heterosexual dating and courting relationships in later life.

RELEVANCE OF THE PROBLEM

For the most part, research on dating and courtship has studied only high school and college aged samples with the 1970s witnessing a marked decline in the dating research, coupled with an increased interest in the process of the dyadic love relationship (Bernardo, 1981). But little has been done to advance understanding of the dating and courtship processes of middle-aged or older persons. Although it is acknowledged that for persons in middle or later adulthood, such dating relationships are most frequently subsequent to divorce or widowhood, the context and meaning of such heterosexual dyadic dating relationships is of no less consequence on the lives of those involved. In fact, in a world of shrinking social roles, dating relationships in late life may have heightened import for the morale and self-concept of the older person.

Research on intimate, heterosexual relationships in later life typically has emphasized sexuality and has tended to ask only those questions that lend themselves to the structured questionnaire format. Although such research efforts are to be praised for their pioneering attempts to add to the small pool of quantitative knowledge concerning later life intimacies, they rarely add to an understanding of the qualitative dimensions of loving and dyadic processes (Brecher, 1984). For example, Brecher provides data on the number of elderly who said they were currently in love. He then further delineates between love relationships that are durable and continual versus those that are sudden or "falling in love" experiences. While this study represents an attempt to qualify the love relationship, it demonstrates the inability of most survey data to probe into the meanings, symbols, and expression of the love relationship in later life. In-depth analysis is needed at this time to explore some of the qualitative dimensions of the dating relationship as it occurs in the later stages of the life course.

Mate selection will not be the focus of this inquiry. The primary reason for this is that although some argue that the numbers of older persons in the United States choosing to marry has increased (Vinick, 1978), it appears to be largely a function of increasing numbers of older persons in the population. In reality, there are about 3 brides out of every 1000 older single women, and about 17 grooms out of every 1000 older single men (Treas, 1976). Although these estimates are not indicative of an "epidemic" of later life marriages, they also do not reflect the propensity to date and court in the older population.

Currently, there are no estimates of the numbers of older persons who engage in formal or informal dating relationships. If, as in college-aged samples, much of the dating that occurs eventually leads to marriage, then the statistics on the number of older brides and grooms might lead one to suspect that little dating is occurring in later life. However, whereas structural and normative factors operate at younger ages to push the dating couple toward the marital relationship, older couples may find social constraints that modify their dating patterns and purposes in the direction of nonmarital commitment. So although it may be argued that large numbers of older persons do not marry in later life (either first-time marriages or remarriages), it does not necessarily imply that frequency of dating behaviors and the numbers of older persons dating are low.

Although the amount and nature of one's need for intimacy varies across the life course with different patterns of intimate attachment emerging for men versus women, the need for intimacy still exists among the elderly (Lowenthal, 1967; Trapmann and Hatfield, 1982). Thus one might expect that dating and courtship are prevalent in older populations. Alternatively, it might be argued that same sex friendships and kinship networks offer adequate outlets for intimate attachments in later life. However, evidence presented by Hochschild (1973) and Litwak and Szelenyi (1975) indicates that such "functional interchangeability" across actors (kin, friends, lovers, spouses, and so on) with respect to the satisfaction of other personal needs is limited. Given this general lack of functional interchangeability across actors, there is no reason to suspect that heterosexual dyadic relationships become less salient as one ages.

METHODOLOGY

In light of the relatively scant body of empirical knowledge concerning dating and courting in later life, it was the intent of this study to explore the dimensions of dating and courting among older populations and to determine the methodological feasibility of such an inquiry.

In the fall of 1983, a membership list of persons age 60 and older who attend a Twin Cities (Minneapolis/St. Paul) singles club was obtained. This singles club for older persons is just one of several such organizations in the Twin Cities area. Membership is open only to those persons age 40 or older. For purposes of this study, only those persons 60 years of age or older were interviewed.

Although the reference point of age 60+ is somewhat arbitrary, interviews were conducted only with persons of this age group as a means of assessing the function of age in dating relationships. Because a sizable body of knowledge exists on college age dating patterns, an attempt to contrast younger with older populations highlights age-related differences. Consequently, middle-age dating behaviors and processes will not be studied, although it is acknowledged that dating during that stage in the life course may produce its own unique patterns of behavior.

There are two primary reasons why the findings as presented in this discussion may not be generalizable to the larger population of single older Americans. First, in-depth face-to-face interviews were conducted with only ten subjects (an equal number of males and females). Keeping in mind the main focus of the study—mainly to explore the various dimensions of dating relationships in later life and determine the methodological feasibility of a larger study—a limited sample size was desirable as a means of further refining instrumentation and assessing the issues of reliability and validity.

The way in which a sample was obtained points to the difficulty in constructing a random, nonbiased sample of older persons who are currently dating. It was determined that a sample of persons actively participating in a singles club may indeed be more prone to date in the traditional sense of the term, perhaps be more sexually active than singles choosing not to belong to a singles club, and to be unique in background characteristics such as health, SES, ethnicity, and levels of community integration. Despite the failure of this sample to produce readily generalizable results, its merit rests in the fact that we are more likely studying dating and courting in the most active or extreme cases that will certainly provide in-depth information about the dating relationship itself and its processes.

The semistructured interviews were conducted in the homes of the older persons on a scheduled basis. Of those persons initially contacted concerning the study, no one refused to be interviewed. This in itself was enlightening, as when the research design was initially proposed there was considerable speculation concerning the willingness of older respondents given the subject area.

Some of the more sensitive topics (for example, incidence of sexual intercourse with dating partner, discussion of sexual behaviors unique to the dating relationship, comparison of present and past relationships) that originally were deemed difficult to discuss by the researchers proved to be discussed readily by the respondents. In fact, as one interviewer observed, the older persons seemed willing and pleased to be able to discuss their dating relationships, as few objective listeners are available in their individual social networks.

The interviews ranged from two to four hours in length. Because couples were interviewed for the most part (but at different times), reliability was assessed more easily. Interviewers subjectively report high levels of correspondence in terms of couples' perceptions of their relationships. Even issues such as power in the relationship, assessment of levels of physical attractiveness between partners, and recall on earlier dating patterns and behaviors appears to be consistent across partners.

The average age of the respondents was 62.7; the length of time they had considered themselves to be on the "dating scene" ranged from 4 months to 19 years. All respondents were white, middle SES, and single at the time of the interview. This reflects the general composition of the singles club from which the sample was drawn, with the exception that the club itself is estimated to have a membership of about 5 women to each man.

FINDINGS

This chapter will focus on levels of romanticism in later life, behaviors associated with dating and courting, and the motives for dating. When the original interviews were conducted, an emphasis on assortativeness of partner selection and the development of dyadic relationships were also central features. However, the preliminary interviews revealed that measurement of these dimensions of dating was extremely difficult. Findings are inconclusive at this point concerning the age generalizability of theories of dating and courtship in these areas. Therefore, this discussion will center on those aspects of later life dating that proved fruitful in the exploratory interviews.

BEHAVIORS ASSOCIATED WITH DATING AND COURTSHIP

Because traditional dating behaviors have changed, sociologists may feel a reluctance to study dating patterns and customs at this time (Murstein, 1980). In younger aged groups, there appears to be a lessening of formal structures. Although the structure of dating has indeed changed over the past decade, dating still exists. The behaviors associated with dating are highly related to historical time, with issues such as how couples meet, where they go on a date, what they talk about, levels of sexual activity, and customs associated with the dating arrangement influenced by changing societal attitudes and norms.

A study by Knox and Wilson (1981) of university students' dating behaviors revealed that the most frequent means of meeting a dating partner was through a friend. The second most likely source of initial meeting was at a party. Dating partners were also frequently introduced through work or class participation. In earlier decades church or club settings may have also been important meeting places.

Interviews with older persons show that they tended to meet dating partners through more formal means, such as singles club dances, participation in other club memberships such as the American Legion, or other formal organizations or activities. Few reported having met their current dating partner through friends or other more informal random encounters. The relatively low emphasis placed on friends, family, or informal introduction to dating partners in later life reveals a marked difference between the young and old in terms of their sources of dating introduction.

As the Knox and Wilson study revealed, the settings for dates of college student were most frequently restaurants, sporting events, parties, or the place of residence of one of the partners. As hypothesized, older persons more often attended voluntary organizations as settings for dates. Primarily, functions such as dances, card parties, and other club activities were mentioned as places for dates. Dancing received priority rating as a frequently mentioned setting for dates in later life. This most likely reflects cohort effects as they relate to preferred activities of older couples.

Interestingly, dating settings in later life appear to have more variety compared to younger age dating patterns. Activities such as camping, canoeing, attending movies or the theater, dinner at restaurants or place of residence, concerts, and trips were frequently mentioned settings for dates. Although not directly comparable to the Knox and Wilson study, this implies that settings for dates may indeed reflect more variety in later life. This may be the result of more financial stability, coupled with more diversity of interests.

Many of the normative behaviors of the dating relationship tended to reflect cohort trends. For example, in the older sample, the man is still expected to drive and pick up the woman for the date. Preference was given for men to pay for the date, but in those relationships that are long-term and that have perceived equity of finances, acceptance of the Dutch treat type of dating arrangement is evidenced. However, even in this arrangement careful consideration of the man's masculine role is given. For example, as one woman put it, "I don't think it's [Dutch treat] good for a man. . . . I don't just treat him. He'll fix my car and then I'll take him out to an expensive play."

Although those persons interviewed felt that it was becoming more acceptable for women to ask men out on dates, none of the women sampled had ever done so. Nor had any of the men ever been asked out by a woman. Although there was acknowledgment of tolerance for shifting dating norms, for the most part, the dating behaviors indicated a strong tendency toward traditional male/female roles in dating patterns and habits.

Consistent with the findings of Macklin (1972) for younger college-aged samples, cohabitation is part of the dating relationship for many older persons. The tendency to maintain two residences is also found, with the dating couple typically spending two to four nights per week together at one of the residences. Reasons for maintaining separate residences are primarily focused on the need to feel independent of the relationship and to keep up appearances for family and friends. One man spoke of his girlfriend's bringing the extend-a-phone to his apartment when she spent the night, so family and friends would not know she was out of her apartment.

Sexuality appears to be a vital part of the dating relationship in later life. Sexual intercourse is expected from the dating partner; this is true for women as well as men. The normative standard of sexuality tends to imply that if sexual intercourse does not occur by the fourth or fifth date, then other dating partners will be sought. The majority of those interviewed report that sexual intercourse is better in later life; there is evidence that new learning can and does take place in the sexual activities and behaviors in later life. Kissing, hugging, and petting behaviors are deemed appropriate in the dating relationship, and do not appear to differ radically from the expression of intimacy at earlier stages in the life cycle. The nuances of the sexual relationship appear to remain constant over time and contribute to overall satisfaction with the sexual aspect of the dyadic relationship.

One of the key differences between older and younger dating partners may be along the dimension of the progression on the relationship. All those interviewed felt that dating in later life took on an accelerated pace. The formation of the dyad was accelerated because of a sense of constricted life space. In other words, relationships formed and crystallized quickly because couples did not have time for "playing games." Men and women alike reported being up front with their motives and feelings early in the relationship. Less emphasis was placed on the "feeling out" of the relationship as their age alone dictated that they should speed up the process of dyad formation. There was also the notion that marital experience or a variety of dating partners had taught them what they wanted in a heterosexual relationship, and were quicker to determine if the present dating partner would fulfill their role expectations.

ROMANTICISM IN LATER LIFE

Symbols of romanticism were an aspect of the dating relationship in later life that all respondents could identify. However, contrary to the research by Treas and VanHilst (1976) on remarried older Americans, which suggests a high level of symbolic romanticism as demonstrated in the large number of June weddings, the preference for religious vows, and the tendency to honeymoon, the interview data did not reflect similarly high levels of romanticism among dating couples. In fact, a surprisingly low emphasis on romanticism in dating relationships was evidenced by both men and women. Although both genders stressed the pragmatic side of the dating relationship—that is, role compatibility and companionship—rather than the romantic side, women were slightly more inclined to discuss romanticism from an emotional framework.

The women interviewed tended to place more value on symbolic romanticism and ideally see romanticism in the relationship, though most acknowledged that it was difficult to obtain in later life. So far as definitions of romance are concerned, traditional definitions of romance prevail for both men and women. They both describe romance as consisting of gifts—flowers, candy, and personal gift exchanges. However, once again women were more likely to express romance in terms of specific behaviors such as hugging, kissing, or verbal pledges of love/desire.

MOTIVES FOR DATING

Beginning with work by Waller (1937), sociologists have explored the motives or functions of the dating relationship for younger ages. Waller's theoretical orientation, although finding nothing positive in the functions of the dating relationship, did point out factors such as prestige, recreation, and sexual education as motives for dating. Burgess and Locke (1940) and Lowrie (1951) further expanded the list of possible functions of dating to include courtship for the purposes of mate selection, a means of obtaining affection, and opportunity for friendly association with the opposite sex.

Prior to collecting the interview data, the researchers speculated that dating for the function of mate selection was not as likely a characteristic of later life dating relationships as of younger. Societal pressure to marry in later life is not likely to be as strong. And the implicit functions of the marital institution itself, legitimization of children and confirmation of sexuality, are not salient issues in later life.

However, the interview data fails to support the hypothesis that dating in later life is not for purposes of mate selection. In fact, the majority of those persons interviewed responded that selection of a marital partner was of prime importance in their underlying reasons for dating. Most expressed the desire to marry in the future, although many stated that they knew they would not marry their present dating partner for a variety of reasons. There was some evidence that the current dating relationship provided the opportunity for meeting potential dating partners. Several respondents reported looking for future dating partners when in the company of their present dating partner. Although long-term commitment and monogamy are the norm among the dating relationships of older persons, the underlying motive to marry is salient enough that precedence is given to the search for "Mr. or Mrs. Right" even when a long-term dating partner is available.

Some older persons did not use the dating relationship as a means of courtship or marital partner selection. There were those individuals who felt that they did not want to remarry in later life as it would mean "giving up something." The things they perceived they might be giving up included independence, financial security, and privacy. Interestingly enough, persons more likely to fear loss of emotional or financial independence were women. Having been in marital relationships in the 1940s through the 1970s, these were women who found themselves outside traditional marital roles for the first time due to widowhood or divorce in later life. Consequently, they were reluctant to give up newfound freedom.

Secondary motives in the dating relationship tend to center around an exchange of intimacies, utilization of the dating relationship as a means of remaining socially active, and relearning to interact with persons of the opposite sex. The issue of self-revelation or intimacy exchange appears to be a motive that is stronger for men than for women. Women characteristically reported that their female friends supplied an outlet for self-revelation. "I have better emotional exchange with other women than with men" one woman explained. Whereas an older man stated, "I have never been able to share my gut feelings with another man." These findings are quite consistent with studies of friendship formation over the life course (Lowenthal and Robinson, 1976).

Prestige appears to be somewhat of a byproduct of the dating relationship, particularly for women. Although not a motivation to begin dating, many of the women stated that their friends were supportive of their dating but a "bit envious." Women did attribute the ability to get dates as luck or good fortune, and an enviable position to other women. Men did not seem to derive a sense of prestige from the dating relationship, largely due to the disproportionate number of older women to men in society such that, as one man put it, "When I was younger I wasn't a popular guy. . . . I can always get a date now."

Related to the issue of prestige derived from dating relationships in later life is the notion of the dating relationship serving to maintain a stable identity in later life. As Sarah Matthews (1979) points out, old women as widows or single individuals have a reduction in the number of roles available to them. Social roles of parent, grandparent, or sibling may lack content. Friendship and heterosexual dating relationships may indeed increase in importance in telling the older woman to define herself in consistent terms. It is particularly interesting that women throughout the life course have been socialized in defining oneself in relation to physical attractiveness and as a counterpart to a man. Consequently, this emphasis on one's sexual and social desirability may indeed be a highly sought image by older women, one that can be confirmed only through the dating and courting relationship. In an attempt to maintain a stable identity in later life, a woman may, as Matthews suggests, selectively interact with those individuals who reinforce her identity as a woman. This perspective may also shed light on the reason that many older women choose not to become involved in heterosexual dating relationships primarily due to a fear of rejection, hence a disruption of self identity.

Older men, on the other hand, may also seek to interact in dating relationships as a means of guaranteeing a stable identity, but due to the demographic disproportion of older men in the population may not derive the same level of prestige or identity confirmation that seems to benefit women. Interview data imply that the stronger motive for men in dating at older ages is in terms of an exchange of intimacies rather than self-definition.

Dating in later life further tended to acquaint persons with the social skills of interaction with members of the opposite sex. Men and women equally reported feeling awkward in initially returning to dating following widowhood or later life divorce. Unsure of the norms of dating behavior and often questioning their own physical attractiveness and sexuality, they felt that initial dating experiences in later life left them feeling like a "teenager" again. However, poise and learning to interact with persons of the opposite sex did follow after some time spent in dating situations.

In summary, primary motives for later life dating appear to be the following: courtship, companionship, maintenance of a stable identity (for women), and an outlet for intimacy exchange (for men). An implicit function of the dating relationship may also be prestige accorded to women in a highly competitive dating system. It should also be emphasized that incongruency exists between the motive of courtship and the ability of the dating relationship to lead to marriage. As discussed earlier, the tendency for both men and women to hold strong role expectations for marital partners makes marriage less likely in later life. This appears to be a stronger factor in determining the low rates of marriage at older ages than are structural barriers that may discourage later life marriage.

SUMMARY

As stated earlier in the chapter, this exploratory study may lack generalizability to some older populations, but it adds much to determining the methodological feasibility of such a study of heterosexual dating relationships in later life. It also highlights some of the key differences and similarities between younger and older persons' dating relationships. Furthermore, it is a starting point for testing the age generalizability of theories of dating and courtship.

Clearly there is a need to understand better the effects of later life dating on levels of adjustment and well-being. As is so plainly shown in the interview data, there exists a need on the part of older persons themselves to learn of normative standards of dating behavior and courtship processes in later life.

Part II

Interdependence in Social Support Systems

8

AFFECTIVITY AND THE INTERWEAVE OF SOCIAL CIRCLES: Life Course Transitions

JAMES C. CREECH
Graduate Student, Sociology
Indiana University

NICHOLAS BABCHUK
Regents Professor of Sociology
University of Nebraska—Lincoln

Over the past forty years, research convincingly demonstrates how critical it is for individuals of every age and at every stage in the life course to have and maintain intimate relationships (e.g., Davis, 1940, 1947; Eisenberg, 1979; Lowenthal, 1964; Lowenthal and Haven, 1968; Spitz, 1945; Strain and Chappell, 1982; Trapmann et al., 1982). Apart from family members, however, little is known concerning who becomes part of the intimate network and the ties that individuals have in various social circles. Although recent studies have dealt with the theme of overlappng social circles (McPherson, 1983; Verbrugge, 1978; York and Lazerwitz, 1983), there has been no concerted effort made to examine this phenomenon since Simmel's (1922) early essay. That will be the focus in the present inquiry, particularly the role played by the life course.

Author's Note: *Partial support for this research came from training grants furnished by the National Institute of Aging (PHS T32 AG 00074-03) and the National Institute of Mental Health (PHS T32 MH 15789-05). The data were collected by Claude S. Fischer and made available through the Inter-University Consortium for Political and Social Research. Helpful comments were made by Lucy Rose Fischer, Harold L. Orbach, Jill Quadagno, Hugh P. Whitt, and participants of a Midwest Council for Social Research in Aging Seminar. A revised version was presented to the annual meeting of the Midwest Sociological Society, Chicago, 1984. Responsibility for the contents of this chapter are borne entirely by us.*

Simmel (1982) develops three lines of argument from the premise that belonging to multiple social circles is a fundamental characteristic of modern societies. First, the various social circles to which an individual is affiliated can be used as a system of coordinates to define the individual. Each social circle helps to identify uniquely an individual with greater precision and less ambiguity. Second, because an individual belongs to several social circles simultaneously means that these circles intersect or overlap with that individual. By extension, then, all social circles are linked, either directly or indirectly, through their members. Third, subsets of members from one social circle frequently will jointly belong to other circles. Thus the multiple social circles in common can facilitate integration into the community.

When examining intimate networks, sociologists have often relied on Cooley's (1909) conception of the primary group. Although rich in connotation, there are, nonetheless, serious shortcomings in his conceptualization because it is essentially denotative. For Cooley, primary groups are equated with kin, friends, and neighbors, and these three collectivities are seen as inclusive. This mode of conceptualizing primary groups has been followed by many contemporary scholars (e.g., Dowd and LaRossa, 1982; Kerckhoff, 1966; Knipscheer, 1979; Litwak and Szelenyi, 1969; Sherman, 1975). Close examination of these three types of groups, however, shows that the individuals who are members can vary considerably in important respects. To illustrate, the relationship of parents who are close to their adolescent and young-adult children, bound to them by a community of fate, by residence, and through commonly shared values, cannot be compared meaningfully as a unit with neighbors or a group of friends. Neither can the shared secrets and intimacies of best friends be equated with other paired relationships, such as between siblings, between cousins, or between a grandparent and grandchild. Nor can the relationships between neighboring apartment dwellers who live across the hall from one another and who meet only occasionally on the stairs or in the elevator, in any way parallel the relationships between close friends who are coincidently neighbors and who have been on intimate terms for years. Indeed, several recent studies have shown that when primariness is assessed separately from the denotative categories, considerable selectivity is evident within the kinship, friendship, and neighborhood groupings (Babchuk and Ballweg, 1971; Hoyt and

Babchuk, 1983; Longino and Lipman, 1981; Marsden and Campbell, 1984).

A point that has frequently been glossed over in the past is that friends, relatives, and neighbors are not mutually exclusive. There is nothing that automatically precludes a neighbor from also being a blood relation and a friend. Furthermore, primary relationships can and do emerge within other social settings. Homans (1950, 1954), Lincoln and Miller (1979), and Warner and Low (1947), for example, have studied the primary ties of co-workers. Additionally, Jacoby (1966) has argued that voluntary associations, particularly expressive ones, provide a rich environment in which primary ties often emerge.

Small group size, frequency of interaction, and a long history of association are sociological properties that contribute significantly as preconditions for primary relations to develop. When these elements function so that persons view each other holistically, are altruistically empathetic when one or the other is confronted with personal problems, seek to aid each other without regard to personal cost, help each other in a crisis, and so forth, then they are on primary terms with each other. In sum, to be intimate, "very close," or primary is for the relationship to be one that is characterized by a predominance of positive affect and in which there is a high degree of mutual concern between members. This way of characterizing primary ties is consistent with Cooley's intent as suggested by Bates and Babchuk (1961).

AFFECTIVITY, AGING, AND SOCIAL CIRCLES

One of the most widely held hypotheses among network theorists is that relationships become progressively more intimate as the number of overlapping affiliations between a given pair increases (Boissevain, 1974; Craven and Wellman, 1973; Mitchell, 1969). This hypothesis is also central in the primary group literature. Specifically, the more primary the tie between individuals, the more predisposed they are to engage mutually in a wide range of activities (Bates and Babchuk, 1961). Though the hypothesis seems most credible, support for it has been problematic. To illustrate, in a study of middle-class couples, Babchuk and Bates (1963: 383) found that the number of activities mutually engaged in "proved to be an insensitive indicator of primariness." In addition, Fischer et al. (1977) found a weak negative association between intimacy and the number of social circles shared by a pair of individuals. These two reports have serious limitations in that the investigators examine only the closest ties (affective homogeneity) that their respondents had, rather than taking into account the wider mutual circles in which the respondents were affiliated (see Milardo, 1983; Wellman, 1981).

Two connections come to mind with respect to intimacy and common membership is social settings. The first is that overlapping affiliations increase the likelihood of interaction, which in turn enhances the probability that a relationship will be primary (see Bates and Babchuk, 1961; Davis, 1948; Hoyt and Babchuk, 1983; Small and Vincent, 1984). The other is the tendency for friendships to form between individuals who are in some manner alike or are homophilous (Lazarsfeld and Merton, 1954). In this regard, common social circles expose persons with similar statuses, values, and so forth (e.g., neighbors tend to belong to the same social class and persons belonging to the National Rifle Association hold similar attitudes and values regarding gun control), which facilitates the formation of intimate relations (see Bates and Babchuk, 1961; Greer, 1955; Hess, 1972; Newcomb, 1961; Small and Vincent, 1894).

Several factors influence the salience of different social circles as sources of primary ties throughout the life course. Among the most important of these are presence of children in the home, residential mobility, and stage in career.

The social relationships of young adults, for example, are characterized by a low level of involvement with others. Although individuals at this stage in life have many acquaintances, they have proportionately few to whom they feel close. This stems in part from the fact that many young adults are in the process of beginning a career and are residentially mobile as a consequence. Thus it is difficult to develop close and enduring ties with persons in the community in which the individual resides (e.g., neighbors, coworkers, voluntary association co-members; Freeman et al., 1957; Tomeh, 1973). The situation is compounded by the tendency of young adults to consider peer relations as more important than family ties (Brown, 1981; Shulman, 1975; also see Fischer and Oliker, 1983).

Prior to and during early middle age, "family-home localism" (Wilensky, 1960) comes to dominate social involvement. That is, families with children tend to limit participation to the home or to activities that include the children (e.g., scouting, 4-H, trips to the zoo; also see Harry, 1970). During this stage, involvement with both nuclear and extended kin increases. Along with this additional family responsibility, career mobility tends to depend less upon geographic mobility, allowing other people in the community to become more important as sources for close social relationships. Several studies support this associational configuration or pattern showing that the greatest involvement with neighbors occurs among parents of young children (Gans, 1967; Keller, 1968).

In late middle age, many forms of social participation reach their peak levels of involvement. Family ties continue to grow in terms of importance even though the children have grown and left home (Cumming and Schneider, 1961; Riley and Foner, 1968; Shulman, 1975). With increased amounts of leisure time created by the empty nest, voluntary association memberships increase (Babchuk and Booth, 1969; Hausknecht, 1962; Sussman, 1955) and with them, co-member relationships. Further, relatively long-term ties to neighbors and co-workers generally make these ties with others important at this stage in life (Hess, 1972).

With old age, Lawton and Simon's environmental docility hypothesis comes increasingly into play. In brief, environmental docility occurs as the elderly lose the ability to move around, whether because of physical, financial, or emotional reasons or some combination of the three (also see Lowenthal and Robinson, 1976; Stueve, 1982). Because of the effect of this constraint, which resembles docility, neighbors become more important in this stage of the life course (Hess, 1972). In addition, other research indicates that kinship continues to grow as a source of intimates and confidants well into old age (Hoyt and Babchuk, 1983; Riley and Foner, 1968; Shulman, 1975).

The literature on organizational involvement, however, is ambiguous. Several studies suggest that co-memberships become substantially less important as measured by declining mean number of voluntary association memberships that characterize individuals in old age (Foskett, 1955; Hausknecht, 1962; Knoke and Thomson, 1977; Tomeh, 1973). But this conclusion is contradicted by inquiries that indicate the following: first, most individuals continue to belong to at least one voluntary association well into their 70s, 80s, and 90s (Babchuk et al., 1979; S. Cutler, 1977); second, the elderly especially affiliate with expressive organizations

(Babchuk et al., 1979; N. Cutler, 1977; Trela and Jackson, 1979); and third, expressive organizations are more conducive to the formation of primary ties (Jacoby, 1966). Taken together, these studies lead to the expectation that the old would find voluntary association co-members an important source of close relationships.

DATA AND METHOD

The data are from the Northern California Community Study. Between August 1977 and February 1978, 1050 noninstitutionalized adults were interviewed. Because the data were originally collected to examine the effect of urbanism on social networks and social attitudes, the sampling frame was constructed to guarantee that a wide range of communities would be represented. Respondents ranged in age from 18 to 91. Detailed information regarding the sampling procedure can be found in Nicholls (1979) and Fischer (1982).

To map the social networks, respondents were asked to name the individuals with whom they associate in a variety of situations (see Jones and Fischer, 1978; McCallister and Fischer, 1978). Additional information, such as shared social circles (e.g., co-worker, neighbor, relative, co-member of VA) and affectivity (acquaintance, friend, close friend), was then obtained about each person listed by the respondent. In a final step, these data were reorganized into a file of 19,417 dyadic social relationships. Arranged in this manner, the data can be viewed as a hypernetwork sample (see McPherson, 1982). A hypernetwork is a network of linkages, usually between a person and something else (in this case, another person). In one form of hypernetwork sampling, the respondent constitutes the basis for clustering in a sample of linkages, thus allowing the present data of dyads to be treated in a manner similar to other cluster samples. In other words, the estimates are expected to be unbiased, but with a loss of efficiency (see Cochran, 1977).

RESULTS

EXTENT OF OVERLAP

From Table 8.1, it can be seen that most social relationships overlapped to some extent. Regardless of sex or stage in the life

TABLE 8.1
Number of Common Social Circles by Life Course Stage and Gender[a]

Number of Common Circles	Younger Single	Younger Couple	Younger Parent	Older Parent	Older Couple	Older Single	Total
Males							
One	39.9	33.9	23.4	19.1	18.1	36.2	28.4
Two	56.7	62.2	73.0	75.9	78.1	62.3	67.9
Three	1.7	3.1	2.9	4.7	3.1	1.2	2.7
Four or more	1.7	.8	.6	.4	.6	.2	.9
	(2584)	(849)	(1904)	(1139)	(1715)	(486)	(8676)
Females							
One	38.7	30.6	24.7	17.1	21.4	27.6	26.9
Two	58.9	67.2	72.5	77.3	73.8	69.8	70.2
Three	1.8	2.0	2.6	5.0	2.7	2.5	2.6
Four or more	.6	.2	.1	.6	.2	.1	.3
	(1892)	(805)	(3190)	(968)	(1904)	(1969)	(10728)
Total							
One	39.4	32.3	24.2	18.2	19.8	29.3	27.6
Two	57.6	64.6	72.7	76.5	76.9	68.3	69.2
Three	1.8	2.5	2.7	4.8	2.9	2.3	2.7
Four or more	1.2	.5	.3	.5	.4	.1	.6
	(4476)	(1654)	(5093)	(2107)	(3618)	(2455)	(19404)

a. Percent; Ns in parentheses.

course, a minimum of 60 percent of all dyads shared 2 or more social circles. A curvilinear pattern of association was also found between the number of overlapping social circles and the measure for the life course. Young singles were found to have the smallest proportion of ties that overlap (60.6 percent). The proportion then rose to a peak of over 80 percent among older parents, before dipping back to about 70 percent for older singles. Although more than 70 percent of all dyads had multiple overlaps, it was interesting to note that less than 4 percent shared 3 or more social circles. Further, only 1 of the 19,417 dyads included in the analysis had as many as 5 ties to one another.

Tables 8.2 and 8.3 present information regarding overlapping social circles and affectivity. In brief, the hypothesis proposed by the social network and primary group theorists is supported. That is, the number of shared social circles and the degree of affectivity tend to co-vary in a positive direction. The strength of this finding is enhanced when both sex and the life course are used as control variables; the pattern of association remains consistent when the effects of the control variables are taken into account.

SOME ADDITIONAL ANALYSES

More than half of the dyads sharing 2 or more social circles had a kinship tie. Moreover, 90 percent of the relationships sharing 3 or more social circles included a tie to family. As would be expected from the literature (Adams, 1968; Bott, 1957; Coult and Habenstein, 1962; Komarovsky, 1973; Robins and Tomanec, 1962), females tended to report a greater proportion of kin connections than males (56 percent versus 48 percent); and a curvilinear pattern developed through the life course with males peaking during the older couple stage and females during the older parent stage. The overall importance of kinship as a social circle was highlighted by its association with affectivity. In dyads that were described as very close or primary, 72 percent included a kinship tie, and this percentage decreased substantially in the categories considered less close (friend: 41 percent; acquaintance: 6 percent).

The number of relationships with neighbors made it the second most named social circle and accounted for about 17 percent of the multiple overlaps. The relative importance of neighbors as a source of friendship, however, is somewhat deceptive. About a third of the dyads in the acquaintance category were neighbors (the largest contributor). Moreover, a smaller proportion of neighbors were

TABLE 8.2
Mean Number of Common Social Circles Controlling for Life Course Stage and Affectivity[a]

	Younger Single	Younger Couple	Younger Parent	Older Parent	Older Couple	Older Single	Total
Acquaintance	1.630 (230)	1.513 (78)	1.739 (161)	1.863 (80)	1.736 (87)	1.517 (58)	1.673 (694)
Friend	1.674 (2598)	1.692 (1012)	1.774 (3114)	1.882 (1200)	1.804 (2038)	1.721 (1497)	1.754 (11459)
Close friend	1.735 (1648)	1.856 (564)	1.939 (1818)	2.009 (827)	1.971 (1494)	1.831 (900)	1.887 (7251)
Total	1.694 (4476)	1.739 (1654)	1.832 (5093)	1.931 (2107)	1.871 (3619)	1.757 (2455)	1.801 (19404)

a. Ns in parentheses.

TABLE 8.3
Mean Number of Common Social Circles Controlling for Life Course Stage and Affectivity, and Gender[a]

	Younger Single	Younger Couple	Younger Parent	Older Parent	Older Couple	Older Single	Total
Acquaintance							
Male	1.566 (143)	1.633 (30)	1.873 (55)	1.783 (46)	1.734 (64)	1.071 (14)	1.659 (352)
Female	1.736 (87)	1.438 (48)	1.670 (106)	1.971 (34)	1.739 (23)	1.659 (44)	1.687 (342)
Friend							
Male	1.684 (1490)	1.694 (526)	1.799 (1194)	1.895 (655)	1.847 (995)	1.635 (312)	1.767 (5172)
Female	1.662 (1108)	1.689 (486)	1.759 (1920)	1.866 (545)	1.762 (1043)	1.744 (1185)	1.743 (6287)
Close Friend							
Male	1.743 (951)	1.816 (293)	1.976 (654)	1.989 (438)	1.995 (656)	1.869 (160)	1.891 (3152)
Female	1.723 (697)	1.900 (271)	1.918 (1164)	2.009 (389)	1.952 (838)	1.831 (740)	1.884 (4099)

a. Ns in parentheses.

named primary than any other social circle. And contrary to prior research on neighboring (e.g., Townsend, 1957), men were found to be slightly more likely than women to name a neighbor (14.0 percent versus 10.7 percent).

Both co-workers and co-members of voluntary associations make up about 12 percent of the multiple overlaps. However, being a co-member appears to be the more important tie. Among the most affectively close dyads, co-members are the most likely (next to kin) to be named. Within the co-member category, 35 percent were considered very close or primary. On the other hand, co-workers were in the social circle second most likely to be regarded as an acquaintance, and less than 20 percent were named as being affectively close.

There were sex differences with regard to the co-worker ties. Not only were men more likely to name co-workers (17.0 percent for men; 9.8 percent for women), but they were also more likely to name co-workers as close. Such individuals ordinarily were of the same sex. Over the life course, we expected ties with co-workers to parallel labor force participation patterns. For men, then, the expected pattern would be curvilinear with a peak sometime in late middle-age. What was observed, however, was a fairly steady decline in the proportion of co-worker relationships with successive life-course stages. On the other hand, women seemed to follow the hypothesized trend much more closely. That is, co-worker ties appear to be less important after marriage and less so again after children—the 2 life stages in which women leave the labor force most frequently.

SUMMARY AND CONCLUSIONS

Although at least 60 percent of all dyads shared 2 or more overlapping circles, only one of the 19,417 had as many as 5. That so few dyads had more than 2 social circles in common, only 4 percent, came as a surprise. From Simmel's earlier theorizing, there was reason to believe that the phenomenon of multiple social circles would be far greater. The findings forcefully emphasize how segmented relations, as measured by social circles, are in our society. Of course, a community of fate that might critically bind persons together in a web of different spheres or arenas really only applies to the family and at that, mainly members of the nuclear unit. In earlier times and in less industrialized societies, sharing a common destiny applied with greater force, not only in binding a cohort together, but families and the community as well.

Structural variables, especially being married and having children, play an important part in understanding the weave between membership in social circles and the life course. For example, the unattached (whether single, divorced, or widowed) are less likely to belong to associations than the attached. Young adults, as noted earlier in this chapter, are not only in the most peripatetic stage in the life course (sometimes resulting in the eschewing of family ties), but are uninvolved in the polity and, as the data show, in voluntary groups. When the married pair have children entering school, they begin to become involved. Inquiry shows that husbands who are affiliated influence their wives to join associations, and parents who are active in groups similarly influence their children, and vice versa. Indeed, there are reciprocal influences in groups such as the Parent-Teacher Association, Scouting, and the like. Other voluntary groups are predicated on couple participation (e.g., young couple organizations).

Involvement in many social circles peaks during the middle years, with the expected result that overlap among these circles is most extensive at this life stage. By contrast, entry into the final years is marked by declining social circle complexity. There are several reasons for the decrease. An obvious example is with retirement when the circle of co-workers is lost; though the relationship may continue, the structured interaction of the workplace is no longer part of the link. A second factor is that similarly aged associates, both kin and nonkin, are unavailable. That is, some die, others move in with their children, join retirement communities, or the like. In addition, there is an increased reliance on the kinship network for social support in old age. Much of this support is cross-generational and without ties to the other social circles of which the elderly person is a member.

A characteristic of activity in expressive voluntary groups, apart from the element of immediacy, is the pleasure it brings. In fact, this quality is the reason why so many voluntary groups exist. The pleasure of belonging, of interacting, is enhanced when the activity is exercised with those with whom one is affectively linked. Even in instrumental associations, the sharing of a cause, a value, or an objective deeply felt might wed individuals more closely together. Herein lies, in part, the explanation why being a co-member of the same group ranked so highly with choosing that co-member as a close friend or confidant. Such involvement could and did occur between intimates in all stages of the life course.

Another element that makes for an important difference in the quality of dyad relations within a voluntary group context is its volitional nature as compared to a pair interacting in the neighborhood or work setting. Even in good times, it is not easy to change jobs and even more difficult to refashion the composition of one's co-workers. And changing neighborhoods and neighbors is problematic. There may well be many in these environments to choose from, but compatibility, age differences, values expressed, opinions, tastes, and experiences impede cultivating relations or interacting apart from the casual encounter. Neighbors and co-workers obviously can be included among the circles of interaction, but selection is rarely predicated on the type of choice that distinguishes the dyad in voluntary-group settings—particularly expressive ones.

9

NETWORK ANALYSIS OF MID-LIFE TRANSITIONS:
A Hypothesis on Phases of Change in Microstructures

JOHN E. O'BRIEN
Associate Professor, Sociology
Portland State University

The purpose of this chapter is to advance a general hypothesis regarding the process of change in social position during adulthood. The "immediate" pattern of social relationships in which an individual is embedded is called a "personal social network" (Mitchell, 1969). The life transition has two aspects: first are the events that trigger it, consisting of avoidable or unavoidable external or internal changes that result in what we call a social "position shift" (Secord and Backman, 1974); second is the series of events by which the personal state of consciousness and the social network is abandoned, modified, dissolved, or replaced. The rather elaborate process of change in relationships with the network around the individual is that with which this chapter is particularly concerned.

Analysis of the case studies and reading of the literature led to the hypothesis that the transition process can be broken down into phases. Those phases are outlined below and support is presented to back the claim regarding their universality. The use of the network perspective contributes in three ways to an understanding of the transitional process. First, changes in network communication provide external evidence of how the transition is progressing. Second, the content of the communication between the individual and others in the network at one time point out how the position

Author's Note: *The helpful assistance of Ralph Cherry and Leonard Cain is gratefully recognized.*

shift will affect subsequent personal well-being and network characteristics. Finally, social networks appear to be dynamic structures that help maintain an overall sense of order in society while individuals negotiate their way in and out of various positions through the life course.

THE CASE STUDIES

This work began with the intention of having university students use case studies to explore the postulate that networks mediate the influences between larger levels of social organization and individual action. To date, the procedure has been applied by approximately 200 students in sociology classes I have offered. Because the case study process was exploratory, the protocol that guided it was broadly cast. Each student was asked to locate an individual over the age of thirty who had undergone (or was in the process of undergoing) a life transition. Included were marriage, divorce, parenthood, empty nest, occupational change, retirement, residential location, entering a nursing home, and the onset of chronic illness. The individual was to be interviewed as were three other persons with a significant relationship to the individual. Particular attention was given to examining the social connections between the focal individual and others in the network. The basic analytical problem was to describe the association between those links with others in the network, the unfolding of the transition, and the consequences of the transition both for the focal individuals and their social relationships.

PREVIOUS RESEARCH ON
LIFE COURSE CHANGE

Research about adult life transitions is reported in many parts of the social science literature. That literature will be divided into three categories: (a) studies of the association between major historical events and concomitant changes in the staging of life changes by large populations of adults; (b) studies of the experience of limited samples of individuals who move into or out of particular social roles; and, (c) studies of the process of personal "adjustment" to the "stressful" experience of changes in social situation by adults.

One type of past study is aimed at investigating how the timing, sequence, or number of transitions is arranged or managed by large classes of similarly situated individuals (Duvall, 1962; Foner and Kertzer, 1978, 1979; Winsborough, 1979). This type of research is aimed at analyzing the response of "cohorts" and "age sets" to powerful historical events. At issue is how entire categories of individuals who, by virtue of having been born at the same period and subsequently experiencing some common economic, social, or technical change, respond with a common modification in how they organize their lives.

These studies are only secondarily concerned with particular transitions and the individuals undergoing them. Instead, emphasis is given to how historical events lead to changes in such factors as the timing of the onset of some transition. Examples of hypotheses that might be tested include the contention that the economic depression of the 1930s resulted in a universal change in the age at which people choose to undertake the transition to marriage; or that the entry of women into the work force during World War II resulted in changes in the decision about how soon after the birth of the last child mothers would choose to enter the work force; or how the development of dependable contraceptives (the "pill") resulted in an entire generation of adults modifying their approach to the transition to parenthood; or how the economic circumstances of the 1960s led the American labor force to develop new ideas about the transition to "early retirement."

This type of research is termed "macrostructural." That means that questions are explored concerning the association between one aspect of the "larger social structure" (the depression as an economic event, labor force demands as a social event, or invention of the birth control pill as a technological event), and how large collections of people live their lives (enter marriages, procreate, or manage their careers). Such studies are not concerned directly with the motives of the particular individuals who are affected by those large-scale changes. Rather, the mere fact that some historic event occurs (e.g., the "depression"), and large numbers of people act unexpectedly (wait additional years before first marrying) are inferentially taken as evidence of cause and effect. The evidence used for this purpose is typically taken from large, already available data sets such as those provided by the Bureau of the Census, the Department of Labor, or the Social Security Administration. Although massive in scale, studies conducted using these types of secondary data often appear "cold" or statistical, providing little feel for the human dynamics of the people involved or in the situation being studied.

A second type of investigation examines the immediate experience of individuals who undergo particular life course changes. Examples include the work of LeMasters (1957), who studied the "crisis" of parenthood; O'Brien (1971), who studied the "decision to divorce"; Lopata (1973a) and Blau (1961), who both examined the events associated with becoming widowed; Streib and Schneider (1971) and Atchley (1976), who studied how workers adjust to retirement; Bultena and Wood (1969), who explored the process of residential relocation by older couples from the "snow belt" to the "sun belt"; and Cobb (1979), who studied how patterns of social relationships are associated with the way individuals handle episodes of major illness.

In these studies, "fresh data" are gathered by interviews with a sample of individuals who are personally involved with some particular transition. The intent is to describe the way the process unfolds and the consequences for those directly involved. Because this research rests on firsthand reports, the social psychological condition of those involved is of major importance. Heavy emphasis is given to their state of mind and their perceptions or reports of what occurred and why. This particular research strategy, focusing on particular individuals in particular social situations, is what is referred to as a study of the "microstructure" or fine detail of social organization. In such work, the written descriptions that follow are often rich in human narrative.

The two styles of past research referred to so far provide a valuable foundation for the work reported here. However, our work approaches the study of transitions in a manner somewhat different from each of those two traditions. As pointed out, the macrolevel studies contribute little to our microlevel understanding of what the transitions are like "in action." Instead, the effects of large historical events are inferred statistically, with little explanation of why or how those major events actually affect individual behavior. Microlevel studies have similar limits, but of a different type. Specifically, these more narrowly focused studies often produce findings that lead one to believe that individual human behavior largely occurs in a structural vacuum; it is as if the only explanation for patterns of social behavior is that quite by coincidence, numerous individuals independently "decide" to carry out the same action in the same fashion.

Attention is now directed to the third type of research on life transitions. These studies rely on use of what may be labeled the "adjustment to crisis" research design. Although important in other ways, the first two categories of past studies contributed only minimally to understanding how human life transitions occur independently of the content of the specific roles involved. Certainly there is good reason to recognize that the event of widowhood is different from divorce, marriage different from retirement, or residential relocation different from changing jobs. But it is also likely that there is a constancy to the underlying force both for the society and for the individual in the face of all such transitions.

The third type of research involves direct investigation of the above proposition. The emphasis is on the means by which individuals cope with what are assumed to be the unpleasant and stressful aspects of transitions. Thus Lowenthal and collaborators (1971, 1975) have investigated a model of "adaptation" to the social stress associated with life changes. They assume that not only do individuals differ in terms of how well they adapt but also in the degree to which they perceive a given transition to be stressful in the first place. Lieberman (1969, 1975) and Lieberman and Tobin (1983) also get into the problem of adaptation to life crisis, focusing particularly on residential relocation into nursing homes as a field of investigation. Still more recently, George (1980) attempted to generalize the "social stress model" of House (1974) in order to develop a tool for understanding the way in which older persons deal with changes in family life, work, and residence. The implicit assumptions of this work are that adult life transitions are more or less stressful, that there is a "better" way to adjust, and that the essential variable that determines the adequacy of that adjustment process is the inner resources of the individual.

The above studies depict the life changes of adulthood as at best gloomy events that test the inner mettle of individuals. But there are other investigators who seem to suggest that with the passage of the adult years, things become downright hopeless. For instance there is the "social breakdown syndrome" notion developed by Kuypers and Bengtson (1973). They claim that after a certain point in life, transitional losses progressively strip individuals of supports and opportunities. This is taken as a sign of personal debility by others, thus establishing a cycle of negative social labeling that further depletes the capacity of the person to cope with future life changes. In an even more extreme sense, Rosow (1976) seems to suggest that the personal style of adults as they age is rather irrelevant to their well-being. At least as he sees it, this is because the status of the adult becomes progressively tenuous as age increases. This tenuous status makes life marginal at best in the face of the common transitions that typify the process of growing old.

In this third style of research, there is the tendency to equate "change" with "loss and pain," which is common in the functionalist thought of British-American social scientists. How valid is the assumption that transitions are stressful? Early work by me (O'Brien, 1970) clearly demonstrated that at least as measured by the "life satisfaction index" (Neugarten et al., 1961), the "transition to divorce" is frequently accompanied by an increase in "morale." A common basis for justifying the contention that life change is stressful is the work of Holmes and Rahe (1967). Their work assigned "stress values" ranging from 0 to 100 to 42 common life changes such as marriage, retirement, or changing schools. But what does that stress index mean? We know, for instance, that the more miles run weekly by road racers, the more food they eat. Furthermore, some people believe that running is stressful. Does that mean that the volume of caloric intake is equivalent to a "stress indicator"? The facts appear to be that either running or eating may be stressful, or not, depending on what is going on elsewhere in the life of the individual. It is the nature of these other factors elsewhere, such as the social network of the individual, that we believe is critical in determining how life transitions are accommodated.

Most of the previously cited work that analyzed the collective or personal circumstances associated with life transitions was not essentially concerned with the transition process per se. Instead, it involved the selection of transitions as "strategic research sites" for studying problems concerning "microissues," such as human motivation and coping skills, or "macroissues," such as the effects of historical social developments on the circumstances of adults. Not that choosing practical problems as sites for investigating more general theoretical questions is unjustified or illogical. For instance, it is well known in all the sciences that it is difficult to understand the underlying forces behind events by observing only their steady state.

A common strategy for studying any "dynamic" system is to analyze the production or breakdown of that system. Systematically studying artificially induced changes is what laboratory experiments are all about. But social scientists are generally unable to manipulate the start-up or breakdown of social systems artificially. Hence it is customary to use naturally occurring change in families, groups, corporations, or communities as quasi-experimental happenings. Thus we might carry out research on divorce to study the dynamics of marital happiness, on retirement to study career involvement, on residential relocation to study friendship circles, or on suicide to study how individuals experience stress. This style of research emphasizes the "negative" case as a window on the "normal" state and leads to a great deal of discussion of unpleasant or "deviant" issues in the social science literature. The reader is reminded that this is a product of restrictions on the processes available to social scientists rather than an indicator of a prurient interest in the unpleasant tissue of everyday life.

In this study, the social network model is used primarily in its theoretical rather than its methodological sense as a conceptual tool for analyzing life course transitions. Although this is just a preliminary effort, the approach holds promise for analyzing how macro social forces express themselves in everyday life (O'Brien and Kahanoff, 1981). The general qualities of life changes are emphasized independently of the particular position shift associated with them. It also necessitates no assumption one way or the other about whether transitions are good or bad for either individuals or society at large.

CASE STUDIES OF
PHASES OF LIFE TRANSITION

While analyzing the case studies, a general pattern was identified that seemed to characterize all the transitions. This pattern incorporated four phases that appeared to be logically connected and progressive in sequence. The four are labeled the "assessment," "search," "encounter," and "new equilibrium" phases. The model is advanced as a hypothesis and is intended to guide further research. Its validity rests first of all on the fact that a few hundred case studies have supported its basic form. Second, it is logically consistent with certain broadly accepted theoretical principles regarding how systems of social organization operate. Finally, the model is such that when individuals undergoing transitions are presented with it, they acknowledge its plausibility even though they were unaware of it during the changes that they personally experienced (Schutz, 1962). The limitation of the model is that it is not currently formulated in a readily "falsifiable" manner. In the following sections, case material is presented to illustrate each phase of the model.

The first is labeled the *assessment phase*, during which the individual attempts to evaluate the pending consequences of the position shift for himself, his social relationships, and future life options. This is the first step in the exit from the prior position. The transition may be triggered by involuntary circumstances with the position having been "abolished" without any choice on the part of the individual. For example, an individual might decide to change jobs; alternatively, the shift might begin with the decision of the employer to "terminate" the individual's job. Regardless of what sets it off, this first phase appears to be an assessment of the situation and an attempt to come to grips with its potential impact.

Even if the focal individual did not report on his state of mind, the initiation of the transition process would be tacitly evident to others with whom he or she is closely related. During the assessment phase, silence is the dominant characteristic of the communication between the focal individual and those in his or her network. When the transition begins, the individual begins to recognize that the old images and patterns of exchange connected with it are out of line with the emerging reality of his or her life. Under these circumstances, it is hardly logical to carry on relationships in a "business as usual" sense.

In one case study, Martin, a 64-year-old single man, was approaching retirement. Whether considered voluntary or not, the role change was certain to occur. Interviews with others who had significant relationships with Martin indicated that their first awareness of changes in connection with this event was that Martin discontinued a number of well-established habits. He no longer stopped at the same coffee shop in the morning; he ceased being a regular in a circle of friends at lunch; he no longer automatically joined in at the tavern after work with his blue-collar buddies. Martin no longer seemed to have much to say. He reported that this style of being "silent" and inactive relative to members of the work-support network began about ten months before he actually retired. He no longer found it very interesting to talk about such matters as the next foreman, future union contracts, vacations, business expansion, or layoffs of the work force. In general, Martin gave the impression that further interaction with work friends was futile and perhaps a bit painful.

Next is a *search phase,* during which the individual reaches out beyond the old network for sources of new information, allies, role models, or reference groups that might ease the transition. During this time, the communication with the old network is generally open but of limited detail. Network members become aware of new involvements and use of time, but are generally not informed about the motives and meanings behind those involvements. As an outgrowth of the process of personal assessment, the individuals in the case studies reported that they began to take action to build some sort of new lives for themselves. Although the timing of this second "action step" may be delayed for a considerable period of time, most of the individuals we studied showed signs of entering this stage within one year. The need to find a new pathway for living apparently leads to the intuitive awareness that the time has come to reach out in new directions, toward new people, places, and things.

Although this phase seems to emerge spontaneously for most individuals, there is no particular assurance that the "search" will lead in positive, productive, or healthy directions. Whereas "common sense" seems to be sufficient to lead most individuals to seek relief by reorganizing their lives, intuition alone does not assure that the pursuit will be efficient in the short run or satisfying in the long run. Whether the success of this "searching" process is governed by intellectual skills, blind chance, or some power beyond the individual has not been established. It is clear, however, that some people come through this phase much more successfully than others.

Martin, for example, did not do at all well in the "search" phase. According to information provided by a fellow worker, his withdrawal from connections with the old work group began about eighteen months prior to retirement. This is nearly double the length of time reported by work friends for this stage compared to what was reported by Martin. A neighbor described how Martin began to change his pattern of activity. He tried to establish "speaking" relationships with others in the apartment building in which he had lived for years as a bachelor. Prior to this time, he had treated those same neighbors with disinterest. They misunderstood his more open approach as odd and rejected his new gestures of neighborliness. Simultaneously, Martin turned to waitresses in local restaurants and bartenders in local establishments. In the end, only the bartenders were approachable. During the last months of employment, Martin was reportedly drinking more often and more excessively, was absent from work more often, and performing more and more poorly on the job. His coworkers reported that he was generally on a "downer."

Lovella, at 68 years of age, came through this second phase of her transition to widowhood much more successfully. Rather than due to conscious good planning, the events by which this happened grew out of pain, suffering, and chance.

Other than the last months of her married life, Lovella lived all her adult years in a small town near the Nebraska farm on which she was reared. However, when her husband developed terminal cancer, he did not wish to disintegrate from the disease "in front" of all his friends back home. They made a permanent move west as a couple, to live with their only son in Portland, Oregon. Eight months later, Lovella was widowed. During the preceding years, she had not been particularly close to her son; the daughters with whom she was "close" were back in Nebraska, as were her church, clubs, and life-long friends. The move from a town of 1,100 population, 75 miles from Omaha, to a fair-sized metropolitan city was an unnerving shock. Buses baffled her and freeways terrified her. She began to coil up inside herself with a deepened sense of depression. She transferred all her care and attention to a poodle that she carried everywhere, took to bed with her, and for which she cooked elaborate meals. And then things changed.

The marriage of Lovella's son had deteriorated, and her daughter-in-law was particularly distressed. The daughter-in-law subsequently received a traffic ticket for which she was ordered to put in some community service hours at the local senior center. The daughter-in-law met the director of the Center and saw evidence of the program and its benefits. She encouraged Lovella to explore the opportunity, and arranged to take her to lunch and meet the director. It turned out that Lovella had been somewhat involved in the Senior Center "back home" in Nebraska. The rest is history: Within two years, not only was she involved in numerous activities and volunteer duties at the Center, but Lovella had courted and married a man she met there.

Next is an *encounter phase* during which the individual confronts the old network members with the emerging reality of his or her "new" social self. During the two prior phases of the transition, the focal individual has gained distance from individuals and groups. Eventually, there is a need to turn back to those old ties to resolve their meaning and significance. In this phase, the old network members must often listen to new "lines" that may include justification or rationalization for the changes that are beginning to occur. Their response may be judgmental or supportive. This is a key part of the negotiation process for the individual. Specifically, it must be decided which, if any, of the old associates will be part of the newly emerging life pattern. And of those continuing ties, how must their content and intensity be modified so as to be supportive of the new social position that the individual is beginning to enter?

Whether it is complex or simple, whether it is done quickly or slowly, the encounter phase seems to be a critical step in the transition process. In the case of Lovella, it was done in a remarkably direct way. Admittedly, she had a great deal of history tied up back home in Nebraska. For fifty years, she had been a member of the same church, the same sewing circle, the same friendship network. But she put it to rest primarily with a single extended visit back to Nebraska. The visit provided her with the chance to reach new understanding about the people and places of her past and to share with them aspects of her new life. But equally significant, the visit apparently gave her the opportunity to see that history in a new way—as the "history" that it was. It held little contemporary relevance to her new life, and this recognition provided her with the freedom to move forward in living.

Examples drawn from a transition at the beginning of adulthood also highlight the dominant features of this phase. Margy, 31 years old, was in the later stage of achieving the status of an emancipated adult. She began to assess her life and its potential 6 years earlier. She had "gone off" and completed college, but returned home to live with her widowed mother of whom she was the only child. Her jobs were not particularly satisfying and she felt "trapped." To try to free herself, she entered the Peace Corps and served for 3 years in Iran. Upon returning to the United States, she again chose to reside with her mother. But she deeply wanted the basis of that living to reflect the changed style of independence that she had gained while abroad.

Interviews with Margy, her mother and her closest female friend highlighted the complexity of this stage of negotiations. She clearly wanted her mother to be part of her new life, but not in the same way. Margy moved into the basement of the family home, and established her own style regarding privacy and the care of her personal affairs. At the same time, however, she and her mother attempted to agree to cooperate in purchasing food, cooking, and household chores needed to maintain common space. This reportedly caused a great deal of strain, resulting in conflict, anger, and guilt on the part of those involved. But eventually, the ties were renegotiated successfully, and after about one year, both mother and daughter reported general satisfaction with the way life was working out.

Sometimes, this stage of "negotiating" through one's past involves reaching a new resolution with individuals and events that have no current reality except in the memory of the party involved. Mrs. N., for instance, was hit with the sudden shock of widowhood following the unexpected heart attack and immediate death of her husband on a golf course. For her, "phase one" of the transition was not only characterized by outward silence, but also by inward denial. Mrs. N. reported that she felt that friends from the past misunderstood her new situation, and she was unwilling or unable even to discuss it as a matter of historical fact. She specifically claimed that she tried to act as if she were still married—to a deceased person whose death she never acknowledged.

During the next, "search" phase, Mrs. N. reported seeking many forms of medical help, including diagnoses and prescriptions. Somehow she believed that this would lead to a "cure" for her predicament. Later, she "searched" for relief by attempting to throw herself into religion with a vigor that one of her sons later reported to border on the fanatical. During this phase, she also first sought paid employment and ultimately was linked through a friend to a "widow-to-widow" group. As an outgrowth of this last contact, she finally began to level with herself and others. But that was not easy, because she had to go back and try to "make things right" not only with others, but also with herself and with "God."

Based upon interviews that occurred five years after the death of her husband, Mrs. N. had a lot of backtracking to do. In the nearly three years that it took for her to reach the "encounter" phase, she had developed a great sense of anger toward both her former husband and toward "God." Later, she had to change her point of view and relieve herself of that pain. Then there were her three children on whom she had inflicted what one of them labeled the "hypochondria" and "religious fanaticism." Somehow they had to be reached and a new, more realistic basis for relating had to be established. The same went for some of her former friends and extended family. Finally, she reported that she had had the need to reexamine her own past roles and the behaviors connected with them; the resentment of her former husband's demanding but successful medical practice; her failure to maintain balanced relationships between herself and her three children; and her tendency to engage in "social club hopping" in order to advertise the stature of her husband's social class and financial success. Making peace with herself by "encountering" her own past and "negotiating" a more realistic system of meanings was no simple task. Bringing the expectations and understandings that she held for herself, her children, and her close acquaintances into harmony with the realities of their current lives was critical for her moving forward with life.

Last is the *new equilibrium phase* in which a new network arises that supports the actor's new style of life in the revised social position. Sometimes this is resisted as the individual knowingly "pretends" to be what he or she is not or attempts to run from the past completely. But those deceptions are difficult to maintain. A much more comfortable resolution appears to be to renegotiate social relationships so that the knowledge, attitudes, and behaviors that express the new position can be shared with and supported by others (Rabin and Brown, 1975). This is what most of the individuals in our case studies did.

Mrs. K. was forced to retire due to cancer at the age of 53. Interviews were conducted with her, with the woman who was her housemate, and with 2 of her sons. Prior to the onset of her illness, Mrs. K. was employed as a high school teacher. She was reportedly very "strong," assuming leadership not only on the job but also in relation to her housemate and grown children. Seven months after the first visit to her doctor, she had had major surgery (which appeared to arrest the disease), was declared disabled, was officially "retired" from her job, and was receiving social security benefits. At the time of the interviews, which was about 2.5 years after the onset of the illness, Mrs. K. had reached a basically stable, new equilibrium around her new position.

In the old equilibrium, Mrs. K. had been a healthy, active, self-sufficient, employed adult who was a leader at work and the main decision maker at home. In addition, at age 53, she had continued to play the role of authoritative parent to her adult children and their families. But that all changed. By age 56, this same individual was disabled, relatively unemployable, retired, and supported by a pension. She exerted no leadership in any aspects of her life, including at home with her still employed housemate. Although far from passive or "shut off," she was on the receiving rather than initiating end in most of her relationships. With her children, she was no longer the dominant matriach, but a pleasant, supportive "grandmother" who found herself for the first time having direct, primary relationships with her grandchildren. Also, while she withdrew from the work network save for a couple of continuing former teacher friends, she substantially increased her involvement in church for both spiritual and social reasons. In this way, the new equilibrium is characterized by what is reported to be acceptance on the part of all those involved, although none of them are relating to Mrs. K. in the fashion to which they once had been accustomed.

There are cases, however, in which the new equilibrium involves a large number of redefined relationships, some of which are far from mutually acceptable. For instance, Maggie, at age 36, left her husband to seek a divorce after 17 years of marriage. According to her own report and that of a close female friend of 18 years, the position shift began 6 years before the actual separation. With the entry of the last of her 3 children into elementary school, she felt relieved of the major obligations for child care. The release from the sense of guilt, duty, and obligation to "stay with it" that she had for many years led to the beginning of the assessment stage for her. The "silence" of it was quite complete, certainly with her husband and children, and generally with other nearby relatives, a number of whom were interviewed in connection with the case study.

The "search" phase was also carried out during the time that the marriage was "intact." During the preceding years she began doing volunteer work, then went on to finish a university degree and also allowed herself to get involved in what she called "preliminary emotional" affairs with men. Although this was at least partly visible to those around her, she continued to be "silent" regarding the true nature of her motives. The "encounter" phase was abrupt: One morning she announced that she "was leaving." In the same abrupt fashion, she declared to all her primary relatives and children that she had "never loved" her husband and had decided to end the pretense of harmony. She moved that day from the family home, away from her husband and children.

The "new equilibrium" is only partly stable. She has "gone public" with the "other man" and now spends great amounts of time with divorced or otherwise liberated or at least accepting friends. Her occupational and social involvements are not at all similar to how she spent the majority of the prior sixteen years. The close contact with her mother, mother-in-law, brother, and others in the extended family are gone. She deals with those individuals in only limited terms. Also, she is only partly involved in the daily lives of her children, a complete switch from what had been the case in the past. She reoccupies the family home as half-time parent during alternate weeks. Whereas her new circle of friends are quite satisfied with this arrangement, the same is far from true with her family members. All of them continue to be disgruntled and confused about how to deal with the new situation.

The "empty nest" transition of Mrs. P., at age 49, was not at all a problem for those involved. The transition began, according to Mrs. P., at the time her youngest of three children left for college. The "assessment" phase was quiet and introspective, with Mrs. P. finding an occasional twinge of sadness arising as she began to recognize the "beginning of the end" of her active involvement with motherhood. She approached the "search" phase in an interesting way. Rather than seeking out for help for herself, she set out to help others to deal with the very same transition she herself was in. She did so by making friends with other women who were also dealing with the "empty nest" challenge. She spent long hours having coffee and talking on the telephone with those individuals, ostensibly in the role of informal sage and advice-giver. Retrospectively, she acknowledged that this turned out to be her way of preparing in advance for the inevitable changes with which she was confronted.

When her third child left for college, she began to experience undeniable changes in her lifestyle. Her use of time, patterns of daily living, and social habits were radically modified. Her husband had felt for years that "his day was coming" and indeed, her readiness for renewed "couplehood," as she called it, was evidently something that her husband appreciated as well. In addition to the increased level of companionship she shared with her husband, she felt a substantial release from the rigid schedule that she had kept for so many years. She contended that for the first time in her adult years, she felt the legitimate opportunity for privacy and taking care of herself. Although this "new equilibrium" involved major changes in how she related with her immediate and extended family, interviews with three of those others revealed nothing but acceptance and support for the change in social position.

SUMMARY OF CASE PRESENTATIONS

This overview of a small set of cases from the many that have been conducted was intended to exemplify the four-phase model of life transitions that is being advanced here. It is hoped that this overview supports the claim that the phases are independent of the particular content of the roles involved. In another tradition, Freud (1953) and Erikson (1963) propose that the most important transitions are those associated with universal, inevitable stages of human growth and development. These stages are believed to occur in a fixed sequence, with the outcome of the earlier stages influencing the style of accommodation to subsequent ones. Whereas their content and sequence are hypothesized to be universal, it is recognized that individuals differed in how they handled them. The fact that different individuals resolve the tasks associated with each stage differently is part of the explanation for why adults display particular personality styles and/or disorders.

In the present model, the phases of transitions are specified independently of the stage of the human life cycle at which they occur. The onset of various transitions is not thought to be necessarily connected to any particular aspect of human development. No assumptions are made as to the sequence of transitions, nor is any postulate advanced about the personal maturation that may be occurring at the same time. Even the four phases within any one transition are not postulated to be rigidly "linear" in sequence. If one were to think of a line connecting the four phases, one would best consider it as a "spiral." Often individuals move cyclically through the phases in a series of intermediate moves, ultimately culminating in the terminal achievement of the "new equilibrium" as described above.

NETWORK STRUCTURE AND THE TRANSITION PROCESS

The four-phase model suggests that individuals "solve" the transition problem in a rather standard fashion. This is because the support networks around positions share common cultural components independent of the particular individuals involved (Levi-

Strauss, 1969; Jenkins, 1979). By reinforcing the individual's enactment of expectations associated with particular positions, the network serves a function on behalf of the larger society. Across all individuals, most networks reinforce compliance with standards of behavior and communication that assure commonness of outlook in family, work, and community life in general.

Not all aspects of living that are supported in this fashion are consistent with quality living or social conventions. Support networks may sustain an individual in a drug pushing career as well as in a computer programming career. Although some positions are thought of as "anti-social," the networks that support them also function to maintain their expression in a way that tends, across all instances, to minimize their social costs.

Network may induce self-expression and intrinsically meaningful experiences or exert pressure for conformity that is not to the liking of the focal individual. Those tendencies both to encourage self-expression and to reinforce standards of culturally acceptable behavior often induce inner confusion, strain, or conflict. This ambivalent pressure to "conform" and "express thyself" simultaneously exerted by networks is also a characteristic of most individuals (Hollis, 1977). For instance, someone may begin what appears later to have been a "false start" on a transition. The silence phase is entered and the individual begins to withdraw commitment and energy from the "old position." But, during this time, the network continues to operate as if the individual were continuing as usual. Similarly, just on a day-to-day basis, individual energy and capability to carry out roles varies a great deal due to emotional, physical, intellectual, or social distraction and distress. Throughout such episodes, networks maintain constant structural patterns so that when the distraction, distress, or disease subsides, the individual can reassume a fully functioning status in the original position.

Networks allow modification of the details of a particular position without entirely losing the position itself. Although the typical shape of the position may be culturally universal, members of networks are often tolerant of considerable minor variation in how they are enacted. As a consequence, as the individual changes through the life course, networks allow considerable modification in the particulars of lifestyle within the structure of a constant set of social positions.

This is surely not offered as a "steady state" model of social life. Indeed, all the processes involved are dynamic for the society, the network, and the individual. When the focal individual begins to undergo a position shift, the heretofore functioning network begins to dissolve. A state of tension develops between the members, all of whom must try to manage encounters with one another without confidence that past ways apply to current circumstances (Glaser and Strauss, 1971). Having begun to lose the institutional anchors that secured their prior relationships, the individuals gradually become, structurally speaking, "strangers" (Turner, 1977). The phases of the transition process as outlined appear to allow this process to unfold gradually and in a less radical or painful way than might otherwise be the case.

Private negotiations (Strauss, 1978), personal choices (Goffman, 1974), and immediate emotions are certainly important factors in everyday life. But it also appears that the pattern and timing of those negotiations and changes are ordered by structural forces from social networks. This leads us to two additional generalizations about social networks.

First is the "social control" process: By translating macro-structural forces into expectations that set broad limits on the way social positions are defined, networks help maintain the general patterns of social life even though countless individuals are undergoing personal transitions.

Second is the "ordered negotiations" process: Network structures help assure that the personal negotiations that occur during transitions are ordered in such a way as to minimize the disruptive potential of the process for those involved.

THE "NEGATIVE" QUALITY OF NETWORKS FOR TRANSITIONS

Networks serve the interests and needs not just of the focal individual, but of all members (O'Brien and Wagner, 1980). They are at risk of becoming obsolete in the event that the individual abandons the positions thus supported. Under such circumstances, we observe a number of responses that suggest that indeed networks are viable systems (Parsons, 1959), with a "life of their own." When that occurs, the consequence for the individual in transition may not be particularly positive.

Networks may "hang up" the individual in mid-transition by blocking the search process or rejecting the new identity that the individual is trying to establish.

If a woman is in a network that supports her "wife" role, widowhood may render it irrelevant to the emergent "single woman" lifestyle. Similar circumstances may occur in connection with the transition from work to retirement, from active parent to empty nest, or from married to single through divorce. One of the ways the network attempts to avoid "obsolescence" is expressed by the manner in which its members accept the new situation of the focal member whose life has changed. For instance, upon the death of the spouse, the short-term "definition of the situation" is that the woman is a widow: a married person with a dead husband. It may happen that the network members will never accept the person as having entered the new position of "single woman." Similarly, the old network may reinforce the identity of the divorcée as a "woman living apart from her husband and the father of her children," rather than as a "single person." Retired men also may be treated as engineers, lawyers, executives, or accountants—"without jobs"—rather than as persons liberated from the demands of jobs in order to pursue their own lives. As a consequence, in the event that the individual does not gain enough distance from the old network, the "new equilibrium" may be restricted in the range of truly new opportunities that it supports.

Competing networks with different "agendas" can force the individual into the frustrating situation of trying to enact contradictory expectations.

In some transitions, one well-developed support network is available for the prior position and another almost "ready made" network is waiting in the wings ready to support the new position. An example might be the transition from "dual career" couple to the "breadwinner-parent at home with baby" couple. Beforehand, one set of friends supports the continuing of work and the striving for career advancement while another set of acquaintances is inquiring, "When will you two finally have a family?" When the time arrives, there often are two baby showers, one by the former work friends and one by the family friends. After the child comes along, there may be visits from members of both networks, with the couple getting one set of messages encouraging full-time parenting as long as possible and other messages urging a quick return to full-time work. Similar concurrent influences may be exerted on older persons considering retirement or a move from the family residence to a condominium or the sun belt. The cross-pressures on individuals in such situations can be difficult to manage.

The sustaining capacity of networks is one source of the "grief" response felt by many involved in the transition process.

Network processes have important effects on the emotional tone associated with life transitions. After a person relocates in social "space," some past social contact and its symbolic reinforcement of "self" will be lost. That drop in support is frequently a source of deep feelings of loss. This means that life transitions as we have defined them almost inevitably involve some element of pain and grief for the focal individual. But the same applies for others in the network. There are many instances of loneliness reported by the old set of work mates or neighbors after a person retires or moves away. Or, emancipation for the young person is often the occasion for grief over the loss of intimacy for the middle-aged parent.

Networks sometimes "start" transitions that the focal individual does not seek.

The initiative for change in positions lies neither with the focal person nor with network members. Both play some part, and the relative dominance of the control appears to depend on the particular transitions. In the case of the "decision" to pursue a recovery from the disease of alcoholism, the individual may set out to make the change voluntarily, or the network may organize an "intervention" to push the individual into the path of change. Sometimes, the changes thus pursued are beneficial; undoubtedly, changing the pattern of life for any suffering individual is desirable regardless of the source of initiative for that change. But in other instances, as when well-meant relatives pressure an elderly individual to retire or relocate residence; the transition that ensues may not be in the best interests of the person. Again, it must be stressed that the members of networks have their own agendas that may or may not fit the best interests of the focal individual.

Networks may cast a label of "deviant" and shun the individual who moves out of the prior position, particularly if some core value is involved.

If the network supported an antidivorce value, but a particular member decided to seek a divorce, then the individual may be expelled from the network. But he or she may also voluntarily leave the network because of the contradiction with his or her own preferences. If the individual has been "purged" by the network, the solidarity and integration among the remaining members may be increased. But if the individual making the divorce choice is central enough to the network and voluntarily leaves it, that action may cause the remaining members to question their ideological stance with a resultant reduction in cohesion. In short, the transitional process itself may have the consequences of increasing the density of ties as network members rally together to render aid or rebuke the focal individual and the changes that are occurring. Conversely, transitions of particular members may reduce interaction among network members as the reason for being of the network dissolves, or as members take different sides in conflicts attendant to the transition.

CONCLUSION

We believe that much can be gained from expanded research using network analysis of midlife transitions. A position shift necessitates a dramatic response on the part of both the primary individual and the personal social network. Although this analysis has only scratched the surface of the issue, it lends support for the following conclusions:

- (a) The transition process appears to consist of a set of four phases labeled assessment, search, encounter, and new equilibrium;
- (b) The basic qualities of the phases of transitions appear to be independent of the content of roles associated with particular transitions;
- (c) The transition phases can be studied by analyzing networks of communication independent of measurement of the inner psychological states of the individuals involved;
- (d) The four-phase approach can supplement attention to episodic matters such as personal coping and adjustment problems by highlighting transitions as holistic events driven in important ways by forces of social organization;
- (e) As forceful systems of social organization, networks have lives of their own. This allows the members of networks to pursue collectively their own agendas that may not be in the best interests of the individual;
- (f) The "social control" and "ordered negotiation" effects of networks help explain the smooth flow of social life in spite of the personal distress of the extremely large number of individuals who are in transitions at any one time.

As suggested by this chapter, networks constrain the otherwise infinite variety of ways that individuals undergo life transitions.

This reduces the degree of disturbance that is observed, minimizing the disruption for both the individual and society. As with all systems of social organization, social networks are thus seen not to deny individuality. Rather, systems of social organization exist because all individuals are not, in detail, alike. While networks sustain the pattern of experience in the structure, individuals can, to a large degree, be busy "doing their own thing."

10
INTERDEPENDENCE IN INFORMAL SUPPORT SYSTEMS: The Case of Elderly, Urban Widows

GLORIA D. HEINEMANN
Coordinator, Interdisciplinary Team Training, Geriatrics Program
Buffalo Veterans Administration Medical Center;
SUNY Buffalo School of Medicine

Individuals, regardless of age, rely upon and contribute to establishing and maintaining primary group ties among kin and nonkin (friends and neighbors) alike. The importance of these informal supports to our social integration and sense of well-being is readily apparent both from published reports of research findings and our own personal experiences. Informal support systems are especially important for elderly persons in that they provide for a wide variety of expressive and instrumental needs that range from occasional social visitation/contact and feelings of affection to full-time caregiving responsibilities. In these relationships with family, friends, and neighbors, the elderly can be either givers or receivers (or both) in the exchanges. That is, they may visit as well as be visited; they may feel affection as well as be the objects of affection; and they may be providers as well as recipients of services or care. In time of need or crisis, elderly persons turn for help first to their informal supports that respond directly and/or serve as links between the elderly and the more formal, bureaucratic support system (e.g., organizations and service agencies; Shanas and Sussman, 1977). The elderly themselves seek help from the formal support system only as a last resort when family, friends, or neighbors are not available to them.

Informal support systems become disrupted in widowhood, and as women live longer than men, they are more likely to be faced with this disruption in old age. The average age at widowhood for women is 56 (Lopata, 1973a; Bengtson et al., 1977); of the noninstitutionalized women aged 65 and over, slightly more than half (52 percent) are widows (Heinemann, 1982a). With the loss of the husband, family members and friends perceive and respond to the widow differently. Thus she must redefine and renegotiate her roles and relationships with them in rebuilding her informal support systems. Says Heinemann (1980: 39):

> The widow begins to develop skills and abilities or use previously dormant ones to repattern life. New goals are set, and life begins to have meaning and purpose again. Gradually, the widow negotiates and reestablishes salient reference groups and social roles into support systems which meet a variety of needs and require similar reciprocation. These support systems reintegrate the widow into the social system and facilitate the development of a positive identity, a new lifestyle, and, often, an altered value system.

Although there is much individual variation with regard to this rebuilding process, some general patterns have been observed. Over time, other family members, often adult children and their families, become increasingly important to the widow and fulfill, in part, some of the functions previously fulfilled by her husband. Friends of a couple-companionate nature are seen less and less frequently, whereas friendships wth other single individuals gradually develop and become meaningful.

Given the importance of informal supports for the elderly generally and elderly widows specifically, it behooves us to understand their structure and function and to discern the relationship between the family and friendship support systems. These then are the aims of this chapter. The major thesis of the chapter is that the family and friendship support systems are interdependent and complementary in nature, and that although there are similarities between the two, each is distinctive enough in its own right to merit separate investigation. In this way, the two informal support systems are less likely to be confused with one another and a clearer understanding of each will result.

This chapter is divided into two major parts. In the first, I define support systems, contrast the family and friendship support systems with regard to their structure and function, and discuss their importance and areas of legitimate overlap. In the second, I present research findings regarding the structure and function of each informal support system for elderly, urban widows. These findings have relevance for and support, in part, the arguments for interdependence and complementarity made in the first part of the chapter.

THE NATURE OF
FAMILY AND FRIENDSHIP

DEFINITIONS

The concept of support system requires definition prior to a discussion of the two informal support systems of family and friendship. Lopata (1979) has defined a support system as the mutual, but not necessarily symmetrical, exchange of resources between individuals or between an individual and groups in society. Exchanges take place in the economic, service, social, and emotional areas. The individual is the organizing agent who selects and negotiates a network of relations that, when activated, becomes a personal support system. Informal support systems refer to those among primary group members (family, friends, and neighbors) as opposed to the formal support system (groups, organizations, and agencies of a bureaucratic nature). Informal support systems provide for both expressive and instrumental needs, whereas the formal support system provides mostly for instrumental needs.

The family encompasses the marital dyad, relatives living under one roof, intergenerational relationships among three and sometimes four generations of kin, sibling relationships, and relationships among affinal and more extended kin. The family in modern society has been characterized as the modified extended family—a network of mutual supports among individual households of persons related by blood and/or marriage (Litwak, 1960a, 1960b; Sussman and Burchinal, 1962; Shanas et al., 1968; Heinemann, 1982a, 1982b, 1982c). As an activated support system, the family's major activities include social visitation, mutual aid, and complementing tasks of and linking family members with other social systems. Family members tend to spend holidays and other ceremonial occasions together. The family, too, is the major source of help in times of difficulty and crisis (Shanas et al., 1968; Shanas, 1979b; Heinemann, 1982c). Aid is sought first from immediate family and then from more distant relatives. Differences in helping patterns exist along sex and social class lines. Women provide more direct services and caregiving to family members, whereas men provide more financial assistance and counsel. Working-class families exchange more direct services and social visits because they are in closer geographic proximity than middle-class families who tend to exchange more economic and, possibly, more emotional aid over greater distances. The elderly are not socially isolated from their families; they interact frequently with adult children and other relatives (Shanas et al., 1968; Shanas, 1979a; Heinemann, 1982b, 1982c). In fact, having a strong family support system is associated with noninstitutional, community living for elderly persons.

The concept of friendship is more amorphous than that of family. For the most part, friendships develop between individuals who have interests, experiences, lifestyles, and values in common. Thus many persons who become friends are of the same sex, age peers, and/or persons with similar social class and occupational backgrounds. Friendship embraces not only the dyadic pair—be it same-sex, cross-sex, platonic, romantic, or confidant in nature— but also subcultures or communities of age peers such as those identified among adolescents and the elderly.[1] Friendships vary with regard to level of affection, openness, trust, sharing, and length of commitment. Two people may be close confidants for many years or, alternatively, neighborly acquaintances who visit occasionally over coffee, provide minor services for one another, and lose contact after relocation. Married persons tend to have more expanded friendship networks than unmarried persons (Mancini, 1980); however, it is unclear from the literature whether men or women have more friends. Women tend to find friendship more meaningful and are more dependent upon it in comparison to men; elderly women are more likely than their male counterparts to have confidant relationships among their friends. Men, on the other hand, rely on their wives as confidants and tend to lose these relationships in widowhood (Strain and Chappell, 1982). Because of the importance of the confidant relationship for the elderly, Hess (1979) believes that women's friendship patterns may be more functional than men's in old age. Friendship networks vary by social class as well. Middle-class persons tend to have loose-knit friendship networks and more resources to make new friends than do their working-class counterparts. For widows, the better educated are less socially isolated and see friends more often than other widows (Lopata, 1973b, 1975; Atchley et al., 1979). Among working-class persons, most friends tend to know one another and most friendships are sex segregated (Hess, 1979). As a support system, friendship buffers against social losses, negative evaluations, and accompanying depression. The confidant relationship, especially, is related to good mental health, high morale, and community living/participation among the elderly (Lowenthal and Haven, 1968). Additionally, friends provide elderly persons with affective assistance, relief from loneliness, and short-term aid in times of illness (Cantor, 1979).

CONTRASTS

As informal support systems, kinship and friendship are alike in some respects and different in others. Rosow (1967) has described them as separate social arenas, and, in fact, it is the differences between the two systems that enable them to complement rather than duplicate one another.

Family relationships extend across generations, and families tend to encourage/facilitate upward mobility of younger generations of kin who become better educated than their parents, take on new careers, and develop new orientations to life. This creates much diversity among family members. Conversely, friendship formation is heavily dependent upon sociohistorical factors and socioenvironmental contexts. Persons at similar turning points in the life course or experiencing the same life stage transitions (e.g., age peers) most often become friends. Furthermore, the amount of social activity and friendship formation in a given geographic area is related to the number of age peers living in that area (Rosow, 1967). Thus intergenerational relationships typify kinship whereas age peer relationships typify friendships; kin tend to be heterogeneous and friends, homogeneous.

Family relationships are either formally legitimated (e.g., marriage, adoption) or predetermined at birth; therefore, they tend to be more stable over time than friendships. Family relationships can remain dormant for relatively long periods of time and still be activated on special occasions or in times of need or crisis. Friendships, on the other hand, are more tenuous because they are voluntary in nature and, thus, in more danger of dissolution (Hess, 1979). In comparison to kinship, friendship requires more mutual choice,[2] initiative, assertiveness, and consensus for development and maintenance.

Exchanges between intergenerational kin tend to occur and become equalized over the life course; however, in instances when one generation, usually the eldest, has experienced social, financial, emotional, or physical loss, immediate exchanges are unequal in value (e.g., caregiving responsibilities in return for what may seem like occasional appreciation or indifference). Exchanges of a more immediate nature are need specific and, therefore, dissimilar in nature (e.g., care of grandchildren so an adult daughter can return to the labor force). Because friendship is more fragile than kinship, exchanges between friends are usually immediate and of equal value or "tit for tat" (Hochschild, 1973). The homogeneity of friendship results in friends providing one another with similar rather than dissimilar services. For example, in Matthew's (1979) study, elderly women living in close proximity often provided one another with baked goods even though each was capable of baking for herself.

Because of the legitimacy and stability of family ties, specific persons rather than the presence of relationships per se are perceived as important. Examples of this come readily to mind: the rebelliousness of children at the idea of a stepmother; the inability of an elderly widow to consider remarriage;[3] and the shock and disapproval of younger generations when an elderly family member does decide to remarry. Certainly, some individuals do have lifetime friendships that are perceived in this same manner; however, with friendship, it is also possible to emphasize the importance of "having relationships" instead of the uniqueness of persons (e.g., those who always have someone with whom to go out or who develop and discard friends as their own life situations change).

While emotional needs of the individual are met by both family and friends alike, kin and peer ties are not interchangeable because each meets different emotional needs for the individual (Hochschild, 1973). Family relationships involving persons of different generations are characterized by identification and projection. For example, children become socioemotional insurance policies for parents and important sources of identity, especially for an elderly mother. These one-sided relationships transcend differences and function to ensure solidarity and a sense of security. In contrast, relationships with friends are characterized by symmetry and equality; they provide not only mutual gratification, but also a sense of integrity and self-worth. They confirm identity rather than function as a source of it.

Although affection characterizes both family relationships and friendships, the two informal support systems have different bases for social contact. Social contact between family members is based upon positive concern and a sense of duty/responsibility (Adams,

1968). Filial piety serves as an example of the combination of motives underlying family relationships. In contrast, the social contact between friends is relatively free from obligation. The interpersonal attraction and mutual selection of friends for companionship result in social contact for its own sake (i.e., for enjoyment). Furthermore, social contact with family members and that with friends have different consequences for the individual. That is, contact with friends is associated with high morale, whereas contact with kin is unrelated to morale (Pihlblad and Adams, 1972; Arling, 1976b). Mancini (1980), exploring the relationship between social contact and morale among friends, found that social contact permits the individual to gain competence in the role of friend, and it is this competence, not merely the contact, that is related to morale. With regard to the family, high morale may be related to accomplishments of children (vicarious identification) rather than to contact with them or other relatives (Lee, 1979).

Finally, exchanges of mutual aid occur in both informal support systems; yet, the specific tasks carried out in each are different in kind. Financial aid and socialization serve as examples. In the area of financial support, family members, not friends, are deemed the appropriate providers. "People look only to their closest family members, primarily children, for financial aid, and there are no functional substitutes for them among other personal associates" (Rosow, 1970: 60). Hochschild (1973) observed that friends may borrow and loan small sums of money from each other, but in a financial crisis, the individual turns to close family members. Shanas and associates (1968, 1982) also found that financial exchanges occur in families, specifically between different generations of kin, and often this financial aid is given in the form of gifts.

Whereas financial aid is the prerogative of kin, late life socialization occurs, for the most part, among friends and neighbors. As friendship formation becomes more localized in retirement, neighbors become meaningful friends of the elderly (Rosow, 1967; Hess, 1972) and important agents of socialization for them (Rosow, 1970; Cantor, 1979). Elderly persons with many old neighbors often name them as important and admired reference figures (Rosow, 1970). These elderly age mates, especially those living in subcultural enclaves (e.g., elderly housing projects, retirement communities, and institutional settings), provide one another with positive role models and behavioral norms.

IMPORTANCE

The viability and importance of each informal support system adds additional support for their complementary nature. Jonas (1979) argues that neither kinship nor friendship is more important than the other and that involvement in the two systems should not be perceived as competitive. Rather, relationships within each system are qualitatively different from one another, and, thus, an individual can be involved in both of them equally. Further support for this perspective is provided by Dono and associates (1979) who explicate a functional specificity model for explaining involvements with family, friends, and neighbors. According to this model, the structural characteristics of each primary group are related to its unique functions. That is, with regard to health and well-being, a neighbor would make day-to-day observations of an elderly widow to ensure that she is well; a close friend or relative living in the same city but not the same neighborhood would do weekly grocery shopping or light housekeeping for her; and an adult child living a considerable distance away would be called to take charge in the event of a serious health crisis.

For those who postulate a hierarchical model to explain involvement in informal support systems (i.e., preference for kin over friends and neighbors for social support; Cantor, 1979), my response is that these preferences may be more hypothetical than real and, more important, apply only to certain subgroups of elderly under specific circumstances. For example, widows with children living in close proximity are less likely than other widows to become involved in neighborhood and community activities. In this situation, loss of the role of spouse results in a restructuring of the relative value of family vis-à-vis other roles. The role of parent often becomes more salient as intimacy once shared with the spouse is sought from adult children. Under these circumstances, then, involvement in other contexts becomes problematic and less rewarding (Trela and Jackson, 1979). Moreover, these same authors note that some elderly do wish to play roles in diverse contexts and, in these instances, family roles do not take primacy over other roles. Hochschild (1973), too, found that elderly most active with children are also most active with nonkin. For these elderly, both kin and nonkin are important in their lives, and there is no evidence that family roles take priority over other roles. Finally, Rosow (1967) states that for elderly persons, friendship patterns tend to be independent of relationships with children; frequency of contact with children and that with friends and neighbors have no reciprocal effect on each other.

LEGITIMATE OVERLAP

Although kinship and friendship do not duplicate one another in the provision of specific kinds of support to individuals, there are legitimate areas of overlap between two informal support systems. These areas of overlap further support for their interdependence.

Probably the most obvious example of overlap between the two informal support systems is the marital dyad—a family relationship that develops from a type of friendship. Like friendship, it is based upon voluntary choice and mutual affection, which may explain why both good quality marriages and contact with friends are related to morale and why wives rather than nonkin are selected as confidants by elderly husbands. This latter situation also serves as a second example of overlap between the two systems in that a relative can be both kin and friend simultaneously, and although this example refers to spouses, this type of relationship is not limited only to spouses.

The following three scenarios across the life course afford further evidence of the legitimate overlap between kinship and friendship. The first scenario (my personal experience) involves grade school children, specifically a class of fourth graders.

> Each day, letters, sometimes three to six pages in length, were written and exchanged by the female members of this fourth grade class. These letters detailed the day-to-day fantasies of adult family life and were written to "make believe" kin rather than real friends or classmates. That is, a letter to one's best friend was addressed to "sister," while letters to girls less well known or less well liked were addressed to "cousin" or "aunt." Family roles were assigned not only on the basis of personal friendship, but also according to popularity within the classroom. Thus the more popular girls tended to be "sisters," and the less popular girls, their more distant relatives. Interestingly, there seemed to be a consensus among the female classmates as to the particular family roles assigned to them. While the male members of the class did not participate in the actual letter writing, they were assigned family roles by their female classmates and were integrated into the imaginary family life described in the letters. One's boyfriend became one's "husband," and other males

were referenced as various in-laws depending upon the family roles conferred on other female members of the class. The family roles assigned to the males also reflected their popularity within the classroom (i.e., popular boys tended to be "husbands," less popular boys, distant relatives).

This confounding of kinship and friendship provides an excellent example of informal learning among children. It seems to have been functional in several respects. First, friends were used to practice and role play for future roles within the family (i.e., anticipatory socialization). Second, the more familiar kinship system—more familiar to the children—was used to legitimate and maintain the less familiar friendship system. Third, an unfamiliar environment of nonkin was structured and stratified into a status hierarchy with a subcultural component based upon family relationships. Thus we learn future family roles through anticipatory socialization and role playing with friends, and we learn to develop our friendship support system by utilizing roles from our more familiar family system.

The second scenario (my personal experience) is taken from the experiences of ten nursing students, all in their early- to mid-twenties. They lived together in a dormitory, were together in all of their classes, and rotated through the various clinical specialties together.

> Five of the ten nursing students spent much of their personal time together. They ate meals together in the hospital cafeteria, congregated in one another's rooms to socialize or play cards in the evenings, and three of the five paired as roommates at different times during the three-year period. The other five members of the group were included in these activities, but not as consistently or intensively. They seemed to enjoy spending more of their time alone than in the company of others. This friendship clique referred to one another in terms of family roles. The big-boned, rather abrasive woman reared on a farm was known as "dad"; the slightly older and more nurturing woman, "mom"; and the other three young-appearing, energetic, and outgoing women of about the same height and weight became "the kids." The other five members were treated as more extended kin although no specific family roles were assigned to them.

Here, again, family roles were utilized among nonrelatives to help define friendships and to distinguish close friends from more distant ones. Furthermore, employing familiar family roles may have been functional in alleviating homesickness and providing a warm, nurturing environment to counteract the stresses related to (1) working with the sick and dying and (2) performing academically at a level high enough to remain in the nursing program.

In the final scenario, reported by Hazan (1983; paraphrase), elderly persons—poor, Jewish, and living in the East End of London—attended a day care center operated by the Jewish Welfare Board.

> These elderly persons of low socioeconomic status were disaffiliated from their families, friends, and neighbors and forced to seek help from the day care center. Within the center, a counterculture developed in which children were condemned as ungrateful and selfish; and topics concerning family affairs were taboo. The center became an isolated haven where old attachments were abandoned. Yet, kinship terminology was used to define the nature of relationships among the individuals. Members referred to each other as "brother" and "sister" and described the atmosphere in the place as "homey" and the overall social scene as "one big family."

According to Hazan, the kinship terminology was utilized to denote equality and nondifferentiation among members—to create an environment very different from what they had experienced in real life. Thus family labels permitted them to perceive one another as equals and buffered them from the harsh realities of poverty, shame, and loss in the larger society.

SUMMARY

In the preceding pages, I have attempted to show that the informal support systems of family and friendship are structurally and functionally different as well as interdependent and complementary in nature. With regard to structure, family ties are legitimated, intergenerational for the most part, and relatively stable over time. Family members are heterogeneous and perceived important for their uniqueness. Immediate exchanges between kin tend to be unequal and dissimilar in nature; however, intergenerational exchanges are often equalized over the life course. In contrast, friends tend to be homogeneous age peers who value one another as unique individuals or for the relationship itself. Friendships require considerable assertiveness and reciprocity for development and maintenance and are less stable than family relationships. Exchanges are immediate and equal in value. Often friends provide one another with the same kind of services.

Emotional needs are met in both informal support systems; however, family relationships provide solidarity and a source of identity; contact is based upon positive concern and obligation. Friendship, however, confirms identity and provides one with a sense of self-worth. Contact with friends is an end in itself in that it provides mutual gratification and enjoyment and is associated with high morale.

Other functions carried out via informal support systems are task specific to each. For example, major financial help is provided by family members only, while adult socialization is the prerogative of friends and subcultural enclaves of unrelated individuals. Because the systems do not duplicate functions, they cannot be substituted directly, nor are they competitive. Their complementary nature ensures that both are equally important to the individual, and involvement in one system has no reciprocal effect on involvement in the other. Loss of spouse may increase the value of kin over nonkin for widows. For some of them, this is temporary until new, meaningful friendships can be developed. Others, however, may remain highly involved with family members due to preference or an inability to convert strangers to friends.

Legitimate overlap exists between the two systems across the life course. Anticipatory socialization into adult family roles takes place among friends; we learn to make and maintain friends by relying upon and utilizing roles from the more familiar kinship system; and we use family terminology, too, to (1) bring warmth and nurturance to unfamiliar or threatening environments or (2) buffer against loss, shame, or negative evaluations in the larger society. These areas of overlap, then, provide additional evidence for the interdependent, complementary nature of family and friendship.

INFORMAL SUPPORT SYSTEMS
OF ELDERLY, URBAN WIDOWS

In this part of the chapter, I present data from a study of urban widows to demonstrate further that the two informal support systems—family and friendship—are interdependent and complementary and cannot be directly substituted for one another.

DESCRIPTION

This secondary analysis was undertaken to investigate the factors associated with strength of the informal support systems of family and friendship and to determine whether the same or different factors are predictive of this strength in a sample of elderly, urban widows. Life stage of the widow was used as a control variable due to the heterogeneity among the elderly population, especially with regard to availability and utilization of informal supports. The models for predicting strength of the informal support systems were expected to vary by type of informal system (i.e., family or friendship) and by life stage of the widow.

Data reported here were collected via a regional survey of previously widowed women residing in the Chicago Standard Metropolitan Statistical Area (SMSA) during 1974.[4] The universe from which the sample was drawn was the Social Security Administration's list of women who were receiving or had received in the past some form of benefit as a result of their husbands' dying. The study was designed so that women from five benefit recipient categories were represented in the sample; data were weighted so that the number of women in each of these categories corresponded to their proportion in this particular universe. In weighting the data, an attempt was made to approximate the original sample size in order that tests of statistical significance could be utilized in the analysis. Subsets of respondents (remarried women and widows under age 60 were excluded) and variables from this study were utilized in this presentation of findings.

The number of active roles the widows had among family members and friends served as the two separate measures of informal support system strength. These variables were constructed by counting the different roles each widow had among kin and nonkin. For a role to be considered active, one of the following conditions had to be met: (a) the respondent had to mention the availability of at least one role partner and had to have engaged in face-to-face interaction with that role partner at a minimum of once a year, or (b) the respondent had to mention the role partner as being a source or recipient of help in at least one of the four areas—financial, service, social, and emotional—identified in the survey instrument. In constructing these measures, the number of different roles was counted rather than frequency of interactions or number of role relationships because these latter two measures are more likely to be associated negatively with aging and because widows who are emotionally dependent upon their children may develop many role relationships with others to compensate for their insatiable desire to be with children and to keep busy (Rosow, 1970). These relationships are likely to be superficial and contribute little to strength of informal support systems.

Focusing this investigation on the number of active roles the widows had among family and friends does not imply that those widows with the largest number of such roles are necessarily the best adapted to widowhood; rather, it does imply that the chances for a successful adaptation are maximized when social networks are broad and varied. The widow who has a variety of active roles among family and friends, then, has full, well-rounded support systems responsive to a wide range of needs and able to provide a considerable number of services.

Within the family, the widows interacted as mothers and mothers-in-law, daughters and daughters-in-law, sisters and sisters-in-law, grandmothers and granddaughters, aunts, cousins, nieces, and other in-laws. Summing these family roles resulted in scores ranging from 0 (widows with no family roles) to a maximum possible of 12 such roles. Among friends, the widows were involved with friends made before the death or illness of the late husband, friends made after the husband's death, intimate cross-sex friends, neighbors, coworkers, and spouses of friends. This variable ranged from 0 (widows with no friendship roles) to a maximum possible of 6 roles.[5]

Multiple regression analysis was used to determine the combined effects of the independent variables on strength of the family and the friendship support systems. Problems of multicollinearity were not an issue because the intercorrelations between independent variables were not above .45.

FINDINGS

The frequency distributions for number of active family and friendship roles among young-old widows—those 60 to 74 years of age—are presented in Figure 10.1. All of these widows had at least 1 active family role; the majority of them had between 2 and 5 such roles. The modal number for this group was 4, and over one-third of the young-old widows had 4 active family roles. None of them, however, had more than 7 roles. While these widows had fewer friendship roles in comparison to family roles, friendship roles

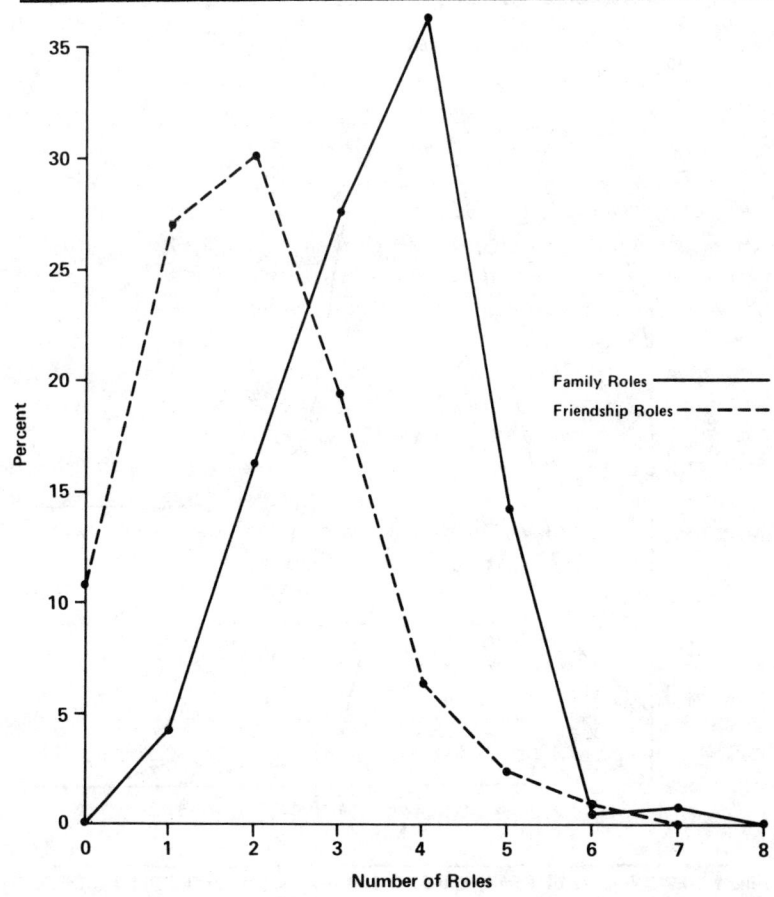

Figure 10.1 Number of Family and Friendship Roles Among Young-Old Widows (60-74)

were prevalent among them. Almost 11 percent had no friendship roles; however, the majority had between 1 and 3 such roles. The modal category was 2 for this group, and slightly over 30 percent of the young-old widows had two active friendship roles. Less than 1 percent of them had the maximum possible of 6 roles.

The old-old widows—those 75 years of age and older—had fewer active roles in both informal support systems than did the young-old widows, and like the young-old widows, they, too, had more family than friendship roles. Almost 4 percent of the old-old

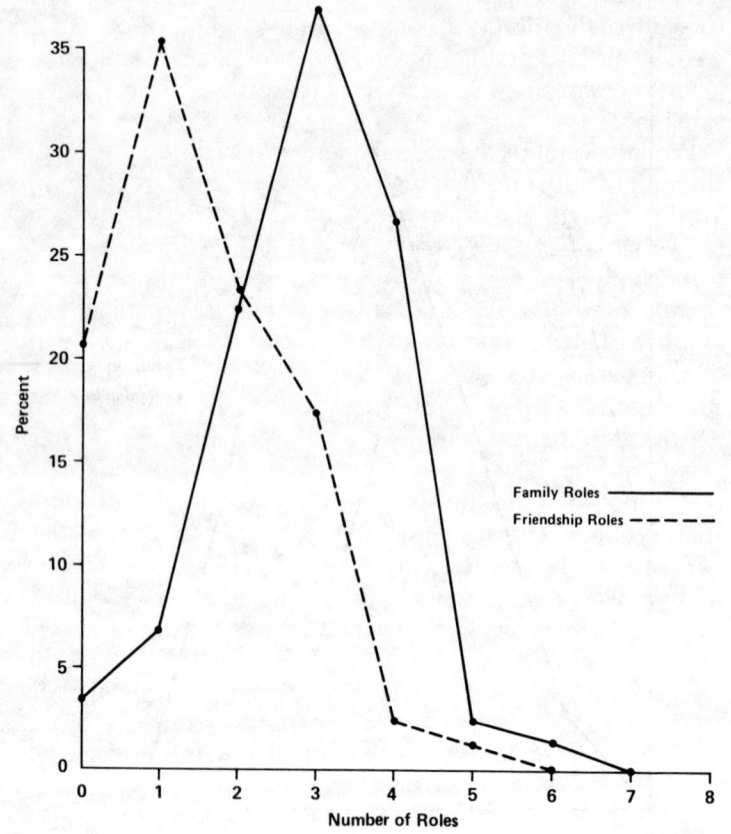

Figure 10.2 Number of Family and Friendship Roles Among Old-Old Widows (75+)

widows were without family roles, while the majority of them had 2 to 4 such roles. Among this group, the modal category was 3, and over a third of the old-old widows had 3 active family roles. None, however, had as many as 7 such roles. Just over 20 percent of these old-old widows had no friendship roles. The majority of them had between 0 and 3 such roles with one being the modal category. Again, over one-third of the old-old widows had 1 and none had as many as 6 active friendship roles (see Figure 10.2).

There were 8 independent variables that were found to be significant predictors of strength of the family support system for the young-old widows. These variables are presented in Table 10.1. The overall model explained 28 percent of the variance in the dependent variable and was significant at the .001 level. With regard to strength of the friendship support system, 5 independent variables were significant predictors, and the model, also significant at the .001 level, explained 32 percent of the variance in this dependent variable.

While several of the independent variables were predictive of strength of both informal support systems, the models for predicting the strength of each were not identical. Three of the independent variables—number of living children, number of social activities in which the widows engaged, and life satisfaction—were significant predictors of both dependent variables; however, number of living children was positively associated with strength of the family support system and negatively associated with strength of the friendship support system. Other variables predictive of strength of the family support system included employment history, income, religious involvement, whether perceived as grieving or not, and idealization of the late husband. Other variables predictive of strength of the friendship support system were education and organizational involvement. Thus young-old widows with strong family support systems tended to have a number of living children, a weak history of employment, low income, and high religious and social involvement. Additionally, they were likely to be perceived as grieving, did not idealize the late husband, and were satisfied with their lives. Young-old widows with strong friendship support systems tended to have relatively few living children, good education, and high social and organizational involvement. They, too, were satisfied with their lives.

For the old-old widows, Table 10.2 shows that 9 independent variables were significant predictors of strength of the family support system. This overall model explained 45 percent of the variance in the dependent variable and was significant at the .001 level. There were 5 variables that were predictive of strength of the friendship support system, and this model also explained 45 percent of the variance in the dependent variable and was significant at the .001 level. Independent variables predictive of strength of both informal support systems included number of living children, income, number of social activities and organizations, and whether perceived as grieving or not. Again, number of living children was positively associated with strength of the family support system and negatively associated with strength of the friendship support system. Other variables in the model predicting

TABLE 10.1
Significant Determinants of Informal Support System Strength
Among Young-Old Widows (60-74)

	Informal Support System Strength	
Independent Variables	Family Beta Weights	Friendship Beta Weights
Number living children	.165***	−.154***
Completed education	_a	_a
Employment history	−.143**	—
Yearly household income	−.192***	—
Religious involvement	.234***	—
Social activities	.347***	.341***
Active organizational memberships	—	.173***
Perceived not grieving	−.196***	—
Idealization of late husband	−.194***	—
Life satisfaction	.094*	.168***
Multiple R	.528	.564
R^2	.279	.318
Overall F	17.806***	39.618***
df	8/368	5/425

NOTE: Standardized beta coefficients from the regression analyses are presented in this and subsequent tables.
a. Not a significant determinant for this informal support system; therefore, not included in the analysis.
*p < .05; **p < .01; ***p < .001

strength of the family support system included age, physical health problems, perception of hostility, and life satisfaction; no additional variables were predictive of strength of the friendship support system. Old-old widows, then, with strong family support systems tended to be at the younger end of the age continuum, to have a number of living children, physical health problems, low income, high social and organizational involvement, and low scores with regard to life satisfaction. Moreover, they were perceived as being hostile rather than grieving. Those old-old widows with strong friendship support systems had few living children, low income, high social and organizational involvement, and were perceived as not grieving.

DISCUSSION

Findings presented above show that the family support system tends to be stronger than the friendship support system among elderly, urban widows regardless of their life stage; however, both

TABLE 10.2
Significant Determinants of Informal Support System Strength Among Young-Old Widows (75+)

	Informal Support System Strength	
Independent Variables	Family Beta Weights	Friendship Beta Weights
Age	−.401***	—a
Number living children	.263***	−.163***
Physical health problems	.136**	—
Yearly household income	−.188**	−.190***
Social activities	.355***	.388***
Active organizational memberships	.302***	.403***
Perceived not grieving	.285***	.123**
Perceived hostility	.307***	—
Life satisfaction	−.258***	—
Multiple R	.670	.673
R^2	.449	.453
Overall F	19.471***	39.247***
df	9/215	5/237

a. Not a significant determinant for this informal support system; therefore, not included in the analysis.
*p < .05; **p < .01; ***p < .001;

informal support systems are viable and coexist simultaneously among these widows. Additionally, models for predicting strength of the informal support systems did vary by type of support system and life stage of the widow. Overall, a greater number of independent variables made unique contributions to the prediction of strength of the family support system than to the prediction of strength of the friendship support system. Additionally, the models were more predictive of strength of informal support systems for the old-old than the young-old widows.

The findings do suggest that the informal support systems of family and friendship are interdependent and complementary in nature. First, extremely similar or directly substitutable systems would be expected to have the same predictors with regard to their strength. Interdependent systems, however, would be expected to have some predictors in common as well as some unique predictors. This latter expectation is, in fact, what these findings indicate (see Tables 10.1 and 10.2).

The findings also suggest that the two informal support systems have different long-range consequences for widows. Low income and the perception of grieving were associated with strength of the family support system for young-old widows, and the presence of physical health problems, hostility, and low life satisfaction were associated with this same dependent variable for old-old widows. Thus family members are accepting of widows' frailties, hardships, dependencies, and negative characteristics. They rally around these vulnerable kin and function as a succoring, nurturant support system. These vulnerabilities, however, are less likely to be related to a strong friendship support system, which requires assertiveness and reciprocal exchanges. Instead, self-initiating behavior (active social participation), time for friendship (fewer living children), and resources/skills for exchange and involvement (higher education levels for young-old widows) were factors related to a strong friendship support system among elderly, urban widows. Yet, in instances of economic vulnerability, friends, too, function as a protective and nurturant support system.[6] That is, low income was associated with a strong friendship support system for old-old widows. This may be due to the generalized economic vulnerability among this life stage group as a whole. Thus the family support system is flexible in that it supports vulnerable kin and provides them with a sense of security; the friendship support system is less flexible in that it requires more from the individual and supports vulnerability only when that vulnerability applies to an age cohort as a whole. This support system fosters a sense of self-worth and accomplishment in the individual. Both of these functions are important, and the loss of either can be detrimental to the general well-being of elderly widows and elderly persons generally.

IMPLICATIONS

In this chapter, I have argued and attempted to show—through a review of the literature and a presentation of data about elderly, urban widows—that the family and friendship support systems are interdependent and complementary in nature.

A clear, insightful understanding of the structure and function of each of these informal support systems can be useful to two groups of people: (1) persons in the helping professions who come in contact with, counsel, or develop programs for widows and (2) persons involved in policymaking with regard to the health and long-term care of the elderly.

Helping professionals should be aware of the various family members, friends, and neighbors available for providing informal support to widows; what factors contribute to strength of the informal support systems; what characteristics or skills a widow has or requires to develop and maintain them; and when and for whom these support systems are flexible and less requiring of the widow's own initiative for their maintenance. Too often, helping programs have underemphasized the importance of friends and neighbors as resources and have overburdened the family with virtually all of the responsibility for a bereaved and grieving relative. Programs could help widows develop some of the skills necessary for or provide an environment conducive to the formation of informal supports. A better understanding on the part of these professionals of how informal support systems function for the widow could facilitate reengagement of widows into the social system.

On a broader level, a number of factors—the high costs of health and long-term care for older persons, the growing numbers of very old persons, and the federal deficits that have resulted in formal service cutbacks to the elderly—have led policymakers to turn their attention to family members as primary caregivers and resources to supplement the diminished formal support system. These policymakers, too, need to be cautioned not to overtax the family support system. They should appreciate the extent to which the family is providing presently for its aging members; they should be able to differentiate appropriate from inappropriate service provisions with regard to the two informal support systems; and they should begin to anticipate how much more the family can be expected to provide before there are serious negative repercussions or before family members themselves will require some form of help from the formal support system, the friendship support system, or both.

NOTES

1. For examples of this latter type of friendship among the elderly, see Hochschild (1973), Gubrium (1975a), and Matthews (1979).

2. Hess and Waring (1978) note that parent/child relations in later life are becoming more voluntaristic. Because future cohorts of elderly will have more resources

than present day elderly, their involvement with children will be based more on mutual choice and respect and less on obligation.

3. According to Glick et al. (1974), this is more characteristic of widows than widowers, who move more quickly into reestablishing a stable life organization based upon remarriage.

4. The Widowhood Support System Survey was conducted in 1974 by Helena Z. Lopata, Loyola University of Chicago, in collaboration with the University of Illinois at Chicago's Survey Research Laboratory. The study was funded by the Social Security Administration.

5. Construction of independent variables is not presented here due to space limitation. All independent variables are continuous with the exception of the variable, physical health problems, which was constructed as a dichotomous variable such that 1 = at least one physical health problem and 0 = no physical health problems. Perception of grief in the widow was constructed such that a high score on the variable is indicative of not grieving; this is inconsistent with the construction of perception of hostility and may be confusing initially to the reader.

6. This is not meant to imply that financial exchanges took place among friends.

11

THE MEDIATING ROLE OF SOCIAL NETWORKS IN THE HOUSING DECISIONS OF THE ELDERLY

ADRIAN RUTH WALTER
Director, Fellowship Program in Applied Gerontology
Gerontological Society of America

Independence is an illusion. From birth to death we depend on others for survival. Human infants are completely at the mercy of caretakers for several years, and biological, economic, and social dependence by children on their families continues, in many cases, through adulthood. Although such influential sociologists as Durkheim (1964), Parsons (1959), and Burgess and Locke (1940) pronounced the end of extended family ties, bonds of dependence and assistance continue throughout life cycles, as research during the last several decades has revealed continuing instrumental and sociable exchanges between the aged and members of their social networks (Shanas and Streib, 1965; Sussman, 1965; Shanas et al., 1968; Litwak, 1969; Maddox, 1979; Crystal, 1982).

The housing situation of older Americans reflects their lifetime successes and failures; the home is where aging occurs. Although no research has yet shown a causal relationship between living arrangements and health or well-being, the housing decision is a basic determinant of the long-term care decision because it is the

Author's Note: *This chapter is adapted from a paper presented in October 1983 to the Association of Collegiate Schools of Planning. The work on which this is based was generously supported by grants from the U.S. Department of Housing and Urban Development, the Department of Urban Studies and Planning of MIT, the Joint Center for Urban Studies of MIT and Harvard University, the Midwest Council for Social Research in Aging, and the University of Missouri-Kansas City Institute. All conclusions and interpretations are entirely my own.*

physical location in which long-term care is made possible or impossible.

Thinking of housing in this enabling sense can turn our attention to its capacity to place both a ceiling and a floor on the elusive but psychologically important concept of "quality of life." For example, residents of a slum hotel may be dry and warm and possibly even fed, but may live in fear of crime or rodents and consider their housing situation to be extremely deficient. Similarly, a resident of a beautifully furnished and immaculate congregate living facility in one of the wealthiest towns in Massachusetts told the author that this solution to her housing problem was the best she could expect, but "who really wants to live in a place like this anyway?" Her dissatisfaction stemmed not from any flaw in the physical environment, which was the best that money and taste could buy, but was instead a comment on the social environment and the near-institutional aura of such a facility, no matter how well appointed.

Housing defines and expresses location in both physical and social space, with spatially referred sentiments (Fried and Gleicher, 1970), implying that housing choices are particularly embedded in social context. Social class is defined at least partly by residential location (Coleman and Neugarten, 1971; Rainwater, 1974; Coleman and Rainwater, 1978; Coleman, 1978), with working-class and minority families more likely to have localized extended family networks than white middle-class families (Bott, 1972; Young and Wilmott, 1957; Sussman and Burchinal, 1962; Rosow, 1968).

Although social networks are contained in the physical dimensions of home and neighborhood, until recently few housing policy analysts and researchers have paid any attention to the nonmonetary factors involved in housing decisions. In particular, the dozens of writers who analyzed the outcomes of the Experimental Housing Allowance Program (EHAP; see Frieden, 1980; U.S. Department of Housing and Urban Development, 1980; Bradbury and Downs, 1981; Struyk and Bendick, 1981, and the citations in these volumes) paid virtually no attention to social factors as they affected the experiment's outcomes. This chapter begins to remedy that omission.

Did families and friends affect the housing choices of the aged in EHAP? If they did, what actual services do these members of social networks perform, and with what effect? These questions are difficult to answer and have seldom been asked. The data base collected during the course of EHAP is used to outline some previously neglected factors that affected the housing choices of the elderly as revealed in the housing allowance experiment, and can help us draw some conclusions for policy and program designers.

WHAT WAS THE
HOUSING ALLOWANCE EXPERIMENT?

In 1970, Congress authorized the U.S. Department of Housing and Urban Development to conduct an experiment to determine whether a program of direct cash grants to eligible families was a feasible alternative to housing construction programs initiated during the New Deal, accelerated in the late 1960s, and suspended by President Nixon in 1973 (Meyerson et al., 1962; Friedmann, 1968; Mandelker, 1973; Keith, 1973; Musgrave, 1973; Weicher, 1973; Hartman, 1975; Frieden, 1980). Fixed-location public housing projects had been criticized as inefficient and unfair, and possibly the cause rather than the cure of housing problems (see Wurster, 1966; Peattie, 1971; Frieden, 1971; Starr, 1971; Wallace, 1972; Aaron, 1973; and Solomon, 1974, to name just a few critics of public and other subsidized housing schemes). For the elderly in particular, there was a feeling that "new rental structures built primarily in urban areas are not responsive to large segments of the elderly who do not wish to move, do not wish to give up ownership status, or do not reside in urban areas" (Welfeld and Struyk, 1978). The potential benefits of this approach are laid out in Solomon (1974); the success of housing allowances in serving a cross-section of low- and moderate-income families is summarized in Frieden (1980).

The allowance, a cash transfer very much like a negative income tax, provides a subsidy to participating families on the basis of income and household size. These allowances could be used to let poor and moderate income families choose their own housing in the private marketplace by boosting their purchasing power with a cash grant earmarked for housing.

The housing allowance is a demand-side subsidy, designed to "[empower] consumers to pursue their own interests in the marketplace" (Downs and Bradbury, 1981: 398). They are based on the premise that what poor people need most is money (see Ryan, 1971), and are distinguished from unrestricted cash subsidies of the type tested in the Seattle and Denver Income Maintenance Experiments (see Hannan et al., 1978) by the housing-related requirements attached to the subsidy. In each of the three components of the experiment, eligible families were enrolled in the program and offered the opportunity to qualify for the allowance, which was paid only if the family already lived in or could find housing acceptable to the program's administrators. Monthly payments were mailed directly to participating families, and could not exceed actual gross rent costs including utilities.

EHAP was a first step in moving the federal government out of the politically difficult business of building new low-cost housing for poor people and into the direct provision of cash grants to eligible low- and moderate-income families of all ages that would boost their purchasing power in the private housing market. Subsidizing existing living arrangements was initiated after a series of political battles during the activist 1960s and early 1970s that tried to limit or halt the construction of new public housing projects in middle-income areas (e.g., Cuomo, 1983; Danielson, 1976) in the attempt to integrate racially and economically segregated neighborhoods and communities. A private-market approach fit the Republican administration's stress on privatization while paying at least lip service to the liberal notion of minimizing the red tape and stigma often associated with governmental subsidy programs.

EHAP was one of many social experiments conducted during the 1960s and 1970s that tested social science theory and method in the crucible of actual provision of public services (Rivlin, 1977; Gilbert et al., 1977), and is therefore an example of social science as the handmaiden of program design. It is also one of the few housing programs that has generated analyzable data.

Households headed by people aged 62 or over constituted between one-fifth and one-third of families eligible for the housing allowance (Frieden, 1980: 23), but research results indicate that the elderly did not benefit from this program in proportion to their eligibility (U.S. Department of Housing and Urban Development, 1980; Struyk and Bendick, 1981). Although the experiment was conducted in twelve cities across the country, this analysis discusses research outcomes in the Demand Experiment cities of Pittsburgh (Allegheny County), Pennslyvania and Phoenix (Maricopa County), Arizona. In Pittsburgh, the elderly (defined as households with heads aged 62 or over) were 37 percent of the eligible population but only 25 percent of households receiving payments; in Phoenix, the elderly constituted 22 percent of eligible families and 21 percent of the families receiving payments.[1]

The aged families under study were free to move or not in response to the offer of the allowance. If their homes met the program's housing requirements, they could remain in place while receiving the allowance; if they wished to use the allowance to improve their housing conditions, they could move; if their current home did not meet the housing requirements and could not be repaired, they would either have to move to a place where the housing did comply or lose the benefits. The steps in the experiment are outlined in Figure 11.1. Behavior was carefully monitored and recorded, allowing patterns to emerge.

Housing allowances acted as a cushion, a "safety net" if you will, one element in a package of support that the elderly compiled for survival in old age. Although housing allowances acted as potential additions to economic resources, they were not evaluated in strictly economic terms, but involved the use of friends and family as "mediating structures" (Berger and Neuhaus, 1977) in the housing decisions.

The idea explored in this chapter by examining mobility rates and repairing and moving behavior is that these activities and consequent ability to qualify for the allowance were far more conditioned on social networks, particularly relatives and landlords, than has been generally realized. For those who did move during the course of the experiment, families and friends provided important instrumental assistance to the aged program participants.

RESIDENTIAL MOBILITY

Because allowances were only available to families living in housing that met health and safety standards, much of the experiment's outcome depended on the willingness or ability of families to move to new homes if their preprogram housing did not qualify, and the elderly were much less likely than were other families to move over the two-year data collection period. This reluctance to move is the major reason why the aged failed to qualify for the allowance.

Rossi (1981: 55) concluded, in a review of findings from the experiment, that "older households are least responsive to the incentives offered by the Experimental Housing Allowance Pro-

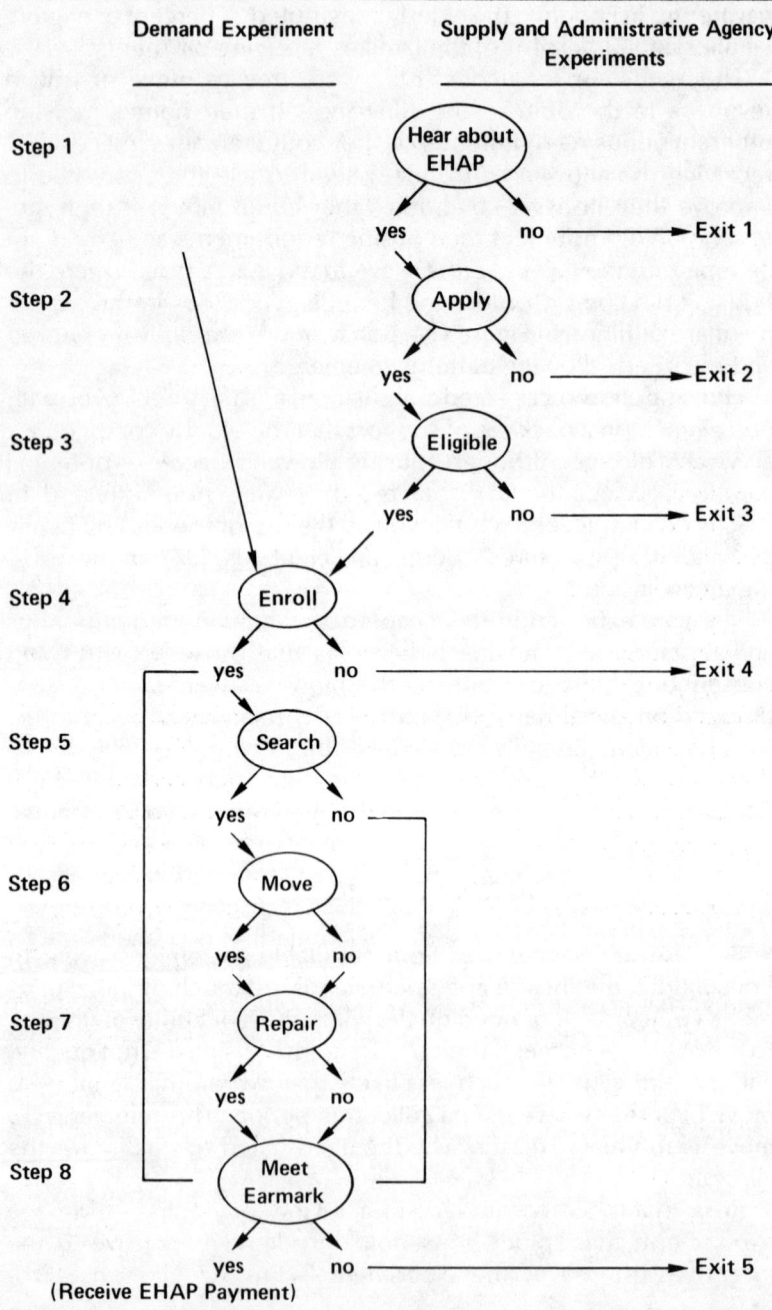

Figure 11.1

gram payments." He seems to define responsiveness as mobility, which is not, of course, the only possible response. Perhaps the most unequivocal finding of the experiment, according to Rossi, is that the older the head of the household, the more stable it was, a finding that holds up under all sorts of ceteris paribus conditions. The main lesson Rossi (1981: 157) found regarding the effect of housing allowances on mobility was the following:

> The major processes that drive residential mobility are not touched very deeply by the experimental treatments. In the aggregate over time, the amounts of moving appear to be stable, changing slowly rather than in response to identifiable short-term trends in the economy at large or the housing market. Since tenure and family life cycle appear to be the major correlates of residential mobility, it seems unlikely that the housing allowance payments are going to have much effect on moving; at best they will accelerate or retard changes that might otherwise have occurred rather than drastically altering the levels of residential mobility for the households to whom housing allowances were offered.

Newman and Duncan (1979) found, in an analysis of national longitudinal data from the Michigan Panel Study of Income Dynamics, that each additional year of age reduced the chance of moving by .3 percentage points, and the age effect was the most powerful of all the variables with an effect on mobility.

The case of "Ruby Jackson," described in Frieden (1980: 55-57) and based on the author's field experience in the Jacksonville, Florida site of the Administrative Agency Experiment (Wolfe and Hamilton, 1977) is the most dramatic illustration of the willingness of the elderly to give up the housing allowance rather than move. Mrs. Jackson, a black widow of 65, lived in a severely substandard single-family home in Jacksonville, Florida that had been built by her husband nearly half a century earlier. The home, which she owned, had no running water or indoor plumbing, and had been condemned by the Jacksonville Housing Code Enforcement Division three years before the allowance program began; from the time the house was condemned, the city's social worker had been trying to get Mrs. Jackson to relocate to more acceptable quarters. Mrs. Jackson had been enrolled in the program, had found a new place to live, and this new apartment had been approved by the administering agency. The day before she was to move she called her counselor and said that she would rather forego the payment than move from her long-term house. Why did she refuse to move, even though she was living in a condemned dwelling? Mrs. Jackson told the author that many of her neighbors deep in the pine woods of northeast Jacksonville were kin to her, and she did not wish to leave them. She was bound to the area by social ties, despite her physically substandard dwelling.

LOW MOBILITY RATES OF AGED

Data from the housing allowance demand experiment show that the elderly clearly preferred to stay in their preprogram housing even if it meant not receiving the housing allowance subsidy. Although over 40 percent of all participants in Pittsburgh and about 66 percent in Phoenix moved during the course of the 2-year experiment, the elderly were about half as likely to move as were younger families.

What do we know about why the elderly do not move very often or very easily? A study of Boston's neighborhoods has shown that familiarity with an area is extremely important in housing decisions (Hollister et al., 1977). In that study, "familiarity with area" was the most cited reason for choosing to buy a new home in a particular area, and for wanting to live in one place rather than another. Familiarity, dealing with the known, and being comfortable are all reasons why people move where they do (MacDonald and Mac-Donald, 1974; Tilly and Brown, 1974).

The negative effects of unwanted moving have been shown to range from increased costs (Hartman, 1964) to extended grief reactions (Fried, 1963) and even premature death (Aldrich and Mendkoff, 1968; Borup et al., 1979). No such dramatic claims are made in this chapter, but they should be kept in mind.

MOBILITY IN THE HOUSING ALLOWANCE EXPERIMENT AND EFFECT ON RECEIVING PAYMENT

The aged in the housing allowance experiment exhibited behavior that was contrary to what economic theory would predict about human response to the offer of an income supplement earmarked to improve housing conditions. Why is moving important in the context of the housing allowance experiment? Families who moved were more likely than were families who did not move to qualify for

TABLE 11.1
Proportion of Families with an Earmarking Requirement
Who Met the Requirement by Moving

Age	Proportion of Families Who Moved		Total Number of Families Who Met the Requirements	
	Number	%	Number	%
Pittsburgh				
18-54	88	52.4	168	100.0
55-59	2	25.0	8	
60-64	5	38.5	8	
65-69	4	28.6	14	
70-74	2	16.7	12	
75 and over	1	10.0	10	
Total	102	45.3	225	100.0
Phoenix				
18-54	134	83.7	160	100.0
55-59	5	62.5	8	
60-64	3	50.0	6	
65-69	7	63.6	4	
70-74	9	56.3	16	
75 and over	4	25.0	16	
Total	162	74.7	217	100.0

SOURCE: Central and Hades Files.

the allowance and receive the subsidy payment, yet the elderly were less likely than were families of other ages to move in order to receive the allowances.

The elderly were most likely to qualify for the allowance payment without moving from their preprogram home. Table 11.1 shows that in Pittsburgh, over half of young families, but only 10 percent of households headed by people aged 75 and over, and in Phoenix over 80 percent of the young, but just 25 percent of the old-old, met the program's requirements after moving to a new home.

What does searching behavior indicate? A completely satisfied family will probably not even look for a new home if offered a housing allowance. Slightly dissatisfied families may look for new housing but not find something suitable due to cost, location, unfamiliarity, or unsuitability to special needs. A family could want desperately to move to a better home but not be able to find something affordable that also meets the experiment's standard for good housing. In other words, a family can look for housing and decide that they can find nothing better than their present home, what can be called a voluntary nonmover, or can involuntarily fail to find a home that meets the program's standards due to discrimination on the basis of a whole host of factors such as race, sex, presence of children, source of income, and age, or just due to a lack of suitable housing in the market, which would be more of a comment on the supply of housing than on either desire to move or effectiveness as searchers.

For families of all ages, moving helped them to qualify for the allowance if they were in a treatment group that required them to live in good housing. Table 11.2 shows that more families who moved qualified for a payment (59.6 percent in Pittsburgh, 66.9 percent in Phoenix) than families who did not move (42 percent in Pittsburgh, 38.5 percent in Phoenix). However, except for one household headed by someone over the age of 75 in Pittsburgh who moved, among the very old moving did not increase the chances of qualifying for the allowance.

Why did families have to move to qualify for the subsidy? High proportions of the elderly who did not move did not qualify for a payment because the home they lived in did not meet the program's standard of acceptable housing. Moving was not necessary for those living in good housing, but people in bad housing had to move to meet the program's requirements. Most of the elderly qualified in their preprogram homes, but many of those living in substandard housing could not repair it up to the standard, and lost the chance to receive the subsidy. In Pittsburgh 69 percent and in Phoenix 42.9 percent of those age 75 and over who did not move did not qualify for the allowance payment (see Table 11.2).

MOVERS HAD FEWER SOCIAL TIES THAN NONMOVERS

Walter (1983) described how in the early steps of qualifying for an allowance payment (Figure 11.1), the elderly with few social ties such as the single, short-term residents, and those without family or friends in their neighborhoods participated in the experiment at a higher rate than did the elderly who had access to other sources of assistance than the housing allowance program.

A network of social ties in an area is thought to be a major reason that the elderly would not move even to receive the allowance

TABLE 11.2
Proportion of Participants Who Moved and Met the Requirement of Families
in Either Minimum Standards or Minimum Rent Treatment Groups

	Moved				Did Not Move				Total			
	Met Earmark		Did Not Meet Earmark		Met Earmark		Did Not Meet Earmark		Met Earmark		Did Not Meet Earmark	
Age	No.	%	No.	%	No.	%	No.	%	No.	%	No.	%
PITTSBURGH												
18-54	88	58.7	62	41.3	80	45.5	96	54.5	168	51.5	158	48.5
55-59	2	66.7	1	33.3	6	37.5	10	62.5	8	42.1	11	57.9
60-64	5	83.3	1	16.7	8	47.1	9	52.9	13	56.5	10	43.5
65-69	4	66.7	2	33.3	10	29.4	24	70.6	14	35.0	26	65.0
70-74	2	40.0	3	60.0	10	47.6	11	52.4	12	46.2	14	53.8
75 and over	1	100.0	0	—	9	31.0	20	69.0	10	33.3	20	66.7
Total	102	59.6	69	40.4	123	42.0	170	58.0	225	48.5	239	51.5
PHOENIX												
18-54	134	66.3	68	33.7	26	35.1	48	64.9	160	58.0	116	42.0
55-59	5	71.4	2	28.6	3	37.5	5	62.5	8	53.3	7	46.7
60-64	3	50.0	3	50.0	3	37.5	5	62.5	6	42.9	8	57.1
65-69	7	77.8	2	22.2	4	28.6	10	71.4	11	47.8	12	52.2
70-74	9	90.0	1	10.0	7	38.9	11	61.1	16	57.1	12	42.9
75 and over	4	50.0	4	50.0	12	57.1	9	42.9	16	55.2	13	44.8
Total	162	66.9	80	33.1	55	38.5	88	61.5	217	56.4	168	43.6

SOURCE: Central and Hades Files.

payment. They valued their nonmonetized and spatially localized social network even to the exclusion of potential monetary help.

Those aged who moved during the two-year period of the demand experiment would be expected either to have low social ties, so that they would not be facing a decreased local assistance system; would move to a place where they could get more help; or would be able to use their nonmonetary resources, that is, family and friends, in a way that enhanced the net resources available to them in their homes. They used their social resources to enhance their monetary resources and receive an allowance payment.

The elderly were making decisions that had much more to do with the social ties available to them in their neighborhoods and in their present homes than were young families. Elderly families who moved during the experiment were less likely to have relatives living in the neighborhood than were nonmovers, but the presence of relatives had almost no effect on the mobility of nonelderly families. Table 11.3 shows that in Pittsburgh, 29 percent of those related to their landlord moved compared to 42.2 percent of those not related to the landlord. In Phoenix, the difference was even more dramatic: 39 percent of those related, but 67.4 percent of those not related to their landlords, moved during the course of the experiment.

The numbers are small, but a look at the age distribution of this variable is instructive. Only 3 families out of the 17 above the age of 70 and related to the landlord moved during the 2-year period, and all 3 were in Phoenix where mobility rates were quite high. However, all of the families who were related to the landlord at the baseline survey were still related at the end of the 2 years, whether or not they moved.

Table 11.4 shows that 100 percent of household heads in Phoenix over the age of 60 and related to the landlord at the baseline survey were still related at the end of 2 years. Even if they moved, they found another place to live that was also owned by a relative.

INSTRUMENTAL ASSISTANCE FROM FRIENDS AND FAMILIES

Even though elderly households overwhelmingly stay in the long-term housing, if they want to move they draw on their social networks for help in finding, repairing, and moving to a new home.

TABLE 11.3
Mobility History of Participants Who Were Related
to Their Landlord at Baseline

Age	Proportion of Families Who Moved		Total Number of Families in the Program	
	No.	%	No.	%
PITTSBURGH				
Related to landlord				
18-54	25	30.5	82	100.0
55-59	1	33.3	3	100.0
60-64	1	50.0	2	100.0
65-69	2	25.0	8	100.0
70-74	0	—	1	100.0
75 and over	0	—	4	100.0
Total	29	29.0	100	100.0
Not related to landlord				
18-54	472	50.1	942	100.0
55-59	24	33.8	71	100.0
60-64	17	29.8	57	100.0
65-69	27	23.3	116	100.0
70-74	19	20.7	92	100.0
75 and over	14	19.2	73	100.0
Total	573	42.2	1351	100.0
PHOENIX				
Related to landlord				
18-54	29	46.8	62	100.0
55-59	0	—	0	100.0
60-64	0	—	4	100.0
65-69	0	—	4	100.0
70-74	1	33.3	3	100.0
75 and over	2	22.2	9	100.0
Total	32	39.0	82	100.0
Not related to landlord				
18-54	686	77.2	889	100.0
55-59	17	45.9	37	100.0
60-64	21	40.4	52	100.0
65-69	28	37.3	75	100.0
70-74	18	32.1	56	100.0
75 and over	18	30.0	60	100.0
Total	788	67.4	1169	100.0

SOURCE: Baseline Survey, Hades and Central Files.

TABLE 11.4
Proportion of Participants Related to Their Landlord at Baseline,
and Still Related to Their Landlord at the End of Two Years

Age	Proportion Related at Two Years (in percentages)	Total Number Active At Two Years (in integers)
PITTSBURGH		
Related at baseline		
18-54	67.1	76
55-59	66.7	3
60-64	50.0	2
65-69	75.0	8
70-74	100.0	1
75 and over	100.0	4
Total	69.1	94
Not related at baseline		
18-54	3.4	878
55-59	0	69
60-64	1.8	56
65-69	2.7	112
70-74	1.1	88
75 and over	2.8	72
Total	2.9	1275
PHOENIX		
Related at baseline		
18-54	70.0	50
55-59	—	0
60-64	100.0	4
65-69	100.0	4
70-74	100.0	3
75 and over	100.0	9
Total	78.6	70
Not related at baseline		
18-54	4.0	705
55-59	0	33
60-64	0	47
65-69	2.7	73
70-74	1.8	55
75 and over	0	56
Total	3.2	969

SOURCE: Baseline and Third Periodic Surveys

This section discusses how the elderly actually use their social networks to fix up their old homes, find a new place to live, and assist with moving. Once a decision is made to move, the assistance of members of the social network is crucial in implementing that decision. Members of social networks help the aged to search, repair, and move (Steps 5, 6, and 7 of Figure 11.1), thus helping them qualify for the allowance payment.

What instrumental assistance is given by friends and families? First, friends and neighbors help with routine repairs. The elderly are more dependent on the help of friends and neighbors in general than are younger households. When something goes wrong in the home, the aged are about half as likely as the young to fix it themselves.

Of the 9 percent of all families in the supply experiment who qualified for payments by repairing their homes, most did the repairs themselves (McDowell, 1979), but elderly households in both Green Bay and South Bend were less likely to do their own work and more likely to rely on help from others. Table 11.5 shows that, for homeowners, in Green Bay 48 percent of the elderly but 76 percent of the nonelderly enrollees, and in South Bend 32 percent of the elderly and 59 percent of the nonelderly, performed their own required repairs. Owners in South Bend were slightly more likely to hire a contractor than were owners in Green Bay, but in both cities the aged were more likely to hire help (18 percent in Green Bay and 23 percent in in South Bend), and also more likely to call on the help of a friend. Elderly owners in the two cities called on friends approximately twice as often as did the nonelderly: 33 percent of the elderly and 14 percent of the nonelderly in Green Bay, and 39 percent of the elderly and 22 percent of the nonelderly in South Bend had friends perform the repairs.

Table 11.5 also shows that elderly renters in Green Bay were more likely (17 percent) than were renters in South Bend (11 percent) to have repairs made by a contractor. In South Bend, the repair was more likely to be done by a friend (18 percent in South Bend and 7 percent in Green Bay). This may be due to higher proportions of minorities in South Bend (Goedert, 1978) and the existence of exchange networks in minority communities (Stack, 1973).

Renters were less likely than were owners to do their own repairs, and elderly renters were even more likely than were the young to call on their landlords (46 percent in Green Bay, 47 percent

TABLE 11.5
Source of Labor for Initial Repairs by Elderly and Nonelderly Enrollees
(in percentages)

City	Enrollee	Landlord	Friend	Contractor	Other	Total No.	%
Green Bay							
Homeowners							
Elderly	48	—	33	18	1	311	100
Nonelderly	76	—	14	10	1	607	100
Renters							
Elderly	30	46	7	17	(a)	211	100
Nonelderly	50	33	10	7	(a)	1,713	100
South Bend							
Homeowners							
Elderly	32	—	39	23	6	1,367	100
Nonelderly	59	—	22	14	4	1,168	100
Renters							
Elderly	22	47	18	11	2	378	100
Nonelderly	42	37	10	10	1	3,215	100

SOURCE: McDowell (1979: 57).

in South Bend) than were the nonelderly (33 percent in Green Bay, 37 percent in South Bend). This confirms the ideas suggested by Walter (1983) on the importance of the relationship with landlords. Nearly half of the elderly renters in the supply experiment relied on their landlords to make the repairs that were necessary to help them qualify for the allowance payment, compared to about a third of the renters. By contrast, nearly half of the elderly homeowners in Green Bay did the repairs themselves. In South Bend, the modal way that elderly homeowners qualified for the allowance was to have a friend do the necessary repairs, again confirming the importance of social ties in meeting the requirements of the program.

FINDING A NEW PLACE TO LIVE

Families who had moved in the three years preceding the baseline survey in the demand experiment were asked how they had located their current unit, and the evidence shows that the modal method of finding a new home was through a friend or relative.

Word of mouth and personal contacts seem to be the best ways to find a new place to live (Granovetter, 1973), and were more important for the elderly than for the nonelderly in the demand experiment. In Pittsburgh, over half of all those who moved in the three years preceding the baseline survey, and about two-thirds of those over the age of 70, found their new homes through information from friends or relatives. In Phoenix, 38.9 percent of all participants, but over half of those over the age of 70, found their present unit through a friend or relative. The second best way to find a new home was by looking in newspapers, and (in Phoenix only) scanning vacancy signs placed in windows. But the overwhelming majority of movers, both before and during the experiment, found their new homes through personal contacts.

The same pattern held for those who moved during the two-year experimental period (Table 11.6). Participants who searched for a new home during the experiment used virtually identical methods as did those who looked before the experiment began. In Pittsburgh, 57.3 percent and in Phoenix, 40.8 percent of movers found their homes with information gleaned from friends or relatives, with word of mouth more effective in Pittsburgh than in Phoenix.

It is interesting that those who looked for a new place to live both before and during the experiment used many methods of searching. They checked bulletin boards, read newspapers, hired realtors, looked at vacancy signs, and asked friends and relatives, but the method that got results was the "personal touch." Table 11.7 shows that 11 percent in both Pittsburgh and Phoenix looked at bulletin boards, 59.5 percent in Pittsburgh and 50.8 percent in Phoenix read newspapers; 51.8 percent in Pittsburgh and 24 percent in Phoenix hired realtors; and 34.6 percent in Pittsburgh and 52.1 percent in Phoenix checked vacancy signs, but those methods were not as productive as using friends or relatives. Other ways of looking for housing were used, but personal networks were the most effective.

DID THE ELDERLY NEED SPECIAL HELP TO QUALIFY FOR A PAYMENT?

A survey of the elderly done for the administrative agency experiment (Wolfe et al., 1977) found that most of the aged had no special problems, and were able to get most of the assistance they needed

TABLE 11.6
How Participants Who Moved During the First Two Years of the Experiment Found Their Present Unit

Age	Friend or Relative		Newspaper		Vacancy Sign		Realtor	
	No.	%	No.	%	No.	%	No.	%
Pittsburgh								
18-54	130	56.5	39	17.0	16	7.0	37	16.1
55-59	6	60.0	2	20.0	1	10.0	1	10.0
60-64	4	80.0	0	—	1	20.0	0	—
65-69	8	72.7	1	9.1	0	—	1	9.1
70-74	3	42.9	1	14.3	1	14.3	2	28.6
75 and over	2	50.0	0	0	0	—	1	25.0
Total	153	57.3	43	16.1	19	7.1	42	15.7
Phoenix								
18-54	159	38.9	86	21.0	108	26.4	44	10.8
55-59	6	60.0	0	—	2	20.0	1	10.0
60-64	5	62.5	1	12.5	2	25.0	0	—
65-69	7	58.3	2	16.7	1	8.3	1	8.3
70-74	4	80.0	0	—	0	—	1	20.0
75 and over	2	50.0	1	25.0	1	25.0	0	—
Total	183	40.8	90	20.1	114	25.4	47	10.5

Age	Knew Former Tenant		Social Worker		Neighborhood Bulletin Board		Total	
	No.	%	No.	%	No.	%	No.	%
Pittsburgh								
18-54	8	3.5	0	—	0	—	230	100.0
55-59	0	—	0	—	0	—	10	100.0
60-64	0	—	0	—	0	—	5	100.0
65-69	1	9.1	0	—	0	—	11	100.0
70-74	0	—	0	—	0	—	7	100.0
75 and over	1	25.0	0	—	0	—	4	100.0
Total	10	3.7	0	—	0	—	267	100.0
Phoenix								
18-54	7	1.7	1	0.2	4	1.0	409	100.0
55-59	0	—	0	—	1	10.0	10	100.0
60-64	0	—	0	—	0	—	8	100.0
65-69	1	8.3	0	—	0	—	12	100.0
70-74	0	—	0	—	0	—	5	100.0
75 and over	0	—	0	—	0	—	4	100.0
Total	8	1.8	1	0.2	5	10.5	448	100.0

SOURCE: Third Periodic Survey

TABLE 11.7

Percentage of All Searchers Using Various Sources of Information to Find Out About Available Units

Age	Bulletin Boards		Friends or Relatives		Newspapers		Realtors		Social Workers		Vacancy Signs	
	No.	%	No.	%	No.	%	No.	%	No.	%	No.	%
Pittsburgh												
18-54	59	12.6	307	65.3	294	62.6	259	55.1	17	3.6	172	36.6
55-59	3	9.7	17	54.8	18	58.1	9	29.0	0	0.0	6	19.4
60-64	2	13.3	8	53.3	8	53.3	8	53.3	1	6.7	6	40.0
65-69	2	8.0	13	52.0	10	40.0	8	32.0	2	8.0	7	28.0
70-74	1	6.7	8	53.3	6	40.0	6	40.0	0	0.0	5	33.3
75 and over	0	0.0	7	70.0	1	10.0	3	30.0	0	0.0	0	0.0
Total	67	11.8	360	63.6	337	59.5	293	51.8	20	3.5	196	34.6
Phoenix												
18-54	64	11.0	275	47.1	309	52.9	145	24.8	15	2.6	311	53.3
55-59	2	15.4	6	46.2	4	30.8	1	7.7	0	0.0	6	46.2
60-64	3	27.3	6	54.5	6	54.5	2	18.2	2	18.2	5	45.5
65-69	2	8.7	8	34.8	6	26.1	4	17.4	1	4.3	10	43.5
70-74	2	25.0	6	75.0	2	25.0	2	25.0	0	0.0	3	37.5
75 and over	0	0.0	3	30.0	3	30.0	2	20.0	0	0.0	3	30.0
Total	73	11.3	304	46.8	330	50.8	156	24.0	18	2.8	338	52.1

SOURCE: Third Periodic Survey.
NOTE: Adds to more than 100 because respondents could give more than one answer.

from outside the administering agency. The help offered by friends or relatives was much greater than help offered by the agency for searchers who either moved or stayed. Assistance was provided by friends and relatives, and most often included notifying the participant of apartments that were available. Friends and relatives also provided transportation assistance, helped the aged to negotiate with landlords, and helped them to make housing decisions.

Table 11.8 is the closest we can come to this data in the demand experiment data base, and it indicates that, although a very small proportion of all families relied on somebody outside the household to make the decision to move to the current unit, a higher proportion of households whose heads were over 70 compared to younger families relied on outside help. However, the numbers are very small and should be used with caution.

CONCLUSION

Social factors affected the mobility of low-income elderly families in the housing allowance experiment in several ways. Although residential stability is the rule among the elderly of almost all ages and social classes, it is generally people with few social ties who move. A minority of elderly-headed households move either during an experimental program or in the society at large. In the experiment, moves were generally local and helped the aged to qualify for the allowance payment. High social resources inhibited moves, as they inhibited participation in the early stages of the experiment (Walter, 1983), but when a decision to move was made, the elderly called on their friends and family to help them out.

In the housing allowance experiment, social networks helped the elderly to qualify for allowance payments. People who moved generally faced higher housing costs, but in the experiment the elderly used nonmonetized assistance from their friends and families to increase their economic resources with an allowance payment. Friends and family were used to help the elderly repair their preprogram units, search for housing, and move into new housing.

The general conclusion is that although the aged are usually reluctant to change their residences, when they do choose to move they call on assistance from outside their households to help them

TABLE 11.8
Who Decided to Move to This Unit, for Movers Only, at Two Years

Age	Respondent No.	%	Spouse or Other Household Member No.	%	Someone Else No.	%	Total No.	%
Pittsburgh								
18-54	230	69.7	95	28.8	5	1.5	330	100.0
55-59	9	50.0	9	50.0	0	—	18	100.0
60-64	6	100.0	0	—	0	—	6	100.0
65-69	11	73.3	3	20.0	1	6.7	15	100.0
70-74	6	54.5	3	27.3	2	18.2	11	100.0
75 and over	3	60.0	1	20.0	1	20.0	5	100.0
Total	265	68.8	111	28.8	9	2.3	385	100.0
Phoenix								
18-54	388	62.8	228	36.9	1	0.2	617	100.0
55-59	9	69.2	4	30.8	0	—	13	100.0
60-64	9	64.3	5	35.7	0	—	14	100.0
65-69	14	87.5	2	12.5	0		16	100.0
70-74	5	62.5	1	12.5	2	25.0	8	100.0
75 and over	5	55.6	3	33.3	1	11.1	9	100.0
Total	430	63.5	243	35.9	4	0.6	677	100.0

SOURCE: Third Periodic Survey

find a new home that is suitable for their economic, physical, and social status. The help, however, is not strictly financial.

POLICY IMPLICATIONS

What does this research imply for the design and implementation of housing assistance programs targeted to the elderly population? Although statistically imprecise, the general message is one of caution. Programs are often designed and implemented based on theories of how humans are expected to behave; only too rarely is there an opportunity to base policy and programs on actual behavioral outcomes. Some lessons that these findings ought to suggest include the following:

- Planning for housing the elderly must take into account, to a much larger extent than had previously been understood, how that housing plan will affect the personal networks of those participating in the housing scheme;

- Planners of housing for the aged should discuss in advance how likely their plan is to succeed given both the low propensity of the aged to move and their dependence on the assistance of family and friends if they do choose to move. Those who do not have such potential sources of aid, or who are reluctant to call on those people, might need additional assistance to help them obtain the benefits for which they are qualified;
- We must guard against overprofessionalization (Gerdt Sundstrom, personal communication). Whenever possible, human services delivered to the elderly should aim at complementarity rather than substitution (for example, assisting kin rather than replacing them, and using informal supports to fill in for gaps in formal service provision). Professionals in aging should look for ways to utilize and strengthen, to the extent possible, existing family and neighborhood ties. Overreliance on familes should be avoided at the same time that this important source of aid is recognized and used when appropriate. Program designers should learn to utilize families creatively, while providing respite care to relieve unbearable burdens;
- When new programs begin, outreach should be targeted not only to the aged themselves, but to their network members who can then pass the word.
- We must keep in mind that those elderly who either do not have any family members left, or who are on bad terms with kin and have few friends, will need extra attention to be well-served by existing programs. Attention should be paid to replacing lost roles and relationships through peer networks that can possibly perform functions similar to those of families and long-term friends.

METHOD

This research is a secondary analysis of data collected by Abt Associates Incorporated under contract to the U.S. Department of Housing and Urban Development, and made available through the Housing Research Data Center in Arlington, Virginia. The relevant variables were extracted from the demand experiment data tapes and new files were constructed. Because of the larger number of treatment groups (25) and small proportion of elderly (about 20 percent), even when treatment groups are merged the sample size is relatively small when doing crosstabulations by age. The conclusions presented in this chapter, then, are suggestive and are consistent with other research by gerontologists and sociologists, and provide insight into some phenomena that are not currently well understood.

NOTE

1. The inter city differences between participants in Phoenix and Pittsburgh were, particularly for mobility-related behavior, greater than the intracity variations among the age groups. These two cities were chosen for the experiment at least partially because they could provide contrast between an older northeastern city (Pittsburgh) and a growing Sunbelt City (Phoenix). Many of the observed behavior differences are a result of that intended contrast. Despite large between-city differences, in the following analysis, observed within-city patterns are remarkably similar.

12

WHO HELPS THE ELDERLY PERSON: A Discussion of Informal and Formal Care

NEENA L. CHAPPELL
Director, Centre on Aging
University of Manitoba

BETTY HAVENS
Provincial Gerontologist
Government of Manitoba

Increasingly, researchers in gerontology are turning their attention to the informal network of the individual (Horowitz, 1981; Johnson and Catalano, 1983; Ward et al., 1984). Most frequently this focuses on the family, but more and more studies are including friends and neighbors, as well as other relatives (Cantor, 1983). This increased attention has coincided with a growing concern about demands on the formal health care system as the population ages. Less frequently, studies focus on the interaction or interdependence between the informal and formal support systems or the role both play in the elderly individual's life. No doubt, this is at least partly due to the complexity of the question.

This chapter presents a preliminary examination of the role of these two systems in the lives of the elderly. It looks first at the concept of interdependence, then at the social network and the formal support network, as well as the role of both systems to-

Authors' Note: *This research was supported in part by the National Health Research and Development Program through a National Health Research Scholar award to Chappell (#6602-1137-48). Data reported here were collected with a grant from the Social Sciences and Humanities Research Council of Canada (#492-79-057) to Chappell.*

gether. Empirical data are presented, centering mostly on assistance from informal and formal sources.

INTERDEPENDENCE

Most frequently the concept of dependence or independence, rather than interdependence, is used in the literature and in conversation. These concepts, however, can be viewed as representing extremes on a continuum, where interdependence could be said to be the norm. Defining the terms, though, is no simple task. The dictionary defines dependence as "relying on another for support" and independence as "not nurturing or relying on something else or on someone else" (Merriam-Webster, 1974: 198, 361). Unfortunately, "requiring support" is no less vague than the terms "independence" and "dependence." The inherent difficulty in the concept, we would suggest, stems from the fact that the very definition of the term is socially derived. Whether a particular behavior is defined as dependent or independent is socially determined. This is confounded by the fact that an individual may be more or less dependent in one area of life but independent in another. For example, an individual may be able to dress or undress him- or herself without assistance but may rely on others for going up and down the stairs, and is therefore considered dependent in the latter task. However, if the individual lives in an environment free of stairs, even though the individual may be unable to perform this particular task, there would be no need for assistance for that individual. Therefore, the person would not be dependent.

In an attempt to understand these concepts, authors have created categories of different types of dependency. For example, Van den Heuvel (1976) discusses the numerous forms dependency can take: physical, mental, emotional, cognitive, social, economic, environmental, and so on. However, he reclassifies these into three broad groupings: practical/physical helplessness, interpersonal or social powerlessness, and psychological need. Clark (1972) describes the concept in terms of six types of dependency: socioeconomic, developmental or transitional, neurotic, dependency of crisis, dependency of nonreciprocal roles, and dependency of a cultural-conditioned character trait. Blenkner (1969) argues that dependencies fall into four categories: economic, physical, mutual, and social.

These authors note that dependencies can be intermixed and interacting, occurring simultaneously as well as at different times and with different impacts. For example, the individual referred to above who is unable to go up and down the stairs is environmentally dependent because the existence of stairs in the environment is a major determinant of the need for assistance. Similarly, psychological or mental dependence may lead to the need for assistance in the social, physical, and economic areas.

Despite the recognition of a multitude of areas of dependency, it is probably fair to say that most of the gerontological literature to date has focused on physical dependency. This no doubt reflects the emphasis on physical assistance within the formal health care system with its medical orientation. Physical dependency is frequently discussed and measured in terms of activities of daily living (Katz et al., 1981) such as assistance required with bathing, dressing/undressing, going to the bathroom, or instrumental activities of daily living (Branch and Jette, 1981) such as going out of doors and shopping. These types of physical dependency are frequently referred to as functional disability. Even for these physical activities, a precise scientific definition eludes the investigator. As Kane and Kane (1981) point out, independence in the task of bathing might be defined as the ability to lather and rinse the whole body, including the back and all extremities. Yet few people irrespective of age can reach their backs without the help of a long-handled scrub brush. Their point is that imposing an overly rigid definition of ability for independent functioning defeats its purpose.

An older mother who comes once a week and does the shopping for her daughter with four young children at home is clearly providing assistance, yet few would contend that the daughter is "dependent" on her mother. That is, whom we consider dependent and why is socially derived and depends on the social context. Examining the area of social dependence and psychological dependence perhaps best illustrates this point. Because everyone engages in interaction of varying kinds and degrees virtually every day, it is difficult to know when that interaction indicates a psychological, emotional, or social dependency. What one individual would consider social dependence, another would not. The mother-daughter relationship referred to above may apply to one daughter in the situation who defines herself as socially dependent and perhaps undesiring of this situation. Another daughter may not consider herself dependent and indeed be grateful for the interaction she has with her mother. Similarly, what would be considered a life of relative social isolation by some may be considered the optimal living situation by others.

Despite the lack of precise scientific definition of dependence, it is nevertheless true that there is an accepted common sense understanding of the term within everyday society. Within this common sense definition it is also no doubt true that dependence is considered an extreme on a continuum with independence at the other extreme. Interdependence no doubt more accurately reflects the real situation than either of these extremes. Furthermore, it is important to understand and remember the complexity of interaction within different spheres of dependency or interdependency, and that the process by which an individual becomes defined as independent or dependent in any of these spheres is itself a social definition.

In addition, the individual's subjective perceptions of his or her situation are particularly important. For example, if an elderly individual believes that he or she is coping well without specific types of assistance from either friends or formal agencies, this may lead him or her to refuse offers of assistance should they arise and could well prevent him or her from seeking such assistance. Similarly, if they perceive themselves as requiring assistance while either their informal network or formal agencies consider them capable of fulfilling these functions, they may become frustrated in their efforts to obtain help.

That is, the concept of interdependence has value within scientific research despite the absence of definitional rigor. One of the reasons for these definitional difficulties is the importance of the subjective dimension of the concept and of the social context for shaping the meaning of the concept for the individual.

INFORMAL NETWORKS

The gerontological literature clearly accepts the importance of social interaction for the elderly. Maintaining close ties with relatives and friends is said to maximize adjustment during old age and increase overall well-being (Chappell, 1983; Kozma and Stones, 1978). Increasingly it is argued that social support mediates stressful events (Larson, 1978; Lemon et al., 1972; Havens, 1968; Cohler and Lieberman, 1980). There is within this literature an emphasis on the family. The family is discussed as providing companionship, affection, and other primary group rewards for its members. It fulfills what Cantor (1975) refers to as the more idiosyncratic human needs (Sussman and Burchinal, 1962). However, more recently others have investigated friendship and neighbor interactions (Wood and Robertson, 1978; Cantor, 1979; Wellman, 1982; Ward et al., 1984).

This literature, however, does not tend to focus on interdependence. Little can be found on reciprocity or mutual interaction. No doubt this reflects the difficulty and the complex methodology that would be preferred for its study. The literature does suggest reciprocity and interdependence but largely indirectly. More frequently the literature examines, for example, the number of individuals in the elderly person's social network (Bultena, 1969; Heltsley and Powers, 1975), who provide what type of assistance to the elderly person (Paringer, 1983), who the individual perceives as his or her confidant, and so on (Treas, 1976; Sherman, 1975; Horowitz and Shindelman, 1981). Fewer investigators have attempted to look directly at reciprocity. Hill (1968) is an example, having studied tasks provided and received between the generations.

In other words, the general concepts of interdependence, interaction, and reciprocity appears to be accepted at the conceptual level within the gerontological literature, or at least would not be denied at this level. We would suggest that one of the reasons empirical data tend not to reflect the concept is the difficulty of adequate measurement. Nevertheless, it can be argued that keeping this concept foremost in mind and examining data explicitly with this question in mind will lead to additional contributions from existing data sets. That is the intent here—to seek a more adequate understanding of the reality of the elderly and a more complete picture of the social context within which they live their lives.

THE FORMAL SUPPORT NETWORK

The formal support system tends to encompass the formal health care system. Although there are increasing efforts to include what may be referred to as less medicalized services—more social and community services within this overall system—it still represents an overemphasis on medical care. While much of this literature focuses on cost containment and the actual members and types of services provided to what proportion of the population (Clark and Collishaw, 1975; Health Statistics Reports from the United States), there is evidence of an emerging discussion concerning the interdependence between the receipt of informal and formal care (Weissart, 1977; Paringer, 1983; Comptroller General, 1977).

This concern has been raised in terms of the provision of formal support services, in particular additional community and social services, leading to a "shirking" of family responsibility for its elderly members. The contrary argument is that the provision of formal community services is necessary for those in need as is respite care for informal caregivers. That is, formal care need not replace or substitute for informal care.

Empirical data referring to these issues, however, are more difficult to find. Brody (1981) does argue that enough is known to state that families seek assistance from the formal system only when the informal network can no longer cope. O'Brien and Wagner (1980) provide some data and conclude that most draw first from informal sources followed by aid from formal agencies and/or organizations. Evidence before the Select Committee on Aging in the United States points out approximately 80 percent of home care provided to the elderly is provided by family members (Biaggi, 1980; NRTA et al., 1980). Brody et al. (1978) report that the presence of family and its availability as a source of care are important factors in delaying if not preventing institutionalization of the chronically ill older person. Branch and Jette (1981) report more assistance from informal than formal sources. The fact that it is those with limited family relationships who are prime candidates for institutionalization when they become sick (Shanas, 1979; Marcus, 1978), however, suggests that formal supports substitute for informal in the absence of the latter.

It is an examination of both social networks and formal assistance in the lives of the elderly population that is the focus of this chapter. The aim is to gain a greater understanding of the interaction of both, specifically in the provision of formal assistance to elderly individuals. The focus on assistance underestimates the role of informal support in the lives of elderly persons. It ignores the emotional and social elements of such interaction, which some argue (Schmidt, 1981) make them preferable to formal services even if the latter are similar in task performance.

DATA AND METHODOLOGY

The data are drawn from 800 elderly respondents living in Winnipeg, Manitoba, Canada. Long-term care institutional residents were excluded from the population prior to drawing the samples. Half of these individuals come from a random sample of those aged 65 and over living in Winnipeg and not receiving formal home care services. The other 400 refer to a random sample of long-term users (those receiving services for a minimum of 5 months) of home care services. The home care users were obtained from a random listing of all users in the central home care office; the nonusers were obtained from a random list obtained from the Manitoba Health Services Commission (which handles all provincial health insurance) after having deleted those receiving home care. Both samples were stratified by area and by age and sex to ensure sufficient numbers of old elderly men for analyses (see also Chappell, 1983; Strain and Chappell, 1982).

The Manitoba Home Care Program is the oldest province-wide, centrally administered, universal no cost to consumer home care program in Canada. It was designed specifically to relieve the inappropriate pressure on acute, extended care and personal care beds resulting from the absence of comprehensive alternative care in the home (Rombout, 1975; National Health and Welfare, 1982). It was started in 1974 in rural parts of the province and in 1975 in urban Winnipeg. It is staffed by professionals, paraprofessionals, and volunteers providing a range of services including homemaking, orderly service, medical supplies, meals-on-wheels, therapy, nursing, and so on to those requiring such services to function adequately at home because of aging, physical health disability, or personal crisis or illness (Government of Manitoba, 1974: I-25).

Respondents in this study were interviewed during the spring, summer, and fall of 1980 with interpreters used for virtually all major language groups. Data were collected on various normative social contexts including household members, relatives outside of the home, unrelated friends, neighbors, and persons seen for specific purposes such as storekeepers. Data were collected on individuals' total social networks as well as on their assistance networks. Data are presented here on their assistance networks as a proportion of their total networks and in terms of reciprocity. The data are presented first on standard types of instrumental assistance, and then on assistance with activities of daily living because the sample of home care users are known to be functionally disabled (Chappell, 1983).

The home care users are estimated to constitute approximately 15 percent of the elderly population in Manitoba. The general descriptions of the social networks and assistance networks will be given for the sample weighted appropriately. Therefore, the nonusers are given an 85 percent weight so that the resulting projections refer to those elderly persons living in Winnipeg, not in long-term institutional care. The 400 users are compared with the 400 nonusers, unweighted, when a comparison of these 2 groups is sought.

Sample characteristics are published elsewhere so are only summarized here (Chappell, 1983; Strain and Chappell, 1982). Those using home care services were more likely to be female rather than male, to be older (75 or over) rather than younger, to have been housewives rather than to have worked in professional or high level management jobs, to be widowed rather than not, and to live in an apartment rather than to live in their own homes. There were, however, no educational, religious, or ethnic group differences between the two groups. The users, in other words, reveal the same general characteristics as users of formal services noted elsewhere (Shanas, 1979; Wan and Weissart, 1981). They tend to be female, older, and widowed. It is also true that the users are significantly less healthy (in terms of functional ability, chronic conditions, and perceived health) and less active than the nonusers.

SOCIAL NETWORKS AND CAREGIVING

The scope of the elderly population's network can be seen in Table 12.1. This refers to the number of people individuals report as available generally in their lives (in the household, as friends, relatives, neighbors, and others seen for instrumental purposes). It is clear that, according to this measure, few elderly persons are totally isolated. No one reports no other people or only one other person in their lives. Only 5 percent of the sample

TABLE 12.1
Social Network[a]

Total Number of Individuals[b]	N	%
2-10	19	5
11-25	101	25
26-40	121	30
41-65	87	22
>65	75	19
Total	403	101

a. Sample includes users of home care services and nonusers. The sample was weighted so that nonusers make up 85 percent of the sample and users make up 15 percent of the sample.
b. Includes number of persons in household, relatives, friends, neighbors, and others seen for instrumental reasons all outside the household. Friends here refer to nonrelatives.

report between 2 and 10 other people. Most (55 percent) report that anywhere from 11 to 40 people are available in their lives.

When the users and nonusers are compared, nonusers have larger overall social networks (mean or $\bar{x}$ for users = 33.2; $\bar{x}$ for nonusers = 48.2; t = -6.29; p < .001). This confirms previous analyses based on overall networks but focusing on specific normative contexts. These analyses (Chappell, 1984) revealed that nonusers have more individuals available to them among household members, relatives outside the household, friends, and persons seen for specific purposes. Not unexpectedly, the differences in so many specific areas add up to differences in the overall network.

Individuals were also asked if they received assistance from or provided assistance to any people with whom they were involved in terms of assistance. Assistance referred to the following: helping with grandchildren; helping out when ill; giving advice about personal problems, job, and so on; financial aid; providing a home for others; household tasks; transportation; emergency aid; and other assistance. Assistance could be either provided to or received by the respondent (each appears separately below).

Table 12.2 turns specifically to the assistance network. Over half of the elderly persons are receiving assistance of some form (231 or 58 percent). Over half also provides some form of assistance to others (221 or 55 percent). Almost half are in a reciprocal relation-

TABLE 12.2
The Assistance Network[a]

	N		%
Reciprocity			
Neither receiving nor providing	68		17
Receiving assistance only	112		28
Receiving and providing assistance	119		30
Providing only	102		25
Total	401		100
Sources (Receipt)		%[b]	
Not receiving assistance	167		42
Receiving from informal sources	170	(73)	43
Receiving from formal sources	14	(6)	3
Receiving from both formal and informal sources	48	(21)	12
Total	399	(100)	100
Sources (Provision)			
Not providing assistance	179		45
Providing to informal sources	204	(93)	51
Providing to formal sources	6	(3)	2
Providing to both formal and informal sources	10	(5)	2
Total	399	(101)	100

a. The sample was weighted so that nonusers make up 85 percent of the total sample and users make up 15 percent of the sample.
b. Percentages in parentheses refer to those in receipt of assistance only (N = 232), and only those providing assistance (N = 220).

ship in regards to assistance, either receiving and providing it or neither receiving nor providing it (187 or 47 percent). As noted above, nonusers are more likely to be providing assistance than are users ($\bar{x} = 1.19$ for nonusers; $\bar{x} = .50$ for users; $t = -8.25$; $p < .000$). On the other hand, users are more likely to be receiving assistance than are nonusers ($\bar{x} = .98$ for nonusers; $\bar{x} = 2.89$ for users; $t = 18.79$; $p < .000$).

Assistance is further examined in terms of source, whether it is provided to or received from formal or informal sources (also see Table 12.3). Over half of the elderly population (58 percent) are receiving some form of assistance. Just over half (55 percent) of the population are receiving assistance from informal sources, and 15 percent from formal sources. However, among those receiving some form of assistance, fully 94 percent receive some assistance from informal sources. Finally, among the 15 percent receiving formal care, 80 percent are also receiving care from informal

TABLE 12.3
Frequency of Assistance Received[a]

	N	%
Not receiving any assistance	167	42
Once	2	1
When occasion arises	49	12
Once a year	25	6
Several times a year	42	10
Once a month	42	10
Several times a month	33	8
Once a week	19	5
Several times a week	11	3
Every day	8	2
Totals	398	99

Group Differences	$\bar{x}$ Nonusers	$\bar{x}$ Users	t	p
Every day	.35	.56	3.25	<.001
Several times a week	.22	.36	3.02	<.01
Once a week	.31	.77	8.36	<.000
Several times a month	.26	.49	4.14	<.000
Once a month		ns		
Several times a year		ns		
Once a year		ns		
When occasion arises		ns		
Once		ns		

a. Sample was weighted so that nonusers make up 85 percent of the sample and users of home care services make up 15 percent of the sample.

sources. That is, these data provide Canadian figures confirming the provision of informal care to the elderly population and the provision of informal care even when formal care is provided.

The data also confirm the greater tendency of the users to receive informal assistance than is true of the nonusers ($\bar{x}$ = .92 for nonusers; $\bar{x}$ = 2.04 for users; t = 11.15; p < .000) and to receive formal assistance than is true of the nonusers ($\bar{x}$ = .07 for nonusers; $\bar{x}$ = 1.05 for users, t = 19.98; p < .000).

Fully 55 percent are involved in the provision of assistance, primarily to informal sources (also see Table 12.3). Users are less likely to provide assistance either to informal ($\bar{x}$ = 1.14 for nonusers; $\bar{x}$ = .48 to users; t = −8.14; p < .000) or to formal sources ($\bar{x}$ = .05 for nonusers; $\bar{x}$ = .02 for users; t = −2.24; p < .05).

Finally, Table 12.3 shows the general frequency of assistance. Few (8 or 2 percent) are receiving assistance every day; few (11 or 3

TABLE 12.4
Frequency of Assistance Provided[a]

	N	%
Not providing any assistance	178	44
Once	4	1
When occasion arises	64	16
Once a year	50	12
Several times a year	43	11
Once a month	23	6
Several times a month	14	3
Once a week	13	3
Several times a week	66	1
Every day	8	2
Totals	403	99

Group Differences	$\bar{x}$ Nonusers	$\bar{x}$ Users		t	p
Every day	.45	.79		3.55	.000
Several times a week			ns		
Once a week			ns		
Several times a month			ns		
Once a month			ns		
Several times a year			ns		
Once a year			ns		
As occasion arises	2.56	2.03		−2.60	.05
Once			ns		

a. Sample was weighted so that nonusers make up 85 percent of the sample and users make up 15 percent of the sample.

percent) are receiving assistance several times a week. As expected, the users are more likely to be receiving assistance more frequently than is true of the nonusers, up to once a month. There are no user/nonuser differences in the receipt of assistance, once a month or less frequently (also see Table 12.4).

The distribution for assistance provided appears in Table 12.4, and is similar to the distribution of assistance received, just discussed. However, the differences between users and nonusers are not as evident in the provision as in the receipt of services. Users are more likely to provide assistance on an everyday basis, but less likely to provide them when the occasion arises. Otherwise no group differences are evident here.

Because the sample of users studied here are characterized by high functional disability (Chappell, 1983), the examination of the

TABLE 12.5
Proportion of Total Network Devoted to Assistance
with Activities of Daily Living[a]

	N	%
(A) Providing or Receiving Assistance		
Not providing or receiving	251	64
1-5	65	17
6-15	49	13
16-25	13	3
>25	11	3
Totals	389	100
(B) Providing Assistance		
Not providing assistance	345	86
1-10	44	11
11-100	12	3
Totals	401	100
(C) Receiving Assistance		
Not receiving assistance	291	76
1-5	45	12
6-15	34	9
16-25	8	2
>25	6	2
Totals	384	101

a. Sample weighted so that nonusers make up 85 percent of the sample and users make up 15 percent of the total sample.

assistance network was repeated specifically for assistance with activities of daily living only. Respondents were asked about assistance with the following: using the telephone, feeding/eating, dressing/undressing, washing/bathing, cutting toenails, taking medication, nursing care, getting about the house, getting in and out of bed, going outdoors in good weather, going outdoors in any weather, going up and down stairs, watching TV/listening to the radio, and preparing meals. As shown in Table 12.5, far fewer individuals were involved in assistance interactions specifically in terms of activities of daily living.

Indeed, only 36 percent are involved in either providing or receiving assistance of this type. Of those involved in such interactions, only 19 percent of the population are involved in activities of daily living assistance with more than 5 percent of their total networks. Furthermore, home care users are much more likely to be involved in such relationships than is true of nonusers ($\bar{x}$ for nonusers = 2.64; $\bar{x}$ for users = 16.23; t = 9.88; p < .000). There is no significant difference between these two groups in those providing assistance for activities of daily living. However, there is again a dramatic difference between the two groups in the receipt of assistance for activities of daily living ($\bar{x}$ for nonusers = 1.46; $\bar{x}$ for users = 14.81; t = 10.12; p < .000). Not unexpectedly, it is the users who are more likely to be receiving assistance for activities of daily living than is true of the nonusers. This is to be expected, given that users are much more likely to be functionally disabled on these particular measures than is true of the nonusers ($\bar{x}$ for nonusers = 1.07; $\bar{x}$ for users = 1.33; t = 20.11; p < .001).

Focusing on the activities of daily living assistance network, the reciprocity of this type of assistance and the sources are provided in Table 12.6. Few are involved in both receiving and providing this type of assistance. Furthermore, more receive assistance (28 percent) than provide it (14 percent). Those who receive assistance with activities of daily living are more likely to receive it from informal sources (21 percent) than from formal sources (14 percent). One-third of those receiving such assistance from informal sources also receive it from formal sources. Not unexpectedly, it is the users who are more likely to receive this type of assistance from informal sources ($\bar{x}$ for nonusers = .33; $\bar{x}$ for users = 1.62; t = 9.37; p < .000) and are more likely to receive it from formal sources as well ($\bar{x}$ for nonusers = .07; $\bar{x}$ for users = 1.32; t = 15.64; p < .000). Only 14 percent of these individuals are providing this type of assistance and all of them are providing it to informal sources, none to formal sources. There are no significant differences between the users and nonusers in this respect, but there are so few individuals in this category that the meaningfulness of exploring group differences may be questioned.

Once again, these data confirm, with representative Canadian data, the existence of the informal care system, and indeed a greater proportion of care provided by this informal system than is found within the formal care system.

The frequency of assistance received is shown in Table 12.7, and that provided is shown in Table 12.8. It is clear that among the small proportion who are receiving assistance with activities of daily living, they are receiving them rather infrequently. Instead, they are equally distributed throughout the range. As expected, the users are more likely to receive these services every day, once a

TABLE 12.6
The Activities of Daily Living Assistance Network[a]

	N	%
Reciprocity		
Neither receiving nor providing	251	63
Receiving assistance only	95	24
Receiving and providing assistance	15	4
Providing only	40	10
Totals	401	101
Sources (Receipt)		
Not receiving assistance	291	73
Receiving from informal sources	55	14
Receiving from formal sources	27	7
Receiving from both formal and informal sources	27	7
Totals	400	100
Sources (Provision)		
Not providing assistance	345	86
Providing to informal sources	55	14
Providing to formal sources	—	—
Providing to both formal and informal sources	—	—
Totals	400	100

a. Sample weighted so that nonusers make up 85 percent of the sample and users make up 15 percent of the total sample.

week, several times a month, and once a month. However, there are no group differences for receipt of these services several times a week or for less frequently than once a month.

The provision of assistance is similarly equally distributed in terms of frequency among a small proportion (only 14 percent) of the population. Differences between users and nonusers did not emerge other than the fact that nonusers are more likely to provide these services on a once a week basis than are users.

CONCLUSIONS

The data presented here have been weighted to represent the community living elderly population in Winnipeg. That is, they represent those aged 65 and over living in metropolitan Winnipeg, and not in long-term institutional care. The data are Canadian and substantiate writings coming out of the United States, arguing that

TABLE 12.7
Frequency of Assistance Received with Activities of Daily Living[a]

	N	%
Not receiving any	289	73
Less than once a month	22	6
Once a month	15	4
Several times a month	18	5
Once a week	23	6
Several times a week	16	4
Every day	11	3
Totals	394	101

Group Differences	$\bar{x}$ Nonusers	$\bar{x}$ Users	t	p
Every day	.48	1.08	3.65	<.000
Several times a week		ns		
Once a week	.32	.84	5.75	<.000
Several times a month	.25	.42	2.15	<.05
Once a month	.23	.40	2.79	<.01
Less than once a month		ns		

a. Sample weighted so that nonusers make up 85 percent of the sample and users make up 15 percent of the total sample.

TABLE 12.8
Frequency of Assistance Provided with Activities of Daily Living[a]

	N	%
Not providing any	344	86
Less than once a month	9	2
Once a month	3	1
Several times a month	10	2
Once a week	11	3
Several times a week	15	4
Every day	9	2
Totals	401	100

Group Differences	$\bar{x}$ Nonusers	$\bar{x}$ Users	t	p
Every day		ns		
Several times a week		ns		
Once a week	.29	.04	−2.99	<.01
Several times a month		ns		
Once a month		ns		
Less than once a month		ns		

a. Sample weighted so that nonusers make up 85 percent of the sample and users make up 15 percent of the total sample.

most elderly persons cope well within the community without an inordinate amount of assistance. Further, they also support the claims that informal care to aging members is alive and well. This is true even when the elderly individuals are recipients of formal care such as that provided by the home care program studied here. It should be pointed out that it is a home care program policy in Manitoba that informal assistance received from family, friends, and neighbors is to be taken into account when determining amount and type of services to be provided by the program. This policy supports complementing informal assistance rather than replacing it. These data could be reflecting the successful implementation of that policy. Before generalizations are made elsewhere, policies guiding the implementation of formal services should be well understood for the particular locale. Nevertheless, the data provide strong empirical support for the claim that, even among those receiving formal care, home care users receive much more assistance from informal sources, and more than do nonusers.

13

SERVICE NEEDS AND SUPPORT NETWORKS OF ELDERLY NATIVE AMERICANS: Family, Friends, and Social Service Agencies

ROBERT JOHN
Graduate Student, Sociology
University of Kansas

It is with some justification that the National Tribal Chairmen's Association titled the final report of the first national Indian conference on aging *The Indian Elder: A Forgotten American*. Native Americans are a neglected minority group, and nowhere is this neglect more evident than in the area of support networks of elderly Native Americans.[1] Academic research on the status and needs of Native American elders has lagged far behind research on other minority elderly. This neglect is most clearly evident in the absence of publications in scholarly journals and the superficial treatment given Native Americans in social gerontological texts in the obligatory chapter devoted to "minority" aging. One need only contrast the amount of information available about other minority groups to realize the relative paucity of information on the Native American aged. This chapter analyzes the service needs and support networks of elderly Native Americans including family, friends, and use of formal social services in both urban and reservation settings.

THE NATIVE AMERICAN FAMILY: EXTENDED OR UNAVAILABLE

A great deal of research on social networks, particularly of kin networks, began in the early 1950s in response to the "isolated nuclear family" thesis that had come to dominate conceptualizations of family life by the mid-1940s, largely through the influence of the work of Louis Wirth, William F. Ogburn, and Talcott Parsons. This thesis specified that the nuclear family, isolated from kin, was the normal family structure in modern, industrial, urban societies, and nearly two decades of research on family networks sought to investigate if this was indeed the case. Because the isolated nuclear family thesis was associated with "urbanism as a way of life," most research during the 1950s and 1960s was done on urban families. Fewer studies were done on rural families (see Powers et al., 1981), fewer still attempted a rural/urban comparison (Key, 1961; Shanas et al., 1968; Winch and Greer, 1968; Straus, 1969; Winch, 1977), and studies of the family network of minorities, with the exception of blacks, are even less numerous. A number of essays (Sussman, 1965; Adams, 1970; Gibson, 1972; Lee, 1980; Lee and Cassidy, 1981; Powers et al., 1981) review and critically evaluate the isolated nuclear family debate and the family network studies that have led to the new consensus reflected in family texts—that the "modified extended family" desiring "intimacy at a distance" is a better characterization of reality (Troll et al., 1979).

Exactly the opposite presumption has characterized statements about the family life of Native Americans. In comparison to the white families that have been the primary focus of family network research, studies of Native American family life start from the opposite, though possibly erroneous, assumption that an intact extended family network is the norm. Indeed, the existence of extended family structures among Native Americans and their roles as a support to aging members is well documented in the anthropological literature, but little literature about American Indian families is of recent origin. This, however, has not deterred gratuitous characterizations of Native American family life. According to a December 1979 staff report to the Federal Council on the Aging:

> Various statements . . . as well as documented reports, attest to the strong traditional bond existing between the Indian family and their older members. Older Indians continue to play an important role in the extended American Indian families. However, according to the National Indian Council on Aging the increasing acculturation of young American Indians has caused the natural support network to erode at a rapid pace. It is important to note that there are still insufficient data to draw definite conclusions [U.S. Department of Health and Human Services, 1979: 32].

The contradictory nature of this statement should be evident. Despite allusions to statements and documented reports that attest to the strength of intergenerational ties, no sources were cited. The most reliable portion of this statement suggests the opposite—that family integration is, in fact, declining, leading to the disruption of the traditional source of support for Indian elders.

The issue of the existence and extent of the family network is important for a number of reasons. As is true of other minorities (U.S. Department of Health and Human Services, 1979), Native Americans, in general, have low formal service utilization, a condition that is not simply attributable to lack of availability or awareness of services. As Dukepoo (1980: 32) notes, "fear, mistrust and insensitivity" of agency personnel are special problems that reduce service use among American Indians, although Powers and Bultena (1974: 253) found similar attitudes among elderly Iowans. Additional impediments include "difficulties with written forms and documents" (Dukepoo, 1980: 33) or what Indians jokingly call "white tape," and the existence of multiple obstacles such as transportation problems, poor health, or inadequate income, that combine to limit utilization rates. If a number of factors hinder use of formal social services, the importance of the family network becomes even more salient or central in providing needed support to aging members.

Recent scholarship has suggested that the Native American family network may be an important source of indirect assistance as well. That is, the family network is not only a direct service provider, but is also instrumental in facilitating formal service use by elderly family members. According to Murdock and Schwartz, the availability of and contact with family members is an important factor in both the perception of needs and the use of services. Murdock and Schwartz (1978: 480-481) conclude that "children may assist elderly persons by both creating greater awareness of the needs for and availability of services, and in directly obtaining the required services." Although they state their conclusions in a tentative manner, Murdock and Schwartz (1978: 481) suggest that "extended families serve to increase the mechanisms for service usage as well as the sources of information concerning services." In their view, family members are not only the primary caregivers within the social network, but also may serve an indispensable mediator role between Native American elders and alien service bureaucracies.

Whether as direct provider or intermediary, then, the existence of an extended family network is no less crucial now compared to the not too distant past when they were the sole source of support of Indian elders. However, existing studies do little to clarify what is occurring within Native American families. John G. Red Horse et al. (1978) offer a typology of "three distinct family patterns" among urban Chippewas, which they label "traditional," "bi-cultural," and "pan-traditional." Although each of these family types differs from the others in terms of language used in the household, religious affiliation, value system, and recreational and cultural activities, all three are characterized as having an extended family network. Red Horse et al. (1978: 69) claim that "extended family networks represent a universal pattern among American Indian nations." Dukepoo (1980), however, documented urban/rural differences in the social networks of elderly Native Americans that suggest a "traditional extended" organization of family life on the reservation and a pattern similar to the white middle class among elderly Native Americans in urban San Diego. Steele (1972), however, alludes to the existence of extended family households among urban Potawatomi, and Williams (1980) claims that extension exists among nonreservation Oklahoma Native Americans in terms of a social network characterized by residential propinquity. Miller (1975), however, concluded the opposite—that compared with reservations, the extended family system was not available to the urban Native Americans she studied in the San Francisco Bay area.

As one might guess, how particular researchers define and measure family extension is a crucial consideration. The two basic measures of family extension are household composition and residential propinquity. Of these, the best measure of family extension is effective or functioning social network based on interaction and proximity of residence (see Sussman, 1959, 1965; Klatzky, 1972; Wilkening et al., 1972; Gibson, 1972; Powers et al., 1981). Generally, however, this measure of family extension is not collected.

METHODS

The data used as the basis of comparison in this chapter are drawn from the first nationwide study of Indian elders conducted during 1980 by the National Indian Council on Aging (NICOA). NICOA employed a cluster type probability sample in which each federally recognized Indian tribe, Alaskan village, as well as urban centers funded by the Administration for Native Americans was considered a cluster. A random sample of these clusters was chosen and then a random sample of individuals was drawn from tribal rolls or a list of urban center program participants. Major problems with this procedure concerning the representativeness of the sample are candidly discussed at length in the NICOA report entitled *American Indian Elderly: A National Profile*. In brief, these major problems include not having accurate population data for sample selection and the failure to gain participation from all of the chosen clusters, in particular the Sioux and Chippewa. Despite the problems, this is the most comprehensive study conducted to date and the findings add to our knowledge of a "group" of elders about which little is known.

Of greater concern than the problems arising from the representativeness of the sample is the failure of NICOA and their consultants to analyze the data fully. NICOA did not employ the urban/reservation dichotomy that is the basic comparison of this chapter. In fact, they fail to provide any cross-classification of the data, and do not report some elementary but crucial summary statistics. The information on the reservation group over 45 and all Indians over 60 years old, which I use in this chapter, come from the NICOA study. However, their report does not provide data for urban Indians over 45 years of age. Because they did provide figures for all Indians over 45 and separate figures for the 45+ reservation group, it was possible to calculate the urban figures and I derived this information myself. All tables included in this chapter have been compiled from National Indian Council on Aging (1981) data.

The basic comparison made throughout the remainder of this chapter is between urban and reservation Indians over the age of 45. Although this would be considered "middle age" by researchers who study the white middle class, there is good reason for focusing on this age group rather than the more traditional age of 60 or 65. As the NICOA study concludes, the status of the 45+ reservation groups closely resembles the status of the 65+ non-Indian population. Elsewhere (John, 1980: 296), I recommend that the federal government confront this issue and provide services to Indian elders based on "the realistic age at which an Indian should be considered 'elderly'," rather than an arbitrary chronological age chosen for bureaucratic convenience. I also argue that using age 60 or 65 as the criterion for designating who is defined as "elderly" has hampered realization of the legislative goals of the Older Americans Act among Native Americans.

As acknowledgment of convention, however, I have provided information on all Indians over 60 years old. The figures on the over 60 age group must be treated with a greal deal of caution because more reservation Indians were sampled and NICOA (1981: 35) stated that these results were unweighted because "the rural/urban population split is not well known." Unlike the data on Native Americans over 45 years of age, it was not possible to calculate urban/reservation differences for Indians over 60. As a result, the figures for Native Americans over 60 are more representative of reservation residents in this age group.

URBAN/RESERVATION DIFFERENCES IN CURRENT STATUS

As many authors point out, accurate figures on the number of Indian elders and their geographic distribution do not exist. According to the best demographic estimates, approximately half of all Native Americans live in urban areas and the other half are rural. It is unclear whether the same is true of Indian elders. In this section, I will compare urban and reservation groups over the age of 45 on several important indicators of their current status. In addition to basic demographic information that addresses some of the issues raised in the previous section, I also attempt to characterize the financial position, social contact, life satisfaction, and health status of the two groups.

Reservation Indians over 45 years of age are substantially[2] less likely to live alone than are urban Indians, and substantially more likely to live in a household with more than 2 members. Only 16.4 percent of reservation residents compared to 25.1 percent of urban Indians report that they live alone, and 30 percent of urban Indians compared to 47 percent of reservation Indians have households with 3 or more members. The reservation group is substantially more likely than urban Indians to have a spouse, child, grandchild, or a sibling present in the household. Reservation Indians are slightly more likely to have a parent or grandparent in their home, and slightly less likely than are urban Indians to report having a friend living with them. Reservation Indians are more likely to be single, married, or widowed, and considerably less likely to be divorced or separated.

Clear differences emerge in terms of financial status as well. When asked how well the amount of money they have takes care of their needs, there was virtually no difference in the responses between urban and reservation groups. Slightly over one-third of both urban and reservation samples replied that their income "poorly" met their needs. Although only a small minority of both groups say that they receive regular financial assistance from family members (Shanas et al., 1968: 206), reservation Indians (5.7 percent) are significantly more likely than urban Indians (2.4 percent) to receive such support. Using another measure of financial need, 48 percent of urban Indians and 73.6 percent of reservation Indians report that they "cannot" or "can barely" meet their payments. Furthermore, although a majority in both groups reported that they usually do not have enough for "little extras," the reservation group was significantly more likely to report this status. A majority of people in both settings also feel that they do not have sufficient resources for future needs, with the reservation group once again significantly more likely to express concern for the future. Similarly, a majority in both settings report that they do not have sufficient financial resources or assets to meet emergency needs, with reservation residents significantly more likely to feel vulnerable in this regard. Given this perception of their financial situation, it is understandable that a majority of both groups agree that they need financial assistance beyond what they already have. Once again, this sentiment was significantly more likely to be expressed by reservation Indians.

There are major differences in the social contacts of the two groups as well. Reservation Indians are less likely to report having a confidant, to have talked with someone on the phone in the last week, to have spent time with someone other than a household member within the last week, and more likely to say that they do not know any people well enough to visit the person's home. Although reservation Indians are slightly more likely to express that they would like to see friends and relatives more often, and report that they have less social contact in general, they are slightly less likely to express feeling lonely "quite often" than are urban Indians.

Urban Indians tend to live further from their "nearest friend or relative" than reservation Indians. However, 33.7 percent and 44.8 percent of urban and reservation Indians respectively report that they live within one mile of this nearest contact. Another 23.3 percent of urban Indians and 24.9 percent of reservation Indians report that this person lives one to five miles away. The comparable proportions for the group over age 60 is 42.2 percent live within one mile, and another 24.4 percent live one to five miles away.

The fact that urban Indians live at somewhat greater distance from their nearest friend or relative apparently does not result in less frequent contact with this person when compared with the reservation group (see Powers et al., 1981). Equal proportions of the reservation and urban samples (41.8 percent) report visiting this person at least several times a week, while 39.2 percent of the 60+ group say they visit this often. A difference does exist for those people who report the least contact with their nearest friend or relative. Reservation Indians (11.1 percent) are twice as likely as urban Indians (5.5 percent) to say that they never visit their nearest friend or relative. An even larger proportion of the 60+ group (13.1 percent) say they never see this person.

Some differences also exist in terms of life satisfaction. Both groups are equally likely (87 percent) to acknowledge that they are "happy most of the time." However, in response to another question, reservation residents were more likely to express feeling lonely much of the time even when they were with people. Reservation residents were also slightly more likely to describe their present life satisfaction as "poor" and considerably less likely to evaluate it as "good" compared to urban Indians. A majority of reservation Indians report that their present life satisfaction is "fair," while a majority of urban Indians describe theirs as "good." Despite this, reservation residents are significantly less likely to express a desire to "leave home," and significantly more likely to express the feeling that their daily lives are full of things that interest them. Reservation Indians are, however, significantly more likely to believe that someone is planning to do evil things to them (13.3 percent), a sentiment that is practically nonexistent among urban residents (1.7 percent).[3] Neither group is more likely than the other to report fitful or disturbed sleep, nor to feel that no one understands them. On balance, one would have to conclude that the life satisfaction of reservation Indians is somewhat lower than their urban counterparts.

Undoubtedly, lower life satisfaction is partly explained by differences in health status, as evidence points to greater health problems and medical needs among reservation Indians. For example, reservation Indians are substantially more likely to feel that they need medical care or treatment beyond what they currently receive. In fact, they are over twice as likely to claim this than are urban Indians (29.1 percent versus 13.6 percent). Furthermore, a higher proportion of reservation Indians report having taken prescription medications within the last month for 14 of 18 types of drugs about which information was gathered. In addition, reservation Indians are significantly more likely to report that they need supportive or prosthetic devices that they currently do not have; the 3 most often mentioned devices were a hearing aid (24.2 percent), glasses (12.9 percent), and a cane (6.5 percent).

Reservation Indians are more likely than urban Indians to report that their health interferes "a great deal" with things they want to do, and less likely to report that their health does not interfere "at all." A plurality of reservation Indians (44.2 percent) report that their health interferes "a little" compared to a plurality of urban Indians (43.4 percent) who report that it does not interfere "at all." Although a majority of both groups say they are covered by health or medical insurance, reservation Indians are significantly less likely to report such coverage. Over 44 percent of reservation Indians compared to 22.5 percent of the urban group have no coverage. When asked how their current health compared to their health 5 years ago, a majority of both groups reported that it was about the same. The major difference between the 2 groups was that urban Indians were more likely to report that their health had improved and less likely to say that it had gotten worse within the last 5 years. Similarly, when asked to rate their overall health at the present time, a plurality of urban Indians (48.3 percent) indicated their health was "good" compared to a plurality of reservation Indians (41.6 percent) who rated their health as "fair." Indeed, the same pattern emerges at the extremes of the continuum as well. Reservation Indians are twice as likely to describe their health as "poor" and urban Indians are nearly twice as likely to evaluate their health as "excellent."[4]

Given these important indicators of status, a clear portrait of the two groups can be described with some precision. The deprivation experienced by reservation Indians is substantially greater than urban Indians. In general, the reservation group is poorer, supports more people on its income, has fewer social contacts, lower life satisfaction, and is in poorer health.

SPECIFIC SERVICE NEEDS AND USE

The greatest service needs for both groups over 45 years of age are for what Powers and Bultena (1974) call nonpersonal (e.g., housework, shopping, transportation) rather than personal (e.g., bathing, dressing, and eating) services. However, the relative levels of needs in the two groups are quite different. The 4 most prevalent activities of daily living for which both urban and reservation groups report that they need some assistance are housework, transportation, using the telephone, and going shopping. In fact, over one-fourth of the reservation sample state that they need some assistance with these four activities. However, the percentage requiring some assistance with the activities of daily living range from twice to over four times as much expressed need among reservation Indians. For example, the greatest service need of both groups is assistance with housework. However, the need is nearly twice as great on reservations. Nearly one-third of people on reservations (29.2 percent) report that they need some help with housework, compared with 15.6 percent of the urban group.

In addition, there is not a single activity of daily life in which a larger proportion of urban Indians report that particular need in comparison with reservation Indians. Indeed, over 10 percent of reservation Indians over 45 years of age report that they need some assistance with 7 of the 13 activities, something that was true for only one of the activities for urban Indians over 45 years old.

When one turns to the issue of perceived need for specific services, the foremost need among all three groups could be termed the need for information and referral assistance (see Table 13.1). Over 40 percent of each of the 3 groups said that they need someone to broker, advise, give information, or help them get available services. Except for this number one service need, the remaining rankings differ among the 3 groups. Once again, compared to the urban group, higher proportions of the reservation sample perceived a need for 11 of the 17 services. Apparently, the need is twice as great for a review of one's overall condition, help with legal matters, regular meal preparation, 24-hour care, nursing care, help with personal hygiene, and training in basic personal skills (including speech therapy and reality orientation) among members of the reservation group. In addition, more than 10 percent of urban Indians perceive a need for 10 of the 17 services, whereas this was true for 11 services for the reservation group and 13 services among Indians over 60 years old.

Furthermore, the top 5 service needs of both the reservation group and Indians over 60 were designated by one-third of the respondents in each group. With few exceptions, the greater perception of service needs among reservation Indians is attributable to lower income, poorer health, or different characteristics of the reservation environment—in particular, a lack of transportation. Alternately, the services cited by a higher proportion of the urban sample are the types of services needed when traditional support and counseling is absent, or those supports needed to negotiate an urban environment.

SOCIAL NETWORK: PATTERNS OF POTENTIAL AND ACTUAL ASSISTANCE

When asked if there is someone who would give help if they were sick or disabled, reservation Indians were less likely to view such help as being available. However, reservation Indians who said that this type of assistance would be available if necessary were more likely than urban Indians to feel that such help would be provided as long as it was needed. When asked to identify the source of this potential assistance, the rank ordering of the three most likely caregivers for both urban and reservation groups were the same. Children were mentioned most often (see Sussman, 1965: 84), followed by the person's spouse, with siblings ranked a distant third. Friends were listed as the fourth likely source of support for the urban group whereas some "other" relative was mentioned by reservation residents.

Both reservation and urban Indians rely equally on their children for this potential service, thus confirming Adams's (1970) statement that the parent-child bond is the most important kin tie, but reservation Indians identified their spouses more frequently than the urban group, a result largely attributable to the greater likelihood that urban Indians do not have a spouse present. For the over-60 group, children clearly predominate as the most important potential caregiver with a spouse second, another relative a distant third, with a sibling and a grandchild as less likely caregivers. The major differences between the two groups' potential support networks are that urban Indians are substantially less likely to say they would

TABLE 13.1
Perceived Need for Specific Services

	Urban 45+	Reservation 45+	All 60+
For someone to broker, advise, give information about available help	47.5	44.0	47.9
Transportation	22.2	40.8	39.0
For regular monitoring by phone or in person (5 times a week)	25.9	33.9	39.4
For doctor or social worker to review overall condition (health, mental health, and financial condition)	16.4	33.5	30.4
Help with routine housework	17.9	30.7	33.1
Education or on-the-job training	25.3	15.6	11.4
Help with legal matters	10.5	22.8	20.9
Have someone regularly prepare meals	7.1	20.0	21.6
24-hour care	5.8	13.5	16.3
Prescription medication for nerves	13.7	9.7	10.5
Nursing care	5.2	12.4	13.8
Help in finding a job	14.6	11.3	8.4
Someone to help with bathing, dressing, eating, going to toilet	3.9	9.0	11.2
Physical therapy	7.2	9.5	11.0
Remedial training or instruction in basic personal skills (speech therapy, reality orientation)	3.8	9.7	9.2
Treatment or counseling for personal or family problems or for nervous or emotional problems	9.7	6.8	7.8
Find another place to live	10.3	5.5	6.8

rely on a spouse and nearly twice as likely to rely on assistance from friends than are reservation Indians. However, a family member was identified as the potential caregiver 88.3 percent and 96 percent of the time for the urban and reservation samples, respectively. Because this question provides an indication of what people believe would occur, the results attest to a modest attitudinal difference between the two groups, and a somewhat greater prominence of family members in the support network of reservation residents. In comparison, 94.3 percent of the sample over age 60 identified a family member as their potential support.

In comparison to the source of support that people identify as part of their potential support network, the actual pattern of assistance is quite clear. Table 13.2 provides a breakdown of the source of assistance for ten services for people who had received

TABLE 13.2
Source of Support for Specific Type of Assistance for Those Who Received Help in Last 6 Months

	Urban (45+)			Reservation (45+)			All (60%)		
	Family or Friends	Hired Help or Agency	Both	Family or Friends	Hired Help or Agency	Both	Family or Friends	Hired Help or Agency	Both
Personal care (bathing, dressing, eating, or toilet)	60.0	20.0	20.0	62.8	16.3	20.9	59.5	16.7	23.8
Nursing care	18.2	63.6	18.2	25.5	44.7	29.8	24.4	43.9	31.7
Physical therapy	—	85.7	14.3	—	62.5	37.5	—	66.7	33.3
24-hour care	57.1	28.6	14.3	75.4	7.2	17.4	72.3	9.2	18.5
Monitored by phone or in person (at least 5 times a week)	95.3	—	4.7	90.8	3.2	5.9	90.6	2.5	6.9
Finding a place to live	36.8	36.8	26.3	47.1	47.1	5.9	35.0	25.0	40.0
Household chores	66.7	14.8	18.5	85.8	5.5	8.7	75.0	10.0	15.0
Someone regularly prepared meals	71.4	14.3	14.3	86.3	3.9	9.8	80.2	6.2	13.6
Legal matters, managing personal affairs or money	33.3	57.1	9.5	55.9	32.4	11.8	56.4	30.9	12.7
Someone brokered, gave information or got help	18.7	60.0	21.3	36.2	41.3	22.5	31.3	44.3	24.4

these services within the last six months. Although it is true that family and friends are important service providers for all three groups (see Sussman and Burchinal, 1962: 237 on family support), Indians on reservations depend on family and friends more than their urban counterparts for nearly all types of assistance.[5] Certainly this is explained in part by the greater availability of social services in urban areas. However, with the single exception of regular monitoring by phone or in person, a higher proportion of residents on reservations depend on family and friends for assistance than do urban Native Americans. In fact, family and friends provide a great deal of the care for the reservation group even for those services such as nursing care and physical therapy that are primarily medical services.

In contrast, with the exception of finding a place to live, urban residents rely on hired help or a social service agency more than reservation residents. Indeed, more than 10 percent of urban Indians report that they received assistance from hired help or an agency for 9 of the 10 services, whereas the same was true for the reservation group for only 6 services. Furthermore, there are only 3 services (finding a place to live, help with household chores, regular preparation of meals) for which a higher proportion of the urban group report reliance on both formal and informal supports than do reservation Indians. In each of these 3 instances, however, reservation Indians report that these services are ones typically provided by family and friends.[6] As might be expected, the pattern of assistance for Indians over 60 years of age closely parallels the reservation group.

The discrepancy between service availability on reservations and in urban areas can be addressed by looking at service utilization during a six-month period. An analysis of actual service use for a six-month period reveals not only the rate of service use in urban and reservation groups, but also the services that are most used and the differences between the two groups. As can be seen in Table 13.3, the exact rank and rate of use vary from group to group but the same services are in the top five for all three groups. Social and recreational programs, regular monitoring by phone or in person, help with household chores, a review of their overall condition, and use of a broker for information or assistance are the five most used services.

Where service utilization rates differ between the two groups, the reason for the difference is clear. Urban Indians show higher utilization rates for all services provided either exclusively or pre-

TABLE 13.3
Service Utilization in Past 6 Months

	Urban 45+	Reservation 45+	All 60+
Organized social or recreational programs (including pow-wows, Indian feasts, or ceremonials)	54.4	48.4	48.3
Employment assistance or counseling	12.9	6.8	6.5
Occupational or on-the-job training	8.0	4.5	2.5
Remedial training or learning basic personal skills (speech therapy, reality orientation)	1.7	1.2	2.0
Counseled for personal, family, nervous, or emotional problems	5.8	5.9	6.2
Took prescription medication for nerves	14.3	8.7	10.3
Help with personal care (bathing, dressing, eating, toilet care)	5.2	9.3	12.5
Nursing care	5.7	9.7	11.2
Physical therapy	4.0	5.3	5.4
24-hour care	8.2	15.1	19.7
Monitoring by phone or in person (at least 5 times a week)	41.3	44.6	52.0
Help finding new place to live	11.6	3.5	6.1
Regular help with routine household chores	15.6	27.9	29.0
Someone regularly prepared meals	12.3	22.9	24.1
Help with legal matters, handling money	14.0	14.9	16.0
Doctor or social worker reviewed overall condition (health, mental health, social, and financial condition)	15.8	27.2	27.0
Someone helped get needed services, gave information about available help	43.9	31.1	38.0

dominantly by formal social service agencies with the exception of those services that tend to be medical services. The difference is most pronounced in the area of employment assistance and training, as well as information and referral services. In contrast, reservation Indians tend to have higher utilization rates for those services provided by family and friends, services in which assistance from family and friends is given in conjunction with services from an agency, or services of a medical nature.[7] Once again, the service utilization pattern of the over-60 age group more closely resembles the reservation pattern.

When asked if someone helped with such things as shopping, housework, bathing, dressing, and getting around, the urban sample was significantly less likely to report these forms of assistance

(28 percent versus 39.6 percent). The source of this help also differed between the two groups. For reservation residents, a child (43.2 percent) or spouse (32.1 percent) was identified as their "major helper," followed by an "other" relative (6.3 percent), a sibling (4.7 percent), or a grandchild (3.2 percent). In comparison, the urban sample identified their spouse (41.3 percent), a child (39.1 percent), followed by a grandchild (6.5 percent), and some "other" relative (6.5 percent) as their "major helper." When one considers the fact that a spouse is less available to urban Indians, several possible conclusions can be drawn from this finding. Either urban Indians are more isolated from their children, or adhere to the value of independence, not wanting to "burden" their children. The absence of children alternative is suggested by the relative salience of grandchildren as their major helper as children are considered the first source of help for these kinds of assistance (see Sussman, 1965; Shanas et al., 1968; Adams, 1970; Powers and Bultena, 1974). The relative absence of help from a sibling also suggests that fewer family members are available to urban residents (see Bultena, 1969), a conclusion that seems supported as reservation residents identified 6 different kin relations as their major helper compared to only 4 such relations by the urban group.

The importance of a child in providing assistance for both personal and nonpersonal tasks is revealed from information provided about secondary sources of help with these same five services. For the most part, the secondary caregiver, when one is available, is a child for both reservation and urban Indians, and some family member was identified by everyone who said that he or she had a second source of support. Of the people who say they receive help, approximately half of the reservation sample compared to less than one-fourth of the urban sample report more than one source of help for these types of support, a circumstance that was true for over 40 percent of the over-60 age group. This piece of evidence suggests that the family network on reservations is larger, and that more people are active in providing services than in urban areas. This is also some indication that responsibilities toward elders on reservations are more likely to be shared rather than the sole responsibility of one family member. Friends, apparently, do not provide these services for either urban or reservation Indians. Indeed, friends were not mentioned by any of the respondents as either primary or secondary caregivers.

CONCLUSION

It is clear from these results that there are major differences between urban and reservation groups in need for services as well as the mix of support received from formal and informal sources. By nearly any measure, the reservation group has greater service needs than urban Indians. In general, reservation residents are poorer, have greater financial concerns, support more people on less income, have fewer social contacts, have somewhat lower life satisfaction, and are in poorer health than urban Indians. And, compared to urban Indians, family is more salient as a direct and sole provider of services to reservation residents for eight of ten services, and family members of reservation residents are more likely than their urban counterparts to share service responsibility with formal sources of support for seven of ten services. Indeed, there is only one service for which a majority of reservation residents report that formal supports are the sole direct service provider compared to four such services for the urban group. Nonetheless, family is important in providing services for both reservation and urban Indians, although the relative demands on the family network are greater on reservations.

In addition, although it is not possible to conclude this with certainty, it appears that friends are not important service providers for either urban or reservation residents for the services on which information was gathered. Given the financial position of most Native Americans, it is likewise probable that hired help is an insignificant service provider compared to services delivered by an agency, although this too is conjecture. What cannot be explained is the reason these differences exist. Would these differences hold if one were to control for availability of services, availability of family and friends, proximity of members of the support network, migratory status, the age composition of the two groups, marital status, or any other intervening variable?

Unfortunately, more research is necessary simply to bring discussion of Native American social networks into current discourse. A number of topics about which something is known among whites, blacks, and even Hispanics are yet to be researched among Native Americans. If this chapter documents the importance of children to Native American elders, how important are friends, siblings, or more distant relatives in their social networks? Is frequency of interaction, type of activities, direction, flow, and types of assistance, or proximity of kin similar or different from what prevails in groups on which research has been conducted? Are there sex differences or asymmetry in contact and assistance within the network? Do the family networks of elderly Native Americans evidence isomorphism with conclusions about social class or ethnic group network characteristics?

Designing a rational social service policy is dependent on such information. But until more research is conducted, it will be difficult to pinpoint those services family are willing and able to provide their aging members as opposed to those services that need to be provided by formal means. Or further, there is a need to design services so as to accentuate the strengths and shore up the weaknesses of the informal network in order for the two systems to complement rather than compete with each other. Such information would also permit more precise identification of the characteristics of people most likely to need formal services, whether these people are predominantly women, widowed or never married, the very elderly, people without a surviving child, or those who suffer multiple chronic health problems as is true of the most needy portion of the elderly population in general. Without such research, the Native American elder will indeed remain a forgotten American.

NOTES

1. I use the terms Native American and Indian interchangeably throughout this chapter to denote all aboriginal people, whether American Indian, Eskimo, or Aleut.

2. I use the two terms "substantially" and "significantly" in a double sense throughout this chapter. These two terms denote that a finding is both a substantively important one and that it is also statistically significant at the .05 level or better based on a test of significance between two proportions. See Bohrnstedt and Knoke (1982: 177ff.) for further discussion of this technique. In comparison, the term "slightly," when used in comparing the two groups, means that the differences were not statistically significant.

3. Rather than view this as evidence of mental illness or paranoia, I interpret this as evidence of the persistence of traditional cultural practices and beliefs on reservations, in particular the making of good and bad medicine.

4. Part of these differences in health status could be attributed to the fact that the urban sample may be younger than the reservation group. However, it was not possible to calculate the mean and median age of the entire sample, and NICOA did not report this information. Using the age of the household head, which was the only age information NICOA reported, does yield some indication of the age distribution of the two groups. The mean age of the household head of the

reservation group was 62.1 years compared to 55.6 years for the urban group. The median age of the household head of the two groups was 62 and 58 for the reservation and urban groups respectively. Although reservation Indians are more likely than urban Indians to be over 75, there is no difference in the proportions under 55 years of age. The major differences between the two groups occur for people between the ages of 55 and 74. My conjecture is that this difference is the result of migration back to the reservation after retirement.

5. Powers and Bultena (1974) provide information to make a limited comparison with Native Americans. Although they identify the source of assistance for both personal and nonpersonal tasks, the number of responses was very small for those people receiving assistance with personal tasks, so it is not possible to compare their findings with those reported here. In general, however, they report that family-friend networks account for nearly 90 percent of the aid received, the remainder supplied by hired help. They found that formal service agencies provided none of these day-to-day services. Of the two nonpersonal tasks that are directly comparable, household chores and meal preparation, Native Americans over 45 years of age in both environments rely on family and friends more for housework and less for meal preparation than the Iowans they surveyed.

6. The results reported here shed some light on the thesis advanced by Murdock and Schwartz about the important intermediary role of family members in service utilization. Although it is not possible to test their thesis about formal service utilization and household composition, it appears that family members are not important brokers in the urban environment. One might suspect, in line with their findings, that this is because more people live alone and there are fewer households with more than two members. My guess is that their suggestions appear to have more relevance for reservation Indians, a hunch that is bolstered by the fact that their study was of reservation Sioux over age 55. However, as the results reported here show, the role of family members as direct service providers to reservation Indians is more important.

7. This higher use of medical services is largely explained by the fact that the Indian Health Service's (IHS) primary responsibility is to serve rural Indians. Although any Indian (recognized as such by the federal government) is eligible to receive IHS medical care, in many cases urban Indians must travel long distances to reach an IHS facility.

Part III

Interdependence in Health and Social Services

14

THE OLDER VOLUNTEER:
The Case for Interdependence

BARBARA PAYNE
Director, Gerontology Center
Georgia State University

C. NEIL BULL
Associate Professor, Sociology
University of Missouri—Kansas City

The relationship between volunteering and aging represents an emerging form of interdependence that both counters the view of older persons as dependent and powerless and supports the idea of older persons' desires for autonomy and independence. Gerontologists have relied heavily upon disengagement, activity, and exchange theories to explain social behavior and the social positions of older persons, including volunteering. These theoretical frameworks obscure the mutually supportive, interdependent networks that not only temper the impact of stress, loss, and hazardous life events experienced by older persons, but also obscure the significant contributions older persons make to interdependent relationships.

In these theories, independence is frequently confused with autonomy and self-reliance, and normal dependencies are not distinguished from abnormal dependencies among older persons (Blenkner, 1969). Furthermore, this dichotomy between independence and dependence has influenced the understanding and enactment of the volunteer role as the "independent" giver serving the "dependent" receiver. Such interpretations are inconsistent with the reported interdependency among adults with family, friends, neighbors, and voluntary organizations (Cohler, 1983; Munnichs, 1976; Henderson, 1977; Morgan, 1983).

Some recent research and journalistic accounts about volunteering report a mutual or interdependent relationship between the volunteer and the recipient (Payne, 1977; Harel et al., 1975; "60

Minutes," CBS Television, February 5, 1984). Gerontologists have begun to investigate theoretically and empirically the concept of interdependency (Munnichs, 1976). Most of the American studies have focused on the interdependent or mutually supportive relationships among adult family members (Cohler, 1983; Mancini, 1980). They report that most older people, even those over 80 years of age, provide material and sociopsychological assistance to their middle-aged and older family members and adult grandchildren. However, not only may participation in family life be less satisfying after middle age, but the continued family responsibility among older persons may be associated with lower morale and increased psychological distress (Cohler and Lieberman, 1980; Hess and Waring, 1978). Some studies (Payne and Bull, 1983; Cohler, 1983) have found that many older people say these family interdependent relationships limit their autonomy and suggest that sympathy with the adult children may be biased. Furthermore, Mancini and others (1980) found that for healthy older persons, contact with friends (peers) was more important to a sense of well-being than increased contact with family members. Unlike the interdependency among adult families, the interrelationship among volunteers and their clients can be entered and exited at will, and they involve friends (peers) as co-volunteers and/or as recipients of services.

In this chapter, the concept of interdependence is applied to the older volunteer and the voluntary organizations through which persons give or receive volunteer services and support. Data are primarily from the Longitudinal Study of the Shepherd's Centers' Older Volunteer we conducted from 1972 to 1983; survey research conducted by ACTION (1974); Harris (1975, 1981); and the Independent Sector (Gallup, 1981). The chapter includes the following: (1) a discussion of the increasing significance of the interdependency of the older volunteer role in voluntary organizations (including churches and other religious organizations), government programs and private-for-profit organizations; (2) a theoretical framework for the micro- and macrolevels of interdependence in volunteerism; and (3) the Shepherd's Center volunteers and organizations as a case study to demonstrate interdependence.

HISTORICAL BACKGROUND

In social gerontology, volunteerism among the elderly has been studied from three perspectives. The first perspective is a part of the research about leisure among the elderly in answer to the question, "what do older people do with their time?" Such studies have had as their primary focus the number of memberships held and the amount of time spent in activities of voluntary organizations (Payne, 1973; Havighurst, 1970). Second, the degree of participation in voluntary organizations and volunteering has been linked with life satisfaction to show how much the variance in satisfaction can be explained by different rates of participation (Adams, 1971; Babic, 1972; Bull and Aucoin, 1975; Cutler, 1976). Third, the types and degrees of participation have been studied as part of various indices of community involvement and as sources of social networks (Neugarten and Tobin, 1961; Graney, 1977; Katz, 1970; Maves, 1981; Morris et al., 1964). These studies were a part of gerontologists' preoccupation with "successful" adaptation to the sociopsychological, physical, and economic losses of aging and with collecting hard data or facts about the activities of older persons (Cavan et al., 1949). None applied the concept of interdependence to participation in the voluntary associations or to volunteering.

It is only in the last few years that a distinction has been made between a volunteer and a voluntary organization participant. A voluntary organization is a not-for-profit organization with a board, a high percentage of volunteers, members, and a limited staff. Volunteers are persons who offer themselves and their time for specified services of their own free will to help others or a voluntary organization; they may also work without pay or for pocket expenses in profit organizations such as hospitals and nursing homes. The voluntary organization participants may attend functions of an organization but not assume volunteer positions to carry out its work.

The most recent development of the volunteer role includes the many informal ways of helping others for no monetary reward, such as regularly providing assistance to an elderly neighbor. That is, volunteer work need not be done within an organization. The Gallup Study conducted for the Independent Sector in 1981 used this expanded definition and included a broad range of activities such as volunteering at a local hospital, baking cookies for a senior center social, ushering at church, working to get a traffic light in a dangerous neighborhood intersection, canvassing for a political candidate, and collecting money for a charity. The efforts to study volunteerism among the elderly continues to be complicated by the inability of researchers to agree on the definition of "volunteer activity" as well as by the varying perceptions of what constitutes volunteer work by service providers and the general public. This narrowness and inconsistency of the traditional definitions used by researchers has resulted in an underestimation of the amount of volunteering, especially among older persons, and volunteerism, especially membership in voluntary associations (including churches), and formal and informal volunteering that are a part of the heritage and experience of most older adults. Volunteerism has played a major role in the history of the United States. Volunteerism is rooted in the observations of DeTocqueville in 1835: "Americans of all ages, all conditions, and all dispositions form associations to build inns, to construct churches, to diffuse books... in this manner they found hospitals, prisons, and schools" (DeTocqueville, 1945).

What began as a local activity for all members of the community in the late nineteenth century developed into numerous national associations in this century. Consequently, the United States is still characterized as a nation of joiners (Hausknecht, 1962; Curtis, 1971).

Voluntary associations were organized to solve specific social problems or issues, for example, the Cancer Society, the March of Dimes (for Polio), and the Red Cross (for disasters). They were also organized for special populations (e.g., ethnic minorities, handicapped). Some of the associations were organized to serve ethnic-, sex-, or age-specific groups such as the YMCA, YWCA, the Boy Scouts, the Girl Scouts, NAACP, Southern Leadership Conference, and the National Organization for Women (NOW). It is not surprising, then, that national voluntary organizations would develop in response to the unique needs and problems of the increasing number of older persons in the United States. The growth of associations organized solely for the benefit of the elderly took place after 1920. The pioneer effort to provide economic support to maintain older persons' autonomy came from the American Association for Old Age Security, organized in 1927. Its goal was to secure private and public pensions for workers who had been forced to retire or needed to retire without pensions. Their platform, presented to Franklin Roosevelt before he became President, contributed to the formulation of social security legislation. After social security was established and operative, the organization disbanded (Pratt, 1976).

Traditionally, volunteering not only has been left to younger and more vigorous adults, usually women, but the older volunteer has been viewed as an intrusion into the well-organized functioning of an agency. Worthington's 1963 review of the literature in both the volunteer bureau field and the aging field identified much on services given to and for the elderly, but little on how older people contributed. In fact, professionals in all fields and the elderly themselves needed to be convinced that older persons could make a significant contribution (Morris et al., 1964: 50). The role of government in social welfare and volunteering, especially in relation to older volunteers, began to change markedly in the late 1960s. Under the Older Americans Act of 1965, a research project, SERVE, was funded by the Administration on Aging and the Community Service Society of New York to determine whether a volunteer role would enrich the lives of the elderly and whether they could contribute valuable, reliable services to community agencies (Sanier and Zander, 1971).

At first, agencies agreed reluctantly to use the older SERVE volunteers. Many staff persons were skeptical about the value of the service provided by older people. Most thought that the older volunteers would be more trouble than they were worth, that they would not be reliable because of illness, and that bad weather would interfere with their attendance. The project SERVE volunteers dispelled these fears and proved the value, capability, and reliability of the older volunteers. Consequently, the SERVE volunteers began not only to change the traditional concept, but also to help establish the practice of older volunteers serving their peers and persons with handicapping conditions.

As a result of the SERVE experience, volunteering has become an important social role for older persons. In 1974, 22 percent of persons 65 years of age and over reported that they did volunteer work compared to 35 percent of those under the age of 65. In addition to those elderly already doing volunteer work, another 10 percent said they would like to volunteer their services (ACTION, 1974). Similar findings were reported in 1981 by NCOA (23 percent) and by Bull (1983). The significantly greater percentage of older persons providing services reported by Gallup (37 percent) reflects the use of the new expanded definition of volunteer activity.

Among the numerous national, regional, and local associations that are dedicated to supporting independence and autonomy of older persons, we have chosen to focus on three examples: (1) The Retired Senior Volunteer Program (RSVP), which is a federal government agency that has developed interdependency with older volunteers among aging agencies and between volunteers; (2) The American Association of Retired Persons (AARP), which is a large, private, national organization, with over 3,500 chapters; and (3) the National Network of Shepherd's Centers.

THE RETIRED SENIOR VOLUNTEER PROGRAM

In 1969, Congress enacted legislation establishing the Retired Senior Volunteer Program (RSVP) modeled on the SERVE Project (Sanier and Zander, 1971; Sanier, 1976). The first appropriation funded 11 pilot RSVP Projects. The success of the program was instantaneous. Within 5 years, more than 700 communities had RSVP programs involving more than 165,000 older volunteers on a regular basis. RSVP has stimulated other public and private older volunteer programs (Bowles, 1976: 81-88). In 1980 there were more than 350,000 RSVP volunteers in all 50 states, Puerto Rico, and the Virgin Islands.

Harel and Shur conducted a case study of the city of Cleveland's RSVP program in 1975 to determine the impact of the federally sponsored older volunteer program on a local community's health and welfare service. They concluded that the importance of the volunteer to the local agencies had grown considerably; in some instances, programs could not operate without the services of the volunteers. These services included the local nutrition program (Title VII, OAA) and the expansion of services to include escort service, gift shops, security guards, tutoring, and telephone reassurance in English and foreign languages. The study reported higher morale among the RSVP volunteers than among those applying from other projects, such as Public Housing. Filipic and Harel (1978) concluded the report with the following interpretation of the program:

> The Retired Senior Volunteer Program has demonstrated the ability to identify older persons with skills which they are willing and able to give to the community as well as those who, while they do not have readily identifiable skills, have expressed a desire to remain contributors to their communities. The program staff serves as the link between the senior volunteer who needs help in finding satisfying and appropriate volunteer assignments and the service agencies that are striving to provide quality service on limited budgets. For those who need help in increasing their skills or acquiring new skills,

program staff serve as a resource to aid the senior volunteer and the agency. In turn, the senior volunteer becomes a link between the community and the service agency as well as an advocate who expresses the agency's goals and objectives and financial needs. The community is the beneficiary of this program that facilitates the involvement of older persons not only because of the hours of service (conservatively 4,000 hours per week in Cleveland and 500,000 hours nationally), but also because the identifiable role in the community brings with it a status of dignity for older persons. The program demonstrates that it makes good sense to invest in organizational efforts to protect and preserve the rights of older persons to become and remain involved in the community in which they live.

RSVP and other older American Volunteer Programs, for example, Foster Grandparents and Senior Companies, provide peer services that support other aging programs in counties, cities, and the federal/state network (programs such as Area Agencies on Aging, Senior Centers, Nutrition Sites, and Meals on Wheels). Many of these agencies have come to rely heavily on the older volunteer for increasing their services or to compensate for budget cuts. The growth of these federal government-initiated and cooperatively locally funded volunteer projects over the past twenty years has led to an interdependency that is thrown out of balance when the governments begin to cut budgets.

AMERICAN ASSOCIATION OF
RETIRED PERSONS

The largest and most influential voluntary association formed by, for, and with older persons is the AARP (prior to 1983 it was NRTA-AARP, National Retired Teacher's Association/American Association of Retired Persons). It was founded in 1947 by a retired school principal, Ethel Percy Andrus, to improve the image and raise the relative status and economic assets of retired persons. By 1955, there were 20,000 members, and in 1984, there were over 13 million members with more than 3,500 chapters, 9 regional offices, and the national office in Washington, D.C. It is an example of the development of an interdependent national organization of older volunteers in which both the volunteers and the members give and receive the benefits of the programs and services. Its large national organization is an interdependent structure of staff and member volunteers. More than 23,000 volunteers carry out AARP's educational, service, and lobbyist programs.

SHEPHERD'S CENTERS

In 1972 a new type of voluntary organization called the Shepherd's Center, dedicated to maintaining independence, purpose, and dignity in the later years, was organized in Kansas City, Missouri by older volunteers and operated by older volunteers as a pilot model project for the ecumenical outreach of the religious congregations within a specified neighborhood service area containing a concentration of older persons. Over a 10-year period, 22 programs and service components were developed by the volunteers to provide a peer network that would enable older persons to remain in their own homes, enhance life satisfaction in later maturity, and enable self-realization through artistic expression, community service, caring relationships, life-long learning, and the discovery of inner resources (Maves, 1982; Cole, 1981). Older volunteer coordinators assisted by committees were responsible for the services and programs. Initially, the senior minister of one of the churches served as the executive director. The rapid growth of the program soon required a minimal paid staff including a full-time paid director to give support, stability, and continuity to the programs without dominating or taking away initiative and responsibility from the volunteers.

The Shepherd's Center was an immediate success, and in 1974 a separate arm of the program, the Mid-American Resource Training Center, was formed to respond to the requests from all parts of the United States for training to start other Shepherd's Centers. More than 50 Centers based on the Shepherd's Center model are currently in operation, and the model has been adopted by The United Methodist Church as its noninstitutional form of ministry to the elderly. The Shepherd's Center model is an example of the function of a non-family primary form of interdependence among older persons and their peers. This approach differs in organizational structure and limited geographical service area from the more formal and institutionalized interdependence among RSVP volunteers and AARP volunteers and members.

OLDER VOLUNTEER LONGITUDINAL STUDY

This project began in 1972 as a one-year participant observation study of the older volunteers who planned and operationalized the Kansas City Shepherd's Center's model. During this period, we designed a five-year longitudinal study of a panel of the first Center volunteers to begin in 1974. In 1976 and 1977, two Centers, the Northside Shepherd's Center and Life Enrichment Services (modeled after the Kansas City Shepherd's Center), were established in Atlanta (the second in a middle-class neighborhood and the first in a low-income, integrated, old working-class neighborhood). It was decided to include these Centers in the research project. Participant observations and the five-year period of annual interviews for these three Centers began in 1976 and were concluded in 1982. A control group of non-Center older volunteers was chosen from the RSVP volunteers in Atlanta and Kansas City.

RESEARCH OBJECTIVES

The study was designed to observe the development of the three Centers' organization by the older volunteers as well as their development of services and programs to accomplish the goals of autonomy and independent living for themselves and their peers. The study of the volunteers was designed to answer the following questions: (1) "How are peer volunteer roles appropriate to link older persons to their peers, to the local community, state and national organizations?" and (2) "What is the relation between the type of organization through which older volunteers enact their roles and the development of interdependent relationships?"

THEORETICAL FRAMEWORK

Continuity theory provided the theoretical framework for the development and enactment of the peer volunteer roles. An adaptation of the role reconstruction model of Bergtson and Kuypers (Payne, 1977) provided the theoretical framework for the enactment of peer volunteer roles. The major assumption is that older persons have a status role pool of skills learned through education, work, the family, leisure activity, community organizations, the church, and so on. These skills can be restructured into new peer volunteer roles that serve to sustain their own autonomy and that of their peers (Payne, 1977).

Warren's (1978) community theory was selected as the framework for the study of the Shepherd's Center organizations and their internal and external interdependencies. Warren's model is an application of social system analysis to community. He defines community as "that combination of social units and systems that perform major social functions having locality relevance." The community is the organization of social activities to afford people daily local access to those broad areas of activity that are necessary in day-to-day living. These activities are organized around five functions that have "locality relevance": (1) production-distribution-consumption; (2) socialization; (3) social control; (4) social participation; and (5) mutual support.

Warren distinguishes between a community's vertical and horizontal patterns, that is, the internal and external aspects relating the system and its social units to each other. The community's vertical patterns are the structural and functional relations of its various hierarchical levels within the system's structure of authority and power. Sometimes the relationship is downward, such as the federal aging agencies established under the Older Americans Act: Administration on Aging to the Regional Office of the Administration on Aging, to State Units on Aging to the Area Agencies on Aging. Sometimes the relationship is upward, for example, from local churches like the Shepherd's Center to Denominational Boards. In the model presented here, the relationships are both upward and downward.

The horizontal pattern is the relationship across the many different units and subsystems to each other. Roughly speaking, the horizontal units tend to be on approximately the same hierarchical level for administration authority and decision making (Payne and Bull, 1983).

METHODOLOGY

The longitudinal design included panels of the first volunteers from each of the three Centers: Kansas City (N = 68); Northside Shepherd's Center (N = 50); and Life Enrichment Services (N = 49). The RSVP control groups were stratified random samples of volunteers in Atlanta (N = 100) and Kansas City (N = 78). Participant observation of the development of the Centers was continued tor for five years in each Center. The panels were interviewed annually for five years. The RSVP control groups were interviewed at two points in the five-year period.

There were two structured interview schedules. The one administered at Time 1 was longer and collected information needed only once, such as prior volunteer experience. The Time 2, 3, 4, and 5 instruments repeated questions from the first interview to measure change and added an open-ended question about significant events or change occurring since the last interview. At the conclusion of the five-year study, the panels were invited to a group discussion session with the researchers and were recognized for their contribution to the research.

The instruments included a measure of ageism (Kogan, 1961), volunteer satisfaction (a 26-item Likert scale developed for the study), alienation, and items to measure reasons for volunteering, self-health evaluations, family composition and interaction, friendships—new and old, memberships and other volunteer activities, the amount of time volunteering, understanding and commitment to the goals of the volunteer program, and the development of social networks to support independent living.

VOLUNTEERISM AND INTERDEPENDENCY

Although the commonly held view of the elderly is that they are dependent members of society, most older people express the strong desire to maintain an independent lifestyle and retain their autonomy. For almost two decades, public policy (Older Americans Act of 1965, 1978) has been directed toward progams intended to support independent living for the elderly. However, Carol Estes (1979) maintains that the federal programs have actually increased dependency, not independency. The missing link in the goals of the elderly and these policy assumptions is an understanding of normal dependencies and the existence of independent relationships to sustain autonomy. If independent living for older persons requires the provision of support services/networks, then we have initiated the normal dependencies that trigger the establishment of independent relationships. All age groups have their normal dependencies and at the same time they strive for independence and autonomy. Reliance on the development of interdependencies is necessary, then, for the achievement of autonomy at any age. Among the elderly, normal dependencies and support needs may be more visible and the struggle for independence more difficult. The functionally independent Shepherd's Centers' volunteers recognized the support needs of their peers and anticipated (or acknowledged) their own. In so doing, they took a giant step toward operationalizing the concept of interdependence.

All the volunteer panel members and the RSVP volunteers reported that their main reason for volunteering was to help their peers stay out of institutions and maintain their autonomy. Also, they wanted to create and maintain the conditions, services, and networks to age in place.

THE NEW OLDER VOLUNTEER ROLE

The volunteer role differs from other social roles in motivation and in performance. It is entered to fill and perform altruistic acts, that is, to help others (mostly nonkin), and to respond to human need without any expectation of financial reward. This characteristic excludes volunteering from the application of exchange theory of roles that predicates all social behavior upon the psychological exchange of rewards (positive reinforcements) and cost (negative reinforcements) and, consequently, to an accumulation of greater power by one of the parties (Blau, 1964). The older volunteers in the studies reviewed in this chapter also do not fit the exchange theory as Dowd (1976) applied it to older persons: "In the case of the aged, decreased social interaction is the eventual result of a series of exchange relationships in which the relative power of the aged vis-à-vis their social environment is gradually diminished until all that remains is the humble capacity to comply." The meaningful productive social interactions of the older volunteers with and for their peers has resulted in the acquisition of increased power and autonomy; furthermore, these volunteers are not disengaged but are actively involved in attacking the major social issues and needs accompanying the increase in the numbers of older persons in society.

The basic altruistic nature of the volunteer roles and voluntary organizations is more like Sorokin's (1954) "love" behavior. The volunteer role has the characteristics of intensity in that the amount of time a volunteer spends varies from a few hours a week, month, or year, to many hours daily. It has "duration" in that some volunteer activities are for a short period of time, for example, versus a lifetime of volunteering. Most of the older volunteers (68 percent) in the Centers' panels and RSVP (85 percent) sample reported prior volunteer experience in providing services, serving on boards, and fund-raising. Many were involved in volunteering for organizations other than their present work for the Centers or RSVP. The volunteer role contains Sorokin's dimension of "purity" in that the major reason given for volunteering by all respondents was "to help others." Other research for reasons for volunteering has found this same "purity" dimension (NCOA, 1975, 1981; Gallup, 1981).

In the earlier analysis of the volunteer role based on two years of the Older Volunteer Longitudinal data, we adapted the Bengtson and Kuyper reconstruction model of social roles for older persons to a restructuring model of the older volunteer roles (Shepherd's Center and RSVP volunteer roles; Payne, 1977). We pointed out that the recycling of past roles through the new older volunteer roles contributed to the volunteers' social independence and interdependence. We concluded that the volunteers created mutual support systems that reduced dependence on family members for social-psychological support. Volunteers gained knowledge about community resources and maintained their skills, which reduced their own anxiety about becoming more dependent.

A simpler version of this process model that isolates the interdependency nature of the volunteer role is shown in Figure 14.1.

Role theory is usually described as action and interaction between two or more actors based on expected and reciprocal relationships. Such reciprocity is a part of the older volunteer role; indeed, it is a necessary part of the role, but it is not sufficient to explain the interdependencies of the roles. The Interdependency Model shows the intersection points of mutual giving and receiving that demonstrate the development of interdependence between the older volunteer and the peer recipient.

The Older Volunteer Longitudinal data support this model. The highest correlations of volunteer satisfaction scale items were between personal satisfaction from helping others and personal expressions of appreciation from the peer receivers and appreciation from others in the community for their services ($p < .05$). Other evidence of the interdependence was the giving of financial sup-

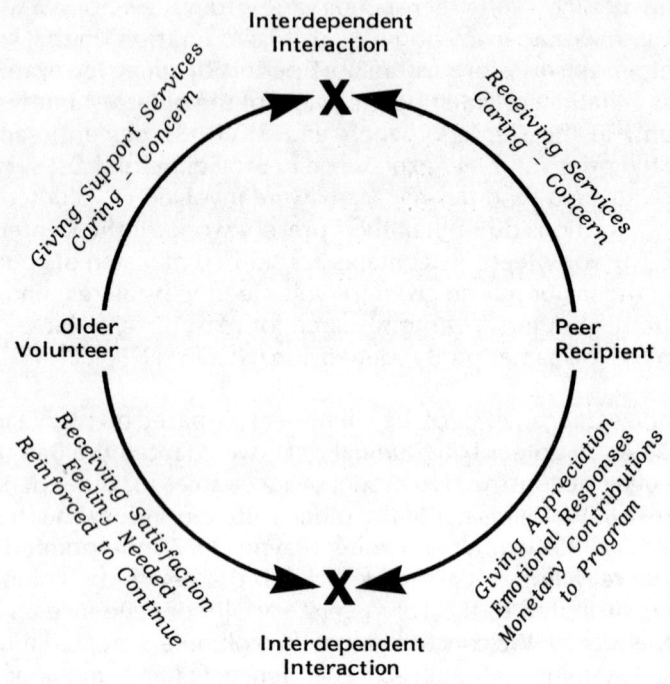

X = Intersection points represent the Interdependent-Interaction

Figure 14.1 The Interdependency of the Older Volunteer

port to the Center's activities by recipients and the volunteers. Many recipients sent contributions for the Center operations and several included the Centers in their wills. During the first five years of operation, each Center began to receive funds as memorials to honor volunteers or recipients when they died.

The interdependence concept among the Shepherd's Centers' volunteers and recipients is supported by cases in which the older volunteer became the peer recipient. Examples of this reversal of roles and interdependence are the cases of panel volunteers Mr. and Mrs. Y and Mr. and Mrs. N.

> Mr. and Mrs. Y filled different volunteer roles, but in the third year of the Kansas City study, Mr. Y developed a terminal illness. With the

help of Mrs. Y and the other volunteers, Mr. Y was able to continue some volunteer activities until a few weeks before his death and appeared on the CBS documentary about the Shepherd's Centers in 1976 (CBS, "Volunteer to Live"). He gave services and he received psychological support for his own dying as well as support services during the final weeks from the Center volunteers. After his death it was the Center volunteers and organization that provided support to Mrs. Y during her bereavement and resumption of her Center volunteer work. Mrs. Y is one of those who made a significant financial contribution to support the Center's service program.

Mr. N was one of the prime movers in the development of the Kansas City Shepherd's Center and filled many key volunteer roles—from coordinator of the "meals on wheels" to Chair of the weekly volunteer coordinators meetings. Mrs. N participated in the Center's educational program and weekly forum. In the fifth year of the study, Mrs. N developed Alzheimer's disease. Mr. N. received social support and companion services for Mrs. N in these early stages of the disease, which permitted him to continue his volunteering and leadership roles in the Center. The Center volunteers learned from this case how to serve as volunteers to older Alzheimer's victims and their family members. Mr. N. gave leadership and services, and he received services for himself and Mrs. N.

The strength of the volunteer interdependency is in the peer and nonfamily ties that maintain the autonomy that is frequently lost in interdependence among adult families. Furthermore, the high volunteer satisfaction reported by all the panel members contributed to the morale of the volunteers. Throughout the five-year study of the panels, the dropout rate was low and mostly related to change in the health of a family member, moving to be near a family member, or to death. The interdependence among the older volunteers is related to the Peer Center Organization and to the community, as we shall see in the following section.

SENIOR CENTERS:
ORGANIZATIONAL INTERDEPENDENCE

One of the earliest solutions proposed to counter the loneliness, isolation, and role losses of older persons was participation in voluntary organizations. Social activity was believed to contribute to the successful adaptation to aging (Havighurst, 1970). More specifically, those interested in older persons recommended neighborhood organizations or centers designed to provide access to social participation and encourage activities by the elderly. Among the first of such neighborhood organizations were the Hodson Center in Brookly, New York and the Golden Age Clubs sponsored by local churches, civic organizations, and city governments.

There has been a proliferation of public and privately operated Centers since the mid-1950s. In 1966, the National Directory of Centers listed only 340 senior centers. By 1980, the number had increased to over 8,000.

These Senior Centers are operated by public and private community agencies, generally with the mixing of funding from government, voluntary, and some corporate dollars. The multipurpose Senior Centers have come to be recognized as major components in the network of community resources. The neighborhood centers provide five kinds of support: (1) access to goods and services provided by Senior Centers staff members as well as or by personnel from other agencies; (2) a social climate that encourages older people to seek and accept services; (3) a focal point from which to reach out to the isolated, friendless, and very frail older people; (4) a bridge linking the elderly to the community at large; and (5) additional resources by providing opportunities for new social roles that utilize their skills and experience (Leanse, 1977).

The Shepherd's Centers are adaptations of the multipurpose senior center model by a nonprofit ecumenical organization of older persons. The difference is in the sponsorship, the organizing principles, and the goals. The primary goal is to utilize older people in organizing, administering, and providing those services required by the elderly to remain in their homes and continue independent living. The organization is ecumenical in that it is a partnership of churches/synagogues incorporated to serve a specific geographical area. The organization is composed primarily of older people who staff and deliver the services. Each center is autonomous. Funding is primarily from the sponsoring organizations and other community gifts. There are six stated purposes (Cole, 1981):

(1) to sustain older people who desire to live independently in their own homes and apartments in the community;
(2) to provide retired people with an opportunity to use their experience, training, and skills in significant social roles;
(3) to enhance life satisfaction in later maturity and enable self-realization through artistic expression, community expression, community service, caring relationships, lifelong learning, and the discovery of inner resources;

(4) to demonstrate life at its best in later maturity so as to provide attractive role models for successful aging;
(5) to advocate the right of older people to a fair share of society's goods, and to assist them in gaining access to services; and
(6) to contribute to knowledge about what is required for successful aging and to experiment with new approaches and programs for meeting the needs of older people.

SHEPHERD'S CENTERS AND ORGANIZATIONAL INTERDEPENDENCE

Warren's five locality relevant functions are proposed as basis to support the daily needs of all citizens. They are also necessary to meet the basic support needs of older persons who desire to age in place. An analysis of the Shepherd's Centers using these five functions (Figure 14.2) shows the interdependence between a center (or centers) and the local community (horizontal) and beyond the local community (vertical).

Figure 14.2 shows three levels of Warren's functions and their vertical and horizontal interdependent patterns. Circle A represents the extra community (vertical) patterns, Circle B the horizontal patterns, and Circle C the internal organization of the Shepherd's Center and the community relevant functions of the Center.

The internal organization of the Shepherd's Center (Circle D) has a social structure of interrelated programs and peer relationships. They have the characteristics of the voluntary association in funding from the private sector, a volunteer board, a minimum of paid staff, service programs, supervision provided by volunteers, and specific social or welfare goals for a specific group.

The Center is organized to contribute in some way to each of the locality relevant functions (Circle C, Figure 14.2). The production-distribution-consumption function exists for and by the elderly to meet their support needs and quality of life needs. Examples are Meals on Wheels, handy-man service, home-housekeeping help, senior companions, hospice, transportation, dial-a-ride, educational programs, support groups, recreation, trips, and self-help groups. The socialization function includes association with peers, sanctions for appropriate social involvement, and aging subculture identity. Shepherd's Centers become a reference group through which older volunteers are labeled by the community as resourceful, useful, valuable, and skilled.

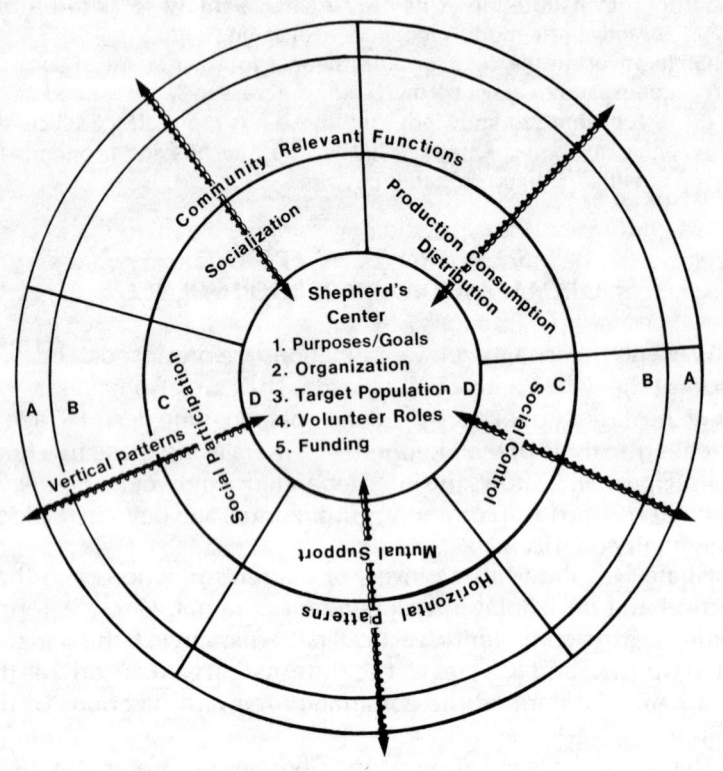

Figure 14.2 A Community Model of a Voluntary Organization and Shepherd's Center

In the area of social control, the Center organization and services enable older volunteers and participants to be in control of their lives, The Centers exert peer pressure, apply meaningful sanctions, develop the older person's positive self-concept, new norms of aging behavior, and provide collective means of solving/controlling aging problems.

Social participation is provided through opportunities for access to various types of social participation with peers who have mutual interests and concerns. These include volunteer roles, adult education, structured participation for isolates, widowed, and newcomers, singles groups, and political participation in local, state, and national elections and issues. Subjects from the Longitudinal Study were elected to and attended the Silver Haired Legislature. Political candidates at all levels participated in the

Center Forums. One older participant served as a legislative intern in a congressman's office. As a group they wrote letters to public officials on issues of concern. Assistance in voting was regularly offered. Some attended or were delegates to state and national White House Conferences on Aging. The Centers functioned to replace or supplement family (primary group) with an informal network of associations.

The mutual support function takes place by enabling access to services for the unique, emerging needs accompanying the physical, psychological, and social processes of aging. In additional to the social and health support services, the new older volunteers reported new friendship networks and confidants. Widowed found help to work through their grief from groups and peers. Through these they learned to live alone.

Community horizontal patterns of input and influence on the Centers' function (Circle B) include a variety of relationships in the production-distribution-consumption of services to the elderly; other community agencies influence, exchange, cooperate, or compete with the Centers, such as the AAA (Area Agency on Aging), city and county councils on aging, city transportation agencies, local units of government providing social and health services, local chapters of AARP (American Association of Retired Persons), and RSVP Programs.

For example, during the first three years, conflict developed between the two Atlanta Centers and other aging community agencies. The conflict involved a county Council on Aging for the suburban Center and the city's Senior Citizens, Inc. for the inner city center. In both instances, it was encroachment and competition for the same private (voluntary) funding. In the suburban center, the aggressiveness of the older staff volunteers led to direct confrontation. This Center and the County Council have apparently resolved their overt differences. The success of the Center is "shared" by the Council. The conflict in the inner city was primarily over participants and function. The inner city Center has a prescribed neighborhood boundary and the Senior Citizens, Inc. is a citywide organization with broader functions including services to neighborhood Centers. On the surface, the conflict is resolved. This was accomplished through other agencies in the city, the AAA, and the county council taking action on behalf of the Shepherd's Center.

The Kansas City Center seems to have escaped such conflict perhaps because the period (1972) in which it was organized preceded the dominance of local aging agencies and the aging network (AAAs and State Agencies). Because the three Shepherd's Centers utilize services from agencies—public and private—and the agencies depend on the Centers to achieve their goals of client service, an organizational interdependence has developed.

Local agents of socialization to elderhood include the local media, adult education within the public school system, colleges, private and public agencies, business community, religious organizations, and professionals (physicians, lawyers, and so on). The Centers' interaction at the community level has an impact on these sources, and they become socializing agents to an elderly population for community organizations; consequently, the local media, TV stations, radio, and press become the vehicles for educating the community to new images of the elderly. These Centers continue to be resources for the media, at every level, for understanding older persons, their potential, and their needs. Evidence of this function from the Longitudinal Study includes the CBS Special, local TV coverage, articles in the local papers, "Guideposts" (October, 1978), and radio interviews.

Agencies and community social units exerting social control affecting elderly are the local social welfare agencies, AAAs, churches, media, and units of local government performing social control functions such as police department, fire department, city hospital, and street maintenance. The Centers provide the focal point for health control programs (flu vaccination, health fairs), crime control programs, defensive driving courses, and so on. The Centers also provide volunteers to promote and deliver the health services.

Center volunteers participate on AAA Advisory Councils, County and State Councils on Aging, and University Gerontology Advisory Councils and present programs about the Center on Aging to churches, civic organizations, professional meetings, and so on. These are new linkages that expand the community participation of the Center participants.

Mutual support for the Centers came from voluntary agencies and foundations, for example, United Way, philanthropic groups, churches, Red Cross, YWCA, YMCA, and libraries. Public agencies provided services for the specialized needs of the elderly, such as AAAs, community welfare agencies (health, mental health councils), and county councils on aging. Support was in the form of services, funding, encouragement/endorsement, and professional staff leadership.

The extra local-vertical patterns of relationships with the Centers relevant to the locality functions are represented in Circle A of

Figure 14.2. The Centers are local production-consumption-distribution outlets for many of the services and programs funded and initiated at the National (Federal) level. For example, the Centers used and integrated into their program the Administration on Aging for Older Americans Act services, such as Meals on Wheels; ACTION, for the Senior Companions program; the National Institute on Aging, for information about the aging process; and the Social Security Administration, for Title XX services. Efforts by national organizations, such as the NRTA-AARP, National Council on Aging, the Federal Council on Aging, federal programs and government policy stemming from the Older Americans Act, and the national media, all contribute to the construction of the national identity of older people that are extra community influences on the Shepherd's Centers' volunteers/participants. The dependency and problem image constructed by some of the national policies and programs (Estes, 1979) are rejected and countered by the Shepherd's Center volunteer programming. The national visibility of the Centers through a CBS documentary and film (widely distributed) and the denominational project are inputs upward to counter these negative aspects of old age. The Centers are becoming socializing agents for local and extra local public and private agencies/organizations about old age.

Types of external social control on the lives of older people include the following: (1) many state agencies such as the State Office or Unit on Aging, health planning services, family and children's services, Medicaid, housing, transportation; and, (2) federal agencies such as the Administration on Aging within the Health and Human Services Administration, the Social Security Administration, the Labor Department, the National Institute on Aging, the National Institute on Mental Health, and the Senate Committee. National private agencies and corporations also have an impact and control on the lives of older people, such as denominational boards, the national media and advertising, insurance companies and their regulations, drug companies, and nursing home chains. The Centers are influenced by these controls and in turn influence them through representation on boards and councils. For example, the Denominational Board administering the Shepherd's Center project has a center staff representative and elects volunteers to the board; volunteers serve on State Councils and State Unit Boards and testify before the Congressional Committees. The success of the National Shepherd's Centers as voluntary organizations using older volunteers places them in a position in the 1980s to determine some of the national policies affecting the support for the independent living of older people. Center volunteers participate as delegates, presenters, and members in a number of national and regional aging meetings such as the National Council on Aging, ACTION, Gerontological Societies, White House Conferences, Denominational Boards, NRTA-AARP, Council of Churches, and National Shepherd's Center Consultations.

The Centers receive vertical support from national funding agencies such as AOA (Administration on Aging), state agencies, private foundations, the Endowment for the Arts, and denominational boards. Advocacy groups such as the Gray Panthers and the AARP Legislative Lobby provide social support and endorsement of the Center's efforts for independence and a quality of life in old age.

CONCLUSION

The older volunteer programs and peer organizations reviewed in this chapter can be expected to become more important in the future as the numbers of older persons continue to increase and as resources to support them decline or are withheld. Reliance on federal funding for most services to maintain independent living can no longer be expected. Older persons will be expected to rely on peer interdependency to provide normal aging dependency needs and social meaning. On a more positive note, the emerging involvement of churches, other religious and voluntary organizations, Junior League, and so on can be expected to assist peer organizations such as the Shepherd's Centers in their efforts to maintain independent lifestyles. Many of the voluntary organizations, including the churches, will be dependent on the older members to carry out the work of the organization. Thus a new form of interdependency will emerge between organizations (for all ages) and older volunteers. Interdependency at the person-to-person level, between organizations, and between older persons and organizations requires monitoring and further research as a significant form of social bonding.

15

THE VOLUNTARY ORGANIZATION AS A SUPPORT SYSTEM IN THE AGING PROCESS

LINDA M. BREYTSPRAAK
Director, Gerontological Studies

BURTON P. HALPERT
Extension Specialist, Gerontology

PHILIP G. OLSON
Professor, Sociology
University of Missouri—Kansas City

By now there is considerable evidence to suggest that those who best weather the social, psychological, and physical transitions of the aging process have extensive social networks and systems of informal social support (e.g., see Cobb, 1979; George, 1980; Kahn, 1979). Indeed, the theme of this volume is suggestive of the heightened importance of social bonds and the supports those bonds imply in later life. In the presence of social supports, individuals can engage in "communicated sharing" whereby they receive information that they are cared for, esteemed and valued, and belong to a network of communication and mutual obligation (Cobb, 1976). Kahn (1979) notes the basic elements of supportive transactions to consist of affect, affirmation, and aid. Thus social

Authors' Note: *We are members of the Center on Aging Studies and the Department of Sociology, University of Missouri, Kansas City. Our names appear alphabetically as each contributed equally to the research for and the writing of this chapter. Special thanks are expressed to Dr. Gail Imig, Director, Home Economics Program, and Ruth Pirch, Child and Family Development Specialist, Missouri Cooperative Extension Services, for their support of the study of Extension Homemaker Clubs; to Julie Pellamn and Tess Sharp for their help in interviewing club members, and to Beverly Urani for her assistance in the data analysis.*

supports may help in both instrumental and expressive ways to buffer stress and facilitate coping and adaptation. In addition, social supports no doubt contribute significantly to a sense of self-identity, control, and general well-being.

There is less consensus about the types of informal support networks that are likely to be most viable within the context of the aging process. There has been much discussion of the importance of the family as a source of support and a buffer against stress (e.g., Shanas, 1979b; Sussman, 1976), as well as some consideration of the role of nonkin neighbors and friends (Cantor, 1979; Ward et al., 1981). The role of the voluntary organization as part of the informal support system also has been considered (Amis and Stern, 1974; Babchuk et al., 1979; Cutler, 1977).

Much of the discussion has centered on a conceptual distinction between family and nonfamily supports. Chappell (1983) has argued that informal support networks also should be distinguished according to whether they have a peer or intergenerational focus. While Chappell's investigation centers on nonfamily peer supports as a neglected area of study, she leaves open the question of whether nonfamily intergenerational relations also may have significance in the aging process.

In this chapter, we investigate the relative strengths of intergenerational versus peer relations in supporting women who are encountering physical, social, and psychological transitions of aging in themselves and close family and friends. The data come from a study of a number of clubs that are part of a larger voluntary organization, and, hence, the focus is primarily on a nonfamily context. Specifically, we will address two interrelated issues: (1) How important is the voluntary organization in lending support to individuals as they face the physical, psychological, and social changes likely to be associated with aging? (2) Is the age structure of the voluntary organization a factor in its ability to provide instrumental and expressive types of social support to individuals? Before proceeding to the data, let us briefly review the research that informs us in posing the issues in this way.

SOURCES OF INFORMAL SUPPORT

Analyses by Litwak and Szelenyi (1969) and Dono et al. (1979) suggest that informal support systems—or what sociologists more typically refer to as primary groups—differentiate structurally and assume a variety of forms. Thus kinship represents a permanent group membership that is best suited to handle nontechnical tasks that require long-term commitments—for example, care during an extended illness. It may not, however, be best suited to deal with time emergencies because it often does not involve face-to-face contact. Compared to the kinship system, neighborhoods are characterized by close geographic proximity and relative short-term commitments, and they are best suited to deal with time emergencies—such as a health emergency. Friendships are distinctive in that they maximize individual choice and affectivity. Presumably, when people are able to select one another freely, there is a high degree of match on such characteristics as age, life status and role, and sex and socioeconomic status (Dono et al., 1979). Structurally, friendships may be the weakest form of informal supports in that they do not have the permanence of kinship ties nor the daily face-to-face contact of neighbors (Litwak and Szelenyi, 1969), but their strength is in their focus on affectivity and their ability to deal with issues centering on the family life cycle and occupation that must be experienced in the same way and time to be of use (Dono et al., 1979). In addressing the relative importance of each kind of social support, Dono et al. (1979) argue for a task-specific model, which relates the structural characteristics of each type of group to its unique functions. This is in contrast to Cantor's (1979) *hierarchical-compensatory model*, which predicts that people have an order of preference for the groups from which they seek support, regardless of the task.

It is in the context of aging issues that the strengths and weaknesses of different kinds of informal support groups may become more clear. In addition, a conceptual distinction between intergenerational and peer supports comes into focus. Many gerontologists have argued the importance of peer supports in later life. Blau (1981) focuses on the significance of role exits in later life (retirement, widowhood) and argues that mutual needs make friendships with peers more significant to one's sense of well-being than relationships with children. In addition, people presumably face a variety of social stigmas in later life from which they may be buffered and more adequately socialized to positive old age roles by associating primarily with their age peers (Hochschild, 1973; Rose, 1962; Rosow, 1974). On the other hand, Dono et al. (1979) argue that some of the effects of aging—for example, increasing rates of physical disability, reduced life expectancy, and the potentially greater mobility and lower income associated with retirement—will make reliance on peer social supports increasingly precarious. Informal peer supports are simply much less likely to be available, especially over the longer run, because they themselves are subject to the same vicissitudes of aging. In studying neighborhood support networks, Ward et al. (1981) found that neighbors who were confidants tended to be age peers, but that age was less important when it came to giving and receiving instrumental or emergency support. Thus age peers may be preferable for meeting one's affective needs, but when aid of a more instrumental sort is needed, intergenerational supports may be more stable and contribute to a greater sense of satisfaction and well-being. The data reported in this chapter shed further light on this issue.

VOLUNTARY ORGANIZATION MEMBERSHIPS AND AGING

We are interested in exploring the issue of peer versus intergenerational support systems within the context of membership in voluntary associations. As Babchuk et al. (1979) observe, voluntary associations. As Babchuk et al. (1979) observe, voluntary associations play a vital role in society, not only in terms of the services and information they may provide to others, but also as an arena for education and expressive behavior for members. Aging apparently does not take a significant toll on participation, even among those over age 80 (Babchuk et al., 1979; Cutler, 1977), except for the very elderly who are less likely to hold multiple memberships and to be active participants (Babchuk et al., 1979).

There are suggestions in the literature, however, that the meaning of membership in voluntary associations shifts with age. Babchuk et al. (1979) found that when types of memberships were categorized according to function as instrumental, instrumental-expressive, or expressive, a sample of persons 65 and over indicated most of their involvements to be in expressive or instrumental-expressive groups. They concluded that most were affiliated with associations having preeminent expressive or personal objectives and were focusing on activities that were integrative at the personality rather than the societal level. In a case study of older women who had belonged over a long period of time to an employed businesswomen's club, LaRossa and Dowd (1980) found that the remarkable durability of the club rested on significant transitions in emphasis on various functions in response to the changing age structure of the club. While leadership training was one of the stated purposes of the club, over time socioemotional supports became increasingly important.

The investigation in this chapter is a case study of a voluntary organization in which women often have retained membership and involvement over a number of decades from their early years as homemakers into old age. It provides an opportunity to consider the implications of "aging in place" for the individual members of the organization. Within the limitations of the data, we will explore various indications that the organization serves as an informal support system—particularly with reference to stresses brought on by the aging process. As already noted, we also will consider whether the organization's age structure (intergenerational or peer focus) makes a difference in its ability to function as a source of instrumental and expressive support.

BACKGROUND OF THE STUDY

In 1983, an investigation was made of 16 homemaker clubs in one metropolitan county of Missouri. These clubs are affiliated with the state Cooperative Extension Service. The initial purpose of this pilot study was to gain insight into and generate hypotheses concerning the social organization of these voluntary organizations, especially as it pertains to the increasing numbers and proportions of elderly members.

The 29 clubs within this county are a small fraction of the 1172 clubs throughout Missouri that together form a larger voluntary organization, Missouri Extension Homemakers Association (MEHA). MEHA is in turn part of a national association, the National Extension Homemakers Council, representing 31,488 clubs in 44 states and 2 territories. The stated objectives of these organizations are (1) to strengthen and improve family functioning, (2) to enhance homemaker skills, and (3) to cultivate and train women to play leadership roles in their communities.

Since its inception in 1914, the Cooperative Extension Service has functioned as advisor to the lay leadership of these homemaker clubs. The extension home economist in each county has served as a technical advisor by providing organizational guidance, information on homemaking and leadership development, and advice on programming at regular meetings.

Despite the links with the Cooperative Extension Service and the affiliation of these clubs through statewide and national organizations, there remains considerable local autonomy and variability in their activities, recruitment procedures, membership turnover, and stability. The research team believed that an in-depth examination of a small sample of these clubs would offer a basis for determining the parameters of these clubs with respect to their aging membership.

METHODOLOGY

From its inception, this study was conceived as an in-depth exploration of a sample of clubs within one geographical area. Rather than seeking quantitative data from which to generalize about all clubs in the state, we chose to gather fine-grained profiles of a few clubs and their members.

With the cooperation of the county extension home economist, a membership list for each club in the county was obtained. These lists contained 2 valuable pieces of data: the age and the length of club membership of each member. With this information, 16 of the 29 clubs were selected for study, spanning the age range of members (from clubs with nearly all members under age 50 to clubs with all members age 65 and older) and the age range of the clubs (from clubs founded as recently as 1977 to those begun in 1926). Although the county from which clubs were selected was part of a metropolitan area, all the clubs selected were from the surrounding suburbs and rural villages. Clubs ranged in size from 10 to 20 members.

In order to get as complete a picture as possible of the patterns of club functioning, data were gathered both through group interviews with the whole club and through individual interviews with club members. Group interviews were conducted by one of the investigators in six of the clubs at a regularly scheduled meeting. The investigator was introduced by a club officer, and then, with the aid of a tape recorder to capture the total discussion, tone, and mood of the answers, asked a series of questions about the club. The same series of questions were asked in all six group interviews. The transcriptions of the group interviews then served as one set of data. Data were collected from another ten clubs through individual interviews.

A total of 35 individual interviews were conducted with 3 or 4 members of each club. Interviewees were selected from club records, and, with the assistance of the extension home economist, an effort was made to obtain a cross-section of the club's membership in terms of age, length of membership in the club, and roles in the club (officers and nonofficers). The questions on the interview schedule paralleled those of the group interview, except that they focused on more specific detail not possible in a group interview. The group interviews focused on the history of the club, activities of the club, personal importance and meaning of the club, recruitment practices, aging-related physical and mental health changes in members and significant others, the perceived response of the club to these changes, and possible interest in special programming on issues related to aging. Individual interviews, in addition to the above topics, also probed friendship patterns among members, degree of involvement in the club, social participation outside this club, and personal characteristics such as income, family status, and education level.

Group interviews were independently coded by four members of the research team according to a set of preestablished categories. Individual interview responses were also coded according to a set of preestablished categories, and, despite the small sample size, crosstabulated on a few variables in search of tentative and suggestive relationships. Because of the small size of the sample, we remain cautious about our findings and interpret them as suggestive rather than definitive. Nevertheless, we are confident enough in them to use some of the information in this analysis of aging and the informal support system.

ANALYSIS

The initial objective of this study was to explore the role of the voluntary organization as a support system in the aging process. Having discovered from the homemaker club rosters that a large proportion of members had joined 30 or more years ago, that the average age of members was over 60 (a national trend), and that many clubs contained founding members dating back more than 50 years, we believed this group would serve as an excellent base for a study. Given the stated objectives of the homemaker clubs—to strengthen the family, to enhance homemaker skills, and to develop leadership skills—it appeared of great significance that a substantial portion of the clubs had aging members, and it suggested that, indeed, these clubs functioned as more than formal organizations to teach skills in homemaking and community leadership. Because this statewide organization, with hundreds of clubs, offered a broad spectrum of age ranges and compositions, we believed a unique opportunity existed for exploring both intergenerational and peer factors as they affect social participation and social support among aging women.

Clubs were selected so as to reflect the age distribution of members: clubs were defined as young, mixed, and old. *Young* clubs are those that have membership composed primarily of women under age 50 and, because of this factor, a large number of the members are working full- or part-time. The age of these clubs ranges from 6 to 25 years, and, as a correlate, the length of membership tends to be under 25 years, with the average being less than 10. *Mixed* clubs have membership nearly evenly divided between the 50-65 and over-65 age groups, and a smaller proportion under 50 years of age. There are fewer employed women in these clubs. The age of these clubs ranges from 15 to 57 years, and length of membership tends to be greater than for the young clubs. *Old* clubs are composed almost entirely of women over age 65. No women are employed, and a larger proportion are widowed. The clubs have been in existence for 30 to 51 years, with a preponderance of longstanding clubs and membership. Of the 16 clubs in which group or individual interviews were conducted, three were classified as young, six as old, and seven as mixed. Of the 35 women who were interviewed individually, 11 were from young clubs, 14 from old clubs, and 10 from mixed clubs.

Many of the women in the three club types perceived themselves, close family, or friends as facing age-related changes in health and mental health, although this varied by age group. In the young clubs only a small proportion noted any such changes in themselves or others. More frequently mentioned were problems with teenage children (e.g., drugs) and divorces involving club members. Women in old clubs reported a wide range of age-related difficulties in themselves and significant others, such as memory loss, hearing and vision deficits, arthritis, heart problems, cancer, diabetes, a general decline in vigor, or difficulties in getting about. Depending somewhat on their own age, women in the mixed clubs were also likely to report problems in some of these same areas.

The mixed and old clubs in particular offered an excellent opportunity to explore both how these voluntary organizations provided support systems for members and a comparison of the degree to which intergenerational (mixed) and peer (old) clubs functioned as support systems.

THE MEANING OF THE CLUBS TO MEMBERS

The importance of the homemaker clubs to members and the bases of that importance were determined from responses to several questions in the individual interviews. Those interviewed were asked to rank their homemaker club against all other clubs in which they actively participated. Club participation in general was fairly active: 55 percent of the women interviewed were active in 4 or more other voluntary organizations, and all were active in at least one other group. In exploring the meaning of club ranking of all organizations mentioned, those homemaker clubs that were perceived as "social"—that is, those in which the principal activity was to get together for conversation and pastime activities—were consistently ranked higher than all others (the other categories of activity being religious, family, recreational, educational, and service). As a corollary of this finding, those homemaker clubs in which members claimed that most of the friends with whom they enjoyed doing things came from within the club were ranked highest by these members, and those in which there were the fewest such friends were ranked lowest by those members. Similarly, those clubs in which women identified their closest confidants as being club members were ranked highest, and those with the fewest were ranked lowest.

When asked to compare the purposes and benefits of the homemaker club with those of other organizations to which they belonged, members of the young clubs identified sociability and self-growth as the principal benefits. Members of old clubs were most likely to indicate that it was education that gave their club its special meaning. Members of mixed clubs identified a variety of meanings, suggesting that the intergenerational clubs may maintain their strength as a social organization from a broader base of factors.

One important dimension of the club meaning to members proved to be friendship patterns. As we have already noted, clubs that were ranked highest relative to other organizational memberships were those in which members claimed the largest number of friends. In addition, friendship patterns were more extensive among those members who had more longstanding memberships in the club. And those women who had fewer other clubs in which they participated had more extensive friendship patterns within the homemaker club, suggesting that the narrower the social network (as measured by number of organizations to which one belongs), the more extensive the friendship network within that smaller arena.

Friendships play an important role in other ways. Among those women reporting the club as being important in helping them with personal or family problems, the largest proportion of them also reported joining the club originally because of a friend. When examined by type of club, the young and mixed clubs showed the most influence of friends in the recruitment process, and it was in the mixed clubs that members most often reported being influenced by friends to join.

The data from these interviews suggest that the homemaker clubs are important social support systems for their members, and, more important, that the intergenerational clubs (mixed) seem to be more viable clubs, having stronger friendship patterns, lending more support to members, and offering members a broader case for participation. To explore this idea further, measures of satisfaction with the club were examined by club type to see if the mixed clubs were indeed more supportive to members.

LEVEL OF SATISFACTION WITH THE CLUB

A number of variables were identified as measures of satisfaction with the homemaker club: what ranking members gave this club in relation to their other organizational memberships; degree of disappointment should the club disband; number of club meetings missed in the past year; changes in degree of participation; level of recruitment; and difficulties in recruitment of new members.

With respect to club rank, the largest proportion of women ranking the homemaker club high were from the mixed clubs. Of those expressing great disappointment should the club disband, the largest proportion also were from mixed clubs. When number of club meetings missed in the past year was examined, members of mixed clubs showed the fewest. When individuals were asked if they perceived their level of participation in the club to have increased, decreased, or remained the same over the past five years, the majority of members of mixed clubs reported an increase; this was not found in either the young or old clubs. With respect to recruitment it was only in the older clubs, which were experiencing gradual erosion of membership through disability and death, that significant problems were reported. Yet they also did not engage in much recruitment activity. Though they were experiencing a decline in membership, they lacked the confidence or know-how to recruit new members. Lack of contacts with younger women and uncertainty about the future of their club contributed to their inability to solve the recruitment problem. In striking contrast, there was virtually no discussion reported in the mixed clubs over recruitment. For these clubs, attrition rates were low, few "vacancies" existed, and when an opening occurred, a replacement was already in place.

The data collected through group interviews largely support the findings reported from individual interviews. The mixed clubs showed a greater breadth of activity, higher levels of vitality, more consistent participation in the statewide homemakers organization, and an apparent balance between expressive and instrumental types of social support to individual members.

INSTRUMENTAL ROLE OF THE CLUB

The analysis so far principally has explored the expressive support offered by the clubs. Clearly, both the old and mixed clubs have been strong forces in providing emotional supports to these women as they age. Length of association among members undoubtedly plays an important role in building and strengthening these ties. However, if we examine the instrumental supports offered in these clubs, a different pattern emerges. In a series of questions directed at identifying areas of programming for future club meetings, it appeared clear that the mixed clubs had the strongest interests in focusing on information helpful in dealing with the aging process (e.g., adapting to widowhood or retirement, understanding physical and mental health changes with aging, loneliness, relating to aging parents). Not only did the old clubs not indicate an interest in these topics, they expressed a sense of helplessness in being able as a group to do anything about the circumstances of their aging.

In another series of questions directed at identifying whether the clubs had already in some ways helped members deal with problems of aging, it was the mixed clubs that reported so most often. In addition to providing expressive support (as in visiting and sending cards to a hospitalized member), there were also reports of more instrumental types of activities, such as taking food into the home or relieving a member in the care of an ill spouse. In both the individual and group interviews, evidence came from the old clubs that their aging members were increasingly unable to offer aid to members due to their frailty, inability to drive, or other physical infirmities, although they did frequently report giving each other emotional support or benefiting from an educational program (e.g., nutrition). Two of the older clubs recognized, as their membership dwindled, that their time as a club was coming to an end.

DISCUSSION AND CONCLUSIONS

The aging process emerges as a dimension of nearly all social groups. As already identified in the work of others, it is of major significance in primary groups—especially kin, friend, and neighbor groupings. We have explored the added significance of voluntary organizations as primary group settings in which the aging process also takes place in order to determine whether it plays a significant role as part of an informal support system.

Support systems, a part of nearly all social groupings, are particularly important in the aging process because aging brings with it a number of possible physical changes that require assistance from others, chronic illness that debilitates, changes in daily living patterns occasioned by physical matters such as eyesight or hearing, and role changes (such as widowhood, retirement, or aloneness) that often call for emotional bolstering from others. The aging process calls for both expressive and instrumental support systems. We know that primary groups in general provide both instrumental and expressive support to women throughout their lives; there is also ample evidence to assert that they play the same role in the aging process of women: Family groups tend to take on the long-term commitments, friends become the expressive supports based on shared interests and companionship, and neighbors respond to instrumental needs occasioned by proximity of residence.

From the data gathered from homemaker clubs, it appears that voluntary organizations can, under special circumstances, function to maximize the overlap of family, friends, and neighbors. From several of the clubs studied, it can be concluded that they serve both as expressive and instrumental support systems.

The age structure of the organization—intergenerational or peer (in our study identified as "mixed" or "old" clubs)—seems to be a determining factor in which kind of support system is most likely to be provided. The old clubs, as their members become increasingly older, become more limited in their ability to provide instrumental support, although they may continue to provide emotional support arising from their longstanding friendships, shared reservoir of experiences in the club, and common values stemming from their generational closeness. In some of the older clubs, members expressed interest in recruiting younger members, expressly for such instrumental purposes as providing transportation to meetings and for other tasks these older women found difficult to do by themselves. At the same time, they expressed ease with members of their own age in the club—an example of the expressive dimension in the group.

Studies cited earlier in this chapter recognized that organizations that "age in place" may change their primary support function from instrumental to expressive. Data from our study clarify this point. Among members from both the mixed and old clubs, more than half of those interviewed responded that their reasons for belonging to the club had changed over the years. The original reason for joining was largely "social." For the mixed and old club members, this changed to largely instrumental reasons such as education, social service, and recreation. However, for old club members it has again become principally expressive. It would appear that due to the diversity of their membership, the mixed clubs are best able to meet both instrumental and expressive support needs.

In this regard, the distinction made between the "young-old" and the "old-old" by Neugarten (1978) is helpful in understanding how and why these organizations change in the kinds of support systems they provide. Clubs made up of young-old women who are still vigorous and active are still able to act as viable support systems (both instrumental and expressive) to their members. Yet structurally they are rather precarious because, as their members become principally old-old women who experience frailty and a decline in vigor, the club is diminished in its ability to provide the kinds of supports most needed by its members. Data from our study suggest that, indeed, the old clubs were passing over that threshold of instrumental supports and could, at best, provide only emotional supports.

Dono et al. (1979) have made the observation that in the course of aging, individuals may initially seek out age peers for their support system (such as moving to an age-homogeneous retirement community), but eventually may be forced to seek out more intergenerational supports (such as children) as frailties develop. Thus a case can be made that intergenerational voluntary organizations offer a more enduring response in the search for support systems in the aging process. Indeed, our data support this point well: The mixed clubs were in most regards the most viable of all the clubs, were most willing to address openly the issues of aging, and were acknowledged by their members as already having provided supports in the aging process.

Although our data remain tentative and preliminary, they strongly suggest a powerful relation between the age structure of the group and the kinds of support systems it can provide.

16

INTERPERSONAL SUPPORT AND HEALTH OF OLDER PEOPLE

MARSHALL J. GRANEY
Associate Professor, Sociology
Wayne State University

This chapter is concerned with stress and interpersonal support in relation to older people's maintaining, losing, and regaining health. Concepts such as interpersonal support, health, and stress are complex, and research findings about their interrelationships have been sometimes ambiguous or even contradictory. Thus it is appropriate that we begin with a review of the concepts of interpersonal support, health, and stress.

INTERPERSONAL SUPPORT, HEALTH, AND STRESS

INTERPERSONAL SUPPORT

In this chapter "interpersonal support" is defined as relationships that are, or are perceived to be, capable of contributing to an individual's competence in coping with psychophysical stress. This area of concern has been conceptualized, with variations in connotation and operationalization, as emotional support (Fuller and Larson, 1980), interpersonal network (Wells and Macdonald, 1981), social network (Langlie, 1977), social resources (Palmore et al., 1979), social support (Cobb, 1976), and social-support network (Wan, 1982). At the present time these various conceptualizations may be considered to be, for the most part, subsumed under the rubric of interpersonal support, as defined above.

Author's Note: *I thank Veronica F. Engle and Jill Quadagno for critiques of this chapter that have been helpful in revising it for publication.*

In the gerontological health literature, interpersonal support has usually been considered in terms of sources of support. In more general literature on health, interpersonal support has been considered in terms of the means by which these sources may attain supportive effects as aids in coping. Each perspective contributes to our understanding of the relationships between interpersonal support and health.

In terms of sources, for example, Lin et al. (1979: 109) define social support as "support accessible to an individual through social ties to other individuals, groups, and the larger community." This general catalog can be elaborated to specify kin, friends, acquaintances, and co-workers (Lin et al., 1979) as well as neighbors and voluntary associations, including mutual help membership groups. Interpersonal support is, however, usually considered as distinctly different from contact with the helping professions. To provide interpersonal support a person must often be a "significant other," linked socially through primary group ties such as the family (especially the spouse and/or children) or peer groups (especially the confidant and close friends). For those without primary group ties through family or friendship, membership support groups, such as mutual help organizations, and community voluntary associations, such as church groups, may be used for similar purposes.

The means by which interpersonal support may figure in the attainment of positive health effects in people's lives have been considered by Langlie (1977) and indirectly, in the study of coping strategies, by Pearlin and Schooler (1978). In Langlie's (1977) view, interpersonal support networks may either (1) exert pressure on the individual to conform to preventative health norms, or (2) provide preventative health information of practical utility. According to Pearlin and Schooler (1978: 2), coping behavior may exert a protective function in three ways: (1) "by eliminating or modifying conditions giving rise to problems," (2) "by perceptually controlling the meaning of experience in a manner that neutralizes its problematic character," and (3) "by keeping the emotional consequences of problems within manageable bounds."

Most members of our society marry at some time during their lives. Whether or not an individual marries, his or her siblings and, perhaps less often, one's own parents may serve as valuable interpersonal support in times of stress. In addition, family ties to children and grandchildren may also provide interpersonal support. The interdependence of generations is clearly recognized in our society (Shanas, 1979a). For example, daughters tend to accept considerable responsibility for assisting healthy but aged parents, and also for parental care in times of illness (Shanas, 1962). Most older people with living children live geographically proximate to at least one child (Shanas et al., 1968). Some older people's children may be too geographically dispersed, however, to serve many supportive functions. (Some parents contribute to family dispersion through their own migration after retirement.) When children do not live close by, the equivocal nature of "intimacy at a distance" arises (Blau, 1973). Although the child and the older parent may, in some sense, feel "close," if they are geographically distant they are available to one another as interpersonal support resources in only a strictly limited sense during dire, short-term problems. Such relationships may be supportive in a perceptual sense, however, in that they can provide feelings of belonging and of being a member of a network of caring people (see Cobb, 1976).

Thus interpersonal support resources provided by the family are not available to everyone. For some older people, who are the victims of abuse, the family may fail as a support system even when it is intact and proximate. For yet others, alienation or geographic distances may intervene, and the most successful aging people will eventually outlive their spouses and, sometimes, even their own children.

HEALTH

Health is conceived here as an extended continuum ranging from a high positive state of wellness, through an intermediate state characterized by the mere absence of symptoms, to an extreme negative state of illness. Unfortunately, and seemingly contrary to this global conception of health, there exist at the present time multiple models of health. The two chief competitors are the functional model, with its focus on the maintenance of function (the basis of wellness), and the medical model, with its focus on disease (the basis of illness).

Wellness

Wellness reflects the individual's capacity to manifest high levels of vigor. According to the World Health Organization advisory committee, as quoted by Shanas and Maddox (1976: 576): "Health in the elderly is best measured in terms of function; . . . degree of fitness rather than extent of pathology may be used as a measure of the amount of services the aged will require from the community."

Services are ordinarily sought only by those who perceive that they need them, and research evidence of two kinds indicates that older people tend to define their own health in terms of functional assessment: (1) older people's attitudes and behaviors, as indicators of functional health, correlate highly with their self-assessments of health (Engle and Graney, 1984); and (2) although the majority of older people's self-assessments of health agree with physicians' assessments, more than one-third of these comparisons disagree (Graney and Zimmerman, 1981). According to the findings of several studies conducted over a substantial period of time, disagreements between older people's and physicians' ratings of older people's health are usually in the direction of self-assessed health being more favorable than physician-assessed health (Graney and Zimmerman, 1980). This difference indicates that the assessors are using different models of health as the basis of their judgments. Physicians make their assessments of older people's health based on comparisons to general medical standards. Functional decline is acknowledged in these standards, but the ideal used as a basis for health evaluation is an absence of disease. Most older people's own comparisons, in contrast, are in terms of their own functional abilities, and within their own age group (in which the presence of one or more chronic diseases is the norm). Thus older people's health self-assessments tend, on the average, to be more favorable and optimistic than physicians' assessments.

Illness

Illness reflects the presence of one or more pathological conditions. The majority of older people function with a burden of one or more chronic diseases such as arthritis, diabetes, or hypertension. Relative to youth or middle age, there is among older people a prevalence of chronic disease as compared to acute episodes of sickness or injury trauma (although the latter are by no means rare; Shanas and Maddox, 1976). In the medical model of health, emphasis is placed on the presence of pathological conditions that are often debilitating and sometimes fatal. In contrast to health assessment based chiefly on functional capacities, indicators of health under the medical model include absence of diagnosed diseases, hospitalization, treatment by a physician, and pain (Lawton et al., 1967).

Functional assessment of health, as emphasized by older people themselves, and medical assessment of health, as emphasized by physicians, are neither wholly independent conceptions of health nor are they unrelated to each other. Both perspectives can be subsumed under a broader, more general model of health. Thus it is reasonable to consider health in terms of both wellness and illness in research on aging, and using the conceptualization of health as an extended continuum includes both wellness and illness. Two later sections of this chapter focus, in turn, on these two parts of the general concept of health.

STRESS

Mechanic (1962: 7) has defined "*stress* as the discomforting responses of persons in particular situations. . . . To the extent that the discomforting response cannot be easily reduced or eliminated, we may expect that it will tend to be of some severity and duration." In recent years, stress has been increasingly implicated in the etiology of illness. For example, many environmental pathogens have come to be seen as endemic; so why are some people susceptible, and others not? A psychosomatic nexus may often be implicated. For example, a disproportionately high incidence of tuberculosis among people who have recently experienced marital breakup or other socioemotional stressors has been found (Rahe and Arthur, 1978).

Stress may originate from many social sources, ranging from the external level of social organizations, as in retirement and its consequent loss of social roles, to the inner thought processes of the individual struggling to come to grips with personal growth and decline. The interpersonal support network is itself frequently implicated in some of the most severe stresses people ordinarily experience: widowhood, children leaving home and/or the geographic area, and one's own changes of residence and associates. Like many other things, the interpersonal support system has both manifest and latent functions. The chief manifest function of the interpersonal support system is evident in its name, and that is clearly a positive influence on health. For example, one's associates may assist in various ways: the avoidance of stressful life changes; generally ameliorating the influence of stress experienced; or specifically mediating between stress and health outcomes (Pearlin and Schooler, 1978). On the other hand, nothing is without its costs. Much of ourselves is invested in our relationships with others, and this may eventually cost losses and grief: Change is inevitable. Thus some stress in old age (but certainly not all) has its origins in older people's being part of an interpersonal support system.

There is generally considered to be a well-established relationship between stress and health. Stress has been implicated as a cause of decline in mental health, functional health, physical health, and in health self-assessments. The role that interpersonal support may play in mediating the effects of stress on health is less certain, however. The positive and negative findings presented in research findings reviewed elsewhere in this chapter tend to show mediating effects considerably smaller than those expected on intuitive or theoretical grounds. This may stem from several factors, including weaknesses in theory (it is, after all, those in greatest need who should be expected to have the most manifest and active interpersonal support networks, and this expectation has not been well accounted for in past research) and methodological problems (many studies are retrospective and/or rely on samples too small to support the forms of data analysis used by the researcher).

CAVEATS

Research reviewed in this chapter is subject to all of the usual caveats common to recent gerontological research. Specifically, limits to generalizability of findings due to the particular historical, cultural, and technical bases of the research need to be considered. Most of the research on stress and health is based on data from contemporary North American settings, and both cross-cultural and minority data are scarce. Further, the scarcity of findings based on long-term prospective research makes the extent to which interpersonal resources mediate between stress and health difficult to assess at the present time.

WELLNESS

In exploring the relationship between social resources and health, many studies have investigated the interpersonal support system as a coping mechanism predisposing to wellness. Although research findings have been mixed, the usual results have shown evidence of a predominantly positive relationship. Unfortunately, even in research with positive findings, the degree to which variations in health have been explained in terms of differences in social resources has been consistently low. Nevertheless, this avenue of research on gerontological health is considered to hold promise.

Langlie (1977) has theorized that interpersonal support may predispose to wellness through exerting pressure on the individual to conform to positive health norms, or by providing preventative health information. Shanas (1979b) has documented that the overwhelming majority of children provide advice and financial support to older parents. Support of this kind contributes, either directly or indirectly, to access to goods and services, balanced nutrition, and other aspects of preventative health care, including physical activity, mental well-being, and interpersonal resources for coping with continuity and change in the lives of older people.

NUTRITION

Cooking for one is not much fun, but many older people find themselves in this situation. Meals are a social time during most of our lives. For older people living alone, however, much of the enjoyment is lost that other people find in considering new foods and recipes, meal planning, shopping, food preparation, and serving an attractive meal to be appreciated, shared, and enjoyed together with one or more companions. Research findings have shown consistently that living with a spouse can make a significant positive contribution to health, and research also shows that living with a spouse or anyone else in the same household can accomplish about the same good effect. Nutrition may be one of the most important factors explaining how sharing a household with another person is beneficial to health.

The search for the appearance, if not the full reality, of a shared meal explains explains part of the nationwide popularity of cafeterias among older people. Cafeterias, more than restaurants, provide a comfortable place to dine alone—yet in the presence of others—and cafeterias, in comparison to restaurants, provide an advantage to older people in greater control over the size of meals and of portions. Even for older people living in shared households, dining out in a cafeteria or a restaurant affords an opportunity for physical activity, mental stimulation, novel foods and experiences, and access to foods that may be impractical to prepare to serve one or two people.

A balanced diet, eaten in congenial surroundings, can contribute much to maintaining or improving physical functioning and social and psychological well-being among older people. Unfortunately, this ideal is too often not the case, and laxative addiction that is common among older people may be due to imbalanced diet and inactivity.

PHYSICAL ABILITY

As with nutrition, there is a social component to the exercise and physical activity needed to maintain the body's systems in good working order. Most people of all ages find that physical activities ranging from bird watching to sex are more fun with someone. Thus health clubs and spas serve a physical exercise function for some older people that is analogous to the nutrition function of cafeterias, as discussed above. For older people with able-bodied associates, jogging with a partner, taking walks together, or going shopping together are all ways that physical activities constitute preventative health behaviors that enhance body health, cement social bonds, and promote mental health.

"Use it or lose it," and "wear out or rust out" are both common prescriptions for physical health heard these days. Social relationships have been found to be related to maintaining functional health of this sort. For example, Wan and Weissert (1981) have found that social support serves as a buffer against declines in physical health status, and that the strength of one's own support network—especially siblings, relatives, and friends—correlates with effective physical functioning.

Both subjective feelings of wellness (health self-assessments) and fewer numbers of days spent ill in bed have been found to be directly correlated to being married (Fenwick and Barresi, 1981). Further research is likely to find, however, that it is the shared household living arrangement rather than one's formal marital status that accomplishes these positive effects. People who share their lives with others have greater competence in the activities of daily living (Wan and Weissert, 1981), and those who share their households with others are less likely to be institutionalized

(Shanas, 1979b; Wan and Weissert, 1981). Older women are more likely than men to be physically inactive or even home-bound, both because of a shortage of men and because of less financial resources. Pooling resources for transportation may provide a partial answer to the problem of inactivity for some older women.

Research on relocation of nursing home residents has found that function is better maintained among those with effective support systems because degree of physical infirmity after relocation has been found to be correlated to social support (Wells and Macdonald, 1981). Even in research with a focus that has been on the medical model of health, social support resources have been found to have what might, in this context, be termed immunity-inducing benefits (Palmore et al., 1979).

MENTAL WELL-BEING

Some research findings have established a relationship between levels of social contact and mental well-being in general. Other findings have illuminated the relationship between particular kinds of social contact, such as marriage and family, and mental well-being. Most research on the relationship between social support and psychological well-being has focused on the degree to which social support serves as a buffer to mitigate adverse health effects of stressful life events such as bereavement, retirement, relocation, of physical health crises.

Close contact with others is a natural stimulant, and the cooperation and conflict that constitute and result from interpersonal interaction serve to exercise mental faculties and are normal parts of life that are missing from the lives of those who lack close association with others. Further, the presence of others is an aid to agenda-setting and other anchorages to the realities of everyday life. Removing older people from familiar environmental and social contacts that serve as reference points and cues in their schedules or rounds of activity is likely to result in confusion and apparent senility. For these reasons, one would expect better orientation to reality, zest for life, decreased likelihood of eccentricities (e.g., "cat ladies") and less addiction to psychoactive substances (e.g., alcohol and tranquilizers) among older people in living arrangements that are shared with other people.

Those people who are physically active have higher levels of vigor as a result. For many, physical exercise serves as a release of tensions and frustrations, and physical stagnation is associated with mental stagnation and fatigue. In addition to the satisfactions of the social relationship component found in many physical activities, strenuous exercise is associated with biochemical changes and increased blood flow that promote an individual's sense of well-being and stimulate mental activity.

Lowenthal and Haven (1968) have found that older people who experience decreased social interaction are more likely to exhibit mental health symptoms of depression. In their study, the important role of confidant was highlighted, with a positive correlation found between having a confidant and mental well-being. Others have emphasized the importance of marriage and family contacts of well-being among both younger people (Gore and Mangione, 1983; Eaton, 1978) and the aged (York and Caslyn, 1977).

Employment is another central social role in the lives of many people, and several studies have examined the ameliorative influence that social support may have in preserving mental health and psychological well-being under conditions of unemployment. Gore (1978) found less evidence of either depression or physical illness symptoms among recently unemployed males who experienced greater social support, and this may have relevance to retired men. In studying retirement's effects, Palmore et al. (1979) found no physical symptom correlates, but did report weak adverse psychological correlates. These problems were said to be especially mild for people with social class and interpersonal resources. More recently, Gore and Mangione (1983) have found both absence of employment and absence of marriage to be correlated to symptoms of depression among younger men and women.

In research on the mitigating effects of social support, one study of the stressful effects of nursing home relocation has found that the presence of at least one person to whom an older person feels close had an ameliorating effect on potential physical and psychological aftereffects of interinstitutional relocation of older people (Wells and Macdonald, 1981). It is encouraging to note that 82 percent of already-institutionalized older people in this study had at least one close family member or friend outside the nursing home, and others without this resource were able to find similar social support among nursing home staff and personnel.

Eaton (1978) found evidence of a higher correlation between stress and symptoms among people living alone, providing evidence of a mediating effect of social support in data on a relatively youthful sample. Similarly, in research across the life cycle, Lin et al. (1979) have found limited evidence of social support mediating between stressors and psychiatric symptoms. In addition, Palmore et al. (1979), in studying psychiatric and physical outcomes associated with retirement, widowhood, empty nest transition, and serious illness, found little evidence of decline among people with interpersonal and socioeconomic support resources. Fuller and Larson (1980), however, found no evidence of interpersonal support mediating between stressful life events and morale or distress among older people. Evidence that older people in the poorest health have the most active support systems, such as that presented in Fuller and Larson (1980), is neither new nor anomalous, nor does it refute the importance of social support. It is, after all, ordinarily the burning buildings that are surrounded by fire trucks. Empirical research that finds only weak or no support for hypotheses about the importance of social support because of weak or even inverse correlations evident between social support and wellness has been too simplistic in its hypotheses, design, and operational procedures. We need to anticipate that a natural tendency toward increased mobilization of social support resources will be evident during the latter stages of the life course.

CONTINUITY AND CHANGE

Successful aging is associated with continuity, and unsuccessful aging is associated with the discontinuities of a life career dissipated through misadventures, false starts, blind alleys, and the stress associated with too many changes in too short a time. Failures—in materials, in health, or in relationships—can occur instantly, but success ordinarily is not an overnight phenomenon. Thus to attain success in many endeavors (such as family life or occupational career) requires persistence and stability over time or, in a word, continuity. Problems arising from discontinuities are the logical basis of an ancient Chinese curse: "May you have an interesting life."

Curse or no curse, change is inevitable. And, owing simply to their greater longevity and duration of exposure, older people must necessarily experience the most change over the course of their lives. Therefore, to age successfully one must not only enjoy continuity, but one must also be able to deal effectively with changes in one's social situation and in one's own body. We ordinarily think of spouses, children, and friends as resources in a social support network, but major stresses are also associated with spouse, children, and friends. In addition to the ordinary conflicts between people that may arise from the problems of daily living, alienation and loss of significant others through geographic mobility or death are not mere possibilities to the older person; they are the inevitable experience of the aged: To live the longest is to have suffered the most losses in these regards.

It is one of the many paradoxes of aging that the social support system that is important for good health in the first place may also precipitate illness through sometimes inducing stress. Eaton (1978), however, has found that the stress induced by subsequent events is less than one might ordinarily expect, a phenomenon that may be considered an "immunity inducing" aspect of prior stress. Thus older people who have had "interesting lives," including active social lives, may be more competent at coping with many kinds of stressful events than their younger counterparts. Much of this increased competence may be due to older people having experienced many past crises accompanied with active social support, and thus having a social support system in place and readily mobilized to help cope with later events.

ILLNESS

Suchman (1965) has conceived of illness behavior and medical care as a process, with as many as five stages: (1) symptom recognition, (2) assumption of the sick role, (3) medical care contact, (4) dependent-patient role, and (5) recovery and rehabilitation. Our consideration of the relevance of interpersonal support systems to illness among older people will be organized according to these stages.

SYMPTOM RECOGNITION

Normal aging includes sensory decline and gradual accommodation to these changes. Such changes may lead to an increased likelihood of failure to recognize the more subtle symptoms of disease as they manifest themselves. Also, symptoms that emerge gradually may be misperceived as part of the normal aging process, and not recognized as pathological. In addition, even patently manifest symptoms that are perceived and recognized as unusual may, nevertheless, not be defined by the older person as pathological. Lay people are uncertain about what constitutes "normal" in the first place, and the differences between normal and pathological with regard to many conditions (such as diabetes) may be matters of degree and opinion. Thus "borderline" examples of some pathologies exist, diabetes being an excellent example, that, if treatable and treated, prevent more serious symptoms from presenting themselves.

The typical older person has at least one chronic disease, and affliction with mutliple chronic diseases is not uncommon, particularly among the "old-old." Thus the presence of one or more conditions that are considered "ill-health" or pathological according to the medical model of health is, in fact, the prevalent state of affairs among older people. As with most people of all ages, older people tend to define health in positive terms of ability or overall function rather than in negative terms such as the presence of disease. Being able to maintain function at normal or at near-normal levels may be an important part of the reason why older people are not quick to define symptoms as illness, or less likely to do so at all. Thus Shanas and Maddox (1976: 598) state that "the functional model provides a more useful conceptual tool than the medical model because it will better predict how pathology is translated into illness behavior and ultimately into the sick role."

ASSUMPTION OF THE SICK ROLE

Generally, assumption of the sick role entails relinquishment of normal roles. Thus assumption of the sick role is partly contingent on the availability of an interpersonal support system to make withdrawal from normal roles a realistic possibility.

The prevalence of heart disease, hypertension, diabetes, arthritis or rheumatism, and emphysema or chronic lung disease among the older population is large in comparison to the assumption of the sick role among older people. These chronic diseases do not ordinarily produce the kinds of symptoms that impair function rapidly, or in an unusual manner, and we hypothesize that it is because function can often be maintained that chronic diseases are less likely to generate a sick role response in the older person. Nevertheless, common sense indicates that the prevalence of sickness behavior increases with age.

In addition to age alone, part of the age difference in assumption of the sick role can be attributed to the larger numbers of women in the older population. There is a sex difference in the likelihood of a person adopting the sick role such that the social psychological distance between the concept "female" and the constellation of attitudes and behaviors that constitute the sick role is arguably smaller than for "male" (Nathanson, 1975). Contrary to biological fact, but prominent among the myths of our culture, women have been defined as the "weaker" sex. The connotations of daintiness or fragility associated with "weaker" may be a self-fulfilling prophecy that encourages assumption of the sick role among women, and discourages like behavior among men. However, evidence of all kinds indicates that (with the obvious exception of muscle power) women are the tougher and more durable of the two sexes (Graney, 1979).

Most data on sickness show men to be less likely than women to assume the sick role. For example, according to research reviewed by Nathanson (1975), women report more mental and physical illness symptoms, have higher incidence of acute illness conditions, greater prevalence of chronic disease conditions, lose more days to restricted activity due to illness, experience more days confined to bed, and report more physician visits. Although some sex differences in sickness data have been statistically but not substantively significant, most of the differences reported by Nathanson (1975) are substantial by any standard. Nathanson (1975, 1977) proposes several hypotheses to account for greater assumption of the sick role among women. Among these, one could argue that the sex role scripts of males in our society preclude their facile use of the sick role and consequent mobilization of available interpersonal support systems. Lower apparent morbidity and higher mortality may be related as cause and effect, however, and death rates contradict sickness measures in a sense because men have the higher mortality rate (Graney, 1979).

Another factor besides traditional sex role scripting that may account in part for the lower morbidity of males is that men's morbidity may be lowered as a wellness-enhancing function of their intact support systems. A substantially larger proportion of older men than women live with their spouses.

MEDICAL CARE CONTACT

Although iatrogenic problems continue to diminish the value of medical treatment from what it might otherwise be, there is little doubt that modern medicine cures more than it kills. Secondary to prevention, contact with physicians leading to early detection, accurate diagnosis, and effective treatment is life-preserving behavior. Men, however, tend not to contact physicians when appropriate symptoms are present. In following their traditional sex role scripts, men have been relatively unwilling to interrupt their rigid work routines, ordinarily the primary source of family income, to present complaints to physicians. Traditional women's daily work schedules have been more flexible, however, although with higher labor force participation rates among women this gender difference may tend to diminish. The traditional housewife, for example, does not punch a time clock, and in her round of shopping and other community activities she creates a pattern into which a visit to a physician's office is a small disruption in normal routine.

DEPENDENT-PATIENT ROLE

In the dependent-patient role, the older person is legitimated in the sick role but is subject to a program of treatment. Older people in the dependent-patient role today are more likely than in the past to be under the care of health care professionals. Medicare and Medicaid have augmented this trend, which was set in motion earlier by such factors as increased professionalization and sophistication of medical practice.

Older people often hold the physician in awe, one might almost say reverence, and many are unlikely to question ineffective medical practice. As a result, older people are often unsophisticated consumers of medical care who can be subjected to expensive but needless tests, pain and suffering due to unnecessary procedures, and dosed with useless drugs with harmful side effects without voicing challenges to the physician. The rebellion against this abuse, when it occurs, can be a flight into chiropractic treatment—which in this case represents the older person's discovery of an alternative, and seemingly more holistic, approach to health. Other older people, however, may gain access to physicians who accept responsibility to provide, as a supplement or substitute for the usual ointments and pills, recommendations for nutritious diet, adequate rest, reduction of stress, and vigorous physical exercise in a prescribed regimen for curing ills, gaining positive health, and maintaining wellness.

There is evidence that the practice of medicine may be becoming more wholistic. For example, concern is rapidly growing for prevention, as distinct from treatment, and the public also seems to be growing increasingly aware of the importance of attending to the "wellness" half of the health continuum. Nevertheless, the present system of health care delivery as diagnosis and treatment of disease will not diminish, but can be expected to grow apace. There will, as a result, remain a substantial need for intermediaries, even interventions, to make older people aware of the positive potentials and benefits available under the medical model, to recruit older people into the bureaucratized diagnosis and treatment centers that characterize this approach to health, and to guide them through the bureaucratic and physical mazes that typify major medical facilities for treating seriously ill older people.

One problem that physicians may personally encounter in attaining the more holistic approach to health needed by older people is that of overcoming the borderline mental illness stigma that psychosomatic linkages have represented in the medical profession in the past. The psychophysical nexus relating stress and lifestyle to illness remains, in general, poorly documented and somewhat controversial.

With greater likelihood, to a greater extent, and for a longer period of time, older people require intermediate support between hospital and home such as may be provided through a convalescent home, long-term care, or nursing home. Among institutionalized older people, recovery has been thought to be more rapid if the institutionalization is perceived by the older person to be temporary (Engle, forthcoming). Even within their own homes, many older people are not sufficiently able to be fully independent with regard to shopping, meal preparation, transportation, or housekeeping. Other older people, who are able to meet these self-maintenance needs, lack companionship. For older men such needs are usually met by the spouse, but because most older women are widows, it is to other family members they must turn as interpersonal support resources. Although this may be functional, there is a inverse correlation between contact with children and life satisfaction among older people. Problems in accommodating role reversals may account for part of this, and adverse comparisons between self and children with regard to health, income, and prospects for the future may serve also as important explanations. Thus having physical needs met by others may bode ill for psychological well-being among older people, and this is particularly relevant to the situation of many older women.

RECOVERY AND REHABILITATION

In the recovery and rehabilitation phase, the treatment program is phased out, and the older person relinquishes the sick role.

The recovery and rehabilitation phase is likely to be extended for older people, requiring increased reliance on interpersonal support resources. Fully effective recovery and rehabilitation is less probable or slower among older people because their pathologies are more likely to be incurable chronic diseases. The symptoms are, however, generally treatable. But with sensory loss, lower levels of educational attainment, and/or interpersonal support resources, the treatment plan may be difficult or impossible for the older person to follow. Even in the case of curable diseases, the lower vigor and slower recovery of the older person are likely to be discouraging to the physician, placing greater dependence for support on the older person's informal support system.

SUMMARY

A considerable literature on the relationship between stress and health has been developed, and some research in this area has addressed the question of mediating effects of interpersonal support resources. Only part of this research is based on data on older people, but data on people of all ages have relevance to the situation of older people. In general, findings establish a positive but weak (in terms of variance explained) ameliorating effect that can be attributed to the support system. This lack of strong evidence may be due to technical research problems, theoretical-methodological problems, or both.

TECHNICAL PROBLEMS

Much research on the mediating influence of interpersonal support resources on the relationship between stress and health has been retrospective rather than prospective, and samples have often been rather small and specialized. The retrospective design does not permit the refinements of measurement and analysis that may be necessary to gain a better understanding of the role of interpersonal support resources in health. Further, theory has overwhelmed method and data in some research in this area to the extent that the size and character of the samples on which data are based are inadequate to support either the form of analysis or the elaborate overanalysis of data attempted by some investigators, leading to weak or inconclusive findings.

THEORETICAL-METHODOLOGICAL PROBLEMS

Research on concepts such as interpersonal support has usually found that perceived rather than objective support affects outcomes. This is probably an issue that lies behind the failure of some research to detect effects. Further development of measures to operationalize Cobb's (1976) conceptualization of social support may improve this situation.

In addition, some research has produced findings of an inverse relationship between interpersonal support and measures of well-being. This research has no doubt detected crisis victims who have mobilized support systems and determined that those with active support are also those who are worst off on a variety of mental and physical health measures. This research fails to account for certain fundamental facts of life. The basis of life is time, and continuity and change operate over time. With regard to continuity and change, older people with active functioning support systems are, of course, often those with the worst health. Thus simplistic and naive operationalizations and research designs cannot help but produce negative or even reverse findings about the actual temporal functioning of social support. In terms of time, what research needs to account for is that support systems are most clearly manifest (or, in unfortunate instances, lacking) in the aftermath of a life change crisis, and such crises are insults to morale and physical function. Only carefully controlled prospective research can measure the degree to which strength in the support system has an ameliorating effect on the outcome of the crises. To deal with this problem further, a distinction needs to be made between manifest and latent interpersonal social support resources, and prospective research needs to be utilized to investigate how latent resources are mobilized to become manifest, and with what effects on health.

PROSPECTS

Despite these problems, many if not most social gerontologists and practitioners in the field of aging are convinced of the importance of interpersonal social support resources to older people. The potential importance of knowledge in this area to the maintenance and improvement of the quality of life of older people is too great to ignore, and this concern may portend the emergence of a major research thrust in social gerontology relating theory, methods and findings in a combination with great potential for application in the lives of older people.

17

SOCIAL SUPPORT AND CHRONIC DISEASE: A Propositional Inventory

SIDNEY M. STAHL
Associate Professor, Sociology
Purdue University

MARILYN K. POTTS
Community/Health Services Research Component Director
Indiana University Multipurpose Arthritis Center

Sociology has contributed significantly to our understanding of disease and illness. The social support concept, in particular, has been widely used in studies of the etiology of chronic disease and the amelioration of its consequences. This chapter specifies the parameters of social support theory and applies them to studies of both the etiology of chronic disease and amelioration of the long-term consequences of such diseases.

This chapter has three objectives. First, the evolution of social support theory related to health, illness, and disease is reviewed. Second, research and theory in the emerging area of social support related to etiology and the care of the physically and mentally ill is reviewed, assessed, and synthesized. This second objective is critical in two regards: (a) it integrates now widely divergent perspectives on social support by proposing a typology of its sources, content, and scope; and (b) it advances social support theory beyond its implications for disease etiology by applying it to the care of the chronically ill, an area in which social support theory has not been systematically applied. This omission is probably due to the area's concern for the patient's well-being; the area of patient care is not known for its intensity of theoretical guidance.

Authors' Note: *This research was supported in part by a Multipurpose Arthritis Center grant from the U.S.P.H.S. (AM 20582).*

Finally, we suggest necessary future directions for social support theory's use in studies of chronic disease etiology and care.

This chapter attempts to reflect the diversity of the social support literature. As with any emerging body of research and theory, conceptual agreement is lacking. We attempt to synthesize this body of knowledge by suggesting propositions for future research and theoretical development of the social support thesis.

The prevalance of chronic diseases in the aging population makes the elaboration of this theoretical issue especially salient for social gerontology. For this reason special attention is focused, where possible, on the applicability of social support for the elderly.

THE EVOLUTION OF SOCIAL SUPPORT THEORY IN MEDICAL SOCIOLOGY

Social support theory in medical sociology was developed to explain the theoretically potent but empirically weak association between social strain and disease. Social support was viewed as a buffer between life crises (social strain) and the development of mental and physical illness. This section elaborates the background for social support theory's development as it evolved from the recognition that social stressors are implicated in disease etiology. This recognition in turn led to the development of stress theory and ultimately to a large body of literature on the effect of life events on illness and disease.

Social support theory itself arose from the promising and productive area of life events research. While social support theory in medical sociology was essentially an outgrowth of life events research, the two areas continue to develop simultaneously. A frontier in medical sociology, which is reflected in this chapter, is the integration of life events research with social support theory.

A caveat is appropriately mentioned here. The social support literature is but one emergent area from life events research. Other theoretical statements for explaining the impact of life events on health, such as those concerning coping styles and the perception of life events, have also developed and are reviewed. Through use of social support theory, such theoretical issues appear to be emerging into a more holistic understanding of the impact of social strain on disease etiology.

SOCIAL STRAIN

Hans Selye's (1956) work is a benchmark in the origins of contemporary theory and research on social stressors, being the first to elaborate clearly the relationship between environmental stimuli and physiological responses. Selye developed the concept of the General Adaptation Syndrome (G.A.S.), which postulates that external stimuli result in the arousal of the biologic system. That arousal is "stress." Failure to adapt to stress, or the general physiological mobilization needed to adapt, results in system exhaustion, or disease.

Selye made two critical points. First, external stimuli are nonspecific. That is, varied social-environmental stimuli can result in stress. This formulation produced research into the nature of social stressors or strain, and resulted ultimately, but not necessarily exclusively, in the development of social support theory. The literature is rich in the elaboration of social and psychological events as stress provoking. Second, Selye stated that it is inappropriate to look for a causal link between a specific social stressor and a specific disease outcome. In resisting a stressor, the entire physiological system is aroused (hence the *General* Adaptation Syndrome), such that resistance to a spectrum of diseases is adversely affected. The end result of stress is system exhaustion. Thus stress produces a medically specific disease without a necessary direct link from stressor to disease.

Selye's strain/stress/disease model resulted in a plethora of investigations of physical and mental diseases. Empirically fruitful models evolved positing that disease results from the inability of the organism to master external threats (Antonovsky, 1979). These are models of adaptation to events viewed as stress provoking by either the participant or the investigator. We turn our attention next to the stimuli considered to be sources of strain.

LIFE EVENTS

The popularity of the strain/stress/disease models focused research on stress provoking environmental and social stimuli. Many of the investigations were not theoretically informed and are found throughout a diverse literature. A number of investigators explored social environments hypothesized as stressful, such as Officer Candidate School (Kreuz et al., 1972). Some looked at psychological attitudes as precipitating physiological and mental breakdown (Schar et al., 1973), while Adler investigated the role of childhood socialization processes as productive of future illness (1974). Social or cultural change was explored as a stress-provoking milieu leading to disease (Aakster, 1974), as were specific crises (Berkman, 1969). Socioeconomic status (Cassel, 1966), occupation (House, 1974), and job loss (Kasl et al., 1968) have been implicated as illness-producing stressors.

The diversity of studies made apparent the need for a more parsimonious theoretical and methodological approach. This need was met by the now widely used Holmes and Rahe Social Readjustment Rating Scale (Holmes and Rahe, 1967). These authors noticed that illness incidence tended to follow a clustering of normal life events requiring change or social readjustment. They compiled a list of 43 life events, presented it to various groups, and found that no matter how significant the event (e.g., death of a spouse), or how mundane (e.g., Christmas), illness followed a clustering of life events. They theorized that life events requiring social readjustment trigger a psychophysiological reaction productive of illness not unlike the stress reaction in Selye's General Adaptation Syndrome.

There followed a wonderful deluge of research, all theoretically and methodologically informed by the original life events research and Social Readjustment Rating Scale, including studies on life events predicting psychiatric symptomatology (Ross and Mirowsky, 1979) and somatic health changes (Rahe et al., 1970). Life events scaling was validated on cross-cultural samples (Harmon et al., 1970). The methodology of assessing life events and social readjustment, and the psychophysics scaling theory used were also investigated (Hough et al., 1976; Ross and Mirowsky, 1979).

Though widely used, life events theory was not without conceptual and methodological problems. Did illness result from the degree of change, from the clustering of life events, or from the life area in which change occurred (Ruch, 1977)? Were independent and dependent variables confounded? That is, do life events precede or result from illness (Rahe et al., 1970)? For example, can a specific life event (theoretically an independent variable) also be a dependent variable contingent on other life events? Or, perhaps more seriously, are certain life events caused by illness, the dependent variable (Thoits, 1981)? For example, divorce may be caused by some psychological disorder, thus reversing the theoretically dictated causal relationship. The need for longitudinal studies was evident. Others raised questions about the valence of the life event. Dohrenwend (1973) found that change, either positive or negative, decreases mental health status, while Ross and Mirowsky (1979) found only negatively valenced life events predictive of mental distress.

Despite these detractions, a relationship was demonstrated repeatedly between the occurrence of life events and the onset of physical or psychiatric symptomatology. Though consistent, the results were trivial. The amount of variance in illness onset explained by life events seldom exceeded five or six percent (Rabkin and Struening, 1976; Tausig, 1982). As Rabkin and Struening argue, research seldom went beyond the linear relationship between life events and illness onset to look at mediating variables (1976). Although life events are predictive of illness, not all who experience events become ill. It became necessary to examine intervening mechanisms that either buffered or exacerbated the impact of life events.

Folkman and Lazarus (1980) looked at coping styles, that is, efforts to master, tolerate, or reduce the effect of life events. Kanner and his colleagues (1981) developed a "daily hassles" concept used to mediate between life events and illness; in the case of psychological symptomatology, "hassles" replaced life events.

Another possible mediating factor is the individual's perception of life events as problematic for social readjustment (Rabkin and Struening, 1976). Although theoretical models for the mediating role of perception for physical (Stahl et al., 1975) and mental illness (Chan, 1977) were developed, recent evidence indicates that perception may be of minimal consequence in predicting illness onset (Tausig, 1982).

Social support research also emerged from the life events concept's inability to explain larger proportions of variance in illness development. The central social support thesis is that illness results from a clustering of life events if the individual lacks adequate social support mechanisms to buffer the effect of this stressor. Those experiencing life events but no subsequent illness are "protected" from their impact by being embedded in a social support system. Since the late 1970s, this thesis has generated prodigious amounts of research in medical sociology, social epidemiology, and social psychology. We now turn to a review of theory, findings, and propositions of social support theory.

SOCIAL SUPPORT: A REVIEW OF THEORY AND RESEARCH

The social support concept is not new to sociology. Its articulation as a series of propositions inviting systematic research in the area of medical sociology and gerontology is, however, a development of the last decade. Durkeim's (1951) essential argument in *Suicide* is that social support provided by the social structure predisposes toward, or buffers the individual from, suicide. The central tenets of sociology can be interpreted in this manner. Group membership provides social support mitigating against the impact of the social and/or physical environment. One of the functions of human social organization is to provide such a buffering effect (Merton, 1957).

This section suggests available types of social support and reviews relevant research and theory regarding social support to explain illness etiology. Additionally, it specifies the theoretical groundwork for using social support as ameliorative of the consequences of chronic illness.

THE NATURE OF SOCIAL SUPPORT

Most literature defines social support by its consequences. That is, social support leads to outcomes such as good health or enhanced probabilities of buffering noxious social stressors. Other literature defines the concept by its characteristics, such as the size of the supporting network or the characteristics of the support provided.

We view social support as a process emanating from the focal individual's location in social networks. Our approach is inherently social psychological in its orientation in that we locate the individual within a series of potentially interlocking networks and examine the meaning of that location for the individual. To understand this symbolic meaning, it is necessary to look at the content and sources of the support provided, and at the interrelatedness, or scope, of these sources. Thoit's (1981) use of the social support concept most adequately meets these criteria. Social support exists and is effective when the social needs of the individual are met.

Social networks provide structure for linkages between individuals and groups. These interactive linkages are used to understand the nature and utility of social support. Thus networks provide the basis for allowing the individual to maintain a social identity through interaction. These identities are hierarchically organized, based on the salience of the given identity for a particular social situation. Through the entanglement of roles (later defined as multiplexity), social support is shaped by the social networks within which an individual is located (Stryker and Serpe, 1982). Thus social support is the extent to which the individual's needs are met through interaction with situation-specific significant others available to meet psychosocial and tangible needs.

The above suggests that neither networks nor the social support provided is static. Identities and their saliences remain in flux. This conceptualization of networks and roles is maintained throughout the following discussion. To understand the social support provided by internal network linkages, we turn to its characteristics.

SOURCES OF SOCIAL SUPPORT

A description of social support sources provides a taxonomy of network components potentially available to the individual. Social support systems are not automatically and immediately activated following the intrusion of some life event. Instead, specific sources of support are elicited in response to particular problems (LaRocco et al., 1980). This thesis is consistent with Stryker and Serpe's (1982) assertion that roles or identities are arranged hierarchically.

In general, sources of social support can be related either to primary or secondary identities. That is, threatened identities associated with primary roles are usually supported by groups such as family or kin, whereas needs associated with more distant means/ends, or secondary identities, are met by groups such as neighbors and occupational groups.

Primary Relationships as
Sources of Social Support

The nuclear family provides the most frequently cited primary relationships related to social support and health. Dean and Lin (1977) speculate that the family moderates the impact of life events by meeting the individual's expressive needs. Poorer mental health is found among the unmarried than among the married (Myers et al., 1975).

In the area of somatic disease, the family serves as an effective social support system during post myocardial infarction careers (Finlayson, 1976). Perceived family support is also related positively to measures of life satisfaction, self-esteem, and participation in social and recreational activities among burn patients (Davidson et al., 1981). Among stroke rehabilitation patients, family support, in the form of predictive empathy, is associated with more rapid progress (Robertson and Suinn, 1968). Furthermore, family cohesion, family expressiveness, spouse support, and the presence of a confidant are positively associated with morale among hemodialysis patients (Diamond, 1979). For the elderly, the family constitutes a critical source of support, resulting in lower general mortality (Blazer, 1982) and reduced need for institutionalization (Lindsey and Hughes, 1981).

Family support appears to contribute to the patient's motivation and/or ability to adhere to medical regimens. In a review of studies, Haynes (1976) notes that family influence is considerable, with "supportive" families being associated with greater compliance. Noncompliance and medication errors are associated with old age, perhaps because the elderly often experience problems of forgetfulness or self-neglect and tend to be treated with multiple medications for more than one condition. Thus the provision of social support is especially relevant for this group.

The family as a source of support for arthritis patients is a significant factor in compliance with a hand splint regimen (Oakes et al., 1970). Similarly, Ferguson and Bole (1979) found that the lack of family support is significant among rheumatoid arthritis patients who believe in the efficacy of the treatment regimen but cannot comply because of family interference.

Stahl et al. (1984) found that the role of a family member facilitates maintaining individuals on antihypertensive therapy. Adherence to a supervised physical activity program for men at risk of coronary heart disease is enhanced by support from participants' wives (Heinzelmann and Bagley, 1970).

Although most evidence suggests that family relationships have a beneficial impact on the chronically ill, such relationships may have adverse consequences. For example, Lewis (1966) found that unemployed men following congestive heart failure had been overprotected by their families. Similarly, perceived preferential treatment by family members has been shown to be significantly associated with the extent of disability (Hyman, 1971).

Hammer (1983) maintains that the family constitutes a "core" primary network, but that extended networks may provide an extension of primary support. Litwak and Szelenyi (1969) note that in a technological society, geographic proximity is not a prerequisite for support by primary groups. Perhaps propinquity at a distance is operative in social support systems involving extended kin.

*Secondary Relationships as
Sources of Social Support*

Studies dealing with the buffering effects of secondary relationships generally focus on the maintenance of lifestyles among the chronically ill. Use of a counselor provided through the care delivery system is effective in expediting return to work following myocardial infarction (Garrity, 1973). Croog and his colleagues (1972) demonstrate that neighbors and the care delivery system are complements to, but not supplements for, kin in providing support following a first myocardial infarction. Davidson et al. (1981) note that family support is associated more strongly with positive psychosocial outcomes than is friend support, which in turn is more effective than peer support.

In addition to lay support systems, health care professionals are important sources of support. Thus a caring, supportive relationship between physician and patient is significantly associated with compliance in arthritis (Geertsen et al., 1973). Similarly, Caplan et al. (1976) find that physician support is positively correlated with motivation to adhere to a hypertension regimen. In a study of patients with a variety of chronic illnesses, DiMatteo and Hays (1981) note that physicians' behaviors, such as their accessibility when needed and their ability to make patients feel "cared about" and "listened to" are important predictors of patients' willingness to return for care.

Peer support groups for people sharing medical problems have become increasingly popular. Based on descriptive, largely anecdotal data, group participation is reported to be beneficial for individuals with a variety of chronic illnesses. Pavlou et al. (1978) note an increase in sociability outside the group, and improved relations between staff, family, and patients after a series of discussion meetings for patients with multiple sclerosis. Similarly, for rheumatoid arthritis patients, Udelman and Udelman (1977) observe that brief group therapy leads to a qualitative improvement in mood, better adaptation to hospitalization, and improved communication with family members. Improved clinic attendance and treatment compliance by people with arthritis results from group participation (Schwartz et al., 1978). Wyka et al. (1980) note that participants in group classes for hypertensive patients adopt an exercise program and experience reduced blood pressure.

In addition, to the above descriptive accounts, several controlled studies demonstrate that groups result in increased knowledge about the disease and its treatment, enhanced self-concept, and improved clinical outcomes. Rheumatoid arthritis patients in group counseling show improved self-concept and more factual knowledge of their disease (Kaplan and Kozin, 1981). Among newly diagnosed cancer patients, group counseling results in significant improvement in self-concept (Ferlic et al., 1979). Rahe and Lind (1971) find that post myocardial infarction patients receiving group therapy demonstrate significantly greater knowledge of their disease and of rehabilitation principles that do those in a control group. More important, the treatment group experienced significantly fewer severe coronary heart disease events, such as rehospitalization, coronary bypass surgery, reinfarction, and death. Finally, Lorig et al. (1981), in a randomized, controlled study of groups of osteoarthritis patients, find that participation results in increased disease knowledge and physical activity, improved compliance with exercise programs, decreased pain, and reduced visits to physicians.

In contrast to the above findings, some studies find inconsequential benefits to group participation. Shearn and Fireman (1983) find that mutual support groups for patients with rheumatoid arthritis produce no improvement in depression level, pain, or disability. Although a controlled group study of patients with rheumatoid arthritis shows that participation results in increased knowledge about the disease, little effect is noted on the patients' self-perceived ability to cope with arthritis, or on compliance with prescribed treatments (Potts and Brandt, 1983).

Combined Sources of Social Support

Social support is most germane when produced by a combination of sources. The greater the integration into a support system, the more effective the social support (Myers et al., 1975). This argument is made also by Stryker and Serpe (1982) and will be elaborated later in the section on the scope of the support system.

Several studies suggest that the most effective social support is provided by networks within which the individual plays multiple roles and thus has many potential sources (Mitchell and Trickett, 1980). For example, Evans and Northwood (1979) note that neighborhood networks, consisting primarily of family and friends, are used for everyday social activities and occasional emergencies. Family sources are used by the elderly for financial and medical help. Notably, the elderly are unable to integrate easily into neighborhood networks. This may explain the findings of a prospective study by Ferraro (1982) who notes a decrement in health among the elderly who relocated. In addition, movers were more likely than nonmovers to be institutionalized, and to experience decreased ability to perform self-care activities.

The disease care delivery system in combination with family support is predictive of rehabilitative success (LaRocco et al., 1980), while work, family, and other social relationships buffer the effect of life events on mental health (Jenkins et al., 1981). In a nine-year follow-up study, Berkman and Syme (1979) demonstrate that the social ties of informal and formal groups, marriage, and church attendance buffer mortality, while DiMatteo and Hays (1981) suggest that social support during serious illness is most effective when it is produced by a combination of primary groups (friends and family) and secondary groups (peer groups and helping professionals).

These studies imply that social support, whether as a buffer against illness or as an ameliorative in disease recovery or care, comes from a variety of sources. While theoretically inelegant and rather straightforward, a review of support sources is a necessary first step toward understanding the nature of social support. Sources of support must be isomorphic with the individual's social roles. Thus those identities having salience for the individual will dictate the most likely and effective sources of support.

CONTENT OF SOCIAL SUPPORT

Just as the sources of social support are multidimensional, so too is the content of support. The focal individual, significant others, and groups within networks each possess potentially unique functions. Therefore, the individual's attachments to specific sources within a network dictate the content of the support provided. Thus source and content, and scope (to be discussed later), are interactive components of social support. This section addresses the nature or content of social support.

The content of social support can be located on a continuum ranging from socioemotional to instrumental. This postulate allows us to view the two end points as not mutually exclusive.

Socioemotional Content

For social support to be effective, the network must be stable over time (Thoits, 1982). During periods of crises the network's stability may be altered, thus confounding its ability to serve an intervening function. Kaplan et al. (1977) suggest that support is maintained during network fluctuation to the extent that the recipient's self-esteem remains intact. Self-esteem, which can be maintained by appropriate sources within networks, is thus an important content area for effective social support. Clearly, an adequate explication of social support requires a highly interactive model.

The above approach suggests that social support can be internal and/or external to the individual. Both self-esteem and the individual's coping style are relevant to the efficacy of social support. Folkman and Lazarus (1980: 223) define coping as "the cognitive and behavioral efforts made to master, tolerate, or reduce . . . demands and conflicts" imposed on the individual. Coping is therefore part of the socioemotional content of social support systems. Because the nature of the event requiring coping dictates either a problem-focused or emotion-focused coping style, knowledge of the source of support is critical in understanding the coping process. For example, secondary groups typically provide only problem-focused coping resources.

The need for socioemotional support to maintain a sense of self is well documented (Fuller and Larson, 1980; Jenkins et al., 1981; Thoits, 1983). The provision of intimacy and an outlet for expressive needs (Dean and Lin, 1977) bolsters the individual's ability to mediate crises and maintain preexisting roles and behaviors. The evidence that emotional support mediates between life events and subsequent illness for the elderly is conflicting (Fuller and Larson, 1980). However, the need for socioemotional support to maintain self-esteem and facilitate coping is a central tenet of social support theory. Primary group relationships seem best suited to meet socioemotional needs such as self esteem.

Instrumental Content

The instrumental content of social support consists of those tangible and informational items required to meet needs. It consists also of the help needed to mobilize the individual's own resources (Lindsey and Hughes, 1981). The provision of physical or tangible help such as services, goods, or financial aid (Croog et al., 1972) constitutes instrumental support by meeting the individual's needs.

Similarly, we view information as instrumental content (Cobb, 1976). Information can be relevant to socioemotional needs, such as reassurance that support is available, or addressed toward instrumental functions, such as suggestions regarding the use of services. Informal networks have helped people locate sources of assistance more effectively than formal social agencies (Evans and Northwood, 1979). Problem-focused feedback (Carveth and Gottlieb, 1979) is information directed toward crisis intervention, and is therefore considered social support.

Several studies show that explicit information transfer by health care providers is an important factor in predicting medical compliance (Svarstad, 1976; Hulka et al., 1976). However, knowledge of the regimen alone, without maintenance of a therapeutic relationship, is not sufficiently motivating, as indicated by the lack of a consistent association between knowledge and compliance. Notably, McKenney et al. (1973) find that when pharmacy counseling services are terminated, compliance decreases to its former level.

The perceived availability of social support is positively associated with its efficacy. Thus provision of support without the recipient's cognizance is less effective than support of which the individual is aware (Stahl et al., 1975; Chan, 1977). This is especially true with respect to socioemotional content (Blazer, 1982). The perception that other's behaviors are directed toward the target individual's socioemotional well-being provides the greatest benefit, although tangible support is also critical (Caplan, 1979).

In summary, research and theory indicate that, except for the provision of certain instrumental content by the care delivery system, primary groups are the most effective providers of social support. However, the identity salience of a given role relevant to a crisis will dictate the importance of a specific support source. Individuals may bring coping strategies appropriate to a role behavior with them into crisis situations, but these strategies are often enhanced by the content of a supportive behavior. While instrumental needs can be met by primary or secondary groups, the critical area of socioemotional support is most effectively provided by primary group members. In addition, the extent to which the individual perceives socioemotional and instrumental support as available will dictate the efficacy of that support.

SCOPE OF SOCIAL SUPPORT

The conceptual issue for this third dimension of social support is the focal person's social integration. The greater the social isolation, the more severe the impact of life events and the greater the probability of illness. To understand the impact of the scope of linkages within the support system, we locate the individual on a continuum ranging from isolated to integrated (Thoits, 1983). The more modest the scope of these linkages, the more isolated the individual (Croog et al., 1972). The scope concept is based on the theoretical perspective of identity salience and commitment. The greater the involvement of others in the system, the greater the individual's commitment to a system relevant identity. In a given situation, the salience of an identity dictates the individual's role behaviors, thus making various components of the social support system more (or less) relevant.

When integrated with source and content, scope provides closure to social support theory as an explication of the relationship between life events and illness or disease etiology. In addition, these three social support components are critical for understanding the system's ability to ameliorate the impact of chronic disease. Diverse names for scope properties are found in the literature. The nomenclature used most frequently will be presented here.

Social support systems possess properties attributable to both the structure of the system and to the linkages within the system. It is necessary to discuss each category separately.

Scope of the
Social Support System's Structure

Two properties attributable to the support system are relevant: its size and density. *Size* refers to the number of system linkages that are tied directly to the focal person and are therefore available to provide social support content. Using sociometric analyses, studies suggest that the greater the number of potentially supportive dyadic relationships, the better the individual's mental health (Dean and Lin, 1977) and the less difficult the coping process during bereavement (Walker et al., 1977).

While network size refers to potential dyadic relationships, *network density* is the number of actual per potential network linkages. Network density, referred to as "anchorage" by Kaplan et al. (1977), provides an estimate of network properties available for social support. Network density is used productively in Walker et al.'s (1977) bereavement research. The relevant hypothesis is that the greater the network density, the more effective the social support. As network density increases, the probability of the availability of support, for whatever content the network represents, also increases.

*Scope of the
Social Support System's Linkages*

Finally, we turn to the social support system's linkages. These linkages, when accumulated, constitute the system's fabric. They represent forms of content provided by a variety of sources. Because linkages define network properties, they have the characteristic of scope.

The most often cited linkage property is the *frequency* of contact between the focal person and other network members. Frequency is typically delimited by a time period, usually from the advent to the solution of a crisis. Frequency is an indicator of the person's integration into a network. The relevant hypothesis is that those with more frequent contacts have better health and experience greater "health protectiveness" (Kaplan et al., 1977). This hypothesis has been demonstrated in several studies. Those with frequent social contacts experience the following: lower mortality (Berkman and Syme, 1979; Blazer, 1982); more rapid help-seeking (McKinlay, 1973); and better mental health (Dean and Lin, 1977; Carveth and Gottlieb, 1979). Thus the greater the frequency of contact, the greater the linkages' buffering effect between life events and subsequent ill health.

This same hypothesis can be cast in terms of identity theory. The more others are involved in an individual's identity, the greater the individual's commitment to that identity. Therefore, the more valued an identity, the greater the buffering and ameliorative effect of social support, given high frequency of contact with those supporting the identity. This hypothesis is related to the next scope concept: *valence*. The greater the positive affective importance of others involved in the network's linkages, the more effective the social support. In this way the social worth of the focal person's identity is enhanced (Thoits, 1983).

A number of studies address valence both theoretically (Carveth and Gottlieb, 1979; Jenkins et al., 1981) and empirically (Berkman and Syme, 1979). Each indicates that a positive valence linkage is more supportive than the frequency of support provided. Although this conclusion may be too simplistic, given the interactive nature of the scope, content, and sources of social support, the valence of a supportive individual is clearly important; time and energy are invested in maintaining network linkages based on affect.

Related to valence is the *intensity* or strength of network linkages. It is hypothesized that the perception of linkage intensity is related directly to the efficacy of social support. Several studies indicate that intensity has a positive health protective effect (Kaplan et al., 1977; Walker et al., 1977).

Another property of the scope of linkages is the *dispersion* of network members. Dispersion is measured typically by the ease with which network members can be contacted. Dispersion is frequently equated with the proximity of linked individuals; however, this is not always a useful formulation. While Kaplan et al. (1977) argue that contact with network members must be direct and immediate, Hammer (1983) faults social support research for its inattention to the core (immediate) network's location in an extended context. Most research, however, finds that the more "reachable" (Dean and Lin, 1977) or proximate the individuals forming network linkages, the greater the supportive effect (McKinlay, 1973; Walker et al., 1977).

An intriguing and useful property of scope is the *multiplexity* concept. This concept is central to both social network and identity theory, but has received little attention in the social support literature. Multiplexity refers to the number of roles served by or represented in the linkage between the focal person and those providing social support. Thoits (1983) refers to multiplexity as identity accumulation. The focal individual is embedded in a number of role relationships, each of which can provide social support. The relevant hypothesis is that the greater the multiplexity, the more effective the support. Both Thoits (1983) and Myers et al. (1975) find an inverse relationship between multiple role identities and psychological distress.

The multiplexity property further supports the isolation thesis discussed earlier. The greater the multiplexity of network linkages, the less isolated the network members. Networks characterized by multiplex linkages assure a higher degree of identity accumulation and more extensive role embeddedness. Therefore, the lower the isolation, the greater the probability of the availability of social support.

Relationship density is related to the multiplexity concept. Relationship density refers to the number of content areas served by a given linkage. The associated hypothesis is that social support is more available and more effective if served by a linkage characterized by high relationship density. If a linkage serves both socioemotional and instrumental needs, it is more effective in its buffering effect on illness than if it serves either alone. Finlayson (1976) demonstrates this hypothesis in men's post myocardial infarction careers. Relationship density is also related to multiplexity; the more role-embedded the individual, the greater the probability that a linkage serves multiple content areas. For example, the role of father serves both socioemotional as well as instrumental content areas and therefore has high relationship density. In addition, the role occupant is most likely also a husband, therefore making the father/husband role linkage one characterized by multiplexity. Separating the potentially interactive effects of multiplexity and relationship density remains a significant issue.

The *reciprocity* of a linkage is determined by the ratio of given to received social support. Kaplan et al. (1977) suggest that linkages characterized by reciprocity are the most health protective. The hypothesis is that the greater the proportion of reciprocal linkages, the better the individual's health. From an exchange theory perspective, reciprocal relationships can draw on debts and accumulated good will capital for the provision of social support.

Several questions arise from the reciprocity hypothesis. Does the content of the reciprocal linkage remain constant in a network characterized by high relationship density? That is, must socioemotional support be repaid in kind? Another intriguing question involves the use of the disease care delivery system and patient groups for the provision of social support. To maximize reciprocity, all parties in the linkage (the patient, the system, or the group) must be able to initiate interaction. However, the disease care delivery system seldom initiates interaction; the patient must initiate the request. Thus the relationship lacks reciprocity. Is the perceived efficacy of that support linkage therefore reduced? The lack of reciprocity in such a system may explain its frequent failure, and suggests an avenue for future research.

The *stability* of a linkage is a property of the social support system's scope. The longer the linkage (or system) has existed, that is, the greater its stability, the more health protective it is. McKinley (1973) suggests that the stability thesis is appropriate only for a friendship linkage. However, the hypothesis is testable using either primary or secondary sources, and for any content area.

A related hypothesis is that a linkage characterized by consistent interaction has a greater health protective value. However, a life event crisis itself has an impact on interaction that can change the system in subtle ways, insofar as coping with crisis is not an everyday occurrence. Therefore, mobilization of social support may destabilize that system in a measurable manner. On the other hand, multiplexity helps avoid chaos at the advent of a crisis. The more multiplex the system's linkages, the less consequential the crisis impact and therefore the more stable the system.

Finally, an ignored property of the scope of linkages is the *homogeneity* or commonality of social attributes among those sharing linkages. The greater its homogeneity, the more health protective the system. Walker et al. (1977) support this hypothesis with respect to the crisis of bereavement. The homogeneity property touches on the larger category of the source of social support. Typically, support sources share attributes with those for whom support is provided, for example, family members. However, sources may vary in their homogeneity, thus providing different content for varying crisis situations.

SUMMARY AND DIRECTIONS FOR FUTURE RESEARCH

Social support theory has significant potential for understanding psychological and somatic disease etiology, and for facilitating the processes of long-term care for chronic disease patients. For that purpose, the preceding synthesis of social support theory and research has presented a diverse range of propositions.

A central theme is the role of identity salience in dictating sources of social support productive of ameliorative processes. Because identity saliences remain in flux, the source, scope, and content of social support varies qualitatively and quantitatively to meet differing situations. The more social support is isomorphic with the individual's social roles, the more effective it will be.

Another theme is the extent to which instrumental and socioemotional needs can be met by primary and secondary groups. If social support is most effectively provided by a combination of sources meeting a variety of needs, then the instrumental function of the disease care delivery system will inadequately fulfill the care, as opposed to cure, component necessary in chronic disease management. Furthermore, if instrumental content is provided in an emotionally supportive context, it will be more effective than if provided in a context devoid of emotional support.

Finally, the greater the extent of social isolation, the greater the adverse impact of chronic disease. Therefore, the more role embedded the patient in a social support system, the greater his or her ability to cope successfully with chronic disease.

The few propositions presented here are only suggestive of many research questions derived from an integration of the source, content, and scope of social support. Of recent developments in social gerontology and medical sociology, the evolution of social support theory from stress-strain-disease research appears most promising. Any effective exploration of social support functions and mechanisms must address the interaction of source, content, and scope of socially supportive relationships.

18

CHRONIC ILLNESS AND CARE PROVISION: A Study of Alzheimer's Disease

RACHEL FILINSON
Assistant Professor, Sociology
Purdue University

To conceptualize the elderly as a group with common problems, it is almost inevitable that one consider their health status and health care. In this chapter, Alzheimer's disease, one of the most prevalent chronic diseases of the older population, is examined using data collected primarily through observational fieldwork. The purposes are to present empirical evidence from research conducted on Alzheimer's disease and to use the evidence heuristically to illustrate certain features of chronic disease as they affect the approach to and care for the chronically ill elderly. In the first section, general characteristics of chronic illness and their implications for care provision will be outlined. This will be followed by a description of Alzheimer's disease and the relevance of the chronic disease framework for an analysis of the research findings. The methods used to gather data will then be briefly summarized. The remainder of the chapter will be devoted to a presentation of data organized to exemplify and clarify the themes touched upon in the preliminary discussion of chronic illness among the elderly.

CHRONIC ILLNESS: A FRAMEWORK

It has been argued that as chronic illness becomes a major health problem, the medical and social provisions that evolved earlier to deal with a different constellation of health problems, primarily episodic, acute, and infectious diseases, become increasingly inappropriate (Illsley, 1981: 327). The literature on chronic illness has highlighted the characteristics of long-term illness that challenge existing models of health care delivery and allocation of responsibilities between family, professionals, and the state. These characteristics have led to an incongruity between the needs of the chronically ill and current forms of care provision.

First, chronic illnesses, because they are resistant to curative treatment, require a shift from an emphasis on cure of the disease to care of the afflicted individual outside the medical setting. Ameliorative interventions must consequently stress the availability of social support resources and the maximizing of individual coping strategies rather than the utilization of technical, medical expertise. As Strauss (1979: 98) has pointed out, "Medicine may contribute, but it is secondary to 'carrying on.'" Because the role of medicine recedes in the management of chronic illness (see Ebert, 1977), treatment is predicated less on the theoretical knowledge of the etiology of disease and more on the practical knowledge of symptoms and their control (Glazier, 1973: 14). A categorical approach, which characterized the medical model, is replaced by a more individualized one. There is a tendency for the experience of the disease and the provision of care to be removed from the public arena and privatized, as the patient and his or her social support network construct their own idiosyncratic modes of dealing with the disease.

A second differentiating feature of chronic illness is that the objectives of care are custodial rather than rehabilitative in nature. Accordingly, there is conflict with the priority given in medicine to rehabilitation. Indeed, many of the services needed by the chronically ill person, particularly personal care services (e.g., bathing or dressing) may be of such low status that they fall outside the domain of the mainstream health professions. When custodial care needs have been met by professionals, there has been consistent criticism that such care fosters dependence in the chronically ill person instead of assisting in retaining independent functioning.[1] The care provided is, in a sense, neither rehabilitative nor maintenance because it may increase debility and handicap of the chronically ill recipient.

A corollary of the custodial component of care is that the needs of the chronically ill are multiple and the social and health dimensions are inseparable (Hickey, 1980). Yet, there is typically no single profession or service organization geared to provide the array of services needed (Birenbaum, 1981). Because of the comprehensiveness of needs, there is risk of overlap of services, overload of services, and fragmentation of care (Katz et al., 1976). Family members must often act as mediators in accessing scarce resources for the chronically ill person and fill the gaps left by the patchwork of services.

A third distinctive characteristic of chronic illness concerns the financial aspects. Chronic diseases by virtue of their duration are expensive, yet current funding systems of health and social care have not been shaped to cover the costs of maintenance care. Financial support for services aimed at assisting the chronically ill to remain in the community have only recently come into vogue. Furthermore, it has been claimed that when health dollars have been spent on maintenance care within institutions, such care has frequently been unnecessary (Morris, 1977: 25; Browne and Olson, 1983: 10). In effect, financial resources are not being channeled to those individuals requiring custodial care while being inappropriately deployed to individuals who could have remained independent in the community.

The significance of these characteristics of chronic illness is that long-term assistance, by default, becomes largely the responsibility of the family and other informal agents. The inability of the medical profession to offer an effective therapy, the difficulties in locating and coordinating high quality professional services, and the exorbitant and/or uncompensated costs of chronic disease result in the main part of the burden being shouldered by family members. Evidence of the burden of care assumed by family members has provided strong support for the debunking of the myth that families fail in their obligations to family members. At the same time, the devastation of family members that has been documented and the increasing dimensions of the problem of chronic illness have called into question the continued viability of this scheme of community care (Lowenthal and Berkman, 1967). The family's ability to provide support in the future may be more and more dependent on their use of outside (state and professional) resources to supplement the care they provide.

The management of long-term care for the chronically ill also raises complex ethical questions. How actively should the patient and his or her supporters attempt to maintain optimal functioning and independence? At what point do the costs of prolonging the life of a chronic disease sufferer outweigh the benefits? Who is responsible for making and arbitrating the decisions? To what extent is intervention by professionals permissible? Are professionals obliged to release and explain all pertinent information to enable clients to make responsible decisions? Is the client the patient, the patient's family, or both? If the afflicted individual is deemed mentally incompetent, how should this limit his or her involvement in health care decisions? The role of health care professionals, family, and patient in determining management of long-term care is ambiguous. Moreover, the effectiveness of decision making can be hindered by the fragmented quality of typifying relationships between family, multiple service providers, and patient (Wetle, 1983).

The conditions of chronic illness outlined above are particularly relevant when applied to the aged. Not only does chronic illness disproportionately affect the elderly (Busse and Pfeiffer, 1973: 95), but the chronically ill share many common features with the elderly. As Zuckerman (1979: 159) has stated, "Combined with aging, chronic illness serves as a 'dumping ground' for a miscellany of unspecified conditions." In the same vein, Illsley (1981) has combined the elderly and the chronically ill into the category of dependency groups because of their similarities. Like the chronically ill, the needs of the older adult are not generalizable and the professions that can assist the elderly constitute a sprawling network (Estes, 1979). The vast number of agencies and individuals with a potential vested interest in promoting the cause of the elderly may paradoxically undermine the cohesiveness of the base of support (Pratt, 1983; Vinyard, 1983).

In addition, the type of assistance needed by the elderly is often outside the remit of the conventional health and social services. As Maddox (1978) has argued, the emphasis on specialization of professionals and organizations and the dominance of medical centers has resulted in a mismatch of the needs of the aging population and the types of care offered. Hence it can be surmised that age does not mitigate the problems of care provision encountered by the chronically ill person; instead, the unwieldy structure that has arisen to serve the elderly is likely to reinforce problems.

Changes in the age structure are expected to exacerbate the disparity between the needs of the chronically ill elderly and the present organization of health and social care. The population of the elderly and the very old elderly has enlarged, thereby increasing the population most vulnerable to chronic illness. The increase in longevity may be due in part to improved survival rates of the chronically ill. While the proportion of elderly and chronically ill elderly has grown, the responsibility of care has been placed on a diminishing number of individuals due to smaller family size, family disruption, and female employment (Treas, 1981). The impact of the altered demographic structure has been a cause for concern for the well-being of "normal" elderly (or instance with respect to the financing of social security). The effects on the chronically ill elderly are likely to be even more acute.

ALZHEIMER'S DISEASE

Alzheimer's disease represents par excellence a chronic disease of growing dimensions due to the "graying" of the population. It is a degenerative, age-penetrated, organic brain disease, the incidence of which increases with increasing age. The disease is characterized by impaired memory, orientation, judgment, and abstract reasoning. At the onset, impairment in cognitive function may go unnoticed. As the disease progresses, however, it leads to degeneration of other systems besides the neurological system so that the afflicted individual may lose the ability to communicate or to perform simple motor tasks. The disease may also be accompanied by distortion of the sufferer's personality.

Despite the obvious destruction to mind and body caused by Alzheimer's disease, it has only been in recent years that the prevalence of the disease has been recognized. The growing awareness is partially attributable to the larger proportion of individuals afflicted with the disease as a result of the lengthening life span. The discovery of Alzheimer's disease must also be associated with changing terminology and an altered perspective on aging. Alzheimer's disease used to refer to an organic brain syndrome occurring before the age of 65, identified clinically by chronic memory failure and pathologically by neurofibrillary plaques and tangles. In older adults, the same clinical or pathological presentation was assumed to be normal aging and was referred to as senility or was given the general descriptive labels of dementia or organic brain syndrome (these labels refer to a cluster of symptoms, not to a specific disease). Alzheimer's disease and senility are now considered to be the same disease, whether the symptoms occur before or after age 65. With the inclusion of those over the age of 65 into the category, Alzheimer's disease has been transformed from a rare disorder into the "disease of the century."

Alzheimer's disease is presently incurable and little can be done to abate the symptoms. The state of the diagnostic art further testifies to the limitations of medical knowledge with respect to Alzheimer's disease. Clinical diagnoses are tentative because no diagnosis can be confirmed until postmortem examination. Diagnosis is presumptive and accomplished by excluding all other diseases that present clinically similar symptoms. Even a pathological examination may be subject to dispute because of the ambiguous interface between aging and chronic memory failure. The differentiation between normal aging and pathological aging is unclear because the physiological changes distinctive of dementing diseases (neurofibrillary tangles and senile plaques) are also associated with normal aging. Furthermore, these physiological changes, which are the ultimate test confirming the presence of the disease, have been shown not to correspond with changes in cognitive function and behavior (see Gurland, 1981). In effect, an individual can have signs of Alzheimer's disease according to a pathological examination of the brain though not manifest the disease; alternatively, symptoms of dementia may be present although pathological findings fail to reveal abnormalities in brain cells.

Because of the incurability, irreversibility, and diagnostic elusiveness of Alzheimer's disease, the role of medical professionals in the management of the disease tends to be reduced while the role of the family is expanded. Management of the disease consists of comprehensive custodial care aimed at assisting the impaired individual in carrying out the activities of daily living. The form assistance will take varies considerably, depending on the stage of the disease and type of impairment. Loss of memory can affect an individual in myriad, unique ways, from forgetting how to control one's bowels, even if motor function remains, to hostility to the family member who is no longer recognized. The capacity of the family to provide total care will reflect their ability to cope with the particular expression of the disease by their relative.

A variety of professional organizations, including local area councils on aging, the Visiting Nurses Association, day care centers, Meals on Wheels, social work departments, and volunteer organizations may be suitable to deliver a part of the extensive maintenance care needed for the person impaired with Alzheimer's disease, although none is specifically geared to do so. However, because the effects of the disease on different individuals are so varied, and the symptoms to be controlled change substantially over the course of the disease, service needs are not easily identifiable or predictable. In addition, the system of care, as it will be elaborated later, is poorly adapted to target and coordinate services in an integrated fashion to meet the individualized needs of an Alzheimer's disease sufferer.

Financial assistance for care of the Alzheimer's victim is limited. Institutional care will not be paid for by Medicare or by many insurance companies unless the patient concurrently has another disease that is rehabilitative. Medicaid will pay for institutional care only if the applicant is judged at a predetermined debility status, below a specified income threshold, and is admitted into a Medicaid facility. Reimbursement for services provided within the home to supplement family care follow the same general guidelines. Medicare will currently compensate in-home services only at the skilled nursing level and only in those cases where there is a potential for rehabilitation. Medicaid does not cover the costs of in-home services in all states and requires that Medicaid vendors (which are not always available) be used. Funds from other sources, such as Title XX, are not extensive and are intended for numerous competing purposes (Gelfand and Olsen, 1980).

Care for the Alzheimer's sufferer can pose a number of ethical dilemmas to the family and professional service-providers (Burnside, 1983; Rabins, 1983). How to present a prognosis to the patient or the family in light of its tentativeness and the hopelessness it can engender is one such conundrum. There has also been uncertainty about the degree of involvement of Alzheimer's disease patients in decisions about their own care. Because the process of decline is gradual and insidious, the extent of impairment, and consequently the competency of the individual, is difficult to assess. The motives of the impaired individual similarly are difficult to interpret. For example, a patient may not swallow food because of an inability to do so or because of a refusal to eat; the ethical implications of force feeding would differ depending on the motive assigned to the patient. Another ethical issue concerns the conflict between the rights of the Alzheimer's patient and the right of those in his or her environment. Antisocial behavior such as night wandering or aggressiveness can disturb those who live with the Alzheimer's victim (family or nursing home resident) and can inadvertently lead to disruption in care arrangements if behavior becomes intolerable. Control of these behaviors through medication or physical restraint, on the other hand, can be seen as cruel and demeaning to persons afflicted with the disease because they are not responsible for their behavior. In effect, respecting the personhood of an individual with Alzheimer's disease can mean depriving others of their freedoms; obversely, maintaining the rights of others can lead to restrictions imposed on the Alzheimer patient.

It should be clear from this brief overview that the features of chronic illness and their effects on care provision, as described earlier, apply to Alzheimer's disease. To reiterate, the family and other informal agents, rather than medical professionals, are instrumental in determining management of the disease, care is primarily custodial in nature and does not come under the aegis of any single service organization or agency, financial assistance for care is limited and the professional service provider and family, in providing care, are confronted with profound ethical problems. In the presentation of data that follows the summary of methods used, these aspects of Alzheimer's disease and the management of care will be explored in further detail.

METHODS

Data were collected from participant observation in support group meetings of relatives of Alzheimer's disease victims over the course of a year in a rural midwestern town and through observations over a six-month period in a V.A. nursing home care unit in the same town. The support group had been formed in the preceding year through the grass roots organization of an initial general meeting that attracted 40 individuals from a radius of 60 miles. During the year, small, bimonthly meetings were held at a local church attended by 3 to 10 members and facilitated by a counselor from the local county council on aging. There were over 60 individuals on the newsletter mailing list by the end of the year. However, only 35 had ever attended a meeting and only 20 had attended more than one meeting. The meetings typically started with a short informational presentation followed by discussion of support group members' experiences. It should be noted that some support group members' relatives had not been diagnosed with Alzheimer's disease and others were clearly diagnosed with other types of dementia (for instance, multi-infarct dementia). The group was intended for relatives or friends of individuals suffering from Alzheimer's disease or related disorders though the focus was almost exclusively on Alzheimer's disease.

The nursing home unit was located in a V.A. hospital along four hallways that extended from a common day room. No barriers separated the nursing home from the rest of the hospital. There were 20 staff members and 54 residents. Only one patient was diagnosed as having Alzheimer's disease though nearly half were considered demented. This was to be expected as the diagnostic label of Alzheimer's disease has not been used liberally until very recently. During the observation period, the turnover of residents was light, with few residents being discharged (or dying) and being replaced by others.

The method used—participant observation—consists of direct, continuing interaction in natural settings through regular participation in the naturally occurring activities of the social group. In the nursing home, active participation was minimal. Although I had expressed interest in being a volunteer, the home was already fully staffed with all the volunteers that were needed. However, because staff did not wear uniforms, I was often mistaken for a staff member by residents (a mistake that I rectified). I also suffered the same confusion that residents did in distinguishing staff because of the large number of individuals being trained in the nursing home who appeared to be permanent staff but were not. I usually sat unobtrusively in the communal day room, the cafeteria, or a lounge room and occasionally accompanied staff into residents' rooms. Approximately 6 of the 54 residents recognized me and would converse with me. Most of the staff knew who I was as I had attended utilization review committee meetings. Without assistance, I knew by name about half of the residents. The others I could not easily recognize because for reasons of discretion, I did not go into the residents' rooms where some spent most of the day. Other residents wandered freely around the hospital or went to town with volunteers.

My participation in the support group was much more active. I presented informational sessions, helped to organize a second general meeting, and prepared the newsletter for the group. I inadvertently became a contact person for individuals interested in the group. All but two of the meetings held over the year were attended.

The disadvantage of the method employed are those characteristic of observational field work studies: Hypotheses cannot be tested and confirmed, findings are not generalizable to the population, there is risk of the observer's active involvement producing bias in observation and interpretation, and risk of contamination of the environment by the observer's presence. Reflexive accounts by the observer of possible sources of bias and respondent validation have been two techniques developed to assess subjective distortion, but they are ultimately dependent on and influenced by the same interpretive skills of the researcher as the research they are supposed to evaluate (Emerson, 1981). Neither technique was used. However, there was an attempt to triangulate observations through questionnaries sent to support group members about care provision for the Alzheimer patient, by structured interviews with physicians in the community likely to encounter Alzheimer's disease (20 primary care physicians, neurologists, and psychiatrists, a nonrandom sample, were interviewed), and by informal interviews with staff in the nursing home.

Despite the disadvantages of the field research method, observational field-work is nevertheless critical for an understanding of chronic illness. There is a strong precedent for the alliance of participant observation method with this substantive area. Erving Goffman (1961) and Anselm Strauss (Glaser and Strauss, 1966)—two of the major contributors to qualitative methodology—were examining mental illness and terminal illness, respectively, in other words, chronic diseases, using field methods. Their works have demonstrated the importance of exploring the subjective meanings of illness in a context where the impact is likely to be idiosyncratic and privatized. As Strauss (1975) has noted, there is more to be gained from the autobiographies of chronically ill individuals than from the literature on the subject. Insight into the biography of chronic illness was sought in the present research through the choice of small-scale, intensive study methods and an emphasis on case studies.

Empirical findings from the research, placed in perspective by a discussion of the literature and of parallel studies in the area, will be organized around three themes. The first concerns the withdrawal of the medical profession from active management of the disease and the implications for care provision. The second considers the functions of the family in care provision and specifically looks at the role of the family as mediator for resources. The last examines the provision of maintenance care in a nursing home.

ALZHEIMER'S DISEASE AND THE RETREAT OF THE MEDICAL PROFESSION

An abundance of recent medical literature has self-consciously examined the profession's approach to Alzheimer's disease. The literature has focused on criticisms of current diagnostic practices on several dimensions rather than on treatment for the obvious reason that Alzheimer's disease is not amenable to treatment. The literature has revealed that diagnosis may not be made at all because benign senescence (decrements in memory considered normal for the elderly) is wrongly assumed (see Sluss et al., 1981; Katzman, 1981). Second, it has highlighted the tendency of not specifying the type of dementia present although there are various implications for cure (see Stroudemire and Thompson, 1981; Seltzer and Sherwin, 1978). Third, it has been claimed that inaccurate diagnoses are prevalent (see Barnes and Raskind, 1981; Wells, 1982; Brink, 1980) though there is no agreement in the literature over the direction of the error, that is, whether reversible dementias are diagnosed mistakenly for irreversible ones, whether the converse is true, or whether the specific type of reversible or irreversible dementia is incorrectly diagnosed. To put it simply, the literature has shown that there is little incentive for the medical profession to deal with the Alzheimer's victim because (1) symptoms manifested may simply be the outcome of aging, (2) there are a number of diseases that must be excluded, and (3) even if recognized as a disease, no cure for Alzheimer's is presently available.

The literature has not in general examined the presentation of diagnosis to family members. The scanty evidence that exists suggests that diagnoses, however precise they may be from a medical point of view, are made more obscure when given to family members or to the patient. In effect, families may attempt to manage without full or with inaccurate knowledge of the disease, not because diagnostic investigation has failed to be exhaustive, but because vague terminology is used. They consequently may pursue a frustrating process of seeking second or more medical opinions. The findings from a University of Michigan study of the subjective experiences of families of Alzheimer's victims (Chenoweth and Spencer, 1983) showed that over 70 percent of their respondents sought more than one consultation. A dementia clinic at the University of Washington has had 1,000 families seeking a second opinion, dissatisfied with the judgment of medical practitioners in 25 states.

Multiple consultations do not guarantee that a name or explanation will be given for the disease and this was borne out by the current investigation. One woman in the study, for instance, inadvertently found out about the disease from talking with her dentist after having recognized the symptoms from a description on the Paul Harvey show. She did not obtain any explanation from the two physicians she had consulted. Another support group member began to realize the seriousness of her husband's disease only when her physician, commenting on her husband's recovery from pneumonia, stated, "It would have been better if he died."

Interviews with physicians corroborated the avoidance of giving a technical name for the disease and prognosis. Physicians would use terms such as memory loss or hardening of the arteries, and because the course of the disease is variable, prognosis was given in the most general terms such as "he won't be getting any better" or "you might consider institutional care." Etiology was deemphasized and the symptoms reported by the family confirmed. The evasive practices are similar to those noted by Quint (1965) describing physician interactions with mastectomy patients and by Glaser and Strauss (1966) describing the disclosure of imminent death to terminally ill patients.

Physicians felt it unreasonable to depress families and put them in a pessimistic frame of mind, particularly because a reversible cause might actually be found. Yet this seemed extremely unlikely because once the label of dementia was given to a patient, and not initially queried, it was rarely disputed. Paradoxically, physicians infrequently diagnosed a new case of Alzheimer's disease (except some neurologists) although they had many patients (usually in nursing homes) who already had the diagnosis of dementia. They tended to accept the label of dementia or senility already given to patients despite its imprecision or possible invalidity.

What are the implications of this approach for the patient and his or her family? Without accurae diagnosis and explanation, families might not respond in a way that was most supportive of their relative. The behavior of the demented individual—frequently unaesthetic, antisocial, bizarre, or violent—was interpreted as a character flaw and a cause for anger and argument. For example, a principal supporter caring for her widowed father has assumed her father to be irresponsible because of his habits of squandering money and driving for long periods of time without any apparent destination. She remembered comments made by her mother (now deceased) that "You don't know what your father is really like" and believed these statements confirmed her judgment of her father's behavior. Her father has received no diagnosis, although he had been recently hospitalized, and there was therefore no reason to link behavior with a disease. Once diagnosis was obtained (after some confusion caused by the coexistence of an overmedication problem), the father's behavior was reinterpreted in light of the explanation of pathology. In addition, the deterioration in the parent's marital relationship preceding the mother's death was attributed to the effects of the disease rather than to the father's irresponsibility, as it has been before diagnosis.

Without a diagnostic label to pin on the disease, the management of the disease is more likely to be an isolating and lonely experience. Moreover, it was common for the principal supporters of the demented person to protect others, especially children, from the realities of the disease, thereby cutting themselves off from their natural support system and adding to their isolation. A daughter of an Alzheimer victim, for instance, did not discover her mother's disease until her father was hospitalized and it became clear that her mother, who was expected to provide convalescent care for her father, was incapable of self-care. A son realized that his mother was ill only after his father called for help from a telephone booth, having been driven from the house by his violent wife. In effect, the disease was recognized in these cases when a crisis forced the principal supporter to seek assistance.

The growth of the Alzheimer's Disease and Related Disorders Association, the national organization that promotes research on the disease, and the formation of affiliated support groups for the relatives of Alzheimer's disease victims have partially reversed the process of isolation.[2] The ADRDA has converted into a disease category a problem that was previously considered a biological inevitability and has united under a single label individuals whose experiences may actually be quite diverse. The recognition of the debility as a disease has served to bring together caregivers in mutual support and to publicize and attract public monies for the benefit of victims and their caregivers.

While the ADRDA has transformed a cluster of symptoms and behaviors into a highly visible disease, there still remain essential differences between Alzheimer's disease and organic diseases well-established and recognized by the medical community. Because of the organization's grass roots base,[3] the disease is subjectively interpreted through negotiation among laypersons (namely, support group members) instead of being objectively defined by medical professionals. The support group process enables a disease definition to emerge, but it does so by downplaying the inherent ambiguity and variability of symptoms of the disease in order to pivot the diverse experiences of the members around a common disease definition. The disease concept is stretched to accommodate the various support group members. Members adapt the broadly defined concept to their own experiences, noting and sorting out where there are similarities and differences. In the support group observed in this study, for example, members reached the conclusion that loss of appetite and aggressive behavior are key features of Alzheimer's disease, a conclusion supported directly by evidence from some members. Other members, who during previous sessions had stated that their relatives were subdued or had increased appetites also supported the theory by either not disputing it or by making remarks such as "My mother has not reached that stage *yet*" or "My father doesn't show the *characteristic* aggressive behavior." In other words, it is the disease concept that brings support group members together and reduces their isolation; nevertheless, due to the elusive and variable nature of the disease, the disease ultimately becomes personalized and adjusted to individual circumstances.

The lack of treatment offered by the medical profession has some of the same effects as the absence of an understandable diagnosis. Families sought additional opinions in the hope of finding a cure, they questioned physicians about experimental drugs reported in newspapers and magazines, and alternatively, they prepared their own nostrums. Treatment, like the disease criteria, became individualized. One support group member, for instance, decided to use a diet for hyperactive children to reduce her husband's aggressiveness as well as initiating her own physical therapy program. In treatment, the burden of care was not assumed, as it would be in acute illnesses (Szasz and Hollender, 1956) by a physician offering a medication, device, or therapy to relieve symptoms. Interviews with physicians and with relatives show that on the contrary, medications were to be avoided to prevent worsening disorientation. The therapy offered was in terms of advice to relatives concerning stabilization of the patient's environment, contact with social services or quasi-medical agencies, and plans for long-term care. Thus treatment consisted of guidelines for the provision of care by laypersons and referral to other professional services.

In summary, the insidiousness of Alzheimer's disease, the slipperiness of memory assessment in the elderly, requiring a thorough knowledge of previous cognitive abilities and a precise assessment of decline, and the variability in severity of symptoms have resulted in vague, uncertain, or invalid diagnoses and have impeded its recognition as a disease. The softer phraseology used to describe the disease to family members and to the patient has further undermined its status as a medical issue. Consequently, the disease has been dealt with privately as personal trouble and has not been considered publicly as a health issue.

CARE WITHIN THE COMMUNITY: THE FAMILY AS MEDIATOR

The role of the family in providing care for the Alzheimer's sufferer has been a prominent topic in both research and publicity about the disease. Family members have been seen as hidden victims, imposing great personal sacrifices to maintain the impaired individual in the community. They have also been valuable informational resources, articulating the devastation caused by the disease because those suffering from the disease are often unable to do so. Nevertheless, exact census figures on the number of families in this situation have yet to be gathered due to the undeveloped epidemiology on the disease. Current figures are based on British studies on dementia (a more general category) using the assumption that half of demented individuals have Alzheimer's disease. It is estimated that over 50 percent of institutionalized elderly are demented in some way (Butler, 1975: 227) and that there are six times as many demented individuals outside of institutions as inside (Kay et al., 1969; Parsons, 1965). Over half of these individuals are residing with family members (Bergmann et al., 1978), the majority of supporters being female relatives (Gilhooly, 1984).

Rich data on family care for Alzheimer's victims have been derived primarily from small-scale intensive studies on nonrandom samples of family caregivers (see Gilhooly, 1984; Zarit et al., 1980;

Zarit and Zarit, 1982; Mace and Rabins, 1981, 1982; Sanford, 1975). These studies have explored the physical, psychological, and financial effects of caregiving, they have isolated the aspects of care most intolerable and stressful to the caregiver, and they have examined factors predicting institutionalization.

The data suggest that Alzheimer's disease determines not only the medical condition of the patient but also reorders the social aspects of the patient's and caregiver's lives, affecting interdependent family relationships, the mental and physical health of family members, and finances. As a result, the impact of the disease and the care provision trajectory depend on the familiar and social context in which the disease occurs as well as the severity of manifest medical symptoms. Two findings from the empirical literature bear this out: (1) morale and feelings of burden by the caregiver are not related to the extent of behavioral impairment nor to the duration of the illness and (2) neither the lack of community services nor the degree of impairment predict institutionalization (though utilization of formal services does enhance mental health and psychological well-being). Researchers have related the ability to cope with the disease effectively and to continue to provide care to the caregiver's problem-solving techniques, tolerance of deviance, availability of social supports and use of formal services, and the relationship between caregiver and patient prior to the event (Zarit and Zarit, 1982; Levine et al., 1983; Gilhooly, 1984). In stark contrast with acute illness, where a uniform treatment plan can be applied, the management of Alzheimer's disease is a product of individual coping skills and resources and ad hoc strategies devised by the caregiver.

Most of the factors influencing effective familial care cannot be substantially altered by intervention except for formal service provision. Increased attention has been given to expanding services in the community to raise the low level of home health care service utilization observed in empirical studies (see Gilhooly, 1984; Chenoweth and Spencer, 1983). Explanations for low utilization have been speculative and have stressed the unavailability and inappropriateness of services and financial obstacles to accessing them. The evidence from the present study indicates that even when services are available, there is a lack of fit between the structure of services and individual needs of persons impaired with Alzheimer's disease.

One of the serious limitations encountered in using these services, particularly in a rural area such as the one in which the study was conducted, is finding an agency offering the range and combination of skills needed. For example, in-home services bring professionals into the home to provide care. Services can range from skilled nursing care to homemaker/chore services, the type of service delivered depending on the particular agency focus. In the area where the research took place, skilled nursing care—the most intensive type of nursing care—was more readily available than personal care or homemaker care services to help sustain the home environment. Yet it is the lack of the latter type of services that can prompt institutional care when it is least appropriate, that is, at the less debilitating stages of the disease. In the research sample, unskilled nursing care was provided by volunteers or friends in the absence of a formal system and was vulnerable to dissolution. For instance, when one Alzheimer patient became hostile to the woman providing homemaker services, her family could find no alternative but to consider institutionalization.

The state in which the study was carried out had begun promoting services at a less intensive (intermediate care) level by loosening up restrictions on Medicaid coverage. Nevertheless, services suited to the wide range of needs of the population have not dramatically flourished despite increased funding. First, in order to obtain Medicaid funding for these services, it is necessary to find a Medicaid vendor. Seed money for start-up of facilities is not provided by Medicaid so that new agencies and organizations are not encouraged to enter the field. Second, the requirements stipulated by Medicaid are rigorous and comprehensive enough to favor existing agencies with full facilities and to discourage others. In the research setting, for example, day care had been offered entirely in nursing homes even though day care centers can exist in a variety of settings including senior centers, hospitals, churches, and schools. The incentive to open day care facilities in nursing homes had been stimulated by the simultaneous cut in Medicaid funding for long-term care. Day care and in-home care services dispensed through the nursing home signified another means of filling up beds.

Use of care offered in nursing home facilities was a consistent theme of discussion in support group meetings throughout the year. There had been reluctance to use this care, despite agreement about its quality and the individualized approach, because of the nursing home setting. Caregivers felt that it would be stigmatizing and threatening for their relatives to be placed in nursing homes for day care. Moreover, they felt services were excessive to their needs and might foster dependence. When other agencies were approached to ask if they would be willing to offer leisure activities in a supervised environment, it was recommended that they take their relatives to a pool hall. Support group members had discussed setting up centers tailored to their needs in churches or schools but the time commitment involved in organizing and reliance on volunteer staff made this unfeasible. In effect, while there were day care centers available, with adequate place, they were not acknowledged as a solution by family members providing care.

Funding sources, like services, were available but unusable because of the local structure of resources. For instance, one support group member remarked that she had been relieved to discover that Medicare was willing to pay for institutional care for her husband only to discover that not a single Medicare home exists in the state. Another member was able to arrange for her insurance company to pay for institutional care although custodial care was not covered by the insurance policy. She was able to argue that institutional care was less expensive than skilled in-home nursing home that would have been necessary to maintain both her mother and her convalescing father at home. The insurance company, however, refused to reimburse care in institutions within the town and the Alzheimer patient was placed 25 miles away from her family.

The set of circumstances in the latter case, including the family's willingness to institutionalize, a comprehensive insurance plan that would pay for care, and the availability of space in a nursing home approved by patient and family, did not apply to many of the other support group members. Discussions that centered on services and funding frequently spotlighted the limited applicability of shared experiences on the practical aspects of the disease. While members could discuss in a general way the need for supplementary care, there was considerable variation on the particular package of services required, the familial care arrangements with which to ally formal services, the financial position of the family, and the ability of family members to tap resources successfully. Family members often followed a solitary path in locating, accessing, and developing resources due to different stages of the disease and intensity of symptoms, varying personal preferences and skills, and idiosyncratic combinations of insurance, pension, and state coverage of health care. Families could educate other support group members about their experiences but often experiences would not be relevant to others or would not be relevant at the time they were related.

To reiterate, the heterogeneous symptoms and stages of Alzheimer's disease combined with the social dimensions make the demands for care diverse and extensive. Formal services to supplement family care are not adequate partially because of the unavailability of services and limitations in funding. In addition, there may be low take-up of services because they cannot be integrated successfully into the care provided by family members due to the specialized or concentrated orientations of services in any one locale and/or to the fluctuating and multiple needs of the patient and family.

NURSING HOMES AND THE PROVISION OF CUSTODIAL CARE

A national nursing home survey conducted in 1977 (U.S. Department of Health and Human Services, 1981) documented that 99 percent of all residents had one or more chronic conditions or impairments and that 57 percent of residents suffered from senility or chronic brain syndrome. Given the nature of the population and its health care problems, to what extent is a nursing home suited to provide the custodial care required by a chronic illness such as Alzheimer's disease?

The medical charts in the nursing home in which observations were made revealed an emphasis on nursing objectives as opposed to medical objectives. Little attention was paid to precise diagnosis and etiology of disease. The charts consisted of several sections—a social work history, nursing notes, weekly nursing assessment of function (including memory and orientation), utilization review committee notes, nutrition and dental notes, admitting histories, and previous histories. The description of individual's mental status in all sections was in terms of symptoms rather than disease, including on admission notes. That is, individuals were demented or senile or had memory loss. Only one had a diagnosis of Alzheimer's disease—a person who had developed the disease when relatively young—and very few had diagnoses of other types of dementia. In addition, there were many inconsistencies between sections. Nurses' weekly reports noted that a patient was always oriented although there was dementia listed as one of the conditions. Similarly, there were discrepancies between social work reports and nursing observations.

The nursing supervisor, when questioned about the process of deciding diagnostic labels, mentioned that a thorough examination was given upon admission. Previous diagnosis of dementia was inherited unless there was reason to question it. It was the physicians' responsibility, not the nurses', to query diagnosis as specific disease categories were not pertinent for delivery of nursing care.

It was clear that disease conditions were relevant only insofar as they affected management of patient through the symptoms manifested. In recent months the nursing home had moved to a system of assessment sheets based entirely on function. There was some concern as well to make more uniform the dementia diagnoses, but mainly in a cosmetic way, that is, to use a label currently in vogue, whether it was used precisely or consistently or not. In the utilization review committee notes, goals set for patients transcended the disease category. There were some exceptions, for example, with respect to prosthesis, but for most patients, care plans revolved around adjustment to the nursing home, maintaining function and promoting sociability.

In watching residents operate, there were many instances in which the label of dementia or memory failure did not reflect in behavior. For instance, three demented residents were very active in nursing home activities, including a complicated and competitive tic tac toe game involving bean bag tossing. They could be seen wheeling around other patients and were capable of arriving on time for scheduled activities. Moreover, individuals who were reported to be well-oriented and retentive would display behavior indicative of memory loss. One resident, for instance, cleaned the cafeteria all day long; once finished he would start again. Another resident considered well-oriented was confused about his birthdate, which he believed the nursing home had changed and made a month earlier. A staff member explained the incident, not by mentioning dementia but by suggesting "He's deaf and very old."

The approach of the nursing home therefore served the need of the chronically ill residents with Alzheimer's disease in that care was individualized to support the person in the environment and to retain independent functioning. There were, however, a number of internally conflicting aspects of the approach. First, in downplaying medical diagnoses and stressing symptoms, there was a risk of therapeutic nihilism. Although I was told that there was systematic reinvestigation of inherited diagnoses for reversible causes of dementia, in fact I never saw this happen. The one exception was instigated by an outside physician who strongly advocated more tests on the grounds that the one Alzheimer patient seemed to have depression, not dementia. The diagnosis was not changed.

Second, despite the extensive efforts of a well-meaning staff and the humanistic philosophy of the nursing home observed, there was ultimately the same kind of rigidity impeding the provision of individualized care to the chronically ill person as occurs in the community. Because the institution is offering a protective environment to a number of individuals with diverse and multiple illnesses, it can only go so far in adjusting its environment to the needs of each resident. After a point, the resident must be adapted to the environment.

There were a number of occasions when this inherent conflict surfaced. For example, there was an activity session intended to preserve verbal communication skills. The session consisted of objects or pictures of objects presented to the participants and their responding to a series of questions posed by the occupational therapist about the object. As communication was the goal, it would seem irrelevant if responses were correct or not. However, allowing nonsensical answers would have increased the confusion of participants. As a result, the sessions increasingly excluded those who could not respond correctly even if they could still verbally communicate. Thus the activity's objective to enhance and preserve communication skills (including disoriented residents) was subverted by an implicit commitment to a uniform reality for the sake of the oriented residents.

Third, there was a dedication to rehabilitative therapy despite the prevalence of chronic conditions among the residents. The view espoused by Brody (1973: 148) describing treatment for institutionalized patients with chronic brain disease captures the perspective of the nursing home:

> While chronic brain damage and senility remain, they are no longer acceptable as inevitable nor do they mean that a person must be consigned to purely custodial care. This study demonstrates the

potential of individualized therapy for the aged; of active treatment even with severely impaired patients suffering from disorientation, confusion and loss of memory.

The enthusiasm for rehabilitation, and the denigration of "purely" custodial care were hindered by two factors: (1) because there is uncertainty in mental impairment over which functions remain and the speed of degeneration, it is not clear when restorative therapy rather than maintenance care is indicated. Does the person still actually have the ability and needs assistance in regaining it, or is it permanently lost and rehabilitation would be frustrating and unrewarding? and (2) there are few mechanisms available for achieving rehabilitation. In the nursing home, rehabilitation of the mentally impaired stressed reality orientation, a broad theory that posits that individuals who are confused can be helped to remain oriented in time and place by reminders or stimuli purposively placed in the environment. Clocks and calendars displayed prominently on walls and repeated mention of time, place, and date in conversations are some techniques used. Despite its widespread popularity, reality orientation is not appropriate for all demented persons and can cause distress to the person whose version of reality is disputed by continual external reminders. For example, one resident reminded of a recent outing in which he had participated was irritated because he could not remember the trip and replied angrily "I don't remember any goddam trip." From an ethical viewpoint, reality orientation can conflict with validation of the resident's version of reality, which is a civil right. The Feil (1980) method, in support of the latter, proposed that helping people face reality may add to their confusion and withdrawal.

In addition, the pursuit of reality orientation was undermined by the structural organization of the nursing home. Much of the daily interaction of residents was directed to the nonmedical clerical staff who worked in the communal day room. It was the nontrained staff who were bombarded by resident inquiries and had to cope with their apparently incoherent remarks. The staff responses were spontaneous and were dictated by the necessity to return to their work, not by concern for reality orientation or validation of the resident's version of reality. Interaction with staff trained in the theory was less frequent, limited to sporadic conversations during medicine rounds or mealtimes. Thus there was no ready system for effectively and routinely utilizing reality orientation methods.

In summary, custodial care for demented persons in a nursing home extends the ambiguous identity of memory impairment as a disease. Care focuses on control of symptoms, including control of disorientation. In some cases the abandoning of disease concepts was inappropriate, for instance, when the search for treatable causes or symptoms was abandoned or when rehabilitative therapies were universally applied, regardless of cause of malfunction.

CONCLUSION

Data on the medical, familial, and institutional care of Alzheimer's sufferers have been used to exemplify the disparity between the health needs of the chronically ill elderly and the current organization of care. While the illustrative material has been based on an intensive study of a small number of cases and should therefore be treated cautiously, there has been an attempt to triangulate data through diverse sources and varied settings. Interviews with physicians, observations and questionnaires from families, and fieldwork in a nursing home confirmed the ambiguity surrounding the disease, the centrality of the family in providing care, and the individualized needs of the patient, reflecting the variability of the disease and the interaction of resources, coping styles, and degree of professional intervention. The lack of fit between these features of the disease and the dominant approach in health care provision that stresses categorical, time-limited, rehabilitative, and strictly medical treatment have also been highlighted by the empirical findings. The findings suggest that an understanding and consideration of individual biography is essential for construction of a care plan and indicated that care provision demands the integrated management of the disease by family, patient, and a combination of medical, quasi-medical, and social service professionals.

NOTES

1. See the Veterans Administration (1982) report that reveals that length of stay in a V.A. nursing home predicts need for assistance with activities of daily living, even when other factors are controlled for.
2. Gilhooly (1984) has observed that the choice of Alzheimer's disease instead of senile dementia or senility for the name of the organization has medicalized and destigmatized the disease.
3. The organization has medically trained persons on its advisory board. However, the organization functions primarily through support groups of laypersons.

19

ALZHEIMER'S DISEASE AS BIOGRAPHICAL WORK

JABER F. GUBRIUM
Professor, Sociology and Anthropology
Marquette University

ROBERT J. LYNOTT
Graduate Student, Sociology and Anthropology
Loyola University

The concept of biography, of life history, has been part of sociological discourse for years, taken by Thomas and Znaniecki (1927) early in the century as a principle for analyzing individual accounts of experience. The later use of "career" (Becker and Strauss, 1956; Goffman, 1961) and "trajectory" (Glaser and Strauss, 1968) displayed the organizational orderliness of adulthood, aging, and dying. Psychologists, too, have leaned heavily on the idea of life history as a framework for describing human development, some emphasizing what Gergen (1980: 34) calls "stability accounts" in which life patterns are set in childhood, others being "ordered change accounts" in which the individual is seen as typically "passing through a series of predetermined, epigenetic stages, often but not necessarily terminating in adolescence." As Starr (1982-1983) points out in his useful summary, until recently, the view of life history across the social and behavioral sciences has been of a more or less passive self subject to outside forces that shape its course of growth.

This chapter takes a contrasting view of biography to describe select features of the Alzheimer's disease (senile dementia) experience, specifically, the application of public exemplars of the disease to construct recognizable yet diverse individual biographies. The emphasis is on biographical work rather than on life history as such. Following an earlier argument (Gubrium and Buckholdt, 1977), biography is treated as a practical activity of those whose concern is the life course. In this view, biography is not so much the presentation of the facts of life that lie ordered in the near or remote past as it is the descriptive product of retrospective and prospective constitution, the representation of individual experience (Schutz and Luckmann, 1974; Yarrow et al., 1955; Kohli, 1981; Warren, 1983; Gubrium and Lynott, 1983). To inspect biography is to display the work that enters into its production and subsequent reproduction.

Alzheimer's disease then is something used—a code—for rendering chronologically and substantively meaningful the general, age-related troubles of late life. By itself, the code, the disease, tells us little about the meaningful articulation of the troubles; it informs us only of an end product, what the troubles recognizably become. The Alzheimer's disease experience is an ongoing application of its code, a process that stretches and transforms its meaning well beyond its diagnosis as a condition of later life; its practical meaning is, in effect, to be found in its telling, its description (Wieder, 1974). Treating Alzheimer's disease as biographical work reveals its pervasively social character, how dependent it is on those concerned, how bonded it is to their diversely related experiences, and, conversely, how much it bonds those together who attempt to make sense of the experiences.

THE DISEASE AND ITS EXPERIENCE

It is not uncommon in the related medical literature to learn that there is both unity and diversity in the disease and its experience. As far as the patient is concerned, it is said that Alzheimer's is both organic and behavioral. Its organicity is marked by neurofibrillary tangles and senile plaques in the brain. Other lesions, such as Hirano and granulovacuolar bodies, also are characteristic (Terry and Wisniewski, 1975). Yet the markers are correlated with age (Terry, 1978). The latter fact underpins the continuing controversy among medical researchers over whether the disease is an entity separate and distinct from aging, on the one hand, or is accelerated or extreme aging itself, on the other (Terry and Wisniewski, 1975; Tomlinson, 1977; Tomlinson et al., 1968, 1970; Katzman, 1981; Katzman and Karasu, 1975). In practice, the disease becomes a unified and distinct entity separate from the neuro-organicity of aging when the facts are interpreted that way; otherwise, its organicity is as diverse as the aging brain itself.

It is noted repeatedly that the disease is also a behavioral entity, a brain/behavior condition. The ostensible neuro-organicity of the disease has its correlate in dementia, a diffuse cognitive deficit without delirium, to be distinguished from, among other conditions, the frequently confounding multi-infarct dementia that commonly presents with a sudden onset, stepwise progression, and focal neurological signs (Wells, 1978). Senile dementia differs from fifty or so other pathological conditions that behaviorally mimic it (Haase, 1977). The presence of neuro-organic markers without clinical evidence of dementia does not warrant an Alzheimer's disease designation (Katzman et al., 1978: 267). Indeed, in the final analysis, as Katzman (1983: 8) puts it, while the disease presents as a "progressive deterioration in intellectual capacity in an otherwise alert individual, [the] deterioration must be sufficient to interfere with social or occupational performance or both." Otherwise, "insufficient" interference is explained by the benign conditions of aging that have their own, not incapacitating, impact on performance, like the characteristic memory loss associated with growing old called "benign senescent forgetfulness" (Kral, 1978). Accordingly, Katzman and others locate the differential diagnosis in the everyday social competence of the suspected patient, further diversifying its symptomatic grounds. While Alzheimer's is considered by some medical researchers to be a separate and distinct disease entity in principle, being a nosological unity, its diagnosis and symptomatology are tied to the diversity of the disease experience wherein evidence must be marshalled to reveal an underlying pathological entity—the task of producing unity out of diversity.

The highly varied character of the presented disease is not taken lightly. Although it is described behaviorally in short pithy statements, said to be a progressive, irreversible process of cognitive decline, its concrete manifestations and chronology are so varied as to raise the question of whether it is too great to accommodate a uniform nosology. Though some are reluctant to distinguish the disease qualitatively from what is called "normal aging" (Terry and Wisniewski, 1975; Tomlinson, 1977; Tomlinson et al., 1968, 1970) and thus nosologically accommodate the variability by, in effect, blurring Alzheimer's distinct disease status, others stretch the Alzheimer's disease entity to encompass subcategories, or different forms, of the disease (see Drachman's comments in Katzman, 1983: 7-28). To our knowledge, the nosological problem never is resolved in the medical literature, with the flat conclusion that Alzheimer's is not a disease entity—an understandable shortstop.

The unity-in-diversity problem isn't limited to medical controversy. Other service providers, patients, and caregivers also face the task of making disease sense out of diverse and related experiences. The problem takes a number of forms. While the disease's lay literature (caregiving handbooks, self-help group newsletters, public information pamphlets) describes the symptoms and course of progress of the disease, at the same time, its varied individual manifestations and chronology are bemoaned. Service providers, public educators, and support group facilitators present the characteristics of the disease and yet offer their sympathies over its manifold symptoms and erratic course of progress. Caregivers and, where they can, patients alike, gather in support groups and in voluntary association meetings to discuss their "common" disease experience and confront their wide-ranging differences. As with medical researchers, what brings them together is their belief and concrete knowledge that something has gone wrong with elders of concern to them, that something ostensibly being a disease, not normal aging. Their tacit cognitive task is to interpret the diverse disease-related facts of their experiences as focally indicative of the typical and recognizable biography of the Alzheimer's patient.

In what follows, we examine the biographical work of those who describe the disease in the diagnosed patient. Biographical work does enter into the interpretive procedures leading to diagnosis. Moreover, some of those concerned virtually undo or at least seriously come to question the disease biography of a loved one long after a formal Alzheimer's diagnosis had been assigned. Biographical work is not tied to diagnosis in any definitive way such that, say, diagnostics governs interpretation. If anything, biographical work organizes and disorganizes the practical reality of the diagnosis, the latter reciprocally serving to confirm or disconfirm the estimated validity of the patient's condition.

Data were gathered in a number of settings and drawn from varied texts as part of a larger study of the descriptive organization of the disease (Gubrium, forthcoming; Lynott, 1983). The Alzheimer's Disease and Related Disorders Association (ADRDA) is a self-help organization with missions of public education, research support, advocacy, and help to caregivers (Stone, 1982; ADRDA, 1982); it is a national network with over 50 local chapters, one in every major city of the country. Sponsored or facilitated by the local chapters are support groups for caregivers and family members of Alzheimer's disease patients. Participant observation was undertaken in meetings and the support groups of local chapters in two cities, with active membership in one of them. As part of a research project aiming to assess the meaning of the family burden in caregiving, fieldwork was conducted for a period of four months in a geriatric day hospital affiliated with an acute care hospital. The day hospital provided a structured, therapeutic environment for nine to twelve Alzheimer's disease patients and offered a weekly support group for their caregivers. Data also were drawn from the extant literature of the ADRDA. Its national headquarters, located in Chicago, publishes a quarterly newsletter informing members and interested outsiders of the latest research findings, legislative successes, and publicity campaigns. Many local chapters publish their own newsletters that combine news from "national" with matters of more immediate concern to caregivers, such as coping tips and profiles of the caregiving experiences. In addition, there is the varied promotional and informational literature available from the ADRDA itself and cooperating agencies such as the National Institute on Aging and the National Institute of Neurological and Communicative Disorders and Stroke. Finally, there is an emerging media sector, manifested in popular magazine articles, newspaper features, public service announcements, and broadcast programming. None of the data sources is isolated from the others. They liberally exchange ideas, sentiments, and techniques in order to combat the "disease of the century," to expose the "silent epidemic" that "dims bright minds."

EXEMPLARS

The work of making sense of the disease experience proceeds along two fronts. On the one side are the objects of concern: the patient's disease and the caregiving burden, together the disease experience. Regularly, references are made to the "two patients" of Alzheimer's disease, the victim and the caregiver. On the other side is the stock of available ideas, images, explanations, sentiments, slogans, and examplars of the disease experience, its shared and growing culture. Focal in this chapter are exemplars of the disease experience, among whom are nationally or locally renowned patients and caregivers whose symptoms and burdens of care provide resources, virtual blueprints or models, for interpreting experienced particulars. The intervening biographical work includes the application of exemplary details to select particulars of the individual disease experience, part of the process of transforming the disease's private troubles into public understandings (Mills, 1959).

Rita Hayworth, the Hollywood actress, is the best known exemplar of the disease. Her story is repeatedly referenced by caregivers and concerned others as an example of what ails particular victims. She is a touchstone for sharing what is understood to be the common details of otherwise unique disease experiences, a story that, in application, serves to produce unity out of diversity.

Details of Hayworth's victimization and the caregiving burden of her daughter, Princess Yasmin Aga Khan, are presented in an article written by Rosemary Santini and Katherine Barrett (1983) in the widely read *Ladies' Home Journal*. While the article refers to "the tragedy of Rita Hayworth," the unfortunate decline of an otherwise "glamorous movie star . . . the love goddess of Hollywood," it also offers the portrait of an Alzheimer's disease patient and her caregiver—a public mirror for personal reflection. Hayworth is still physically attractive, an older woman with "dark brown eyes," of "stylish" dress. But she now stares ahead fixedly, seems bewildered and confused. As Rita's daughter reports (Santini and Barrett, 1983: 84-85):

> It's so hard to know what she's feeling, what's going on inside. I don't know what she can understand, but there are fleeting moments when I'm sure that she's at least somewhat aware.
>
> I do know that she needs the security of my love, that in some way I bring her joy. And I visit her as often as I can because I need to be there for her, to tell her I love her, to tell her everything is all right.

The article turns to the disease's characteristics, its brain/behavior markers. Increasingly familiar slogans are used to relay the message of "what it's like," like a "funeral that never ends," "a slow death" (p. 85):

> It is called Alzheimer's Disease, and because it affects the outer layer of the brain—creating a chaotic tangle of nerve filaments—a patient's intellectual ability is eventually destroyed. Other victim's relatives have likened it to "a slow death," a "funeral that never

ends." Often they speak of their afflicted wives or husbands or parents in the past tense. Like Yasmin, 33, they describe the agony of not being recognized, or their feeling that a stranger has inhabited the body of their loved one.

It is reported that Rita is now in the final stages of the disease for which there is no prevention or cure, that inexorably leads to a vegetative existence and eventually to death.

A portrait of the caregiver as victim is offered too. Resembling her mother, Yasmin is beautiful, "an extremely attractive woman, a classical singer who temporarily abandoned her own career a year ago to devote herself to her mother's care and to the Alzheimer's Disease and Related Disorders Association." With this, we get an inkling of the burden of care, the virtual "36-hour day" it requires, as the popular slogan and handbook title put it (Mace and Rabins, 1981). Not only is the burden of care time-consuming, it is emotionally draining and agonizing. Witnessing the mental demise of a loved one takes a terrible toll. Financially, the disease is devastating for most. As the article explains, because of her wealth, Yasmin can afford round-the-clock care for her mother; most other families are not as fortunate, raising the spector of financial ruin and the eventual need to institutionalize the patient.

The course of the disease experience also is presented. Yasmin describes Rita's "stormy" career, her bouts with alcohol, the relentless coverage by the press of her drinking excesses and otherwise "bizarre" behavior, and her five difficult marriages. As the article reports,

> Everyone seemed to agree that Rita was drinking heavily, and when she entered the Silver Hills alcoholic treatment center in Connecticut in 1977 few people were surprised. "At that point, I also thought alcohol was her problem," says Yasmin. "I thought it was really destroying her brain."

But as the article and Yasmin herself contend in retrospect, no one knew that what was "really" affecting Rita was Alzheimer's disease. Now that Rita has been diagnosed as having the disease, her lifelong troubles are interpreted and aligned to fit the biographical needs of a pathological condition with an insidious onset that leads to "slow, agonizing changes" and eventual death. What had been reasonably explained before as the temperamental and alcoholic excesses of a Hollywood star now was, with equal certainty, "really" Alzheimer's disease all along (see Garfinkel, 1967). The authors explain (p. 141):

> If, as Yasmin suspects, Rita began suffering from Alzheimer's as long ago as twenty-five years, it could explain a great deal about her difficult personal life. . . . In retrospect, it could very well be that because of Alzheimer's she began to lack the judgment to pick her friends wisely.
>
> Looking back, the evidence of Alzheimer's may already have been showing up when Yasmin was a child. . . . There *were* hints of the tragedy that was to come.

Thus Yasmin and the authors of the article exemplify part of the biographical work that enters into the recognition of the insidious onset and course of the "dread disease." In application, others who make sense of their own individual disease experiences not only use the Rita Hayworth story as a recognizable instance of what they all share but reproduce the biographical work of the story, reconfirming the unity of the disease experience.

The Rita Hayworth story is a centerpiece of the disease's public culture. It is relayed in national and local ADRDA newsletters and is frequently cited for purposes of disease recognition in the print and broadcast media. When a question arises about what the disease is that a particular patient has or of which an individual caregiver speaks, it is commonly explained that it is the Rita Hayworth disease or what Rita Hayworth has, its publicly recognized details making apparent the individual particulars of the case at hand.

There are, of course, other exemplars of the disease experience. There are the now widely known home-grown cases such as caregiver Bobbie Glaze's (1982) story, a founder of the ADRDA and its national chairperson for program development, and Jerome Stone's (1982) personal tragedy, the first and current President of the ADRDA whose wife contracted the disease. There are the increasingly familiar faces that appear time and again in the frequently shown videotape *Someone I Once Knew,* a film that spotlights five different victims of Alzheimer's disease and their caregivers. Diverse as their experiences are, they all have the disease and share its burdens. There are many local examplars, too, whose stories have spread through the routine borrowing of news and coping items among ADRDA chapters, reprinted in their newsletters. Some become virtual standards by which to compare or assess the condition of individual victims and the care provided for them.

In one of the local ADRDA chapters studied, a caregiver—call her "Emma"—had become a martyr of the disease culture. As referenced and told, her story was commonplace at chapter meetings and support groups. Individual chapter officers and members exemplified the Alzheimer's disease experience by describing the "way it is" by means of Emma's burden of care. Emma's former employer, now her husband, had contracted the disease. She had been and was still devoted to him. His condition grew grave, virtually vegetative. Yet Emma refused to give him up, to place him in a nursing home. She set up 24-hour care in her own home and became a "36-hour" caregiver. Her living room resembled a nursing station with hospital bed and bodily care apparatus about. As best she could, she provided him with affection, company, and succor, feeding, bathing, dressing, cleaning, and sleeping with him. She made his care the center of her life. He, on the other hand, was now the "mere shell of his former self," mute and gaunt, recognizing nothing and no one. While touted by most as a martyr, her story for others was foolhardy, a portrait of what it can all become if one does not face up to the disease.

Beside the standing exemplars are the ad hoc cases that serve as circumstantial grounds for comparing diverse experiences. For example, while the five "anonymous" faces in the film *Someone I Once Knew* are widely available for application to particular disease experiences, the latter become, in their own right, exemplary on occasion. Select caregivers' experiences that are laid out in detail for all to appreciate in a support group or local ADRDA chapter meeting readily serve as temporarily well-known instances of what it's like to, say, go through a funeral that never ends.

APPLICATION

Exemplars and their application have a dialectical relationship. Examplars are products of the collective work of representing disease-related experiences. Those concerned offer examples of what it's like when they intend to communicate about themselves as victims, caregivers, or service providers. Whether celebrities, home-grown, or circumstantial, exemplars are recognizable means of sharing particulars—collective representations (Durkheim, 1973). In turn, exemplars are said to typify the particulars of individual experiences such that original particulars become the exemplary grounds for making themselves recognizable. Exemplars not only are cognitive and empirical artifacts of disease experiences, in application they serve to link, to bond, the experiences together as features of a single entity: the disease.

Application has many facets that both ramify and articulate exemplars. Four are considered: elaboration, typification, the use of indefinite terms, and synchronization.

ELABORATION

As noted by medical researchers (Katzman, 1983) and laypersons, there is some question of whether Alzheimer's is one disease entity or several. There are two ways to deal with the question analytically: elaborate the conception of the disease to account for the diverse experiences to which it applies, or abandon the disease concept as a unifying principle because the experiences it ostensibly contains overshoot its capacity to organize them parsimoniously. By and large, the question is resolved through elaboration. It is suggested in the medical literature, in ADRDA newsletters, and in local public education forums like ADRDA chapter meetings that there may be three, four, or as many as fifty different forms of Alzheimer's disease.

An example of the resolution is drawn from one of the support groups studied, a component of the geriatric day hospital's program, in which an especially well-informed nurse frequently shared the latest research findings with participants. She was an extremely sympathetic facilitators who felt, however, that caregivers should not be given false hope about so-called medical breakthroughs or miracle cures but, rather, be apprised of the complexities of, and limitations in, the disease's understanding. On one occasion, support group participants were explaining to a newcomer how the disease manifested itself in their respective patients. It soon became clear that there was considerable difference among them, not easily explained in terms of the chronology of a single disease. There were some whose victim had had the disease for years, who differed from each other as much as from those who had recently contracted it. There were patients who had been relatively stable for some time and others whose symptoms had altered dramatically in a short period. There were those whose symptoms were not even recognizable in others. The newcomer, whose sister had the disease, was puzzled and admittedly "just dizzy" with all she was learning.

At this point, the nurse who had been listening with concern, spoke up. She turned to the newcomer and explained that what the newcomer was feeling upon hearing all of this was a common reaction, noting further that all of the participants continued to discover new things about Alzheimer's disease, from the researchers and from each other. She went on to explain that the "little known" disease was insidious and took many forms, each patient and burden being "an individual thing." The nurse pointed out that Alzheimer's disease defies easy description, that although it was often said to have distinct stages in its course of progress, there were many exceptions. She then remarked:

> Who knows, in a few years we might come to realize that there are many types of Alzheimer's disease, like Type-A Alzheimer's, Type-B Alzheimer's, Type-C, like that. The more I see of this thing, the more I'm convinced myself that's the disease. Really, it shows up differently for everyone.

The nurse proceeded to elaborate several types without formally naming them. She introduced the first one in this way: "One type is, I'd say, like what Larry has, Gladys's husband." Gladys is a regular participant of the support group. Her husband has had Alzheimer's disease for several years. The nurse described him as having the type of Alzheimer's with a relatively clear onset that reaches a plateau and "just sits there." To this, Gladys added, "That's my Larry all right; 'steady Larry,' I call him." The nurse then explained that a second type is like what Rita Hayworth has, where you've been going downhill for years and years but nobody seems to know it's Alzheimer's. The "symptoms" are explained away, said to be caused by something like the patient's growing stubbornness or some such "normal" condition. Responding to this, the newcomer stated that she had read about Rita Hayworth and, in fact, had wondered if her sister had the same thing, even though there were clear differences. The nurse cautioned that she didn't think the newcomer's sister really had that type but, rather, was more like a third type, represented by yet another support group participant's family member with the disease.

The elaboration of the disease did not end there. The nurse proceeded to specify five or six types in some detail, each time making use of a more or less known exemplar. As she talked, her experienced audience joined in and further elaborated the unnamed types, concretely specifying their particulars out of what they individually knew about the disease, its management, and care. In their ways, each contributed theoretically and empirically to the disease and, in so doing, served to diversify the entity to account for the unity of variable experiences. As such, they conducted the work of seeing a single biography in their troubled lives, an Alzheimer's disease biography. Each patient had the disease in a particular way. As the discussion came to a close, the nurse concluded that, though she had described a few forms of the disease, there were probably as many as thirty or forty different types, predicting that that is probably what will be found in years to come as more and more becomes known about it.

It was clear that the nurse was not only conceptually elaborating the disease to clear things for the newcomer to the support group but for all of those gathered. The disease as an entity, as it applied to the lives of those who listened, was presented as *their* unifying biography, the principle of life history that made it sensible for them to be so different yet so much alike. Each of the participants, not just the newcomer, contributed to both the designation of the unity-in-diversity problem and its resolution through elaboration. Indeed, at one point in the proceedings, the nurse was urged to consider yet another type, a sixth one, at the behest of a participating caregiver who pointed out that the nurse had forgotten Emma's husband, whose well-known vegetative condition was not represented by anyone's patient in the group, not even by someone like Howard's wife Sophie, who was just as far along yet so different.

It should be noted that this nurse's elaboration was not unique as biographical work. Alzheimer's disease is similarly elaborated by everyone concerned, from medical researchers to other service providers and caregivers. To the extent exemplars are widely recognized, their application by all serves to elaborate the disease as the distinct entity unifying the many experiences of concern. Lesser known exemplars, too, serve biographical work as more immediate or delimited means of recognition.

TYPIFICATION

Elaboration yields a resource for description, for representing what the disease is, what it is not, and how its forms compare with each other. Yet, at the same time, select elaborations render particular experiences sensible by specifying the type of experiences they are. The process of documentation, for those concerned, reflexively mirrors in generalizations—sharable representations—the common meaning of individual encounters with the disease.

In another support group studied, participants were less constant in attendance than in the preceding one. Although there was a faithful core of regulars, a good share of each month's participants were newcomers or less familiar faces. It was more commonplace in this support group to receive introductions and to hear new disease stories. Support group meetings were facilitated by successive introductions, a way of beginning the discussion.

On one occasion, as usual, several participants had introduced themselves, explained their relationship to the Alzheimer's victim in their care, and described what their respective patients were like. There were many differences among them, varied combinations of courses of progress, timing, duration, clarity and rapidity of onset, symptoms, and burdens of care. It behooved each successive participant to compare his patient with others in order to convey particular disease experiences meaningfully. One participant, call her "Bea," had attended local ADRDA chapter meetings but was a newcomer to the support group. As she reported, she was attending mainly out of interest for her best friend's mother, adding that her own aunt had Alzheimer's disease and was now living in a local nursing home.

Bea described her friend's travail in caring for the mother. The friend worked part-time and scheduled around the job for the home care of her mother, a familiar enough problem. Bea reported the "awful burden" the mother presented, causing the friend to have no time of her own. At that point, one of the other participants interjected impatiently, "Well, what's the mother like? Can your friend communicate with her? I hope this isn't another martyr story." Bea paused for a moment and then began to explain, referring to the well-known film, *Someone I Once Knew*.

> You've all seen that film *Someone I Once Knew*? [Several participants assured her they all had.] Well, I was just thinking the other day how much Velma [the mother] is like one of the patients in the movie. You know the older woman. [A participant blurted sarcastically that they're all old, causing some laughter and all around good humor.] Yes, I know they're all old. You know the older, white-haired woman that can't seem to stay still? She paces the floor and her daughter's at the end of her rope. Well, that fits Velma to a T. Velma's

like her. She paces all the time, back and forth, back and forth. It's neverending. Katherine [the daughter] has had to put up those baby gates everywhere too so that Velma doesn't fall down the stairs or wander off and . . .

At this time, one of the facilitators, also a caregiver, interrupted Bea and pointed out,

> I know the type! That's right. They're just like what's-her-name in the film. They don't know what they're doing, where they're going. They don't know who you are; they don't even know who they are themselves. Jesus, are they ever hard nuts to crack! If they'd only stay still. They're the wanderers. That kind of Alzheimer's I don't wish on anyone [She knocks on wood].

The sequence of introductions then stopped for a time as participants discussed the now familiar type of patient that Bea had pinpointed. Many comments were made about the way *they* are, explanations offered for why *they* behave as they do, and prognostications shared over *their* future prospects as victims of the disease. Repeated references to "they" and to "them" tacitly communicated a common category of concern, communally acknowledging in each account that it was "them," that type of patient, not others, some other type, that was being described and discussed.

Acknowledged recognition of the type led to personal elaboration. For example, following one's comment that she certainly did know that type of Alzheimer's patient, the type exemplified by the particular case portrayed in the film, she then shared select details of that type of patient with the group. This in turn generated further, concrete elaborations of the type as others took up the process of filling particulars out of additional experiences. In this way, the exemplar not only served to typify, make recognizable and sharable, what Velma was like, but each personal elaboration concretized the category used to unify diverse experiences, displaying the pervasively empirical quality of typification.

The process of typification does not stop with the application of an exemplary biography. Further usage elaborates earlier typifications, spawning typifications of the typical, a process in the practical analytics of searching for detailed understanding. For example, when a participant acknowledged that, in fact, they all knew very well what "that type of patient" was like, the spokesperson routinely elaborated the type in further clarification. But what was clarified was not always composed in the same way that another person had clarified the acknowledged type. This generated subtypes—variations on the type thus being elaborated, how *the* type might manifest itself in some patients and how in others. As such, some patients became a form of that type while other patients were another form of the same type—typical wanderers all—admittedly exemplified by the film's wanderer. The process of subtypification was such that its unifying ramifications served to approximate the diverse details of the very experiences it was understood to organize, the disease thereby virtually becoming its particulars, another sense of collective representation.

THE USE OF INDEFINITE TERMS

This brings us to the use of indefinite terms in the production of a common disease biography. In the preceding paragraph, we noted that typifications were indefinitely linked with individual particulars, meaning that the variety of experiences to which a type applied could appear in many guises yet be underpinned by a single entity. It is commonplace among those concerned with the disease to describe the disease's manifestations in terms of what it may become, how it might show up at any time, what its symptoms could be. While those concerned are certain of what the disease experience is like in their own and some others' lives, the certainty is always linked, in practice, with the proviso of something else it could be.

The use of indefinite terms is part of the oral and written discourse about the disease, from the texts and talk of medical researchers to the personal documents and conversations of caregivers. Usage can be found in related medical research papers; in descriptions of the disease, its stages and symptoms, as they appear in ADRDA newsletters; and in the many pamphlets and handbooks that explain Alzheimer's disease and its management.

A knowledgeable geriatric physician who described Alzheimer's disease to a large group of service providers gathered to learn the latest information at a public conference, used indefinite terms in the same way they are applied in text and conversation. The largely nursing audience was informed of how the disease manifested itself. At one point, the geriatrician explained,

> Alzheimer's is the single most devastating disease of the elderly. Its insidious onset and course of progress strike out in various ways. The disease may present as severe language debility, an inability to

form words or sentences. In others, there is no apparent linguistic pathology, even into its later stages, but there may be a crippling memory loss. For some, the disease presents as incontinence, slovenliness, and general disorganization. In others, there may be a paranoid type of reaction.

Other speakers elaborated the symptoms that present the disease, conditionally linking the diverse manifestations. While, to some extent, conditions specified reflected the service idioms of their providers, the use of indefinite terms was common to all. Service providers of identical discipline presented reasonable links between their own range of descriptions in the same way. What one physician described as the typical way the disease might present itself medically in some patients, another physician portrayed as the contrasting, even opposite, yet typical medical form it could take in others.

The use of indefinite terms bridges opposites without contradiction. As such, while the symptoms of Alzheimer's may be, say, language deficit or verbosity, wandering or sedentariness, combativeness or withdrawal, the seemingly contradictory conditions are reasonable manifestations of the disease because they are described as possibilities, not certainties. In fact, a perusal of various symptomatologies of the disease suggests that the disease may manifest itself over the entire range of everyday experiential particulars, from the inability to use a checkbook to forgetting how to tie shoelaces. Accordingly, indefinite terms provide remarkable flexibility in the selection of typical disease characteristics, further resolving the unity-in-diversity problem.

SYNCHRONIZATION

Those concerned with recognizing the pathological meaning of general age-related troubles work at it, but they do not work at it aimlessly. What they apply, and soon discover or rediscover, is a sense of timing, a disease chronology, in principle, one with a relatively clear beginning and a systematic course of progress. The course may be delineated further into stages, phases, or earlier and later parts. Though it may be indicated repeatedly that Alzheimer's disease has an insidious onset, that quality is the result of the lack of a means of handily detecting its emergence, not of a missing origin as such. The search for onset, thus, is a reasonable, albeit perhaps difficult, pursuit. While it is said that the disease itself is an inexorable process of cognitive and, eventually, physical decline until death, its course of progress is manifested in a variety of ways in individual patients. This, too, provides for the reasoned yet highly complex search for the path the disease will take in individual patients. The integral biographical work is a process of synchronization.

Exemplars are a considerable chronological resource in biographical work. They not only typify symptoms but they display and thereby communicate diverse disease timings. Yet the question of which specific exemplar provides the semblance of particular cases is not a plain matter of matching exemplary onsets and courses of progress with individual experiences with the disease over time. Which exemplar aptly displays "what it's like" always involves interpretation, at times concerted negotiation.

This brings us to the dual character of synchronization. While course of progress is ostensibly about the precise timing of the disease's onset and development, knowledge of that is articulated through the synchronizing efforts of those who concern themselves with it, through the work of assigning the same timing to onset and course. When those concerned do synchronize their, say, sense of the disease's onset in a loved one, the disease's actual onset is revealed—until, of course, someone with a like concern challenges the timing from a different clocking. The dual character of synchronization implies that what is insidious about onset and erratic about courses of progress is as much an artifact of synchronization as of synchrony, of disease biography as a described course of illness, in the literal sense of biography.

Time and again, in the support groups studied, those concerned entertained the question of onset. This was of interest to both caregivers and service providers, onset being a useful basis from which to estimate the changing needs of both patient and caregiver. Likewise, it is apparent that the systematic attempt to locate a sense of timing concerns those with professional research interests in disease intervention. Cohen (1979), for one, presents an intriguing technique for estimating the disease's onset based on informant estimates entered onto a "Determination of Illness Graph for Onset of Dementing Illness." Although Cohen's is an important first step in the objective attempt to estimate onset, it is not clear how the differential estimates of informants are to be synchronized, which brings us full circle to the problem of the biographical work of locating unity in diversity as it applies to timing.

Consider an instance of the problem as it occurred in one of the support groups studied. A regular participant—call him "Harold"—had a rather definite sense of the onset of Alzheimer's in his wife Cynthia. Both in the proceedings and in one-to-one conversation, he was admittedly fairly certain that the disease began about four years before when Cynthia began to forget where she had put things in the house. Harold said that his wife started to act much like the well-known husband of a local ADRDA chapter officer, forgetting simple things at first, like putting her wedding ring down somewhere before she washed the dishes and not remembering where she had placed it. Harold reports that it soon was apparent that her forgetfulness was worsening, again, "just like" the exemplary husband. Later, still like the husband, Cynthia began the typical accusations. She blamed Harold for misplacing her ring, at times even accusing him of deliberately hiding it from her. While Harold was quite distraught by the accusations, it was retrospectively understandable, as he reported, given what "typically happens as the disease sets in."

Occasionally, Harold's daughter, Martha, would participate in the support group. The question of onset, of course, was not a focal topic of conversation at each meeting but it did arise one time during the study when both Harold and Martha were in attendance. As usual, Harold spoke of the disease's onset in Cynthia and compared it with the well-known husband. Hearing this, Martha respectfully disagreed. Turning to her father, she asked,

> Dad, don't you think that it started much earlier than that? Mike [her brother] and I were talking about this the other day and I think that Mother had symptoms at least ten years ago when she was still working. Remember how she would come home and complain about how everyone at work was down on her because of the way she filed things? Remember how we all blamed it on that woman she worked with, who we didn't much like anyhow? I really think now that it's more like the Rita Hayworth thing, like Mother had it for a long, long time but we just didn't notice it.

Harold admitted that his daughter, and son, might be right, that he hadn't really given that possibility much thought.

At this point, several participants joined into the discussion and, using various exemplars, more or less popular, engaged in a familiar conversation, the negotiation of the onset of disease biography, this time Cynthia's. The topic was to come up again among the regular participants. Indeed, it was of concern to everyone as each patient's biography, from time to time, became a chronological problem. For Cynthia, like others, the onset of her disease grew out of the well-intentioned attempt to locate it by Harold, Martha, Mike, and others who took up the work of setting its origin.

Synchronization is not peculiar to the biographical work of Alzheimer's disease. It is an integral aspect of the attempt to sort out diverse timings in the assessment of any disease or life event where chronology is distinctive. Roth (1963), for example, described the bargained synchronization that, in the course of self-interested negotiations, served to realize the institutional timing of individual progress in recovering from tuberculosis. However it is organized, synchronization is, and at the same time produces, collective representation, recognizable temporal unity out of individual chronologies.

SOCIAL BONDING

Social order is regularly described as a set or pattern of linkages—bonds—between actors who are more or less interdependent individuals whose repeatedly and expectantly organized actions form society or sectors thereof. The practice of everyday life, of which biographical work is a part, suggests that this is far-fetched. The social reality called Alzheimer's disease, for example, does not in any direct way link its related experiences together. Whatever links come to exist between the experiences are products of the interpretive conditions (e.g., exemplars) and practice (e.g., typifications) of those concerned.

At best, the concerned do not simply gaze upon, refer to, or talk about the diseased lives they confront in themselves or others. As manifestations of a recognizable and common disease experience, the lives are products of the biographical labor that enters into their "realization," in both senses of that term, products that in their empirical articulation also confront their concerned practitioners as the discovered realities of interest to them. Within the social dialectics of its biographical work, Alzheimer's disease is a form of social bonding, with a practical product that literally represents itself (see Bittner, 1973: 123). Be it Martha, Rita Hayworth, Velma, or another, together they stand as collective representatives of the disease, symbolically yet concretely depictive of the work that ties them together.

20

HOSPICE:
Interdependence of the Dying with Their Community

HARRY S. SHANIS
Evaluation Specialist
General Accounting Office

Currently the experience of dying in the United States is unique compared to other historical periods in terms of the ages and locations of the dying. In general, people are living longer before they die. Presently, about two-thirds of those who die in the United States are over the age of sixty. (Marshall, 1980). In contrast, in Andover, Massachusetts, throughout the eighteenth century less than two-thirds of the population lived to reach their twentieth birthday (Greven, 1970). In addition, the setting where death takes place has changed. The trend during the second half of the twentieth century is that fewer people were dying in the home (Cartwright, 1973). As many as two-thirds of all deaths are taking place in hospitals and the trend is continuing (Lerner, 1970; Kastenbaum, 1977; Lofland, 1978). About one-fourth of these people were transfered from nursing homes to the hospital when their illness became acute (Kastenbaum and Candy, 1973; Palmore, 1976; Lesnoff-Caravaglia, 1978-1979).

The experience of dying in a hospital has been described mostly in derogatory terms (Buckingham et al., 1976). Robert Buckingham researched the terminal patient using participant observation. He went to extensive measures by losing a large amount of weight and taking medication to simulate the symptoms of cancer so that he would be admitted into a hospital. While deceiving hospital staff as a cancer patient, he found virtually no doctor or staff communica-

Author's Note: *The research for this chapter was conducted with the aid of a NIMH Post-Doc fellowship at the University of Missouri–Columbia School of Medicine.*

tion with patients. There was lack of adequate eye contact or other signs of closeness. Patients were referred to by the name of a disease and the negative aspects of their conditions were accentuated. Glaser and Strauss (1965) found a similar phenomenon. They described a time when the hospital staff felt nothing more could be done as the "social death" of the patient. During that time, for all intents and purposes, the staff treated the patient as though already dead. Health professionals are socialized to act as healers. When this role is no longer a possibility, the staff of hospitals are threatened by feelings of inadequacy. There is no room in their prescribed roles for caring for these patients with simple human feeling because this would mean coming face-to-face with their failures (Mauksch, 1975).

The bureaucratic social structure of hospitals controls the dying process, alienating the patient and others (Blauner, 1966). Those in the medical profession who frequently are exposed to the death of patients systematically distance themselves from their patients. Even the language that hospital staff use presents a way of depersonalizing death (Sudnow, 1967).

These accounts of dying in a hospital would suggest advantages for dying in another setting. But a major disadvantage of dying outside of a hospital and in the home is that the presence of a terminal patient is a burden to others. Nevertheless, families are usually glad to care for the patient despite the added work it entails (Cartwright, 1973). Dying patients who were in hospitals and others who were in their homes were asked what setting they preferred. Both groups overwhelmingly desired their homes (Kalish and Reynolds 1976; Hinton, 1967). Not only do patients have a preference for where they want to die, but they attempt to see that this is carried out (Calkins, 1972). Patients want to know information about their situation in order to increase their ability to make the correct decisions (Roth, 1963). When terminal patients cannot control the course of their diseases or treatments, they may revert to disruptions of their present treatments (Simmons and Given, 1972). Overall, terminal patients want to continue to determine how they live so that their lives will make sense to themselves. In other words, people want "to write the last chapters of their autobiography" (Marshall, 1980).

Hospice care offers an alternative way of dying, addressing with its goals the issues concerned with control, treatment, lifestyle, and environment of the patient. Hospice care was developed by the English physician Cicely Saunder, who founded St. Christopher's Hospice in 1967, in suburban London for the care of dying patients with uncontrolled pain. Adopting this concept, the National Cancer Institute sponsored hospices in America in 1974, beginning with Hospice, Inc. in New Haven, Connecticut. The number of hospices are still growing with the aid of the National Hospice Organization's educational, developmental, and political advocacy activities.

The hospice way of death is an intervention technique directed toward enabling a terminal patient to die with dignity, with minimal pain in a familiar environment, which may be the patient's home, a separate wing of a hospital, or a special building. These goals of hospice are accomplished by an interdisciplinary team of health professionals, usually including a nurse, social worker, physician, and clergy, as well as volunteers from a variety of backgrounds. Each hospice usually has a number of these teams. All of these workers must go through intensive training sessions. Members of the team become involved directly when they are needed, depending on the personalized needs of the patient. Most hospice teams meet weekly to discuss all of the patients on the caseload. The team has a nurse on call 24 hours a day in case of a medical emergency. Hospice requires that the patient have a primary care provider: a relative, a friend, or a paid nurse who can give concentrated care to the patient. Those who provide primary care are instructed, assisted, and guided by the trained professionals of the hospice team. Hospices usually require that their patients have prognoses of about two to six months to live. Therefore, most of the hospice patients have cancer and are older than sixty. The reason for the maximum length of time is so that the members of the hospice team do not get too attached to their patient. Also, a relatively extensive length of care saps the hospice's limited resources. The minimum time requirement is set up by many hospices to allow enough time for the hospice team member to understand the patient's situation, which is necessary for sensitive intervention.

The major differences between traditional hospital treatment and hospice care is that the hospice technique maintains the interdependence of the terminal patient's personal network. However, most of the hospice studies focus just on the dying individual.

Buckingham and Foley (1978) found that dying patients cared for in their home by a hospice team had less anxiety, depression, and hostility toward their families (usually a spouse) compared to those living in the home but not receiving hospice care. Silver (1981) measured the well-being of hospice patients each week. She found that the longer the treatment, the more improvement. This suggests that referrals may be more beneficial if made earlier. Hinton (1981) compared patients situated in a general hospital ward, a foundation home, a hospice in-patient wing, and in the home receiving hospice in terms of the patients' own assessments of their moods and attitudes toward their care. Hospice patients had less depression, anxiety, and anger. They were more pleased with the therapy, staff, setting, and communication than those patients not receiving hospice care. In an earlier study, Hinton (1979) found that compared to those in a hospital setting, patients at home experienced a little more anxiety and irritability, but gave more praise to this outpatient system than inpatients gave to their services. Grad and Sainsburg (1968) had similar conclusions in a comparable study. Parkes (1980) conducted a matched study comparing those receiving domicilary service at St. Christopher's Hospice with a control group situated in their homes. Individuals were matched by age, sex, social class, duration of active treatment, and severity of pain before the terminal phase. Although those in the treatment group were more ill (had more physical problems) and did not live as long, they spent a smaller proportion of their time in the hospital.

A study of four rural hospices in the Midwestern United States revealed that three types of interdependence were necessary for viable survival of the hospices. Interdependence is defined as a cooperative relationship among people or organizations providing mutual benefits to those involved. The most basic type of interdependence involved a coordination of the patient with his or her primary network, usually the family. The hospice concept specifies the patient's personal relations as the primary caregivers. Another type of interdependence existed among the members of the interdisciplinary hospice team that supported the patient's network. The third type of interdependence was among the four hospice organizations and their environments.

The first part of this analysis shows how the teams of four rural hospices pursued the major goals of hospice, which involved maintaining the relationship between the patient and his or her network. The second part shows the necessary compatibility required among hospice and significant components in its environment in order for survival.

METHOD

Case studies were conducted focusing on four hospices located in rural Missouri. These hospices delivered care in the patient's home using multidisciplinary teams. Two of the hospices served the same town. The other two hospices served different towns. The four hospices were run by community boards that consisted of the working volunteers who went into the patients' homes and other citizens representing various sectors of their communities, such as college professors, funeral parlor directors, and politicians. Both the hospice, which was partially subsidized by local churches, and another hospice, which had some connection to the town's public health services, had half-time directors. One of the other hospices that was affiliated with a visiting nursing association had a volunteer director. The fourth hospice, which was affiliated with a hospital, could only sometimes pay the director and even then paid no more than for a half-time position. All of the other members of the hospice teams were volunteers including the physicians. The volunteers who were not health care professionals were predominately women in their thirties who were not working at paid full-time jobs, but taking care of their young children in their homes.

Members of the hospice teams were interviewed with open-ended questions for the purpose of understanding how the hospices emerged, their philosophy of care to the terminally ill, their experiences with recent patients, and major problems that threatened the hospice's survival. Also, physicians in the communities were interviewed about their referral practices. Another aspect of the data collection involved attending weekly case review sessions where the members of the hospice teams who had contact with the patients would present progress reports on the status of their patients. In these meetings, the entire team discussed plans for the future care of the patient. At any given time each of the hospices were caring for about 3 or 4 patients.

Throughout the 6 months of field work, 23 patients were cared for by the 4 hospices.

ACCOMPLISHING THE GOALS OF HOSPICE

According to the National Cancer Institute, the goals of a hospice program are to do the following:

(1) ease the physical discomfort of the terminal cancer patient by employing pharmaceutical and advanced clinical techniques for effective symptom control;
(2) ease the psychological discomfort of the terminal cancer patient through programs allowing for active participation in scheduled activities or periods of peaceful withdrawal as determined by the patient, and
(3) aid in maintaining the emotional equilibrium of the patient and the family as they go through the traumatic life experience of progressive disease and ultimately the final separation of death (Cohen, 1979).

These three goals of hospice were pursued by the four hospices using specific techniques. Ease of physical discomfort was accomplished by the hospice technique of prescribing medication. The hospice team caring for the patient in a setting familiar to the patient helped accomplish all three goals. Bereavement follow-up helped with the final goal of maintaining emotional equilibrium in the patient's network.

The first goal of hospice is to deliver palliative care to the patient through medication. Relief of pain is essential before the other goals of hospice can be achieved. Each of the four hospices had a physician who had specialized experience in prescribing medication according to the hospice philosophy. The hospice method of prescribing medication for the control of chronic pain advocates preventing pain before it occurs. Drugs administered as needed (PRN) are appropriate for the care of acute pain, not chronic pain. Hospice medication prescriptions that involve strong drugs such as morphine are unique for the terminal patient. Hospice physicians and nurses must have specialized knowledge about the terminal patient's medication. To illustrate, in the last 24 hours of the patient's life, less medication is required to reduce pain (Lyman and Scott, 1970). Also, addiction to drugs is not a problem because terminal patients do not usually live that long. However, many physicians do not know that morphine taken orally is not addictive even if the patient does live longer than expected. Morphine is usually strong enough to alleviate the pain of the cancer patient. Among the four hospices, appropriate prescription of medication helped to eliminate pain while maintaining the patient's mental awareness. These hospices permitted the patient and the patient's care providers to participate in the decision making of medication use.

The success of the medication prescription contributed to the patient's ability to continue communicating with others. When the patient experienced intense pain, pain was all the patient could think about. The patient's temper would be on edge, which caused him or her to complain, argue, or withdraw. This type of behavior placed an additional burden on the family. The correct prescription buffered this agitation so that the patient could stay in the home. However, too much medication interfered with mental capacities, thus disturbing normal interaction. The medication prescription affected the patient's ability to converse with others and participate in activities.

Although a familiar environment had obvious advantages over a sterile, restricting, alienating hospital room, at times the terminal patient's presence in the home was a tremendous burden on the patient's support network. Even though the purpose of the hospice team was to support the patient's network in this difficult undertaking, at times respite care was necessary to relieve the caregiving network. This required the patient to go into the hospital so that the caregiver could take a break from his or her task. Throughout the ordeal the hospice team was available to contribute a whole array of services to back up the network. Despite some difficult demands by the terminal patient on his or her network, with the assistance of hospice, the patient was able to continue to live in a familiar environment.

Patients were admitted into the hospital for respite care to relieve the family on the average about a tenth of the time they lived at home. One of the volunteers told me, "Sometimes the burden of the patient in the home becomes too much for the family even with my assistance along with volunteers and the county nurse helping out. So, the patient goes into the hospital to give us all a rest for a few days."

The hospice team provided support to the patient's personal network so that even during the crisis situation, the group was able to continue to act interdependently rather than dependently, which is the ultimate aim of the three goals of hospice. Each member of the interdisciplinary hospice teams contributed a specific skill to assist in the care of the patient so that the patient's informal support group could be maintained. The physician prescribed the medication. The social workers helped connect the patients and their network with services in the community. During times of added stress, the psychologist, a social worker, a clerical person, or spiritual advisor facilitated communication and eased the tension between the patient and others. The volunteers who were not health professionals helped with moral support, conversed with the patients and the members of their networks, and performed household tasks to free this time for the members of the network.

The team guided, instructed, and assisted the patient and the patient's network rather than manipulating the situation. The hospice team encouraged the participation of the patient's opinion, such as with the prescription of medication. In all aspects of the patient's care, the hospice teams gave control to the patients and their network, in contrast to the hospital where the patient has virtually no control.

In one of the rural hospices researched, the neighbors, family, and friends of terminal patients wanted to be trained as volunteers so that they could care for particular patients. The other hospices had volunteer teams already established for their patients. However, members of this community wanted to personalize care further by having only people who knew the patient provide the care. A volunteer insisted, "We want our neighbors to be cared for by friends." This notion required many more hours of intense volunteer training for the patient's personal network, but helped to maintain the interdependent quality of the patient's network. Because the members of the network were trained, they became more involved with the patient's care, enabling a continuation of relationships among the individuals of the patient's network.

Excessive pain was suppressed for all of the patients except for one patient who experienced intense pain. This patient was given the strongest legal drug, but she was still in agony. She had a very strong will to live despite the pain. While other patients avoided pain, if not by the medication then by sleeping, this patient stayed awake in order to relate to family and friends. Seeing the patient in this state brought them great distress. The situation would have been no better in a hospital except that the patient would not have been close to the ones she loved. In this case the family preferred to have the patient at home. One solution for future patients of this type would be to have stronger legal drugs, such as heroin for these extreme cases.

The setting where the patient died was a major means for the hospice to accomplish a modification of the second and third goals. All of the hospices in this research delivered care in the home. In the patient's home the patient was involved in the rhythm of everyday life because of the close proximity to family, friends, and neighbors. These hospices aimed at allowing the patient to remain involved in activities as well as the freedom to withdraw and to maintain the patient's equilibrium with his or her family. This is a variation of the second goal in that the National Cancer Organization's goal referred to structured activities. None of the four hospices tried to confine the behavior of their patients to structured activity. The hospice teams made it possible for terminal patients to live in a physical and social environment where individuals could pursue as close to a normal lifestyle as possible.

The third goal only referred to the patient's family. However, the patients in this research had personal networks beyond the family. Some of the patients' family members went to their jobs and returned home in the evening. Others stayed home to perform household tasks. Friends and neighbors came to visit throughout the day. Some just dropped in unannounced whereas others telephoned first.

As the patients were at home, they could participate in activities or at least observe. In some cases in each of the hospices, when the patient was bedridden, the patient's bed was moved into a central place in the home where people could be observed while involved in their daily activities and where others were easily accessible.

Several patients were living at home but continued their jobs during the day. When their symptoms appeared, preventing them from going to work, they had the support to stay at home. The home environment where the patient lived before he or she became terminally ill allowed for a continuation of a life integrated with the lives of family friends and neighbors. A woman who had a prognosis of less than six months to live contacted one of the hospices. The medical director prescribed medication to reduce her pain from the cancer symptoms. This allowed her to work at her job up to the day she died. This patient required little assistance from the hospice team. However, she felt assured that the hospice team was available for her if she needed them and for her family after her death. The security and moral support provided by the hospice encouraged her to live as she really desired.

Unlike in the traditional hospital environment, the patient who was cared for by hospice in the home was not restricted by bureaucratic rules. There were unlimited visiting hours with no minimum age and no restrictions on pets or personal possessions. Patients came and went as they pleased. In this personal environment, patients were not disturbed by hospital staff or patients who were not connected to their lives. While in a hospital, the patient is a vulnerable prey to whomever decides to drop in the room. In contrast, hospice volunteers and family members were asked by patients to only permit certain individuals to enter their homes at particular times. Patients have freedom in their homes to withdraw or engage when they want. Indicative of the privacy in the home, a patient said, "I like being with people, but nowadays I need more time to think. Being in my home helps me control when I can be alone." The familiarity of the home contained rich memories that were comforting. The patient and his or her network experienced many elements of their lives undergoing changes during this time. The familiar home environment was one less major change for the patient to adjust to during this traumatic time.

The third goal of hospice is for the team to maintain the equilibrium of the patient network while respecting its interdependence. Maintaining equilibrium among the patient's personal network while the patient was dying and after the death required a restructuring of the network. Consistent with the hospice technique in carrying this out, the team provided the network with as much control as they could handle. The hospice team facilitated communication within the patient's network so that roles and responsibilities could be transferred, dropped, and gained. In a few instances mediation by a member of the hospice was necessary. In one case a sister of a terminal patient came from the coast to the midwest requesting to see and talk with the patient. However, the patient did not want to see his sister with whom he had not talked for over five years. In this situation the coordinator, a nurse, intervened and satisfied the wishes of each of the relatives. It turned out that the sister wanted to see her brother only because she thought he wanted to see her. The director of the hospice spoke with the patient and his sister and found out that they both would be content not to get together. Miscommunications occurred often under these stressful circumstances. In a few instances when hospice was not providing care at the beginning of a dispute, it was too late for the team to help solve the problem.

Assistance by the hospice team enabled the patient's network to prolong assigning new roles to replace the space that would be left by the loss of the patient and to have freedom to interact more with the patient. The volunteers on the teams who were not health professionals substituted for the network members by performing some of the routine daily tasks such as shopping, babysitting, and cleaning. This allowed the individuals of the network extra time to adapt to the changing situation. Thus the patient's family and friends had more time to complete unfinished business involving financial matters, expressions of emotions, and exchange of information. According to the members of the hospice teams, successful leave-taking by the patient's network seemed to reduce anxiety after the patient's death. The nature of the leave-taking affected how the bereaved felt after the patient died. The team attempted to help the patient's network establish a new equilibrium in a micro-world that would not include the patient.

The hospice team followed up on their assistance to the network after the patient died. Memories of the patient were shared among the hospice team, family, and friends. The trained and experienced hospice team helped the loved ones understand what they had experienced during the terminal illness and after the death. The team empathized with the loved ones, having known the patient themselves. In a number of cases the family and friends of the patient established friendships with the members of the hospice team. After the patient died family and friends were encouraged to continue these contacts with members of the hospice team. Consequently, the patient's death did not cause an abrupt halt to these meaningful relationships.

The different hospice teams varied as to the types of services they provided for the bereaved. To some extent, their techniques differed because of each of the teams own creative ways of expressing loss, but the hospices were also restricted by limited finances and time. One of the hospices had an annual memorial service for bereaved of all of the patients who had died under the care of the hospice. Another hospice called the bereaved monthly for a year to discern if they required social services. The third hospice served the bereaved by organizing a support group. The fourth hospice sent sympathy cards and then followed up with cards to remind the bereaved that the hospice was there if needed.

HOSPICE ENVIRONMENT

The hospice had to find a niche in their environments in order to survive. According to the research of the four rural hospices, the key factors in the environment that affected the way the hospices survived were the following: a supply of patients with appropriate characteristics, community attitudes, the willingness of the members of a hospice team, physician's attitudes, the receptiveness of hospital(s) and health care agencies, and substantial funds. Each of these elements affected the others. This analysis of the emergence and survival of hospice is consistent with the life cycle approach (Kimberly et al., 1981) within the organizational literature that stresses the influence of the environmental context on the life course of an organization.

A sufficient supply of patients was necessary to maintain the active operations of the hospice teams. Most of the patients who used these four hospices were over sixty years of age and had cancer. Each of the communities where these hospices were located had an adequate number of people dying of cancer. In addition to having terminal individuals in the community who had specific characteristics, these individuals had to choose hospice care and to be referred to a hospice by the physicians who originally treated them. Mostly oncologists and general practitioners referred patients to the hospice. The physician only made an appropriate referral when the physician had a thorough understanding of the specific hospice ideology and services of a particular hospice.

Two of the directors of the hospices studied reported that when their hospices began physicians either did not refer appropriate patients or else referred them to the hospice literally the last few days of the patients' lives. Gradually, as the physicians learned more about hospice care in general and the hospice in their community, they referred patients much earlier. Physicians were socialized throughout their entire careers to follow the Hippocratic Oath, which in part requires them to pursue the act of saving the lives of their patients at all times. Most physicians at first found hospice ideology contrary to the Oath. After experience with hospice many of these physicians were able to refer the terminal patient much earlier because most began to think that referring the patients to hospice did not mean giving up on the patient who had a chance to live. Rather, they reported that they viewed hospice as a way to care for a terminally ill patient while still maintaining the patient's dignity and providing comfort. The hospices that were researched encouraged their physicians to work with the hospice team instead of releasing the patient completely to the hospice's care. The relationship between the hospice team and a physician from outside of the hospice team was sensitive to confrontation because the unconventional ways in which the hospice operated often conflicted with the physician's method. The cooperation of the physicians who potentially made referrals was vital.

An oncologist who treated over 80 percent of the cancer patients in one of the communities did not agree with the methods of the hospice that served his community. He perceived that the hospice would take the patient from his care, stop treatment, and give up all hope of survival. The oncologist's view was based on an actual experience that occurred when he transferred one of his patients to the hospice. The hospice had not dealt with the oncologist in a diplomatic manner. The hospice excluded the oncologist from involvement in the case and actually changed the patient's medication. This type of tension occurred with at least a couple of the physicians in each of the communities that the hospices served. However, it was a much more severe situation with the oncologist because he treated such a large proportion of the potential hospice patients. The other hospices attempted to work out arrangements with their community's physicians, encouraging them to participate in the care. The range of involvement in the care by physicians varied from a minor consulting role to a very active continuing relationship.

At one hospice, the amount of involvement by the patient's personal physicians modified the dynamics of the hospice team's intervention. This hospice had no trouble receiving referrals from the physicians in the community, although at first, referrals occurred during the final days before death. However, the physicians who referred patients did not have the time to attend the weekly hospice team meetings that were necessary for continued involvement with the patients. As a result, the medical director had medical responsibility for all of the hospice patients. The medical director unsuccessfully attempted to delegate the tasks that would have been performed by the primary physician among himself and the rest of the members of the team. During a hospice retreat at the house of the medical director, a patient called and then within an hour her family called also to get medical advice. It became obvious because of this incident that the medical director was overburdened because he was performing the tasks that the patients' personal physicians might have performed if they were involved. A hospice protocol was established at that meeting to distribute the after-hours calls among all of the members of the hospice team.

The community's support, in addition to the physicians' acceptance of hospice, was essential for the survival of hospice. The patient and the patient's network had to have confidence that the hospice would ease the difficulty of their situation or else they did not desire hospice services. Community attitudes were based on other factors. Because these hospices were located in the "Bible belt," attitudes toward hospice were strongly influenced by religious beliefs. However, religious beliefs had opposite effects on the attitudes of the citizens of two communities. One of the hospices was actually financially and morally supported by the leaders and congregations of local churches. Another hospice had the congregation of a couple of churches not only refuse to use the hospice but they discouraged other members of the community to use hospice care. Community attitudes affected various aspects of the hospice operations. Not only did the patients come from the community, but also volunteers and health professionals who make up the hospice team were recruited from the community.

The two hospices that were in the same community competed for volunteers and patients, sometimes in an unprofessional manner. Many of the citizens, for whom this was their first exposure to hospice, decided not to use hospice services because of incidents such as these. As a result of not getting volunteers, one of these hospices discontinued services. This hospice may reopen as part of a wing of the cancer hospital that partially supported them. If this occurs the hospital would probably seek Medicare reimbursements. This would be a symbiotic relationship between the hospital, which had many empty beds, and the hospice, which needed financial support and patient referrals. The other hospice continued to exist probably because it was connected to a visiting nurses service from which it could receive referrals. Though both of the hospices were providing free services, the community's image of hospice seemed to affect the hospice's ability to attract patients. In turn, the image of the hospice affected the hospice's very existence.

Another component of the environment with which the hospices had to interface comprised the hospitals and health care agencies. The hospice, the health care delivery organizations, and the hospitals often took turns with the same patients or provided services to patients at the same time. Hospitals usually admitted the hospice patients at least twice to inpatient care while they were being cared for by hospice. This meant that the treatment provided by the hospitals, health care agencies, and hospice had to be compatible. Unless the health professionals had confidence in the other services, they did not make referrals. The hospice teams tended to favor one hospital over another when their patients required inpatient services because of the type of care the hospitals provided. The hospices also depended on the approval of the hospitals and health agencies for referrals. Two of the hospices made special efforts to contact specific people at the area hospitals and health care agencies to explain about their hospice services. These public relations gestures have paid off because their relations to other care facilities appear to be better than those of other hospices.

The hospices that did not have home health workers or nurses as part of their organization had to coordinate with agencies that provided that care. These agencies had their own ideology and methods of operating that the hospice had to consider. For example, the hospice director of one of the hospices thought that the patients and families were feeling that workers from various agencies were randomly converging on their home. Consequently, the hospice director wanted everyone including the county nurses to say that they were part of the hospice. However, the county nursing association did not want to lose their identity in the community after spending over ten years to become established. During a board meeting discussion, one of the county nurses said, "We are paid by county nursing, not the hospice. So I'm not going to say I am part of the hospice." Working out these types of logistics involving coordination with agencies and hospitals was vital to the very survival of a hospice.

Generally, none of the four hospices were financially stable. One of the hospices has folded though it may be revived; the future of the other three hospices is precarious. The financial support of the hospice is another essential element to survival in the environment. These hospices were relatively low cost operations, but they still required money, as little as it may be, in order to survive. One of the hospices was supported by area churches, another by a cancer hospital, the third by a visiting nurses association and the fourth by local hospitals. The board of churches that governed and partially financed one of the hospices restricts the type of fundraising allowed by the hospice. The church board did not want to be associated with activities that might have compromised their public image and religious convictions. In addition to the major sources of financial support the four hospices received some private donations. The contributions from the bereaved were generally small but were accompanied by expressions of deep gratitude that served as inspiration for the hospice teams. None of the members of the hospice teams in this study were paid for their services except for the directors. The directors were never paid more than the equivalent of a half-time salary, though they often worked much more than 20 hours a week for the hospice. Office space, including telephones, was usually donated by churches or hospitals. A monthly fee for 24-hour beeper service was required in order for the nurses to be on call 24 hours a day, 7 days a week. Transportation was usually paid by volunteers, but in some cases this expense came out of hospice funds. The hospices were supported solely by volunteer work and contributions by organizations and private individuals. This unstable source of support placed these hospices in vulnerable situations. When one of the hospices was threatened with the loss of financial backing from the community churches, the hospice had to consider an offer to become affiliated with a hospital. Without the hospital's support the hospice may not survive, but the change of authority to a hospital board would jeopardize the independence and grassroots quality of the present hospice.

Limited funds required these hospices to use volunteers. The fact that the workers were volunteers seemed to have a positive effect on their relationships with patients. The patients came to regard them more as friends or family than hired workers. Many of the volunteers experienced the death of someone close before they joined the hospice. These hospices required a one-year waiting period before the bereaved could volunteer. The volunteer spirit certainly was a salient quality of the hospice teams. Attracting volunteers required good leaders in the hospice. The hospice that stopped services did so, among the other reasons previously mentioned, because individuals were no longer volunteering. This difficulty in recruiting volunteers may be caused by a number of reasons. It seemed that participation in hospice policymaking or at least agreement with the policy may have been a major influence on recruiting and maintaining volunteers. A volunteer nurse from the hospice that may have to affiliate itself with a hospital said, "I am not going to work for nothing for a private profit-making hospital." The hospices' limited funds and reliance on volunteer work set up an atmosphere of shared responsibility and shared authority among the entire group. This shared participation among the entire staff may be jeopardized by government and private intervention.

Medicare reimbursement for hospice services began in the fall of 1983 to support hospice care as a less expensive alternative to the inpatient care of the terminally ill (Pear, 1983). For the larger hospices in cities, this funding may stabilize finances. Hospices will benefit from the funding if they are able to handle the necessary bureaucratic paperwork and meet the rigid restrictions of the certification requirements. The larger hospices may be the only ones that can accomplish this task. The smaller hospices, at least the ones that were the focus of this research, decided independently not to apply for medicare reimbursements. They did not have the administrative staff to complete the necessary paperwork nor did they have the equipment and staff to comply completely with certification requirements. The four hospice boards independently decided that unless they were economically solvent, Medicare reimbursements were a risk they could not afford to take. According to Medicare regulations, if a hospice takes care of a patient, the patient is their financial responsibility until that patient dies. Hospice patients with extreme complications, requiring extensive inpatient services could place one of these small rural hospices deeply in debt because Medicare places a ceiling on individual reimbursements. Hospices will have to be very certain of the diagnosis. Also, the use of Medicare reimbursements by the hospices would compromise the present volunteer spirit and discriminate against specific types of patients. Funding would go toward paying some workers and not others which would cause conflict between volunteers and paid workers. Once workers are paid the hospice may have to only take in patients who could pay their way in order to continue paying the workers. Having paid workers might very well change the relationship between the workers and patients and between the workers and the patient's network. However, despite these possible alternations of hospice under Medicare, the future of hospice is uncertain without some type of financial backing.

CONCLUSION

This chapter showed how four hospices serving rural communities accomplished the major goals of the hospice philosophy and how the hospices found a niche in the community environment. The goals of hospice are to bring about physical comfort to the patient through palliative care; facilitate the activity or withdrawal of the patient, whichever is desired by the patient; and aid the patient and his or her network in maintaining a psychoemotional balance. Generally, the goals of hospice are focused on using multidisciplinary teams of volunteers to assist the patient and his or her network so that they may continue to interrelate and continue their lives in a familiar environment. Prescriptions of palliative medication by the hospice team physician allowed the patient to continue living with others. The patients and their networks with the help of hospice continued their lives to some extent as it was before the illness. However, to varying degrees, the physical symptoms of the terminal illness interfered with their lives. Also, the patients and their networks used their time for necessary farewells and to make arrangements for adapting to the loss of a person in the network. Bereavement care helped to ensure that the patient's network could stand on its own after the death.

This analysis of hospice demonstrates the necessity for research that includes not only the patient but the patient's network as well. The quality of life provided by hospice must be couched in terms of all of the individuals who are influenced. The experience of dying in a hospital tends to exclude family and friends. However, as the hospice technique attempts to keep intact the patient's network, shouldn't the network be the unit of analysis? Actually, consistent with hospice's critique of traditional hospital treatment of the terminal patient, one could learn a lot about the treatment by studying the entire network. This research revealed how four hospices helped to keep the patient and his or her network intact while the patient was dying and after the patient's death. The hospices attempted to personalize care by breaking down the hierarchical relationship between caregiver and patient. The alternative of hospice care placed more of the responsibility of caregiving with the family instead of completely with health professionals. However, this arrangement is not necessarily a less dependent one for the patient with his or her family as caregiver. My further research will involve interviews with patients and members of the patient's network to investigate these issues.

The second part of this analysis showed how the four hospices survived within their health environments. One of the hospices discontinued its services during the time the research was being carried out. The future of the other three hospices was precarious. The main factors influencing their survival status were the following: adequate number of appropriate patients, the community's attitude, willingness of hospice members, physicians' attitudes, relationship to hospital(s) and health care delivery agencies, and funding sources. These hospices were attempting to establish themselves in an environment of traditional health care delivery that is directed at curing an individual rather than caring for a patient and his or her network. Thus, it was necessary for the hospices to be sensitive about the image they project to the environment.

In addition to having an inconsistent medical ideology with the other elements in the environment, financial funding is also problematic. Funding from sources such as Medicare or hospitals may require compromises to the hospice ideology. A limitation of Medicare reimbursement is that it is restricted to patients with specific requirements with regard to financial status and nature of the illness. These small hospices may not be able to survive with their present funding and Medicare does not seem to be a viable solution. Preemption by new funding sources may bring about a diluted version of hospice in nursing homes, in hospitals, and in conjunction with home care agencies. Hospices would then lose their autonomy, a central focus of hospice philosophy. Hospice care as it operated in the four hospices would no longer exist unless hospices receive funding that is compatible with their goals.

21

SOCIAL FACTORS IN INSTITUTIONAL LIVING

EVA KAHANA
Director, Elderly Care Research Center

BOAZ KAHANA
Director, Mental Health and Aging Training Program

ROSALIE F. YOUNG
Researcher, Sociology
Wayne State University

The social world of institutionalized elderly is typically considered in terms of a circumscribed set of social interactions centered around staff-patient, patient-patient, and visitor-patient exchanges. There has been extensive documentation within the gerontological literature of the shrinking social interactions of the institutionalized elderly (Tobin and Lieberman, 1976; Gubrium, 1975a). Yet a more thorough consideration of the social world of the institutionalized older person reveals a complex set of social paradoxes, contingencies, and influences that touch upon diverse aspects of human interconnectedness.

The potential stress presented by institutional life has been well documented in the gerontological literature. Goffman's (1961) classic work has identified characteristics of total institutions that may result in stripping residents of their previous social and personal identity. Townsend (1962) noted the social paradox of life in institutions where the older resident remains alone amidst crowded conditions of living. Lieberman and Tobin (1983) have documented the sense of separation and rejection experienced by many institutionalized elderly.

Negative psychosocial effects of institutional living have been attributed to diverse influences ranging from relocation stress (Tobin and Lieberman, 1976) to inactivity (Gottesman and Bourstrom,

1974), overmedication (Gresham, 1976), excessive staff turnover (Kiyak and Kahana, 1983), and dehumanizing treatment by staff (Gubrium, 1975; Kahana, 1975). An underlying concern with such a broad spectrum of potentially negative environmental influences is the assumption that the more vulnerable the older person, the more severely he or she may be affected by adverse environmental conditions (Lawton, 1980).

It has been argued generally that long-term care institutions have a depersonalizing effect on residents (Coe, 1965; Lieberman, 1969) that diminishes patterns of social interaction. Yet recent studies of institutionalization have raised questions about previous assumptions regarding negative effects and decline brought about by institutional placements (Spasoff et al., 1978; Kahana and Kahana, 1984). It is now recognized that specific characteristics of persons entering institutions as well as specific features of the environment must be understood in considering the impact of institutionalization on the elderly. Accordingly, under the right circumstances, institutional life may present some potentials for positive growth experiences while it also clearly requires readaptation and may impose constraints on lifestyles of the elderly (Kahana and Kahana, 1984).

When old people enter institutions, the social relationships that previously sustained their social identities in the community become less accessible. At the same time, by entering an institution, people who previously were isolated due to limitations of mobility are nearer to others and in a social context where there is a potential for developing new relationships. Data on relocation of older persons into special housing environments indicate that the interpersonal environment of a congregate setting can provide opportunities for interaction with others that in turn enhance well-being of residents (Carp, 1968). There may be a natural drop in some interactions due to a change in accessibility to old friends and relatives, but a potential rise in other interactions due to the nearness of others in the institution. However, new social opportunities as well as constraints on social relationships are influenced by the policies and procedures of the institutions into which they have moved. The impact of these constraints and opportunities may be expected to vary based upon characteristics of the resident, the institutional social environment, and previous social relationships of the resident.

Research by anthropologists in age-homogeneous communities, Fry (1979) and Hendel-Sebestyen (1979) reveal that age may indeed provide a foundation for community. Data appears consistent in this regard, based on studies of mobile home parks, high-rise public housing, and retirement communities (Keith, 1982). Research suggests that older people in these settings engage in extensive social interactions, feeling part of a collectivity.

As these findings suggest, there is a broad spectrum of social concerns that have an impact on and shape the social world of the institutionalized person and can influence institutional outcomes. Diverse preinstitutional social and personal factors affect both entry decisions and social behavior in the institution.

These concerns actually relate to the location of social factors in the institutional paradigm. They can be among the antecedents, correlates, outcomes, or predictors of institutional behavior. Figure 21.1 illustrates this paradigm.

In this chapter, we aim to review and integrate previous research related to social aspects of institutional life. In addition, data will be presented from a recently completed longitudinal study of the initial year of institutional living (Kahana and Kahana, 1978). Researchers had followed prospective residents from the preinstitutional stage through their initial adjustments and through the first year of life in the institution. Older persons entering diverse institutional environments were also compared with a group of residents entering a senior citizens' housing site. The study encompassed self-reports of the elderly regarding life in the institution, perspectives of staff, and interviewers' observations about social interactions with respondents.

The literature reviewed and the research presented address only selected aspects of the proposed paradigm. In particular, little attention has been paid to the variation in the nature of long-term care institutions. Whereas one study may refer to skilled nursing homes, another may be based on personal care homes or homes for the aged. The preponderance of research relevant to social interactions of the institutionalized aged has been based on mildly impaired ambulatory residents receiving basic nursing care.

Attention should also be called to ambiguities involved in definition of variables and limitations of prevailing measurement approaches. This assessment of institutional social interactions may refer to the number of verbal exchanges among residents, to the number of self-reported friends within the institution, or to the number of confidants available to respondents. Actual measures typically focus on counting numbers of visitations, joint activities, friends, or confidants. Generally, little research has addressed the symbolic meaning of social ties or the emotional gratification specifically derived from interpersonal interactions. Furthermore, gerontological studies seldom employ formal network analysis in considering the social world of the institutionalized aged.

In spite of the above noted limitations, elements of previous research may be considered in the broader framework outlined in the conceptual model. In this manner, both gaps in knowledge and potentially useful areas for future research on the social world of the institutionalized elderly may be identified.

REVIEW OF PREVIOUS WORK

PREINSTITUTIONAL FACTORS

Social and Personal Factors

Diverse background factors have been cited to contribute to decisions of the elderly to enter institutions (Tobin and Lieberman, 1976). Some researchers have focused primarily on personal frailty, ill health, and inability for continued independent living (Hickey, 1980). Others have emphasized lack of informal and/or formal social supports as most important in bringing about institutionalization (Gelfand and Olsen, 1980; Lowenthal and Haven, 1968). The very process of institutionalization may be seen as symbolizing society's withdrawal from the older person (Riley and Foner, 1968).

It is increasingly recognized, however, that an interaction between personal vulnerability and loss or inadequacy of social supports is ultimately most likely to bring about institutional placements (Lawton, 1980). In a national survey of the health of older persons, Shanas (1962) found that greater numbers of functionally impaired older persons continue living independently in the community than are placed in institutions. Those remaining in the community in spite of severe incapacity are able to do so because of the availability of formal and/or informal social supports.

Changes in social systems of elderly persons were found to be the most important precipitants of institutionalization in the work by Tobin and Lieberman (1976). Of those entering institutions from the community, 60 percent had experienced adverse changes in social relations. In considering factors that made institutional settings potentially desirable to elderly seeking entry to institutions, Pincus (1968) found (1) desire for care and security, (2) desire for

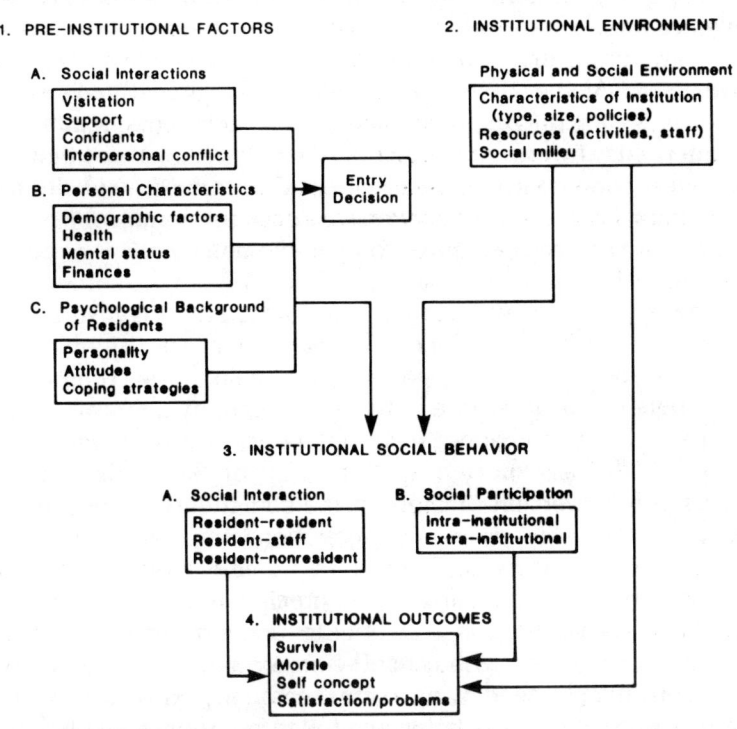

Figure 21.1 Model of Social Factors in Institutional Life

people or companionship, and (3) desire for activities to be the most important factors.

In a study of factors related to institutionalization of community aged, Lowenthal (1964) found that social isolation and an absence of supportive interpersonal relationships differentiated those aged who entered institutional facilities from those who were able to remain in the community in spite of personal frailty. Based on data from the same investigation, Lowenthal and Haven (1968) concluded that lack of a confidant was a critical factor precipitating admission of elderly to a mental hospital. These findings also fit with reports of Kramer et al. (1967) indicating that rates of first admission to psychiatric facilities are lower for older persons living with friends and relatives than for those living alone.

Supporting the above view are findings that loneliness was often given as a reason for seeking institutional placement by respondents awaiting entry to institutions for the aged (Tobin and Lieberman, 1976). At the same time, institutionalized aged have been reported to exhibit greater loneliness than their community living counterparts (Townsend, 1962). Focusing on personal psychological antecedents of institutionalization, Goldfarb (1969) attributed institutional placements to excessive dependency needs.

Tobin and Lieberman (1976) compared elderly persons awaiting institutionalization with a matched group living in the community and not seeking to enter institutions. Those entering institutions were not found to experience life events that were significantly different from those who were able to remain in the community. The single major difference between community and waiting list aged was adverse change in the relationship with a significant other, which was reported by 47 percent of waiting list elderly versus only 18 percent of those in the community. A second important difference was in the larger percentage of waiting list persons experiencing difficulties in homemaking. It is quite possible that institutionalization is precipitated when there are simultaneous decrements in abilities to function and in social support available. Fewer significant others were mentioned by waiting list elderly than by aged living in the community. Nevertheless, no real evidence of social isolation was found in interviews with those on the waiting list to institutions. In evaluating the meaning of the data, it is important to note that the nature of "negative changes with significant others" was not specified. It is also possible that reported negative changes in significant others do not reflect an actual decline in availability of social supports. Instead, they may be a function of respondents' feelings of being abandoned (Brody, 1977). It is also interesting to note that older persons who have the most available social supports express greatest opposition to entering institutions (Shanas, 1962).

A little explored factor in institutional entry decisions is concern by the elderly about being a burden to others. Although this concern is often voiced by the elderly, it has not been stressed in the literature. One exception is the observation by Kalish (1969) that older persons who anticipate impending death may seek to accelerate institutionalization to relieve their families of the burden of care. Physicians and other health care providers may also play an important role in institutionalization of older persons, ranging from the actual decision making to legitimizing family discussions about institutionalization of the older person (Hickey, 1980).

In summary, the data on social factors in entry to institutions tend to support Lawton's (1980) view that the deteriorating balance between ability for self care and social supports is usually responsible for institutional placements.

Psychological Background of Residents

There is generally a paucity of research directed at understanding personal antecedents of institutional social life. Research by Kosberg (1973) reveals that institutional resources may frequently be a function of resident characteristics. Accordingly, he found that minority elderly and those with limited financial resources are often institutionalized in facilities lacking in resources. These elderly are also more frequently placed in institutions that are geographically distant from their previous homes and families than are more affluent elderly. Thus personal characteristics of residents may have an impact on opportunities for social interactions in institutional settings.

Those elderly who had been socially isolated prior to entering institutions appear to have greatest difficulty in learning social norms of the institutions (Granick and Nahemow, 1961). This group was also found most likely to encounter problems and conflicts in interacting with other residents. Using a dependency model, Goldfarb (1969) argues that institutions' failure to meet residents' dependency needs results in negative postinstitutional outcomes.

INSTITUTIONAL ENVIRONMENT

Goffman's (1961) classical treatise, *Asylums*, describes the "moral career" of the institutionalized person through depicting the life of the inmate of a mental hospital. He argues that interactions with others in an institutional setting strip the inmate of his previous identity.

In describing the "total" institution, Goffman refers to a coercive social aspect of the institutional situation where every phase of the resident's daily activity is carried out in the immediate company of a large batch of others, all of whom are treated alike and are required to do the same activities together.

The physical and social environment of the institutional setting clearly plays an important role in defining social opportunities and lives of the institutionalized elderly. There is a sizable body of research addressing the role of physical environmental characteristics in shaping the social life of the resident. There is relatively little research, however, dealing with the impact of the social environment of institutions on resident social interactions.

Institutional social interactions among residents appear to be facilitated by spatial proximity and by organized group activities (Riley and Foner, 1968). In a study by Friedman (1966), it was found that friendship choices were most common among residents living on the same floor.

There is conflicting evidence regarding size of institutions and their impact on social interactions. In a study by Curry and Ratliff (1973), residents of larger homes appeared more isolated than those in small homes, both in terms of interactions with other residents and staff. In contrast, Lemke and Moos (1980) found greater social participation and resident involvement in decision making among residents of larger homes.

Some research evidence tends to support the hypothesis (Ward, 1984) that social withdrawal of institutionalized aged may be a response to lack of physical privacy. Conversely, it has been argued that private rooms in nursing homes may increase social interaction among residents (Lawton, 1970; Goldfarb, 1977). Underlying these expectations is the notion that territoriality is an important determinant of social behaviors.

The value of territorial markers in enhancing social interactions has been tested in an experimental study (Nelson and Paluck, 1980) that placed visual boundaries (strips of yellow tape) to divide semi-private rooms in nursing homes. Results indicated that self-esteem increased and clinical indices of maladjustment decreased among the experimental group of mentally impaired nursing home residents. No comparable changes were found in a control group that did not receive territorial markers.

In another effort at environmental manipulation (Sommer, 1970) to increase resident social interaction, furniture was rearranged in the dayroom of a home for the aged so as to decrease territorial norms that reinforced isolation. In response to a more attractive and better organized physical setting, observed verbal interactions were found to increase. However, residents also demonstrated some degree of confusion and resistance to change. These findings are congruent with results of earlier research (Lipman, 1968) that suggested that enforced proximity and fixed seating arrangements discouraged social interactions in institutional settings.

The importance of social environmental factors in affecting social behavior of the elderly was explored in a study by Kiyak and Kahana (1979). In a study of 13 homes for the aged in the Detroit Metropolitan area, a striking discrepancy was found between institutional policies regarding contact with the outside world and the degree to which residents took advantage of their freedoms. In the face of privileges such as leaving for the day, unrestricted visiting hours, owning a private phone, and visiting a family doctor, residents in many cases did not explore these options for social interactions. It appeared that informal norms may have a greater effect on residents' behavior than do formal policies in the institution.

Institutional norms have been considered as potential predictors of the degree of intimacy or distance between residents. These can regulate the degree of contact and the type of interaction occurring among residents and also between staff and residents (Lieberman and Tobin, 1983).

Provision of socially oriented group activities has been shown to increase general level of engagement by the elderly. McCormack and Whitehead (1981) found that such group activities result in greater increases in activity level than do individual activities or conditions of nonintervention. Greater institutional totality and regimentation of residents has been found to diminish patterns of interaction in institutions (Bennett, 1963). In another early study, social conflict was reported to promote social interaction in a Jewish home for the aged (Jacobs, 1969).

INSTITUTIONAL SOCIAL BEHAVIOR

Resident-Resident Social Interactions

Consistent with generally negative views of institutional life, early studies point to both the paucity and poor quality of social life in institutions. Townsend (1962: 328-329) describes the interpersonal paradox of institutional life wherein the older resident remains alone amid crowded conditions of living.

> In the institutions people live communally with a minimum of privacy and yet their relationships with each other are slender. Many subsist in a kind of defensive shell of isolation. The social experiences are limited and the staff lead a rather separate existence from them. They are deprived of intimate family relationships and can rarely find substitutes which seem to be more than a pale imitation of those enjoyed by most people living in the general community.

Loss of access to old friends has been considered to combine with problems in making new ones to diminish social interactions of the institutionalized aged (Ward, 1982).

Yet in considering legitimate goals of an institution, the elimination of isolation and opportunities for developing social contacts have been cited as major objectives (Hickey, 1980). Those elderly who had been socially isolated prior to entering institutions appear to have greatest difficulty in learning social norms of the institutions (Granick and Nahemow, 1961). This group was also found most likely to encounter problems and conflicts in interacting with other residents.

Goffman (1961) outlines the dynamics of social interaction among residents of total institutions. He argues that initial perceptions of one another tend to be negative. After the initial period of institutional adaptation, a "fraternization" process begins. This process allows formation of social bonds that are not colored by negative attributes of other residents. Based on in-depth qualitative observations of a nursing home, Gubrium (1975b) depicted residents as spending a considerable portion of their time and effort etiher maintaining or avoiding social ties. Cliques, reflecting efforts at establishing friendships and supports, were commonly found on individual floors. At the same time, efforts were often directed at avoidance of certain residents. These resident-resident interactions were seldom encouraged by staff.

A study by Baltes et al. (1983) investigated interactions of elderly residents and their social partners in a nursing home providing intermediate care. Based on 4,943 observations of 40 residents, 50 percent of interactions occurred with staff, 35 percent involved other residents while 15 percent ocurred with nonresidents. This research did not distinguish between interactions occurring among residents versus those involving both staff and residents, suggesting that there is little difference in interaction patterns among these groups. Interactional profiles were also found to be similar across length of institutionalization, sex, and health of residents. When residents exhibited dependent behaviors, social partners (both staff and other residents) typically responded by showing support. There were no consistent responses by social partners in response to independent self-care behaviors shown by residents.

Staff-Resident Interactions

In exploring staff-resident interactions, two primary areas have been investigated. On the one hand, focus has been on the degree of staff-resident interactions. On the other, the quality and nature of these interactions have been explored. Most of those few studies that empirically explored staff-resident interactions have used observational methodologies. The specific nature of staff-resident interaction has been considered primarily in terms of dependency-inducing or caretaking behaviors by staff (Behn and Stewart, 1982; Kiyak and Kahana, 1984).

Gottesman and Bourestrom (1974) studied 1144 residents in 40 nursing homes in Michigan. Behavioral observations revealed that, during a 2-day period, 73 percent had no social contact with anyone on the staff. Only 17 percent of the time were residents observed in contact with any other person, and only 7.5 percent of the time were they in contact with persons other than staff. Gubrium (1975), in an in-depth qualitative study of a single nursing home, provides valuable insights into the nature and dynamics of staff-resident interactions. Top staff were found to use 4 sources of knowledge to learn about residents. These included charts, anecdotes, incidental information, and "serious interviews." This latter source is the only one based on interpersonal contact with residents.

Watson and Maxwell (1977) found that severity of physical and medical impairment of residents is closely related to withholding of care and assistance by institutional staff. Differences in racial composition of residents and staff also affect social interactions between residents and staff. Accordingly, in a home with predominantly white, Jewish residents, white personnel were found to demonstrate significantly more expressive interactions whereas black personnel engaged in more instrumental behaviors (Watson and Maxwell, 1977).

Staff behavior and interaction with the elderly were studied observationally by Kiyak and Kahana (1984) in four institutions. Results revealed that the most common social interactions involved behaviors in which staff treated residents as equals. Dependency-inducing behavior was minimal, while at the same time, staff exhibited positive affect toward residents.

A different impression is conveyed by research considering dependency on staff from the residents' perspective. Research by

Spasoff et al. (1978), based on a longitudinal study of institutionalized elderly, indicates that residents develop increasing dependency on the staff during the course of the first year of institutional living.

With regard to self-reports of residents' or patients' interactions with staff, the majority of studies report resident satisfaction with treatment by staff (Kahana and Kahana, 1984). It should be noted, however, that these reports may be tainted by social desirability factors. Accordingly, it has been argued (Blau, 1973) that the elderly appear passive and "mellow" in order to avoid alienating those on whom they depend for their interpersonal ties.

While studies have generally focused on routine interactions among residents and staff, there is little evidence for establishment of actual social ties or emotional bonds between the two groups. One reason for lack of deeper involvement may be the differential perceptions of residents by staff and the residents themselves. In a study by Kahana and Coe (1969), residents were found to express views of self related to previous social roles and past experiences. In contrast, staff assumed a strictly management-oriented view of residents, considering them primarily in terms of degree of care they required.

It is important to note that the above discussion employed a homogeneous view of staff. Yet it is well known that residents primarily interact with lower level staff, particularly aides (Gottesman and Bourestrom, 1974). Top staff, on the other hand, play an important role in determining norms and social climate of the institution (Gubrium, 1975). Furthermore, residents often have great difficulty in reaching or communicating with professional staff who may have to be approached through intermediaries (Goffman, 1961). In future research it will be important to differentiate interactions between individual residents, resident groups, and different types and levels of staff.

Resident-Nonresident Interactions

Although institutionalization has often been depicted as reflecting abandonment of the aged by members of the family (Brody, 1977), recent research on the subject does not support this view. In a study by Seelbach and Hansen (1980), institutionalized elderly persons resembled noninstitutionalized aged and expressed overwhelmingly satisfaction with family relations. These data are also consistent with results obtained by Smith and Bengtson (1979) regarding improved family solidarity subsequent to institutionalization. In a series of open-ended interviews with 100 institutionalized elderly patients and their middle-aged children, it was found by these researchers that, from the perspective of both generations, family ties either continued or were strengthened by the institutionalization. These data were interpreted as contrary to commonly held beliefs that institutional living strains family ties. We argue that improvements in family ties are likely to occur because institutionalization eases the demands and strains placed by an elderly parent on his or her children.

Research by York and Calyson (1977) also confirms the notion that families continue to be involved with institutionalized residents both prior to the move and subsequent to institutionalization. Families also demonstrated willingness to participate in educational and therapeutic programs provided by the facilities. Those elderly receiving regular and frequent visitors were generally found to receive better care from staff (Gelfand, 1968).

In considering growing support for the view that families remain involved in diverse aspects of patient care, some caution should be exercised. These studies generally employ a survey orientation, samples are often small, and data stress quantity rather than quality of resident family interactions.

While research on family relations of the institutionalized aged reveals active visitation patterns, it appears far more difficult for residents living in institutions to continue maintaining contact with previous friends. Kahana and Harel (1972) found that 76 percent of those interviewed want to continue associations with old friends. Nevertheless, barriers exist in terms of accessibility of the institution to elderly who have transportation and health problems and few friends can continue regular visitation. Even among family members, visitation tends to be restricted to those sufficiently mobile and involved to take the active step of coming to the institution. It is noteworthy, for example (Kahana, 1976), that little actual visitation with grandchildren occurs after institutionalization. A study of the meaning of grandparenthood for the institutionalized aged nevertheless calls attention to the symbolic meaning of relationship for this group even in situations where actual interaction is diminished or absent.

While these data point to potential benefits and importance of resident-nonresident interactions, it is important to note that in fact such interactions constitute only a small minority of residents' day to day interactions.

Hendrick and Hendrick (1981) express concern regarding negative impact on visitors of interactions with the institutionalized aged. They suggest that visitors often complain about a sense of distance between themselves and the resident or resident's lack of awareness of events outside the institution.

INSTITUTIONAL OUTCOMES AND THE ROLE OF SOCIAL FACTORS

An extensive literature exists on the impact of residential relocation on the elderly. Much of this literature focuses on outcomes that pertain to resident survival. High mortality rates of the institutionalized aged are frequently noted and have been regarded by Kasl (1972) as evidence of the negative health consequences of environmental change. However, findings are contradictory. Aldrich and Mendkoff (1968) found significantly increased mortality but other researchers have demonstrated that mortality rates are not affected by relocation (Borup et al., 1978; Grey, 1978; Gutmann and Herbert, 1976; Jossman, 1967; Kowalski, 1978; Zwenz and Csank, 1975). The advanced age of the institutionalized aged certainly is a factor in both health problems and death rates (Verbrugge, 1983).

Other institutional effects have also been considered. These often concern psychosocial outcomes. Psychological effects such as a sense of separation or rejection have been documented (Lieberman and Tobin, 1983). Depersonalization is another result of institutional living, according to Coe (1965). However, in comparisons of institutionalized aged and those awaiting institutionalization, most of the psychological qualities attributed to the effects of institutional living were already present in most who were waiting (Tobin and Lieberman, 1976). These and other works give us a mixed picture of the effects of institutionalization in that they generally support a more positive view of the status of the institutionalized aged.

Recent studies have investigated factors that can mediate adverse effects of institutionalization. Social support and interaction has been considered to be potentially and actually useful in facilitating more positive outcomes. Availability of social supports seems to play an important role in mitigating the effects of deteriorating physical and mental functioning (Wan and Weissert, 1981). In one study, institutionalization per se was not found to have significant effects on residents' self-esteem, but self-esteem was found to covary with social interactions (Newman, 1964).

Pastalan (1972), based on an extensive review of research on home-to-institution relocation, concludes that those elderly who sought interactions following their move adjusted better than those who withdrew from activities.

A recent study by Wells and MacDonald (1981) focused on residents' interaction with family, staff, and other residents. Interpersonal networks of 56 residents in a home for the aged were divided into 3 network categories (close residents, close staff, and close family and friends). Measures of life satisfaction and physical and mental impairment were obtained before and after relocation. Data indicate that close primary relationships were associated with successful adjustment to relocation. However, relocation decreased the average number of relationships. Significant correlations between primary relationships and overall impairment scores are also observed, leading the researchers to conclude that interpersonal networks are a salient dimension in relocation of the elderly.

A somewhat different view regarding the role of contact with the family on postinstitutionalizational well-being is suggested by the work of Walsh and Kiracofe (1980). Their research reflects the view that when social networks of the institutionalized aged change, there is a shift away from relatives as salient members of the social network. We suggest that this shift in salient relationships away from the family may represent an important factor for successful adjustment in retirement homes.

EMPIRICAL STUDY OF
COPING WITH INSTITUTIONAL LIFE

Having reviewed previous research related to social factors in institutional life, we will now turn to a more detailed presentation of an empirical study completed by the investigators that addresses several elements of the model outlined above. This research may be viewed as a case study that highlights both problems and potentials in focusing on the social world of the institutionalized aged. It should be noted that the central focus of the research was on the relationship of diverse coping strategies to postinstitutional outcomes. Nevertheless, extensive information was obtained concerning diverse aspects of the social world of elderly entering institutions.

SAMPLE AND PROCEDURES

Data presented in this research were obtained from a 4-wave longitudinal study of elderly adaptation to institutionalization (Kahana and Kahana, 1979). 253 older adults entering 14 long-term facilities in two midwestern cities were interviewed just prior to relocation or shortly after. A comparison group was made up from 35 persons who moved into an apartment complex for the aged. In addition to premove assessments, interviews took place 2 weeks, 3 months, and 8 months after the move.

Fourteen institutions in two cities made up the facilities. These were both proprietary and nonprofit charitable or religious institutions. They were centered in two metropolitan areas and were primarily located in an urban environment with some suburban and rural representation. Half combined nursing home licensure with home for the aged or board and care home licensure. Eleven were religiously sponsored (5 Jewish, 4 Protestant, 2 Catholic institutions), and four were nonsectarian, but religious sponsorship did not limit residence to adherents of that faith. There was an average bed capacity of 203, and none of the facilities had fewer than 100 beds. Respondents were newly admitted clients to self-care or intermediate care divisions of institutions. Only ambulatory residents who were able to participate in an interview were included in the sample.

Respondents were fairly typical of those described in previous research on institutionalized aged. The mean age of the sample was 79.2 years. A total of 75 percent of the institutionalized respondents were female—61 percent had been widowed, 13 percent were married, 9 percent divorced or separated, and 10 percent had never married. They were not seriously limited in either health or mental functioning. Health scores averaged 6.4 on a scale of 4 to 8, a scale in which low scores represented good health. Mental status was at the level of 7.5 on a scale ranging from 0 to 10 where 0 reflected total disorientation to time, place, and person. It is noteworthy that these persons were more impaired physically and mentally then noninstitutionally bound older persons.

MEASURES

The study employed multimethod assessment strategies including resident interviews and staff and interviewer ratings of respondents. The variables that constituted the focus of the study correspond to some of the components of the model of social factors in institutional life presented earlier. Preinstitutional social factors, institutional social behavior, and postinstitutional well-being were major study variables. In terms of the social world of the residents, five sets of indices were developed: (1) socially oriented reasons for entering the institution, (2) socially relevant coping strategies, (3) social participation, (4) social interaction, and (5) socially oriented problems encountered in the facilities. In addition, indices of psychosocial well-being were considered. These included health (Rosow Health Scale), morale (Lawton Morale Scale), self-esteem (Coopersmith's Esteem Inventory), and mental status (Mental Status Questionnaire).

Types of reasons respondents reported for institutional entry were determined. These related to personal-emotional, social, residential, or health concerns. A subscale of the Elderly Care Research Center Coping Scale (Kahana et al., 1982) was considered as an index of socially oriented coping strategies. These included the following: talking with others about the problem; getting together with people who have the same problem; complaining about the problem to people with authority; and depending on trusted people to deal with the problem.

Self-reported social participation was considered in terms of the number of group activities in which residents engaged. These ranged from sedentary activities to those requiring physical endurance such as dancing and recreational classes. Residents' self reports regarding number of persons they talked to, felt close to, visited with, and received assistance from made up indices of social interaction. Respondent reports of personal, social, and environmental difficulties were secured. Residents' responses to open-ended questions regarding problems encountered in the institution were coded in terms of staff-related, resident-related, self-related, outsider-related, and environment-related problems.

RESULTS

Results of this study presented a more benign portrait of institutional life than that observed in a number of previous works (Lieberman, 1969; Gubrium, 1975). Residents not only survived the move and early adjustment period, but generally found life in a congregate facility to be no worse than they expected and, in many instances, better than they expected. Their morale, self-esteem, and health all remained at moderate levels or increased slightly during the first year of institutional living. These indices of well-being did not differ substantially from those of elderly who relocated to the senior citizens' housing site.

Major differences prevailed between the institutionalized and noninstitutionalized group insofar as age and reason for move. Nursing home residents were significantly older and more likely to have moved for health or interpersonal reasons. There were also substantial differences in health status and psychosocial well-being in that morale, physical health, and mental status all differed significantly prior to relocation. Higher scores in these areas were reported among those moving to the senior citizens' apartment.

Some interesting patterns of changes were noted three months after move for both the institutionalized and senior housing groups. Each group gained in self-esteem and health and showed a slight improvement in mental status. However, differences in morale favoring community elderly were no longer observable 3 months after the move. During the initial 3-month period following move, morale of nursing home residents increased slightly, whereas community living elderly showed a slight decline. Therefore, at the end of the 3-month period, the groups differed significantly only with respect to mental functioning. These data underscore the general observation that institutional life does not adversely affect psychosocial well-being of the elderly.

The present data analyses do not extend to an in-depth consideration of interinstitutional differences. It should be noted, however, that residents in different institutions represented a broad spectrum of physical and mental health conditions with significant differences observed in mean health and mental status scores among residents of the 14 facilities. Correspondingly, there were also differences in social opportunities and social participation. Sampling procedures favored relatively physically and mentally intact elderly. It is likely that more illness and psychopathology prevail when residents of skilled nursing facilities are considered who typically enter in more impaired condition. Caution must also be exercised in generalizing from findings of relative stability in the present study to groups of frail elderly who may enter institutions with major functional limitations.

**PREINSTITUTIONAL FACTORS:
SOCIAL AND PERSONAL**

In contrast to the portrayal of isolated elderly who enter institutions (Lowenthal and Haven, 1968), most persons in the study did not live alone and had family or friends nearby. There were other people with whom they visited, talked, were helped by, or lived. Only about one of ten respondents (11 percent) reported that there was no one they felt particularly close to. Social support was available and generally provided by families. Less than half (48 percent) lived alone, one-third (31 percent) with children or other relatives, and 13 percent resided with spouses. Just prior to institutionalization, respondents mentioned family members as persons they felt closest to—children (34 percent), spouses (7 percent), or other relatives (23 percent). Friends and neighbors were cited as confidants by only 23 percent of respondents.

Those awaiting entry to institutions reported fairly active visitation patterns. More than half (58 percent) reported visitations at least once weekly and 32 percent indicated several visitors or visits made in the last month. However, family, friends, and neighbors made up the visiting network of 55 percent. Helpers had been available to most respondents (61 percent) during the year prior to institutionalization. Children were the major source of aid. Nevertheless, it is noteworthy that 39 percent of those entering institutions neither sought nor received assistance.

Consideration of close relationships, however, provides a portrait of relative deprivation and isolation; one-fourth (24 percent) did not have confidants and the majority had only one other person they talked to regularly (mean score of 1.03 for the institutionalized group). Similar results were found for persons to whom respondents felt close. The number ranged from none to four, but averaged 1.5. Only 7 percent were close to three or more people.

When differences in confidants and close interpersonal relationships were considered between institutionalized and community living aged, the relative isolation of elderly entering institutions was confirmed. Significant differences were observed both in number of people they were close to and number of people available to discuss problems. In addition, institutionalized aged had significantly fewer visitors than did elderly entering a senior residence. These findings confirm the conclusions of previous studies regarding the role of social isolation and absence of confidants as an important factor in institutional placements of the elderly.

Social factors were quite influential in entry decisions. They served as the primary motivating factors for the move for almost one-half (48 percent) of the respondents. In contrast, personal-emotional factors and health needs were mentioned by 10 percent and 20 percent of the sample, respectively, and residential-environmental considerations were cited by 22 percent. Among the socially oriented entry reasons mentioned were rejection by children, death of a spouse, not wanting to be a burden, concern over being alone, and desire for greater interpersonal integration. This type of response was reflected by such statements as: "I wanted to be out of the way of my son and daughter-in-law but I don't want to be alone," "I'm hoping to meet people my age and get interested in living again," "I'm alone so I should be someplace where they will check on me."

In striking contrast were the reasons mentioned for entry to the elderly apartment facility. Less than one-third (29 percent) of tenants cited socially relevant reasons for moving into senior citizens' housing. Neighborhood and housing considerations ranked first among the noninstitutionalized group. Rarely cited were health and personal-emotional factors, each mentioned by less than 5 percent of respondents.

Entry decisions to institutions often involved significant others. More respondents shared decision making with others (48 percent) than made the decision alone (39 percent). Other persons were the sole deciders in 10 percent of the cases. Family members were most frequently reported as those helping to make the entry decisions.

Specifically, children were most often involved, mentioned by 28 percent of the cases. In contrast, professionals were rarely involved, noted by only 9 percent of those entering institutions. These results are in contrast to observations in the medical sociology literature (Hickey, 1980) about the importance of physicians in entry decisions. Some of these differences may be based on sampling strategy in the present study where only respondents entering institutions from independent living arrangements were included in the sample.

PSYCHOLOGICAL BACKGROUND OF RESIDENTS

Most of those anticipating move to an institution appeared willing or even eager to move (80 percent) and expected their stay to be permanent (82 percent). Residents tended to report that they entered homes with fairly clear expectations. A total of 79 percent of the respondents visited the home themselves, and for 67 percent of these older persons, their relatives also visited the home prior to the move. Although for most of the respondents the visit was not a comprehensive one, the majority (57.9 percent) did have a tour of the residence and talked to the staff (65.7 percent).

Social orientation of respondents prior to institutionalization was reflected in our study in socially focused coping strategies. When diverse coping strategies were compared, four socially focused items were among the most frequently endorsed by residents. Only one of the four social coping strategies ranked below the top third of the 22-item array. The foremost of these was talking with others about the problem. This was selected by almost three-fourths (72 percent) of respondents. These results indicate that interpersonal contact plays a very important role in instrumental problem resolutions of the elderly. They indirectly support Goffman's (1961) notions that interpersonal integration represents a crucial technique for coping with life in institutions.

INSTITUTIONAL SOCIAL CONTACTS AND BEHAVIOR

Three months after entry to the institution, social interaction of residents was assessed. Some contact with others both inside and outside the institution were found to be common. Few residents reported no one to whom they generally talked (12 percent) or were close to (7 percent). Yet social contacts were also generally limited. The number of persons residents talked to or were close to resembled premove figures. A total of 48 percent reported regular conversations with only one other person. Mean numbers of persons talked to was 1.2 and people close to was 1.5. Married persons were close to more people and talked to greater numbers than did the nonmarried. Although sex differences were not significant, it is noteworthy that women appeared less socially isolated than were men.

Respondents were frequently visited in the institution. Indeed, more than six of ten (64 percent) reported visits at least once a week from their most regular visitor. Major visitors were family members. Relatives were the only visitors that 27 percent of the sample received, but 13 percent were never visited by families, reporting all visitors as nonkin. Children were most frequently mentioned as visitors, 40 percent citing children. They were also noted as individuals with whom residents were most likely to talk things over.

Families were involved with respondents in other ways, particularly in providing assistance. Despite the availability of staff in the institutional setting, 17 percent of those receiving aid reported a family member as their first choice of aid.

Interaction between residents and staff was considered based on both staff and resident reports. Frequent contact with residents was cited by staff two weeks after institutionalization. Staff reported knowing about one-third of the respondents well (38 percent) and over half (58 percent) slightly. In evaluating resident adjustment, staff reported that two of ten persons (19 percent) experienced great difficulty in the first days after admission and that there were adjustment problems in 57 percent of the cases.

Staff reports regarding care provided confirmed the generally intact physical and mental status of the sample. Whereas 36 percent required almost no care and just 6 percent very much, over half (56 percent) were considered to need little or some care.

Resident reports three months after entry generally indicated no problematic staff interaction. Only about one of ten (13 percent) mentioned difficulties with staff, and these tended to involve nurses and their attitudes toward residents. Half of those with staff complaints reported that nurses were curt. These data confirm earlier research suggesting that institutional aged generally portray little dissatisfaction with staff.

SOCIAL PARTICIPATION

The majority of respondents reported that they participated in some organized social activity of the institution. The range of these activities was quite wide, encompassing both sedentary and active recreational pursuits. Religious services, movies, choral groups, exercise classes, and trips outside the institution were among activities mentioned, although not all institutions offered all. Most frequently engaged in were participatory activities such as games and bingo. Hobbies and religious participation respectively were cited as ranking second and third.

Three distinct patterns of social participation were observable. A small number of residents (17 percent) were involved in 4 or more activities, portraying a very active level of participation. The majority (48 percent) reported engaging in 1 to 3 different social activities. It is interesting to note that one-third of the sample did not participate in any organized activities of the institution. The range of activities engaged in reflects only one aspect of participation. It is possible, of course, that for some residents regular participation in even one activity affords opportunities for intense social involvement. Some marital status differences in activity levels were observed. The married were most likely to portray very high levels of participation (four or more activities), with 24 percent of the married group versus 16 percent of the nonmarried exhibiting this pattern.

When differences in social participation according to marital status are coupled with findings of greater visitation and social interaction among the married, these data suggest that having a spouse may provide the institutionalized older person with a stable base of social support and interaction. Married individuals appear to be more socially engaged both in terms of visitations and conversation patterns than any of the nonmarried categories of widowed, divorced, separated, or never married.

INTERPERSONAL CONFLICT

The present study also provides some basic descriptive data regarding the prevalence and nature of the difficulties or conflict experienced by residents in a variety of institutional environments. Among the difficulties reported, interpersonal problems were not as common as those relating to personal or environmental concerns. Interpersonal problems were reported by 34 percent of respondents while 51 percent and 43 percent respectively mentioned personal or environmental difficulties. A total of 21 percent experienced problems with family and friends and 13 percent with staff.

The most frequent type of conflict with other residents involved roommates (54 percent of those with interpersonal problems were found to have this type of difficulty). Problems with family tended to involve lack of visitation rather than interactional difficulties. Thus it is lack of contact rather than conflict that characterizes problems in family-resident relations.

When we compared these problems with type of entry decision (socially relevant or nonsocially relevant reasons), little congruence was noted. Persons who moved for interpersonal reasons were no more likely to have problems with other residents than those who entered for other reasons (29 percent of each group reported resident problems). However, they were somewhat more likely to experience problems with family insofar as frequency of contact. Of those who moved for socially related reasons, 21 percent reported problems with family or friends compared to 13 percent of those moving for other reasons. This may indicate that interpersonal conflict within the family that may have contributed to the entry decision can persist even as the person remains institutionalized.

CHANGE IN SOCIAL BEHAVIOR
SUBSEQUENT TO INSTITUTIONALIZATION

In view of the vast changes institutional life brings, changes in social behavior were expected. Indeed there was some small gain in social contact after institutionalization. However, findings from this study indicate stability in the social interactions of the elderly. No significant change occurred in either numbers of people respondents were close to (preinstitutional mean of 1.48, institutional mean of 1.52) or total number of people talked to (means of 1.03 and 1.21 preinstitutional and institutional). This general portrait of postinstitutional stability confirms findings of Lieberman and Tobin (1983).

Family visitation also changed little. At neither time period did family members represent the only visitors. Only about one-fourth of the respondents reported pre- and postinstitutional visits to be by family only. As could be anticipated, family aid patterns changed after institutionalization. Whereas over 50 percent of the preinstitutional assistance had been given by families, there was a sharp drop to 17 percent after relocation, which may reflect the availability of assistance from staff or other residents.

Although institutionalization can provide new opportunities for social interaction, the vast majority of persons felt close to the same person 3 months after entry as prior to relocation (73 percent). However, married respondents were much more likely to mention no change in confidants (80 percent) than did the nonmarried. Only about six of ten of the latter retained the same person as a confidant. Married respondents generally talked to their spouse about matters of concern while widowed respondents talked to children and never married to relatives.

Although the modal pattern observed was stability in social interactions, a notable one-third of the residents expanded or contracted their social contacts by increasing or decreasing their networks by two or more persons. The expanders and contractors were almost equal in number (34 expanders and 35 contractors), each accounting for 18 percent.

In considering what differentiated the three groups, some interesting contrasts emerged. Age proved to be an important variable with expanders being older. Thus expanders averaged 82 years in contrast to the mean age of 75 for contractors and 79 for the stable group. Sex and marital status did not prove important.

The greater likelihood of older respondents to expand social interactions may be due to limited interpersonal opportunities of the very old living independently in the community. They are likely to suffer from lack of access to friends and even unavailability of social activities and partners. For this group, institutionalization may afford renewed social opportunities and they can expand their social world after entry.

Based on the expectation that increasing social interactions may enhance psychosocial well-being, the three groups reflecting different patterns of change in social interactions were also compared for changes in morale in that greater social contact could be beneficial. Findings indicate that the majority of each group remained stable. Social expanders were no more likely to demonstrate enhanced morale than were contractors or stables. These data point to only limited utilization of social opportunities afforded by communal, age heterogeneous environments of institutions by new residents. It is interesting to note, however, that the very old demonstrate greatest likelihood of availing themselves of new social opportunities.

CHANGES IN COPING

In considering coping style of residents after institutionalization, the basic pattern found was one of stability. Three of the four socially oriented coping strategies considered changed little. Likelihood of usage three months after institutionalization was almost identical to what had been the case prior to entry. However, one strategy, complaining to people in charge, showed a linear increase in usage, rising from a preentry level of 42 percent to 59 percent. This change points to situational factors that may enhance the salience of some social coping strategies. Specifically, congregate living may require the elderly to engage those in charge in attempting to deal with problem situations. Data in terms of general stability of coping confirm the notion that coping strategies have traitlike as well as situation-specific components (Kahana et al., 1982).

Several noteworthy findings also emerged pointing to the important role of diverse coping strategies in predicting survival and psychosocial outcomes. In the larger study, coping strategies were considered in terms of instrumental, affective, and escapist modes of coping.

Data analyses indicated the prevalence of instrumental coping strategies among elderly respondents. These and avoidance/escape strategies were found to be related to positive outcomes such as survival, high morale, and self-concept. In contrast, affective coping strategies (i.e., emotional expressions) were related to negative postinstitutional outcomes. Thus it appears that the institutionalized older person who is willing and able to take instrumental action in dealing with problem situations fared well, as did the person who tended to deny stress.

Respondents' social participation during institutional life was related to psychosocial factors such as health, mental status, self-esteem, and morale. Preentry health and mental status were both found to have little correlation with self-reported social activity at T_3. Neither predicted greater social activity. However, three months after entry, social participation and some of the psychosocial measures were significantly correlated. Respondents' morale and MSQ were associated with social participation. Persons with greater involvement in social activity demonstrated higher morale ($r = .19$, $P < .01$) and mental functioning ($r = .14$, $p < .05$).

Psychosocial outcomes of residents who were more socially isolated prior to entry versus the more socially engaged did not appear to vary greatly. There were no significant differences in self-esteem, morale, or health three months after relocation among persons who had no visitors or were close to no one and those with visitors and others they were close to.

Based on the correlational nature of these data, directions for causality can only be inferred and the actual role of social activity in enhancing morale or mental alertness avails further study.

DISCUSSION AND CONCLUSIONS

In contrast to previous literature about constricting effects of institutional living, this research points to many opportunities for social contact. Older persons living in institutions who receive frequent visitors from outside have generally pleasing interactions with other residents and staff and participate in activities available at the facility. There is also a category of older people for whom there is an initial expansion of social contacts and redefinition or extension of previous social relationships with family and friends. For this group the crisis of institutionalization may have mobilized latent social resources for these older persons much as it did for those Lowenthal and Berkman (1967) studied in San Francisco.

Findings of the present study did not provide a portrait of the relatively intact recently institutionalized elderly as isolated, withdrawn, or stripped of opportunities for social interaction. Nevertheless, the social opportunities potentially posed by age-homogeneous communities did not appear to materialize in institutional settings. There is little evidence based on the data reported for widespread emergence of close and meaningful social ties among the institutionalized elderly. Social opportunities for expanding interactions were utilized by a minority. A comparable minority also reported shrinking of their social world. For most elderly, the first year of institutional life is characterized by both relative psychological and social stability.

Numerous factors interact in a complex fashion to shape the interpersonal world of the older resident. These include initiatives from others, for example, family, friends, staff, or even other residents. Initiative from the older person based on personal orientation and psychological characteristics may represent another. The institutional physical and social environment may serve to facilitate or thwart such initiatives. In the present study, it was not possible to specify the degree to which external and internal variables determine expansion or contraction of social relationships. Nevertheless, in the framework of this longitudinal study, it is possible to consider correlates of changes in social interaction patterns.

The study reviewed also calls attention to differential perspectives on the social world of the elderly institutionalized person when considered from vantage points of the resident, staff, and outside observers. A multi-method study design allows for consideration of these diverse elements. Nevertheless, an in-depth analysis of the personal or symbolic meaning of social ties was not clearly articulated by these data.

Perceptions of the qualitative value of interactions assume importance on par with actual behavior. Especially when options are limited, perceiving social support as accessible rather than remote may help to reduce some aspects of cognitive dissonance. It is also quite possible that the behavior of friends and relatives is actually quite different after the move even where visitation and formal ties continue. Information about the existence of social conflict in the institution primarily as involving other residents also calls attention to the complex dimensionality of social relations. Previous research has focused on social interactions among residents generally only as reflecting "fraternization" or friendship ties. The role of social conflict both as a precipitant of institutionalization and an aspect of institutional living deserves additional attention in future research. Conversely, greater emphasis on the nature and meaning of helping by the elderly of one another also represents an area of study with potential heuristic value.

In considering previous studies dealing with social life of the institutionalized aged, a dual pattern seems to emerge. Holistic studies of life in institutions that were conducted in the 1960s and 1970s point to a rather negative picture of diminished social ties and abandonment of the institutionalized aged by family and friends. In contrast, more recent empirical research that generally examines only selected aspects of the social interactions of institutionalized aged depicts stability or improvement in social contacts subsequent to institutionalization.

The increased social interactions, which are possible in institutions, as well as the greater attention afforded to the elderly by health care professionals, may be the ingredients that contribute to the well-being of the elderly in good quality institutions. Different conclusions arrived at by different studies may also be a function of secular changes because reports are often based on different cohorts. Furthermore, qualitative studies may provide holistic and impressionistic views of institutional life while quantitative reports present reliable data on only parts of the gestalt.

Qualitative studies consistently portray the institutionalized aged as active participants in their social world, seeking to maintain interpersonal engagement interaction. Yet they reveal relatively little about the intensity or meaning of social ties for their group.

In considering social problems, as well as social opportunities inherent in institutional living, it should be noted that communal living may be difficult for older persons even outside of institutions. Streib (1979), in his review of alternative communal living arrangements for older persons, points out that both the social structure and existence of private possessions may make adjustment to congregate life problematic.

Research on institutions has been criticized as being of variable quality. Methodological problems abound. Samples may be restricted to a few unrepresentative facilities that are interested in sponsoring or permitting research.

As our research pointed out, considerable differences exist in institutions. Not only are the physical and social environment diverse, but residents differ in characteristics. Some facilities serve the more impaired elderly while others are orientated toward ambulatory, alert persons. Therefore, interinstitutional differences should be addressed in reports about the effects of institutionalization. An additional problem is posed by the fact that control groups are seldom available and there is little comparability of measurement across studies (Riley and Foner, 1968). Furthermore, inherent in much of the research on institutions are the conceptual problems of separating effects of selection, relocation, and institutionalization (Lieberman, 1969).

In addition to methodological problems in studies of the social world of the institutionalized aged, there is a general absence of clear conceptual guidelines or theoretical orientations to guide research in this area. Both qualitative and quantitative studies tend to be descriptive and reflect an empirical orientation.

Even existing potentially relevant frameworks such as those articulated by sociologists (Goffman, 1961) and psychologists (Seligman, 1969) are seldom specifically tested in research on institutions. Articulation of the conceptual framework within which research is embedded represents a necessary first step toward advancing our understanding rather than just our data base about the social world of the institutionalized aged. In the introduction of this chapter, we aimed to take a small step in the direction of explicating the domains relevant to the study of social factors among the institutionalized aged. It should be noted that our own data drawn from a larger study exploring theoretical issues of coping among the institutionalized aged only addressed a few aspects of these domains. We are currently in the process of designing research that will meaningfully tie together qualitative and quantitative approaches in understanding the social world of the institutionalized aged.

In spite of the limitations outlined, data based on diverse studies confirm the view that close social relations are relatively uncommon among older persons in institutions. This absence of close interpersonal ties may not be a function of institutionalization per se. Instead, it is likely to reflect diminished social opportunities with significant others as persons age, which may have precipitated institutionalization in the first place.

It is also important to note that characteristics of institutionalized aged have been changing in recent years and may be projected to change further in the future. As community alternatives are increasingly available to even the frail elderly, residents of institutions are likely to become older and more vulnerable, often requiring skilled nursing care. For elderly whose mobility is restricted and who suffer from severe physical and mental impairment, social opportunities of institutional living may also be increasingly limited. Interactions with visitors and staff may take a special importance for this group of frail elders. Yet even as the nature of the social world of those living in institutions may be altered, the importance of interdependence and social relations is certain to prevail.

REFERENCES

Aakster, C.W. (1974) "Psycho-social stress and health disturbances." Social Science and Medicine 8: 77-90.
Aaron, Henry (1973) Shelter and Subsidies. Washington, DC: The Brookings Institution.
ACTION (1974) Americans Volunteer (1965). Washington, DC: ACTION.
Adams, Bert N. (1968) "The middle-class adult and his widowed or still married mother." Social Problems 16: 50-59.
——(1970) "Isolation, function, and beyond: American kinship in the 1960's." Journal of Marriage and the Family 32: 575-597.
Adams, David L. (1971) "Correlates of satisfaction among the elderly." The Gerontologist 2 (Winter): 64-68.
Adler, Robert (1974) "The role of developmental factors in susceptability to disease." International Journal of Psychiatry in Medicine 5: 367-376.
ADRDA [Alzheimer's Disease and Related Disorders Association] (1982) A Disease of the Century: The Case for the Alzheimer's Disease and Related Disorders Association and Its Fight Against Alzheimer's and Related Diseases. Chicago: ADRDA.
Albrecht, S.L., H.M., Bahr, and B.A. Chadwick (1979) "Changing family and sex roles: An assessment of age differences." Journal of Marriage and the Family 41: 41-50.
Aldrich, C. Knight and Ethel Mendkoff (1968) "Relocation of the aged and disabled: A mortality study," pp. 401-408 in B.L. Neugarten (ed.) Middle Age and Aging: A Reader in Social Psychology. Chicago: University of Chicago Press.
Altergott, K. (1980) "Variety in daily life: Time allocation and the structure of role relationships." Ph.D. Dissertation, University of Minnesota.
Amis, W.D. and S.E. Stern (1974) "A critical examination of theory and functions of voluntary associations." Journal of Voluntary Research 3: 91-99.
Antonovsky, Aaron (1979) Health, Stress, and Coping. San Francisco: Jossey-Bass.
Arling, G. (1976a) "Resistance to isolation among elderly widows." International Journal of Aging and Human Development 7: 67-86.
——(1976b) "The elderly widow and her family, neighbors and friends." Journal of Marriage and the Family 38: 757-768.
Atchley, R.C. (1976) The Sociology of Retirement. New York: Plenum.
——Linda Pignatiello, and Ellen C. Shaw (1979) "Interactions with family and friends: Marital status and occupational differences among older women." Research on Aging 1, 1: 83-95.
Babchuk, Nicholas (1978) "Aging and primary relations." International Journal of Aging and Human Development 9, 2: 137-151.
——and John Ballweg (1971) "Primary extended kin relations of Negro couples." Sociological Quarterly 12: 69-77.
Babchuk, Nicholas and Alan Bates (1963) "Primary relations of middle-class couples." American Sociological Review 28: 377-384.
Babchuk, Nicholas and Alan Booth (1969) "Voluntary association membership: A longitudinal approach." American Sociological Review 34: 31-45.

Babchuk, N., G. Peters, D.R. Hoyt, and M. Kaiser (1979) "The voluntary associations of the aged." Journal of Gerontology 34: 579-587.
Babic, Anna L. (1972) "The older volunteer: Expectations and satisfactions." The Gerontologist 12 (Spring): 87-90.
Back, Kurt W. and Linda Bourque (1970) "Life graphs: Aging and cohort effect." Journal of Gerontology 25: 249-255.
Baltes, M.M., S. Honn, E.M. Baron, M.J. Orzech, and D. Lago (1983) "On the social ecology of dependence and independence in elderly nursing home residents: A replication and extension." Journal of Gerontology 38, 5: 556-564.
Barnes, R. and M.A. Raskind (1981) "DSM-III criteria and the clinical diagnosis of dementia: A nursing home study." Journal of Gerontology 36: 20-27.
Baruch, Grace and R. Barnett (1983) "Adult daughters' relationships with their mothers." Journal of Marriage and the Family 45, 3: 601-606.
Bates, Alan (1942) "Parental roles in courtship." Social Forces 20: 483-486.
Bates, Alan and Nicholas Babchuk (1961) "The primary group: A reappraisal." Sociological Quarterly 2: 181-191.
Beck, Scott H. (1982) "Adjustment to and satisfaction with retirement." Journal of Gerontology 37: 616-624.
Becker, Howard S. and Anselm L. Strauss (1956) "Careers, personality, and adult socialization." American Journal of Sociology 62: 253-263.
Behn, J.D. and B.J. Stewart (1982) "A behavioral study of the service provision encounter." Presented at the 35th Annual Meeting of the Gerontological Society of America, Boston, November.
Bendick, Marc, Jr., and Anne D. Squire (1981) "The three experiments," pp. 51-78 in R.J. Struyk and M. Bendick, Jr. (eds.) Housing Vouchers for the Poor: Lessons From a National Experiment. Washington, DC: The Urban Institute Press.
Bengtson, V.L. (1973) The Social Psychology of Aging. New York: Bobbs-Merrill.
Bengtson, V.L., P.L. Kasschau, and P.K. Ragan (1977) "The impact of social structure on aging individuals," pp. 327-353 in J.E. Birren and K.V. Schaie (eds.), Handbook of the Psychology of Aging. New York: Van Nostrand Reinhold.
Bennett, R. (1963) "The meaning of institutional life." The Gerontologist 3: 117-125.
Berardo, F. (1967) "Social adaptation to widowhood among a rural-urban aged population." Washington State University: Agricultural Experiment Station Bulletin 689, December.
———(1970) "Survivorship and social isolation: The case of the aged widower." The Family Coordinator 19: 11-25.
Berger, Peter L. and Richard John Neuhaus (1977) To Empower People: The Role of Mediating Structures in Public Policy. Washington, DC: The American Enterprise Institute for Public Policy Research.
Bergmann, K., E.M. Foster, A.W. Justice, and V. Matthews (1978) "Management of the demented elderly patient in the community." British Journal of Psychiatry 32: 441-449.
Berkman, Lisa F. and S. Leonard Syme (1979) "Social networks, host resistance, and mortality: A nine-year follow-up study of Alameda county residents." American Journal of Epidemiology 109: 186-204.
Berkman, Paul L. (1969) "Spouseless motherhood, psychological stress, and physical morbidity." Journal of Health and Social Behavior 10: 323-334.
Bernardo, Felix (1981) "Family research and theory: Emergent topics in the 70's and the prospects for the 80's." Journal of Marriage and the Family 43: 251-254.
Biaggi, M. (1980) Testimony before the Select Committee on Aging, House of Representatives, 96th Congress, Washington, U.S. Congress, D.C.
Birenbaum, A. (1981) Health Care and Society. Montclair, NJ: Allanheld Osmun.
Bittner, Egon (1973) "Objectivity and realism in sociology," pp. 109-125 in G. Psathas (ed.) Phenomenological Sociology: Issues and Applications. New York: Wiley.
Blau, P. (1964) Exchange and Power in Social Life. New York: John Wiley.
———(1977) Inequality and Heterogeneity. New York: Free Press.

——(1982) "Structural sociology and network analyses: An overview," in P. Marsden and N. Lin (eds.) Social Structure and Network Analysis. Beverly Hills, CA: Sage.
Blau, Z. (1961) "Structural constraints on friendship in old age." American Sociology Review 26, 3: 429-439.
Blau, Zena S. (1973) Old Age in a Changing Society. New York: Franklin Watts.
——(1981) Aging in a Changing Society. New York: Franklin Watts.
Blauner, R. (1966) "Death and social structure." Psychiatry 29: 387-394.
Blazer, Dan G. (1982) "Social support and mortality in an elderly community population." American Journal of Epidemiology 115: 684-694.
Blenkner, Margaret (1969) "The normal dependencies of aging," in The Dependencies of Old People (Occasional paper in Gerontology #6). Ann Arbor, MI: Institute of Gerontology, University of Michigan (August).
Blood, Robert (1956) "Uniformities and diversities in campus dating preferences." Marriage and Family Living 18: 37-45.
Bock, E. (1972) "Aging and suicide: Significance of marital, kinship and alternative relations." Family Coordinator 21: 71-79.
Bohrnstedt, George W., and David Knoke (1982) Statistics for Social Data Analysis. Itasca, IL: Peacock.
Boissevain, Jeremy (1974) Friends of Friends. Oxford: Basic Blackwell.
Borup, J. H., D. Gallego, and P. Heffernan (1978) Geriatric Relocation. Ogden, UT: Weber State College Press.
——(1979) "Relocation and its effect on mortality." The Gerontologist 19: 135-140.
Bossard, James (1932) "Residential propinquity as a factor in marriage selection." American Journal of Sociology 38: 219-224.
Bott, Elizabeth (1972) Family and Social Network: Roles, Norms, and External Relationships in Ordinary Urban Families. New York: Free Press.
Bowles, Lynn (1976) "Older persons as providers of services: Three federal programs." Social Policy (November/December): 81-88.
Bradbury, Katherine L. and Anthony Downs [eds.] (1981) Do Housing Allowances Work? Washington, DC: The Brookings Institution.
Branch, L. G. and A. M. Jette (1981) "Elders' use of informal long-term care assistance." Presented at the annual meeting of the Gerontological Society of America, Toronto.
Brecher, Edward (1984) Love, Sex, and Aging. Boston: Little, Brown.
Brim, O. G., Jr. (1976) "Theories of the male midlife crisis." Counseling Psychologist 6: 2-9.
Brink, T. L. (1980) "The myth of the senility myth." Journal of the National Medical Association 72: 1042-1043.
Brody, E. (1973) "Help for the mentally impaired aged person—The treatment of excess disabilities," pp. 134-149 in J. Segal (ed.) Mental Health Program Reports 6. Washington, DC: DHEW.
Brody, E. M. (1977) Long-term Care of Older People. New York: Human Sciences Press.
——(1981) " 'Women in the middle' and family help to older people." The Gerontologist 21: 471-480.
Brody, S. J., S. W. Poulshock, and C. F. Masciocchi (1978) "The Family Caring Unit: A Major Consideration in the Long-term Support System." The Gerontologist 18: 556-561.
Brown, B. Bradford (1981) "A life-span approach to friendship: Age-related dimensions of an ageless relationship," pp. 23-50 in H. Lopata and D. Maines (eds.) Research in the Interweave of Social Roles: Friendship. New York: JAI.
Browne, W. P. and L. K. Olson (1983) "An introduction to public policy and aging," pp. 3-18 in W. P. Browne and L. K. Olson (eds.) Aging and Public Policy. Westport, CT: Greenwood.
Brubaker, T. H. and C. B. Hennon (1982) "Responsibility for household tasks: Comparing dual earner and dual retired marriages," pp. 205-219 in M. Szinovacz (ed.) Women's Retirement: Policy Implications of Recent Research. Beverly Hills, CA: Sage.
Buckingham, Robert W. and Susan H. Foley (1978) "A guide to evaluation research in terminal care programs," in Glen W. Davidson (ed.) The Hospice Development and Administration. Washington, DC: Hemisphere.

Buckingham, Robert, Sylvia Lack, and Balfour Mount (1976) "Living with the dying: Use of the technique of participant observation." Canadian Medical Association Journal 115: 1211-1212.
Bull, C. Neil (1983) "The relationship between voluntary association participation volunteering, and mood." Presented at 36th Annual Meeting of Gerontological Society of America, San Francisco, November.
Bull, C. Neil and Jackie B. Aucoin (1975) "Voluntary association participation and life satisfaction: A replication note." Journal of Gerontology 30, 1: 73-76.
Bultena, G.L. (1969) "Rural-urban differences in the familial interaction of the aged." Rural Sociology 34: 5-15.
Bultena, G. and V. Wood (1969) "The American retirement community: Bane or blessing?" Journal of Gerontology 24: 209-217.
Burgess, E. and H. Locke (1940) The Family. New York: American Book Company.
Burke, R. and T. Weir (1982) "Husband-wife helping relationships as moderators of experienced stress: 'The mental hygiene' function in marriage," in H. McCubbin et al. (eds.) Family Stress, Coping, and Social Support. Springfield, IL: Charles C Thomas.
Burnside, I. (1983) "Ethical issues arising in nursing." Presented at the Annual Meeting of the Gerontological Society of America, San Francisco.
Burr, W.R. (1973) Theory Construction and the Sociology of the Family. New York: John Wiley.
Busse, E.W. and E. Pfeiffer (1973) Mental Illness in Later Life. Washington, DC: American Psychiatric Association.
Butler, R.N. (1975) Why Survive? Being Old In America. New York: Harper and Row.
Bytheway, William (1981) "The variation with age of age differences in marriage." Journal of Marriage and the Family 43: 923-927.
Calkins, K. (1972) "Shouldering a Burden." Omega 3, 1: 23-36.
Cameron, P. (1968) "Masculinity/femininity of the aged." Journal of Gerontology 23: 63-65.
———(1976) "Masculinity/femininity of the generation: As self-reported as stereotypically appraised." International Journal of Aging and Human Development 7: 143-151.
Cantor, M.H. (1975) "Life space and the social support system of the inner city elderly of New York." The Gerontologist 15: 23-27.
———(1979) "Neighbours and friends: An overlooked resource in the informal support system." Research on Aging 1: 434-463.
———(1983) "Strain among caregivers: A study of experience in the United States." The Gerontologist 23: 597-604.
Caplan, Robert D. (1979) "Patient, provider, and organization: Hypothesized determinants of adherence," pp. 75-110 in S.J. Cohen (ed.) New Directions in Patient Compliance. Lexington, MA: Lexington.
———Elizabeth A.R. Robinson, John R.P. French, Jr., John R. Caldwell, and Marybeth Shinn (1976) "Adhering to medical regimens: Pilot experiments in patient education and social support." Ann Arbor, MI: Institute for Social Research.
Cargan, Leonard and Y.M. Melko (1982) Singles: Myths and Realities. Beverly Hills, CA: Sage.
Carp, F.M. (1968) "Person-environment congruence in engagement." The Gerontologist 8: 184-188.
Cartwright, A. (1973) Life Before Death. London: Routledge and Kegan Paul.
Carveth, W. Bruce and Benjamin H. Gottlieb (1979) "The measurement of social support and its relation to stress." Canadian Journal of Behavioral Science 11: 179-188.
Cassel, John (1966) "Social class and mental disorders: An analysis of the limitations and potentialities of current epidemiological approaches," pp. 42-53 in Mental Health and the Lower Social Classes (Florida State University Study No. 49). Tallahassee, FL: Florida State University.
Cavan, Ruth S., E. Burgess, R. Havighurst, and H. Goldhamer (1949) Personal Adjustment in Old Age. Chicago: Science Research Associates, Inc.
Chan, Kwok Bun (1977) "Individual differences in reactions to stress and their personality and situational determinants: Some implications for community mental health." Social Science and Medicine 11: 89-103.

References

Chappell, N. L. (1983) "Informal support networks among the elderly." Research on Aging 5: 77-100.

———(forthcoming) "Social support and the receipt of home care services." The Gerontologist.

Chenoweth, B. and B. Spencer (1983) "Alzheimer's disease: Subjective experiences of families." Presented at the Annual Meeting of the Gerontological Society of America, San Francisco.

Chesser, Barbara (1980) "Analysis of wedding rituals: An attempt to make weddings more meaningful." Family Relations 29, 2: 204-209.

Clark, J. and N. Collishaw (1975) "Canada's older population." Staff paper, Ottawa: Long Range Health Planning, National Health and Welfare.

Clark, M. (1972) "Cultural values and dependency in later life," in D. O. Cowgill and L. Holmes (eds.) Aging and Modernization. New York: Appleton-Century-Crofts.

———and B. G. Anderson (1967) Culture and Aging: An Anthropological Study of Older Americans. Springfield, IL: Charles C Thomas.

Cleveland, M. (1976) "Sex in marriage: Age 40 and beyond." Family Coordinator 25, 3: 233-240.

Cobb, Sidney (1976) "Social support as a moderator of life stress." Psychosomatic medicine 38: 300-314.

———(1979) "Social support and health through the life course," in M. W. Riley (ed.) Aging from Birth to Death. Boulder, CO: Westview.

Cochran, William (1977) Sampling Techniques. New York: Wiley.

Coe, R. M. (1965) "Self-conception and institutionalization," in A. M. Rose and W. A. Peterson (eds.) Older People and Their Social World. Philadelphia: F. A. Davis.

Cohen, Donna (1979) "Assessment and diagnosis of dementing illness." Presented at the Brookdale Institute of Gerontology and Adult Human Development, Jerusalem, Israel, December.

Cohen, Kenneth P. (1979) Hospice: Prescription for Terminal Care. Germantown, MD: Aspen Systems.

Cohler, Bertram J. (1983) "Autonomy and interdependence in the family of adulthood: A psychological perspective." The Gerontologist 23, 1: 33-39.

———and Henry J. Grunebaum (1981) Mothers, Grandmothers, and Daughters. New York: Wiley Interscience Publishers.

Cohler, Bertram J. and M. A. Lieberman (1980) "Social relations and mental health." Research on Aging 2: 445-469.

Cole, Elbert (1981) "Lay ministries with older adults," pp. 250-266 in Wm. Clements (ed.) Ministry with the Aging. San Francisco: Harper & Row.

Coleman, Richard P. (1978) Seven Levels of Housing: An Exploration in Public Imagery. Cambridge, MA: Joint Center for Urban Studies of the Massachusetts Institute of Technology and Harvard University, Working Paper #49.

———and Bernice L. Neugarten (1971) Social Status in the City. San Francisco: Jossey-Bass.

Coleman, Richard P., Lee Rainwater, with Kent A. McClelland (1978) Social Standing in America: New Dimensions of Class. New York: Basic.

Comptroller General of the U.S. (1977) "The well-being of older people in Cleveland, Ohio." Washington, DC: U.S. General Accounting Office.

Conner, Karen A., Edward Powers, and Gordon L. Bultena (1979) "Social interaction and life satisfaction: an empirical assessment of late life patterns." Journal of Gerontology 34: 116-121.

Cooley, Charles H. (1909) Social Organization. New York: Scribner.

Coombs, Robert and William Kerkel (1966) "Sex differences in dating aspirations and satisfaction with computer selected partners." Journal of Marriage and the Family 28: 62-66.

Coopersmith, S. (1967) The Antecedents of Self-Esteem. San Francisco: W. H. Freeman.

Coser, Rose Laub (1966) "Role distance, sociological ambivalence and transitional status systems." American Journal of Sociology 72: 173-187.

Coult, Allan and Robert Habenstein (1962) "The study of extended kinship in urban society." Sociological Quarterly 3: 141-145.

Craven, Paul and Barry Wellman (1973) "The network city." Sociological Inquiry 43: 57-88.

Crawford, M. (1971) "Retirement and disengagement." Human Relations 24: 255-278.
Croog, Sydney H., Alberta Lipson, and Sol Levine (1972) "Help patterns in severe illness: The roles of kin network, non-family resources, and institutions." Journal of Marriage and the Family 34: 32-41.
Crosby, F. (1982) Relative Deprivation and Working Women. New York: Oxford University Press.
Crystal, Steven (1982) America's Old Age Crisis: Public Policy and the Two Worlds of Aging. New York: Basic.
Cubbitt, Tessa (1973) "Network density among urban families," pp. 67-82 in J. Boissevain and J.C. Mitchell (eds.) Network Analysis: Studies in Human Interaction. The Hague: Moton.
Cumming, Elaine and David Schneider (1961) "Sibling solidarity: A property of American kinship." American Anthropologist 63: 498-507.
Cuomo, Mario (1983) Forest Hills Diary: The Crisis of Low-Income Housing. New York: Random.
Current Population Reports (1978) 1976 Survey of Institutionalized Persons: A Study of Persons Receiving Long-term Care. U.S. Department of Commerce, Bureau of the Census, Series P-23, No. 69, June.
Curry T. and Ratliff, B. (1973) "The effects of nursing home size on resident isolation and life satisfaction." The Gerontologist 13: 295-298.
Curtis, J. (1971) "Voluntary association joining: A cross-national comparative note." American Sociological Review 36 (October): 872-880.
Cutler, Neal (1977) "Toward an age-appropriate typology for the study of participation of older persons in voluntary associations." Presented at the annual meeting of the Gerontological Society, San Francisco, CA.
Cutler, S.J. (1973) "Voluntary association participation and life satisfaction: A cautionary research note." Journal of Gerontology 28: 96-100.
———(1976) "Membership in different types of voluntary associations and psychological well-being." The Gerontologist 16 (August): 335-339.
———(1977) "Aging and voluntary association participation." Journal of Gerontology 32: 470-479.
Danielson, Michael (1976) The Politics of Exclusion. New York: Columbia University Press.
Danis, Benjamin G. and Barbara Silverstone (1981) "The impact of caregiving: A difference between wives and daughters?" Presented at the 34th Annual Meeting of the Gerontological Society, November.
Davidson, Terrence N., M. Leora Bowden, Daniel Tholen, Michael H. James, and Irving Feller (1981) "Social support and post-burn adjustment." Archives of Physical Medicine and Rehabilitation 62: 274-278.
Davis, Kingsley (1940) "Extreme social isolation of a child." American Journal of Sociology 45: 554-565.
———(1947) "Final note on a case of extreme isolation." American Journal of Sociology 52: 432-437.
———(1948) Human Society. New York: Macmillan.
Dean, Alfred and Nan Lin (1977) "The stress-buffering role of social support." The Journal of Nervous and Mental Disease 165: 403-417.
DeTocqueville, A. (1945) Democracy in America. New York: Alfred A. Knopf.
Diamond, Margaret (1979) "Social support and adaptation to chronic illness: The case of maintenance hemodialysis." Research in Nursing and Health 2: 101-108.
DiMatteo, M. Robin and Ron Hays (1981) "Social support and serious illness," pp. 117-148 in B.H. Gottlieb (ed.) Social Networks and Social Support. Beverly Hills, CA: Sage.
Dobson, C. (1983) "Sex-role and marital role expectations," pp. 109-126 in T.H. Brubaker (ed.) Family Relationships in Later Life. Beverly Hills, CA: Sage.
Dohrenwend, Barbara Snell (1973) "Life events as stressors: A methodological inquiry." Journal of Health and Social Behavior 14: 167-175.
Dono, John E., C.M. Falbe, B.L. Kail, E. Litwak, R.H. Sherman, and D. Siegel (1979) "Primary groups in old age: Structure and function." Research on Aging 1, 4: 403-433.
Dowd, James (1975) "Aging and exchange: A preface to theory." Journal of Gerontology 30: 584-594.

———(1980) Stratification Among the Aged. Monterey, CA: Brooks/Cole.
———and Ralph LaRossa (1982) "Primary group contact and elderly morale: An exchange/power analysis." Sociology and Social Research 66: 184-197.
Downs, Anthony and Katherine L. Bradbury (1981) "Conference discussion," pp. 375-404 in K. L. Bradbury and A. Downs (eds.) Do Housing Allowances Work? Washington, DC: The Brookings Institution.
Dukepoo, Frank C. (1980) The Elder American Indian. San Diego: San Diego State University, Campanile Press.
Dunlop, Burton D. (1980) "Expanded home-based care for the impaired elderly: Solution or pipe dream?" American Journal of Public Health 70: 514-519.
Durkheim, Emile (1951) Suicide: A Study in Sociology. Glencoe: The Free Press.
———(1964) The Division of Labor in Society. New York: The Free Press.
———(1973) On Morality and Society (Robert N. Bellah, ed.). Chicago: University of Chicago Press.
Duvall, E. M. (1962) Family Development. Philadelphia: J. B. Lippincott & Co.
Eaton, William W. (1978) "Life events, social supports, and psychiatric symptoms: A Re-analysis of the New Haven data." Journal of Health and Social Behavior 19: 230-234.
Ebert, R. H. (1977) "Medical education in the United States." Daedalus 106: 171-184.
Edwards, John N. and David L. Klemmack (1973) "Correlates of life satisfaction: A reexamination." Journal of Gerontology 28: 497-502.
Ehrmann, Winston (1959) Premarital Dating Behavior. New York: Holt, Rinehart & Winston.
Eisenberg, L. (1979) "A friend, not an apple, a day will keep the doctor away." American Journal of Medicine 66: 551-553.
Emerson, R. M. (1981) "Observational field work." Annual Review of Sociology 7: 351-378.
Elder, Glen (1975) "Age differentiation and the life course." Annual Review of Sociology 1: 165-190.
Elwell, F. and Alice D. Maltbie-Crannell (1981) "The impact of role loss upon coping resources and life satisfaction of the elderly." Journal of Gerontology 36: 223-232.
Engle, Veronica F. (1984) "Stability of mental status and function four days following relocation to a nursing home." Research in Nursing and Health.
———and Marshall J. Graney (1984) "Self-assessed and functional health of older women." International Journal of Aging and Human Development.
Ericksen, J. A., W. L. Yancey, and E. P. Ericksen (1979) "The division of labor." Journal of Marriage and the Family 41: 301-313.
Erikson, E. (1963) Childhood and Society. New York: W. W. Norton.
Estes, Carol (1979) The Aging Enterprise. San Francisco: Jossey-Bass.
Evans, Ron L. and Lawrence K. Northwood (1979) "The utility of natural help relationships." Social Science and Medicine 13A: 789-795.
Farkas, G. (1976) "Education, wage rates, and the division of labor between husband and wife." Journal of Marriage and The Family 38: 473-483.
Feil, N. (1980) Validation/Fantasy Therapy: New Manual Tells How to Help Disoriented Old-Old. Cleveland: Edward Feil.
Feingold, Alan (1982) "Physical attractiveness and romantic evolvement." Psychological Reports 50: 802.
Fenwick, R. and C. M. Barresi (1981) "Health consequences of marital status change among the elderly." Journal of Health and Social Behavior 22: 106-116.
Ferguson, Kristi and Giles G. Bole (1979) "Family support, health beliefs, and therapeutic compliance in patients with rheumatoid arthritis." Patient Counselling and Health Education 1: 101-105.
Ferlic, Mary, Anne Goldman, and B. J. Kennedy (1979) "Group counseling in adult patients with advanced cancer." Cancer 43: 760-766.
Ferraro, Kenneth F. (1982) "The health consequences of relocation among the aged in the community." Journal of Gerontology 38: 90-96.
———and C. Barresi (1982) "The impact of widowhood on the social relations of Older persons." Research on Aging 4 (June): 227-247.

Filipic, Lois and Zev Harel (1978) "Roles and functions of RSVP." Volunteer Administration 10 (Winter).

Finlayson, Angela (1976) "Social networks as coping resources. Lay help and consultation patterns used by women in husbands' post-infarction career." Social Science and Medicine 10: 97-103.

Fischer, Claude (1977a) "Perspectives on community and personal relations," pp. 1-16 in C.S. Fischer et al. Networks and Places: Social Relations in the Urban Setting. New York: The Free Press.

——(1977b) "Network analysis and urban studies," pp. 17-37 in C.S. Fischer et al. Networks and Places: Social Relations in the Urban Setting. New York: The Free Press.

——(1982) To Dwell Among Friends: Personal Networks in Town and City. Chicago: University of Chicago Press.

——and Stacy Oliker (1983) "A research note on friendship, gender, and the life cycle." Social Forces 62: 124-133.

Fischer, Claude, Robert Jackson, C. Ann Stueve, Kathleen Gerson, and Lynne Jones (1977) Networks and Places: Social Relations in the Urban Setting. New York: Free Press.

Fischer, Lucy R. (1981) "Transitions in the mother-daughter relationship." Journal of Marriage and the Family 43: 613-622.

Fischer, Lucy Rose, with Carol Hoffman (forthcoming) "Who cares for the elderly: The dilemma of family support." In M. Lewis and J. Miller (eds.) Social Problems and Public Policies. JAI.

Folkman, Susan and Richard S. Lazarus (1980) "An analysis of coping in a middle-aged community sample." Journal of Health and Social Behavior 21: 219-239.

Foner, A. and D.I. Kertzer (1978) "Transitions over the life course: Lessons From age-set societies." American Journal of Sociology 83: 1081-1104.

——(1979) "Intrinsic and extrinsic sources of change in life-course transitions," In M.W. Riley (ed.) Aging From Birth to Death. Boulder, CO: Westview.

Foskett, John (1955) "Social structure and social participation." American Sociological Review 20: 431-438.

Freeman, Howard, Edwin Novak, and Leo Reader (1957) "Correlations of membership in voluntary associations." American Sociological Review 22: 528-533.

Freud, S. (1953) The Standard Edition of the Complete Psychological Works. London: Hogarth.

Fried, Marc (1963) "Grieving for a lost home," pp. 151-171 in L.J. Duhl (ed.) The Urban Condition: People and Policy in the Metropolis. New York: Basic.

——and Peggy Gleicher (1970) "Some sources of residential satisfaction in an urban slum," pp. 730-746 in R. Gutman and D. Popenoe (eds.) Neighborhood, City and Metropolis: An Integrated Reader in Urban Sociology. New York: Random House.

Frieden, Bernard J. (1971) "Improving federal housing subsidies: Summary report," pp. 489-523 in U.S. Congress, Housing Committee on Banking and Currency, Papers Submitted to Subcommittee on Housing Panels, 92 Cong., 1st Sess., Part 2.

——with Adrian Ruth Walter (1980) "What have we learned from the housing allowance experiment?" Cambridge, MA: Joint Center for Urban Studies of the Massachusetts Institute of Technology and Harvard University, Working Paper No. 62.

Friedman, Edward P. (1966) "Spatial proximity and social interaction in a home for the aged." Journal of Gerontology 21: 566-570.

Friedmann, Lawrence M. (1968) Government and Slum Housing: A Century of Frustration. Chicago: Rand McNally.

Fry, C. (1979) "Structural conditions affecting community formation among the aged." Anthropological Quarterly 52, 1: 7-18. (special issue, J. Keith [ed.], The Ethnography of Old Age)

Fuller, Sara S. and Sandra B. Larson (1980) "Life events, emotional support, and health of older people." Research in Nursing and Health 9: 81-89.

Gadow, Sally (1983) "Frailty and strength: The dialectic in aging." The Gerontologist 23, 2: 144-147.

Gallup Organization, Inc. (1981) "Americans Volunteer." (Poll conducted for Independent Sector). Princeton, NJ: Author.

Gans, Herbert (1967) The Levittowners. New York: Vintage.

Garfinkel, Harold (1967) Studies in Ethnomethodology. Englewood Cliffs, NJ: Prentice-Hall.

Garrity, Thomas F. (1973) "Vocational adjustment after first myocardial infarction; comparative assessment of several variables suggested in the literature." Social Science and Medicine 7: 705-717.

Geerken, M. and W. Gove (1983) At Home and At Work. Beverly Hills, CA: Sage.

Geertsen, H. Reed, Robert M. Gray, and John R. Ward (1973) "Patient non-compliance within the context of seeking medical care for arthritis." Journal of Chronic Diseases 26: 689-698.

Gelfand, D. E. (1968) "Visiting patterns and social adjustment in an old age home." The Gerontologist 8: 272-275.

―――and J. K. Olsen (1980) The Aging Network: Programs and Services. New York: Springer.

George, L. K. (1980) Role Transitions in Later Life. Monterey, CA: Brooks/Cole.

―――and George L. Maddox (1977) "Subjective adaptation to loss of the work role: A longitudinal study." Journal of Gerontology 32: 456-462.

Gergen, Kenneth L. (1980) "The emerging crisis in life-span developmental theory," pp. 31-63 in P. B. Baltes and O. G. Brim (eds.) Life-Span Development and Behavior. New York: Academic.

Gibbs, J. M. (1978) "Role changes associated with widowhood among middle and upper-class women." Mid-American Review of Sociology 3: 17-33.

Gibson, Geoffrey (1972) "Kin family network: Overheralded structure in past conceptualization of family functioning." Journal of Marriage and the Family 34: 13-24.

Gilbert, John P., Richard J. Light, and Frederick Mosteller (1977) "Assessing social innovations: An empirical base for policy," pp. 185-241 in W. B. Fairley and F. Mosteller (eds.) Statistics and Public Police. Reading, MA: Addison-Wesley.

Gilhooly, M. L. M. (1984) "The social dimensions of senile dementia," in I. Hanley and J. Hodge (eds.) Psychological Approaches and the Care of the Elderly. London: Croom Helm.

Givens, B., C. W. Givens, and L. E. Simoni (1979) "Relations of processes of care to patient outcomes." Nursing Research 28, 20.

Glaser, Barney and Anselm Strauss (1965) "The social loss of dying patients." American Journal of Nursing 63: 119-121.

―――(1966) Awareness of Dying. Chicago: Aldine.

―――(1968) Time for Dying. Chicago: Aldine.

―――(1971) Status Passages. New York: Aldine-Atherton.

Glaze, Bobbie (1982) "A never-ending funeral: One family's struggle." Generations 7: 41, 52.

Glazier, W. (1973) "The task of medicine." Scientific American (April): 13-17.

Glick, Ira O., Robert S. Weiss, and C. Murray Parkes (1974) The First Year of Bereavement. New York: John Wiley.

Glick, Paul F. and A. S. Norton (1977) Population Reports. Washington, DC: Bureau of the Census.

Goedert, Jeanne E. (1978) Generalizing from the Experimental Housing Allowance Program, An Assessment of Site Representatives. Washington, DC: The Urban Institute.

Goffman, Erving (1961) Asylums. Garden City, NY: Doubleday.

―――(1974) Frame Analysis. New York: Harper & Row.

Goldfarb, A. I. (1969) "Predicting mortality in the institutionalized aged." Archives of General Psychiatry 21: 172-176.

―――(1977) "Institutional care of the aged," in E. W. Busse and E. Pfeiffer (eds.) Behavior and Adaptation in Late Life. Boston: Little, Brown.

Goldstein, M. (1979) "The sociology of mental health and illness." Annual Review of Sociology 5: 381-409.

Gore, Susan (1978) "The effect of social support in moderating health consequences of unemployment." Journal of Health and Social Behavior 19: 157-165.

―――and Thomas W. Mangione (1983) "Social roles, sex roles, and psychological distress: Additive and interactive models of sex differences." Journal of Health and Social Behavior 24: 300-312.

Gottesman, L. E. and N. C. Bourestrom (1974) "Why nursing homes do what they do." The Gerontologist 14: 501-506.

Gove, W. (1972) "The relationship between sex roles, marital status and mental illness." Social Forces 51: 34-44.

Government of Manitoba (1974) "A home care program for Manitoba." Manitoba: Division of Research, Planning and Program Development, Manitoba Department of Health and Social Development, April.

Grad, J. and P. Sainsburg (1968) "The effects that patients have on their families in a community care and a control psychiatric service—A two year follow up." British Journal of Psychiatry 114: 265-278.

Graney, Marshall, J. (1975) "Happiness and social participation in aging." Journal of Gerontology 30, 6: 701-706.

———(1979) "An Exploration of Social Factors Influencing the Sex Differential in Mortality." Sociological Symposium 28: 1-26.

———and Renee M. Zimmerman (1980) "Health self-report correlates among older people in national random sample data." Mid-American Review of Sociology 5: 47-59.

———(1981) "Causes and consequences of health self-report variations among older people." International Journal of Aging and Human Development 24: 291-300.

Granick, R. and Nahemow, L.D. (1961) "Preadmission isolation as a factor in adjustment to an old age home," pp. 285-302 in P.H. Zubin and J. Zubin (eds.) Psychopathology of Aging. New York: Grune & Stratton.

Granovetter, Mark S. (1973) "The strength of weak ties." American Journal of Sociology 78: 1360-1380.

Greer, Scott (1955) Social Organization. New York: Random House.

Gresham, M.L. (1976) "The infantilization of the elderly: A developing concept." Nursing Forum 15: 195-210.

Greven, P., Jr. (1970) Four Generations: Population, Land, Family in Colonial Andover, Massachusetts. Ithaca, NY: Cornell University Press.

Gubrium, Jaber F. (1974) "Marital desolation and the evaluation of everyday life in old age." Journal of Marriage and the Family 36: 107-113.

———(1975a) "Being single in old age." International Journal of Aging and Human Development 1: 29-41.

———(1975b) Living and Dying at Murray Manor. New York: St. Martin's Press.

———(forthcoming) Oldtimers and Alzheimer's: The Descriptive Organization of Senility. Milwaukee: Marquette University.

———and David R. Buckholdt (1977) Toward Maturity: The Social Processing of Human Development. San Francisco: Jossey-Bass.

Gubrium, Jaber F. and Robert J. Lynott (1983) "Rethinking life satisfaction." Human Organization 42: 30-38.

Guideposts Associates, Inc. (1978) "Volunteer to live." Guideposts. New York: October.

Gurland, B.J. (1981) "The borderland of dementia: The influence of sociocultural characteristics on rates of dementia occurring in the senium," pp. 61-80 in N. Miller and G.D. Cohen (eds.) Clinical Aspects of Alzheimer's Disease and Senile Dementia. New York: Raven.

Gutmann, D.L. (1975) "Parenthood: Key to the comparative psychology of the life cycle." pp. 167-184 in N. Datan and L. Ginsburg (eds.) Developmental Psychology: Normative Life Crisis. New York: Academic.

———(1977) "The cross-cultural perspective: Notes toward a comparative psychology of aging," pp. 167-184 in J.E. Birren and K.W. Schaie (eds.) Handbook of the Psychology of Aging. New York: Van Nostrand Reinhold.

Haase, Gunter R. (1977) "Diseases presenting as dementia," pp. 26-67 in C.E. Wells (ed.) Dementia. Philadelphia: F.A. Davis.

Hammer, Muriel (1983) " 'Core' and 'extended' social networks in relation to health and illness." Social Science and Medicine 17: 405-411.

Hannan, Michael T., Nancy Brandon Tuma, and Lyle P. Groeneveld (1978) "Income and independence effect on marital dissolution: Results from the Seattle and Denver income maintenance experiments." American Journal of Sociology 84: 611-633.

Harel, Z., E. Kahana, and E. Felton (1975) "The international congress on gerontology proceedings." Jerusalem, Israel.

Hares, Z. and D. Schur (1975) Retired Senior Volunteer Biography: A Preliminary Investigation. Cleveland, OH: Benjamin Rose.

Hareven, Tamara (1978) "Cycles, courses and cohorts: Reflections on theoretical and methodological approaches to the historical study of family development." Journal of Social History 12: 97-109.
Harmon, David K., Minoru Masuda, and Thomas H. Holmes (1970) "The social readjustment rating scale: A cross-cultural study of Western Europeans and Americans." Journal of Psychosomatic Research 14: 391-400.
Harry, Joseph (1970) "Family localism and social participation." American Journal of Sociology 75: 821-827.
Hartman, Chester (1964) "The housing of relocated families." Journal of the American Institute of Planners 30: 266-286.
———(1975) Housing and Social Policy. Englewood Cliffs, NJ: Prentice-Hall.
Harvey, Carol D. and Howard M. Bahr (1974) "Widowhood, morale, and affiliation." Journal of Marriage and the Family 36: 586-591.
Hausknecht, Murray (1962) The Joiners: A Sociological Description of Voluntary Association Membership in the United States. New York: The Bedminister Press.
Havens, B. (1968) "An investigation of activities patterns and adjustment in an aging population." The Gerontologist 8: 201-206.
Havighurst, Robert (1970) "Leisure and aging," pp. 165-174 in A. M. Hoffman (ed.) The Daily Needs and Interests of Older People. Springfield, IL: Charles C Thomas.
Haynes, R. Brian (1976) "A critical review of the 'determinants' of patient compliance with therapeutic regimens," pp. 26-39 in D. L. Sackett and R. B. Haynes (eds.) Compliance with Therapeutic Regimens. Baltimore: The Johns Hopkins University Press.
Hazan, Haim (1983) "Discontinuity and identity: A case study of social reintegration among the aged." Research on Aging 5, 4: 473-489.
Heinemann, Gloria D. (1980) "Determinants of primary support system strength among urban, widowed women: Does life stage make a difference?" Ph.D. dissertation, Department of Sociology, University of Illinois at Chicago.
———(1982a) "Family structure and family resources in old age," pp. 193-222 in E. Shanas with the assistance of G. D. Heinemann, National Survey of the Aged. U.S. Department of Health and Human Services, Office of Human Development Services, Administration on Aging, DHHS Publication No. (OHDS) 83-20425, December. Washington, DC: Government Printing Office.
———(1982b) "Living arrangements of older persons and their proximity to adult children," pp. 223-255 in E. Shanas with the assistance of G. D. Heinemann, National Survey of the Aged. U.S. Department of Health and Human Services, Office of Human Development Services, Administration on Aging, DHHS Publication No. (OHDS) 83-20425, December. Washington, DC: Government Printing Office.
———(1982c) "Family contacts and family help patterns in old age," pp. 257-300 in E. Shanas with the assistance of G. D. Heinemann, National Survey of the Aged. U.S. Department of Health and Human Services, Office of Human Development Services, Administration on Aging, DHHS Publication No. (OHDS) 83-20425, December. Washington, DC: Government Printing Office.
Heinzelmann, Fred and Richard W. Bagley (1970) "Response to physical activity programs and their effects on health behavior." Public Health Reports 85: 905-911.
Heiss, Jerold (1960) "Variations in courtship progress among high school students." Marriage and Family Living 22: 165-170.
Heller, Barbara R., Frederick J. Walsh, and Kathleen M. Wilson (1981) "Seniors helping seniors: Training older adults as new personnel resources in home health care." Journal of Gerontological Nursing 7, 9: 552-555.
Heltsley, M. E. and R. C. Powers (1975) "Social interaction and perceived adequacy of interaction of the rural aged." The Gerontologist 15: 533-536.
Hendel-Sebestyen, G. (1979) "Role diversity: Toward the development of community in a total institutional setting." Anthropology Quarterly 52, 1: 19-28. (special issue J. Keith [ed.] The Ethnography of Old Age)
Henderson, S. (1977) "The social network's support neuroses: The function of attachment in adult life." Journal of Psychiatry 131: 185-191.

Henretta, John C. and Richard T. Campbell (1976) "Net worth as an aspect of status." American Journal of Sociology 41: 981-992.
Hess, Beth B. (1972) "Friendship," pp. 357-396 in M.W. Riley et al. (eds.) Aging and Society: A Sociology of Age Stratification Vol. 3. New York: Russell Sage Foundation.
———(1979) "Sex roles, friendship, and the life course." Research on Aging 1, 4: 494-515.
——— and J. Waring (1978) "Changing family patterns of aging and family bonds in later life." The Family Coordinator 27: 303-314.
Hickey, T. (1980) Health and Aging. Monterey, CA: Brooks/Cole.
Hill, R. (1968) "Decision-making and the family life cycle," pp. 286-295 in B. Neugarten (ed.) Middle Age and Aging. Chicago: University of Chicago Press.
Hinchcliffe, M., D. Hooper, and F. Roberts (1978) The Melancholy Marriage. Chichester: Wiley.
Hinton, J.M. (1967) Dying. Harmondsworth: Penguin.
———(1979) "Comparison of places and policies for terminal care." Lancet 1: 29.
———(1981) "The adult patient reactions to hospice care," In Dame Cicely Saunders et al. (eds.) Hospice: The Living Idea. Philadelphia: W.B. Saunders.
Hite, Shere (1976) The Hite Report: A Nationwide Study on Female Sexuality. New York: Macmillan.
———(1981) The Hite Report on Male Sexuality. New York: Knopf.
Hobart, Charles (1958) "The incidence of romanticism during courtship." Social Forces 36: 362-367.
Hochschild, Arlie R. (1973) The Unexpected Community. Portraits of an Old Age Subculture. Englewood Cliffs, NJ: Prentice-Hall.
Hollis, M. (1977) Models of Man. London: Cambridge University Press.
Hollister, Robert M., with Deborah Auger, Adrian Ruth Walter, and Timothy Pattison (1978) Measuring Neighborhood Confidence. Cambridge, MA: Department of Urban Studies and Planning, Massachusetts Institute of Technology.
Holmes, T.H. and R.H. Rahe (1967) "The social readjustment rating scale." Journal of Psychosomatic Research.
Homans, George C. (1950) The Human Group. New York: Harcourt Brace Jovanovich.
———(1954) "The cash posters: A study of a group of working girls." American Sociological Review 19: 724-733.
———(1961) Social Behavior: Its Elementary Forms. New York: Harcourt Brace Jovanovich.
Horowitz, A. (1981) "Sons and daughters as caregivers to older parents: Differences in role performance and consequences." Presented to the Gerontological Society of America. Toronto.
——— and L.W. Shindelman (1981) "Reciprocity and affection: Past influence on current caregiving." Presented to the Gerontological Society of America, Toronto.
Hough, Richard L., Dianne Timbers Fairbank, and Alma M. Garcia (1976) "Problems in the ratio measurement of life stress." Journal of Health and Social Behavior 17: 70-82.
House, J.S. (1974) "Occupational stress and coronary heart disease: A review and theoretical integration." Journal of Health and Social Behavior 15: 12-27.
——— and C. Robbins (1983) "Age, psychological stress, and health," in M. Riley et al. (eds.) Aging in Society: Selected Reviews of Recent Research. Hillsdale, NJ: Lawrence Erlbaum.
Hoyt, Danny and Nicholas Babchuk (1983) "Adult kinship networks: Selective formation of intimate ties with kin." Social Forces 62: 84-101.
Hoyt, Danny R., Marvin A. Kaiser, George R. Peters, and Nicholas Babchuk (1980) "Life satisfaction and activity theory: A multidimensional approach." Journal of Gerontology 35: 935-941.
Hulka, Barbara S., John C. Cassel, Laurence L. Kupper, and James A. Burdette (1976) "Communication, compliance, and concordance between physicians and patients with prescribed medications." American Journal of Public Health 66: 847-853.
Hurst, Charles E. and David A. Guldin (1981) "The effects of intra-individual and inter-spouse status inconsistency on life satisfaction among older persons." Journal of Gerontology 36: 112-121.
Hyman, Martin D. (1971) "Disability and patients' perceptions of preferential treatment: Some preliminary findings." Journal of Chronic Diseases 24: 329-342.

Illsley, R. (1981) "Problems of dependency groups: The case of the elderly, the handicapped and the chronically ill." Social Science and Medicine 15A: 327-332.
Jackson, Robert Max, Claude S. Fischer, and Lynne McCallister Jones (1977) "The dimensions of social networks," pp. 39-58 in C. S. Fischer et al., Networks and Places: Social Relations in the Urban Setting. New York: The Free Press.
Jacobsohn, Peter and Adam Matheny (1962) "Mate selection in open marriage systems." International Journal of Comparative Sociology 3: 98-123.
Jacoby, Arthur (1966) "Personal influence and primary relationships: Their effect on associational membership." Sociological Quarterly 7: 76-84.
Jasnau, K. F. (1967) "Individualized versus mass transfer of non-psychotic geriatric patients from mental hospitals to nursing homes with special reference to the death rate." Journal of the American Geriatric Society 15: 280-284.
Jenkins, A. (1979) The Social Theory of Claude Levi-Strauss. New York: St. Martin's Press.
Jenkins, R., A. H. Mann, and E. Belsey (1981) "The background, design and use of a short interview to assess social stress and support in research and clinical settings." Social Sciences and Medicine 15E: 195-203.
John, Robert (1980) "The older Americans act and the elderly Native American." Journal of Minority Aging 5: 293-298.
Johnson, C. L. and D. J. Catalano (1983) "A longitudinal study of family supports to impaired elderly." The Gerontologist 23: 612-618.
Johnson, Elizabeth S. and Barbara J. Bursk (1977) "Relationships between the elderly and their adult children." The Gerontologist 17: 90-96.
Jonas, K. (1979) "Factors in development of community among elderly persons in age-segregated housing: Relationships between involvement in friendship roles within the community and external social roles." Anthropological Quarterly 52: 29-38.
Jones, Lynne and Claude Fischer (1978) "Studying egocentric networks by mass survey." Working paper No. 284, Institute of Urban and Regional Development, University of California, Berkeley, CA.
Juster, F. Thomas, Paul Courant, Greg J. Duncan, John P. Robinson, and Frank P. Stafford (1977) Time Use in Economics and Social Accounts. Ann Arbor, MI: Survey Research Center.
Kahana, E. (1975) "Environmental adaptation of the aged," in T. Byerts (ed.) Housing and Environment for the Elderly. Washington, DC: Gerontological Society of America.
——— and Z. Harel (1972) "Social and behavioral principles in residential care settings for the aged: The Residents' perspective. Part II." Position paper prepared for presentation at the Annual Meeting of the Orthopsychiatric Association, Detroit, April.
Kahana, E. and B. Kahana (1984) "Institutionalization of the aged woman: Bane or blessing?" in M. Haug et al. (eds.) The Physical and Mental Health of Aged Women. New York: Springer.
———(1979) Strategies of Coping in Institutional Environments. Final progress report, NIMH grant number MH24959-04.
Kahana, E., T. Fairchild, and B. Kahana (1982) "Adaptation," in D. J. Mangen and W. A. Peterson (eds.) Clinical and Social Psychology; Vol. I. Research Instruments in Social Gerontology. Minneapolis: University of Minnesota Press.
Kahn, R. (1979) "Aging and social support," in M. Riley (ed.) Aging From Birth to Death: Interdisciplinary Perspectives. Boulder, CO: Westview.
——— and T. Antonucci (1981) "Convoys of social support: A life course approach," in S. Kiesler et al. (eds.) Aging: Social Change. New York: Academic.
Kahn, R. L., M. Pollack, and A. I. Goldfarb (1961) "Factors related to individual differences in mental status of institutionalized aged," in P. Hock and J. Zubin (eds.) Psychopathology of Aging. New York: Grune & Stratton.
Kalish, R. A. [ed.] (1969) "The dependencies of old people." Inst. Gerontology, University of Michigan—Wayne State University, Ann Arbor, Occasional Papers in Gerontology, b.
——— and D. Reynolds (1976) Death and Ethnicity: A Psychocultural Study. Los Angeles: University of Southern California Press.
Kane, R. A. and R. L. Kane (1981) Assessing the Elderly: A Practical Guide to Measurement. Toronto: Lexington.

Kanner, Allen D., James C. Coyne, Catherine Shaefer, and Richard S. Lazarus (1981) "Comparison of two modes of stress measurement: Daily hassles and uplifts versus major life events." Journal of Behavioral Medicine 4: 1-39.

Kaplan, Berton H., John C. Cassel, and Susan Gore (1977) "Social support and health." Medical Care 15 (Suppl.): 47-58.

Kaplan, Shari and Franklin Kozin (1981) "A controlled study of group counseling in rheumatoid arthritis." Journal of Rheumatology 8: 91-99.

Kasl, Stanislav V., Sidney Cobb, and George W. Brooks (1968) "Changes in serum uric acid and cholesterol levels in men undergoing job loss." Journal of American Medical Association 206: 1500-1507.

Kastenbaum, R. (1977) Death, Society and Human Experience. St. Louis: The C.V. Mosby Company.

———and S. Candy (1973) "The four percent fallacy: A methodological and empirical critique of extended care facility program statistics." Aging and Human Development 4, 1: 15-21.

Katz, A. H. (1970) "Self-help organization and volunteer participation in social welfare." Social Work 15: 51-60.

Katz, S., J. Papsidero, and L. Halstead (1976) "Team care and chronic illness: A framework for teaching comprehensive health care," pp. 45-58 in D.W. Clark and T. F. Williams (eds.) Teaching of Chronic Illness and Aging. Washington, DC: DHEW.

Katz, S., A. B. Ford, R. W. Moskowitz, B. A. Jackson, and M. W. Jaffee (1981) "Studies of illness in the aged. The index of ADL: A standardized measure of biological and psychosocial function." Journal of the American Medical Association 185: 94ff.

Katzman, Robert (1981) "Early detection of senile dementia." Hospital Practice 16: 61-76.

———(1982) "The complex problem of diagnosis." Generations 7: 8-10.

———[ed.] (1983) Banbury Report 15: Biological Aspects of Alzheimer's Disease. Cold Spring Harbor, NY: Cold Spring Harbor Laboratory.

———and T. B. Karasu (1975) "Differential diagnosis of dementia," pp. 103-134 in W. Field (ed.) Neurological and Sensory Disorders in the Elderly. New York: Stratton.

Katzman, Robert, Robert D. Terry, and Katherine L. Bick [eds.] (1978) Alzheimer's Disease: Senile Dementia and Related Disorders. New York: Raven.

Kay, D. W. K., K. Bergmann, E. M. Foster, A. A. McKechnie, and M. Roth (1979) "Mental illness and hospital usage in the elderly: A random sample followed up." Comprehensive Psychiatry 11: 26-35.

Keating, N. and P. Cole (1980) "What do I do with him 24 hours a day? Changes in the housewife role after retirement." The Gerontologist 20: 84-89.

Keith, J. (1982) Old People as People: Social and Cultural Influences on Aging and Old Age. Little Brown Series on Gerontology. Boston: Little, Brown.

Keith, Nathaniel (1973) Politics and the Housing Crisis Since 1930. New York: Universe.

Keith, P. M. and T. H. Brubaker (1977) "Sex-role expectations associated with specific household tasks: Perceived age and employment differences." Psychological Reports 41: 15-18.

———(1979) "Male household roles in later life: A look at masculinity and marital relationships." The Family Coordinator 28: 297-502.

———(1980) "Adolescent perception of household work: Expectations by sex, age and employment situation." Adolescence 15: 171-182.

Keith, P. M., E. A. Powers, and W. J. Goudy (1981) "Older men in employed and retired families." Alternative Lifestyles 4: 228-241.

Keith, P. M., C. D. Dobson, W. J. Goudy, and E. A. Powers (1981) "Older men: Occupation, employment status, household involvement, and well-being." Journal of Family Issues 2: 336-349.

Keller, Suzanne (1968) The Urban Neighborhood. New York: Random House.

Kemper, R. L. (1978) The Community in America. Chicago: Rand McNally.

Kennedy, Stephen D. and Jean MacMillan (1980) Participation Under Alternative Housing Allowance Programs: Evidence from the Housing Allowance Demand Experiment. Cambridge, MA: Abt Associates.

References

Kephart, William (1972) The Family, Society and the Individual. Boston: Houghton Mifflin Co.
Kerckhoff, Alan (1966) "Family patterns and morale in retirement," pp. 173-192 in I. Simpson and J. McKinney (eds.) Social Aspects of Aging. Durham, NC: Duke University Press.
——— and Keith Davis (1962) "Value consensus and need complimentarity in mate selection." American Sociological Review 27, 3: 295-303.
Kerlinger, Fred N. and Elazar J. Pedhazur (1973) Multiple Regression in Behavioral Research. New York: Holt, Rinehart & Winston.
Kessler, R. and H. Essex (1982) "Marital status and depression: The importance of coping resources." Social Forces 61 (December): 484-507.
Key, William H. (1961) "Rural-urban differences and the family." Sociological Quarterly 2: 49-56.
Kim, Jae-On and Frank J. Kohout (1975) "Multiple regression analysis: Subprogram regression," pp. 320-367 in N. H. Nie et al., Statistical Package for the Social Sciences. New York: McGraw-Hill.
Kimberly, J. R., R. H. Miles, and Associates (1980) The Organizational Life Cycle. San Francisco: Jossey-Bass.
Kivett, V. (1978) "Loneliness and the rural widow." The Family Coordinator 27: 389-394.
Kiyak, H. A. and E. Kahana (1979) "The role of informal norms in determining institutional totality in homes for the aged." Long Term Care and Health Services Administration Quarterly 3, 2: 102-110.
———(1982) "Attitudes and behavior of staff in facilities for the aged." Presented at the 35th Annual Scientific Meeting of the Gerontological Society of America, Boston, November.
———(1983) "Personal and job related predictors of employee turnover in facilities for the elderly." Presented at the 36th Annual Scientific Meeting of the Gerontological Society of America, San Francisco, November.
Klatzky, Sheila R. (1972) Patterns of Contact with Relatives. Washington, DC: American Sociological Association.
Klemmack, D. L. and L. L. Roff (1980) "Heterosexual alternatives to marriage: Appropriateness for older persons." Alternative Lifestyles 3: 137-148.
Knipscheer, Kees (1979) "The primary relations in old age: Children, brothers/sisters, other relatives, friends and neighbours," pp. 119-138 in G. Dooghe and J. Helander (eds.) Family Life in Old Age. The Hague: Martinus Nijhoff.
Knoke, David and Randall Thomson (1977) "Voluntary association membership trends and the family life cycle." Social Forces 56: 48-65.
Knox, David and Kenneth Wilson (1981) "Dating behaviors of university students." Family Relations 30: 255-258.
Kogan, N. (1961) "Attitudes toward old people: The development of a scale and an examination." Journal of Abnormal and Social Psychology 62: 44-45.
Kohen, J. (1983) "Old but not alone: Informal social supports among the elderly by marital status and sex." Journal of Gerontology 23, 1: 57-63.
Kohli, Martin (1981) "Biography: Account, text, method," pp. 61-75 in D. Bertaux (ed.) Biography and Society. Beverly Hills, CA: Sage.
Komarovsky, Mirra (1973) "Cultural contradiction and sex roles: The masculine case." American Journal of Sociology 78: 873-884.
Kosberg, J. I. (1973) "The nursing home: A social work paradox." Social Work 18: 104-110.
Kozma, A. and M. J. Stones (1978) "Some research issues and findings in the study of psychological well-being in the aged." Canadian Psychological Review 19: 241-249.
Kral, V. A. (1978) "Benign senescent forgetfulness," pp. 47-51 in R. Katzman et al. (eds.) Alzheimer's Disease: Senile Dementia and Related Disorders. New York: Raven.
Kreuz, Leo E., Robert M. Rose, and J. Richard Jennings (1972) "Suppression of plasma testosterone levels and psychological stress." Archives of General Psychiatry 26: 479-482.
Kuypers, J. A. and V. Bengtson (1973) "Social breakdown and competence." Human Development 16: 181-201.
Langlie, Jean K. (1977) "Social networks, health beliefs and preventative health behavior." Journal of Health and Social Behavior 18: 244-260.
LaRocco, James M., James S. House, and John R. P. French, Jr. (1980) "Social support, occupational stress, and health." Journal of Health and Social Behavior 21: 202-218.

LaRossa, Ralph (1981) "Negotiating role strain: The transition to parenthood." Presented at the Workshop on Theory Construction and Research Methodology, National Council of Family Relations, Milwaukee, October.
———and J. J. Dowd (1980) "Aging in a women's club: The voluntary association as a social support system." Alternative Lifestyles 3: 185-206.
Larson, R. (1978) "Thirty years of research on the subjective well-being of older Americans." Journal of Gerontology 33: 109-125.
Lawton, M. Powell (1970) "Ecology and aging," in L. A. Pastalan and D. H. Carson (eds.) Spatial Behavior of Older People. Ann Arbor, MI: University of Michigan-Wayne State University Institute of Gerontology.
———(1975) "The Philadelphia geriatric center morale scale: A revision." Journal of Gerontology 30: 85-89.
———(1980) Aging and the Environment. San Francisco: Jossey-Bass.
———and Bonnie Simon (1968) "The ecology of social relationships in housing for the elderly." Gerontologist 8: 108-115.
Lawton, M. Powell, Morton Ward, and Silvia Yaffe (1967) "Indices of health in an aging population." Journal of Gerontology 22: 334-342.
Lazarsfeld, Paul and Robert Merton (1964) "Friendship as a social process: A substantive and methodological analysis," in M. Berger et al. (eds.) Freedom and Control in Modern Society. Princeton: Van Nostrand.
Leanse, Joyce (1977) "The senior center, individuals and community," in R. A. Kalish (ed.) The Later Years: Social Applications of Gerontology. Monterey, CA: Brooks/Cole.
Lee, Gary R. (1979) "Children and the elderly: Interaction and morale." Research on Aging 1, 3: 335-360.
———(1980) "Kinship in the seventies: A decade review of research and theory." Journal of Marriage and the Family 42: 193-204.
———and Margaret L. Cassidy (1981) "Kinship systems and extended family ties," pp. 57-71 in R. T. Coward and W. M. Smith, Jr. (eds.) The Family in Rural Society. Boulder, CO: Westview.
Lee, Gary R. and Eugene Ellithorpe (1982) "Intergenerational exchange and subjective well-being among the elderly." Journal of Marriage and the Family 44: 217-224.
LeMasters, E. E. (1957) "Parenthood as crisis." Journal of Marriage and the Family 19: 325-355.
Lemke, S. and R. Moos (1980) "Assessing the institutional policies of sheltered care settings." Journal of Gerontology 35: 96-107.
Lemon, B. W., V. L. Bengston, and J. A. Peterson (1972) "An exploration of the activity theory of aging: Activity types and life satisfaction among in-movers to a retirement community." Journal of Gerontology 27: 511-523.
Leonard, Wilber M., II (1977) "Sociological and social-psychological correlates of anomia among a random sample of aged." Journal of Gerontology 32: 303-310.
Lerner, M. (1970) "When, why and where people die," pp. 5-29 in O. G. Brim, Jr., et al. (eds.) The Dying Patient. New York: Russell Sage Foundation.
Lesnoff-Caravglia, C. (1978-1979) "The five percent fallacy." International Journal of Aging and Human Development 9, 2: 187-192.
Levine, N., D. Dastoor, and C. Gendron (1983) "Coping with dementia: A pilot study." Journal of American Geriatrics Society 31: 12-18.
Levi-Strauss, C. (1969) The Elementary Structures of Kinship. London: Eyre & Spottiswoode.
Lewis, Charles E. (1966) "Factors influencing the return to work of men with congestive heart failure." Journal of Chronic Diseases 19: 1193-1209.
Lewis, Robert (1972) "A developmental framework for the analysis of premarital dyadic formation." Family Process 11: 17-48.
———(1973) "A longitudinal test of a developmental framework for premarital dyadic formation." Journal of Marriage and the Family 35: 16-25.
Liang, Jersey (1982) "Sex differences in life satisfaction among the elderly." Journal of Gerontology 37: 100-108.

References

———Louis Dvorkin, Eva Kahana, and Florence Marzian (1980) "Social integration and morale: A re-examination." Journal of Gerontology 35: 746-757.

Lieberman, M. A. (1969) "Institutionalization of the aged: Effects on behavior." Journal of Gerontology 24: 330-340.

———(1975) "Adoptive processes in late life," in N. Datan and L.H. Ginsberg (eds.) Life Span Developmental Psychology: Normative Life Crises. New York: Academic.

———and S. S. Tobin (1983) The Experience of Old Age, Stress, Coping, and Survival. New York: Basic.

Lin, Nan, Ronald S. Simeone, Walter E. Ensel, and Wen Kuo (1979) "Social support, stressful life events, and illness: A model and an empirical test." Journal of Health and Social Behavior 20: 108-119.

Lincoln, James and Jon Miller (1979) "Work and friendship ties in organizations: A comparative analysis of relational networks." Administrative Science Quarterly 24: 181-199.

Lindsey, Ada M. and Elizabeth M. Hughes (1981) "Social support and alternatives to institutionalization for the at-risk elderly." Journal of the American Geriatrics Society 29: 308-315.

Lipman, A. (1968) "A socioarchitectural view in three old people's homes." Gerontologia Clinica 10: 88-101.

Litwak, Eugene (1960a) "Occupational mobility and extended family cohesion." American Sociological Review 25 (February): 9-21.

———(1960b) "Geographic mobility and extended family cohesion." American Sociological Review 25 (June): 385-394.

———(1965) "Extended kin relations in an industrial democratic society," pp. 290-323 in E. Shanas and G. F. Streib (eds.) Social Structure and the Family: Generational Relations. Englewood Cliffs, NJ: Prentice-Hall.

———(1969) "Occupational mobility and extended family cohesion." American Sociological Review 25: 9-24.

———and Ivan Szeleny (1975) "Primary group structures and their function: Kin, neighbors, and friends." American Sociological Review 33: 20-30.

Livson, F. B. (1983) "Gender identity: A life span view of sex role development," pp. 105-127 in R. B. Weg (ed.) Sexuality in the Later Years. New York: Academic.

Lock, Harvey, Harvey Burgess, and M. M. Thomas (1963) The Family From Institution to Companionship. New York: The American Book Co.

Lofland, L. H. (1978) The Craft of Dying: The Modern Face of Death. Beverly Hills, CA: Sage.

Lohmann, Nancy (1977) "Correlations of life satisfaction, morale, and adjustment measures." Journal of Gerontology 32: 73-75.

Longino, C. and A. Lipman (1981) "Married and spouseless men and women in planned retirement communities: Support network differences." Journal of Marriage and Family 43, 1: 169-177.

Lopata, H. Z. "The social involvement of American widows." American Behavioral Scientist 14: 41-58.

———(1970b) "Widows as a minority group." The Gerontologist 2: 67-77.

———(1973a) Widowhood in an American City. Cambridge, MA: Schenkman.

———(1973b) "The effect of schooling on social contacts of urban women." American Journal of Sociology 79, 3: 604-619.

———(1975) "Support systems of elderly urbanites: Chicago of the 1970s." The Gerontologist 15, 1: 35-41.

———(1978) "The absence of community resources in support systems of urban widows." The Family Coordinator 27: 383-388.

———(1979) Women as Widows: Support Systems. New York: Elsevier North Holland.

Lorig, Kate, Robert Guy Kraines, and Halsted R. Holman (1981) "A randomized, prospective, controlled study of the effects of health education for people with arthritis." Arthritis and Rheumatism 24 (Suppl.): S90 (abstract).

Loughton, Celeste (1980) "Eros and the elderly." The Gerontologist 20: 182-186.

Lowenthal, Marjorie (1964a) "Social isolation and mental illness in old age." American Sociological Review 29: 54-70.
———(1964b) Lives in Distress. New York: Basic.
———and P. L. Berkman (1967) Aging and Mental Disorder in San Francisco: A Social Psychiatric Study. San Francisco: Jossey-Bass.
Lowenthal, Marjorie F. and Clayton Haven (1968) "Interaction and adaptation: Intimacy as a critical variable." American Sociological Review 33, 1: 20-30.
Lowenthal, M. and B. Robinson (1976) "Social networks and social isolation," In R. Binstock and E. Shanas (eds.) Handbook of Aging and the Social Sciences. New York: Van Nostrand Reinholdt.
Lowenthal, M. F., M. Thurnher, and D. Chiriboga (1975) Four Stages of Life. San Francisco: Jossey-Bass.
Lowenthal, M. R. (1971) "Intentionality: Toward a framework for the study of adaptation in adulthood." Aging and Human Development 2: 79-95.
Lowrie, Samuel (1951) "Dating theories and student responses." American Sociological Review 16: 334-340.
Lyman, S. and M. Scott (1970) "On the time track," pp. 189-212 in S. Lyman and M. Scott (eds.) A Sociology of the Absurd. New York: Appleton-Century-Crofts.
Lynott, Robert J. (1983) "Alzheimer's disease and institutionalization: The ongoing construction of a decision." Journal of Family Issues 4, 4: 559-574.
Mace, Nancy L. and Peter V. Rabins. (1981) The 36-Hour Day. Baltimore: Johns Hopkins University Press.
———(1982) "Areas of stress on families of dementia patients." Presented at the Annual Meeting of the Gerontological Society of America, Boston.
Macklin, Eleanor D. (1972) "Heterosexual cohabitation among unmarried college students." Family Coordinator 22 (October): 463-473.
Maddox, George (1978) "The social and cultural context of aging," pp. 20-46 in G. Usdin and C. K. Hofling (eds.) Aging: The Process and the People. New York: Brunner/Mazel.
———(1979) "Sociology of later life," pp. 113-135 in Alex Inkeles et al. (eds.) Annual Review of Sociology. Palo Alto, CA: Annual Reviews.
Mancini, Jay A. (1980) "Friend interaction, competence, and morale in old age." Research on Aging 2, 4: 416-431.
———and William Quinn (1980) "Social network interaction among older adults: Implications for life satisfaction." Human Relations 33, 8: 543-554.
Mandelker, Daniel R. (1973) Housing Subsidies in the United States and England. Indianapolis: Bobbs-Merrill.
Marcus, L. (1978) "The situation of the elderly and their families' problems and solutions, the old and their families: Myths and reality." Prepared for the National Symposium on Aging, Ottawa, October.
Markides, Kvriakos S. and Harry W. Martin (1979) "A causal model of life satisfaction among the elderly." Journal of Gerontology 34: 86-93.
Marsden, Peter and Karen Campbell (1984) "Measuring tie strength." Social Forces (in press).
Marshall, Victor W. (1980) Last Chapters, A Sociology of Aging and Dying. Monterey, CA: Brooks/Cole.
Masters, W. H. and V. E. Johnson (1966) Human Sexual Response. Boston: Little, Brown.
Matthews, Sarah H. (1979) The Social World of Old Women. Beverly Hills, CA: Sage.
Mauksch, Hans O. (1975) "The organizational context of dying," In E. Kubler-Ross (ed.) Death, The Final Stage of Growth. Englewood Cliffs, NJ: Prentice-Hall.
Mauss, Marcel (1967) The Gift: Forms and Foundations of Exchange in Archaic Societies. New York: W. W. Norton.
Maves, Paul B. (1981) Older Volunteers in Church and Community. Valley Forge, PA: Judson.
———(1982) "Programming for older adults: A church response," In M. Okum (ed.) New Directions for Continuing Education: Programs for Older Adults. San Francisco: Jossey-Bass.

McCallister, Lynne and Claude Fischer (1978) "A procedure for studying personal networks." Sociological Methods and Research 7: 131-148.
McCormack, D. and Whitehead, A. (1981) "The effect of providing recreational activities on the engagement level of long-stay geriatric patients." Age and Aging 10: 287-291.
MacDonald, John S. and Leatrice D. MacDonald (1974) "Chain migration, ethnic neighborhood formation, and social networks," pp. 226-336 in C. Tilly (ed.) An Urban World. Boston: Little, Brown.
McDowell, James L. (1979) Housing Allowances and Housing Improvements: Early Tidings. Santa Monica: Rand (Rand-N-1198-HUD).
McKenney, James M., Judith M. Slining, H. Richard Henderson, Douglas Devins, and Martin Barr (1973) "The effect of clinical pharmacy services on patients with essential hypertension." Circulation 48: 1104-1111.
McKinlay, John B. (1973) "Social networks, lay consultation and help-seeking behavior." Social Forces 51: 275-292.
MacMillan, Jean (1979) The Decision to Move—Evidence from the Demand Experiment. Cambridge, MA: Abt Associates.
McPherson, J. Miller (1982) "Hypernetwork sampling." Social Networks 3: 225-249.
——— (1983) "An ecology of affiliation." American Sociological Review 43: 519-532.
Mechanic, David (1962) Students Under Stress. New York: Free Press.
Merriam-Webster (1977) Webster's New Collegiate Dictionary. Toronto: Thomas Allen & Son.
Merton, Robert K. (1957) Social Theory and Social Structure. New York: Free Press.
Meyerson, Martin, Barbara Terrett, and William L. C. Wheaton (1962) Housing, People and Cities. New York: McGraw-Hill.
Milardo, Robert (1983) "Social networks and pair relationships: A review of substantive and measurement issues." Sociology and Social Research 68: 1-18.
Miller, Dorothy (1975) American Indian Socialization to Urban Life. San Francisco: Institute for Scientific Analysis.
Mills, C. Wright (1959) The Sociological Imagination. New York: Oxford University Press.
Mindel, Charles H. and Roosevelt Wright, Jr. (1982) "Satisfaction in multigenerational households." Journal of Gerontology 37: 483-489.
Minnigerode, F. A. and J. A. Lee (1978) "Young adults' perceptions of social sex roles across the life span." Sex Roles 4: 563-569.
Mitchell, J. Clyde (1969) Social networks in urban situations. Manchester: University of Manchester Press.
Mitchell, Roger E. and Edison J. Trickett (1980) "Task force report: Social networks as mediators of social support. An analysis of the effects and determinants of social networks." Community Mental Health Journal 16: 27-44.
Morgan, Leslie A. (1976) "A re-examination of widowhood and morale." Journal of Gerontology 31: 687-695.
——— (1983) "Intergenerational financial support: Retirement-age males, 1971-1975." The Gerontologist 23 (November): 160-166.
Morris, R. (1977) "The human service function and local government," pp. 5-36 in W. Anderson et al. (eds.) Managing Human Services. Washington, DC: International City Management Association.
Morris, Robert, Camille Lambert, Jr., and Mildred Berman (1964) "New roles for the elderly." Papers in Social Welfare. Waltham, MA: Brandeis University.
Munnichs, J. M. A. (1976) Dependency or Interdependency in Old Age. The Hague: Martinus Nijhoff.
Murdock, Steve H. and Donald F. Schwartz (1978) "Family structure and use of agency services: An examination of patterns among elderly Native Americans." The Gerontologist 18, 5: 475-481.
Murstein, Bernard I. (1961) "The complementary need hypothesis in newlyweds and middle-aged married couples." Journal of Abnormal and Social Psychology 63: 196-197.
——— (1971) Theories of Attraction and Love. New York: Springer.

———(1976) Who Will Marry Whom? Theories and Research in Marital Choice. New York: Springer.

———(1980) "Mate Selection in the 1970's." Journal of Marriage and the Family 42: 777-792.

Musgrave, Richard A. (1973) "Policies of housing support: Rationale and instruments," in U.S. Department of Housing and Urban Development, Housing in the Seventies Volume 1, Working Papers.

Myers, Jerome K., Jacob J. Lindenthal, and Max P. Pepper (1975) "Life events, social integration and psychiatric symptomatology." Journal of Health and Social Behavior 16: 421-427.

Nathanson, Constance A. (1975) "Illness and the feminine role: A theoretical review." Social Science and Medicine 9: 57-62.

———(1977) "Sex, illness, and medical care: A review of data, theory and method." Social Science and Medicine 11: 13-25.

National Council on Aging (1975) The Myth and Reality of Aging in America. Washington, DC: Tha National Council on Aging.

———(1981) Aging in the Eighties: America in Transition. Washington, DC:: The National Council on Aging.

National Health and Welfare (1982) Manitoba/Canada Home Care Study: An Overview of the Results. Ottawa: Policy, Planning and Information Branch.

National Indian Council on Aging (1981) American Indian Elderly: A National Profile. Albuquerque, NM: Author.

National Tribal Chairmen's Association (1978) The Indian Elder: A Forgotten American. Phoenix, AZ: Author.

Nelson, M. N. and R. J. Paluck (1980) "Territorial markings, self-concept, and mental status of the institutionalized elderly." The Gerontologist 20, 1: 96-107.

Neugarten, B. L. (1968) Middle Age and Aging. Chicago: Chicago University Press.

Neugarten, B. L. (1978) "The rise of the young-old," in R. Gross et al. (eds.) The New Old: Struggling for Decent Aging. Garden City, NY: Anchor.

———R. L. Havighurst, and S. Tobin (1961) "The measurement of life satisfaction." The Journal of Gerontology 16: 134-143.

Newcomb, Theodore (1961) The Acquaintance Process. New York: Holt, Rinehart & Winston.

Newman, N. C. (1964) "Institutionalization, interaction, and self-conception in aging." Master's thesis, University of Minnesota.

Newman, Sandra J. and Greg J. Duncan (1979) "Residential problems, dissatisfaction and mobility." American Association Journal (April): 154-166.

Nicholls, William (1979) "Sampling and field work methods of the Northern California communities study." Survey Research Center, University of California, Berkeley, CA.

NRTA/AARP & Wakefield Washington Associates (1980) "Family support systems and the aging." Policy report submitted to the Select Committee on Aging, House of Representatives, 96th Congress, Washington, D.C.

Oakes, Thomas W., John R. Ward, Robert M. Gray, Melville R. Klauber, and Phillip M. Moody (1970) "Family expectations and arthritis patient compliance to a hand resting splint regimen." Journal of Chronic Diseases 22: 757-764.

O'Brien, J. E. (1970) "The Decision to Divorce." Ph.D. dissertation. The University of Wisconsin.

———(1971) "Violence in Divorce Prone Families." Journal of Marriage and the Family 33: 692-698.

———and M. Kahanoff (1981) "A framework for assessing the design of social network studies." Presented at the annual meeting of the Society for Applied Anthropology, Edinborough, Scotland.

O'Brien, J. E. and D. L. Wagner (1980) "Help-seeking by the frail elderly: Problems in network analysis." The Gerontologist 20: 78-83.

Olbrich, E. and U. Lehr (1976) "Social roles and contacts in old age: Consistency and patterns of change." Contrib. Human Development 3: 113-126.

O'Rand, Angela M. (1982) "Socioeconomic status and poverty," pp. 281-341 in D. J. Mangen and W. A. Peterson (eds.) Research Instruments in Social Gerontology: Social Roles and Social Participation. Minneapolis: University of Minnesota Press.

Palmore, Erdman (1976) "Total chance of institutionalization among the aged." The Gerontologist 16, 6: 504-507.
———(1978) "When can age, period, and cohort be separated?" Social Forces 57: 282-292.
———William P. Cleveland, John B. Nowlin, Dietolf Ramm, and Ilene C. Siegler (1979) "Stress and adaptation in later life." Journal of Gerontology 34: 841-851.
Paringer, L. (1983) The Forgotten Costs of Informal Long-term Care. Washington, DC: The Urban Institute.
Parkes, C. Murray (1980) "Terminal care: Evaluation of an advisory domiciliary service at St. Christopher's hospice." Postgraduate Medical Journal 56: 685-689.
Parron, E. M. and L. E. Troll (1978) "Golden wedding couples: Effects of retirement on intimacy in long standing marriages." Alternative Lifestyles 1: 447-464.
Parsons, P. L. (1965) "Mental health of Swansea's old folk." British Journal of Preventive Social Medicine 19: 43-47.
Parsons, Talcott (1949) Essays in Sociological Theory, Pure and Applied. Glencoe, IL: Free Press.
———(1951) The Social System. New York: Free Press.
———(1959) "The social structure of the family," in R. N. Anshen (ed.) The Family: Its Function and Destiny. New York: Harper & Row.
Pastalan, L. (1972) "Studies on relocating the elderly." Presented at the Gerontological Society's annual meeting, San Juan, Puerto Rico.
Paterson, Chris and Terry Pettijohn (1982) "Age and human mate selection." Psychological Reports 51: 70.
Pavlou, M., M. Hartings, and F. A. Davis (1978) "Discussion groups for medical patients: A vehicle for improved coping." Psychotherapy and Psychosomatics 30: 105-115.
Payne, Barbara P. (1973) "Voluntary association of the elderly." Presented to the Society of Social Problems, New York, NY.
———(1977) "The older volunteer: Social role continuity and development." The Gerontologist 17 (Fall): 355-361.
———and C. Neil Bull (1983) Report of Longitudinal Study of the Older Volunteer. (unpublished)
Pear, Robert (1983) "U.S. acts to cut benefit to dying in hospice care." New York Times.
Pearlin, L. and J. Johnson (1977) "Marital status, life-strains, and depression." American Sociological Review 42: 704-715.
———and Carmi Schooler (1978) "The structure of coping." Journal of Health and Social Behavior 19: 2-21.
Peattie, Lisa R. (1971) "Public housing: Urban slums under public management," in P. Orleans and W. Ellis (eds.) Race, Change, and Urban Society Vol. V., Urban Affairs Annual Reviews. Beverly Hills, CA: Sage.
Peck, R. C. (1968) "Psychological developments in the second half of life," in B. Neugarten (ed.) Middle Age and Aging. Chicago: University of Chicago Press.
Peterson, John and Constance Miller (1980) "Physical attractiveness and marriage adjustment in older American couples." The Journal of Psychology 105: 247-252.
Petrowsky, M. (1976) "Marital status, sex and the social networks of the elderly." Journal of Marriage and Family (November): 749-756.
Phillips, Bernard S. (1957) "A role theory approach to adjustment in old age." American Sociological Review 22: 212-217.
Pihlblad, C. T. and David L. Adams (1972) "Widowhood, social participation, and life satisfaction." Aging and Human Development 3, 2: 323-330.
Pihlblad, C. T. and Robert L. McNamara (1965) "Social adjustment of elderly people in three small towns," pp. 49-73 in A. M. Rose and W. A. Peterson (eds.) Older People and Their Social World. Philadelphia: F. A. Davis.
Pihlblad, C. T., Richard M. Hessler, and Harold Freshley (1976) "The rural elderly 8 years later: Changes in life satisfaction, living arrangements and health status." Columbia, MO: The University of Missouri—Columbia.
Potts, Marilyn and Kenneth D. Brandt (1983) "Analysis of education: support groups for patients with rheumatoid arthritis." Patient Counselling and Health Education 4: 161-166.

Powers, Edward A. and Gordon L. Bultena (1974) "Correspondence between anticipated and actual uses of public services by the aged." Social Service Review 48: 245-254.

―――(1976) "Sex differences in intimate friendships of old age." Journal of Marriage and the Family 38: 739-747.

Powers, Edward A., Patricia M. Keith, and Willis J. Goudy (1979) "Family relationships and friendships among the rural aged," pp. 80-101 in T.O. Bverts et al. (eds.) Environmental Context of Aging: Life-Styles, Environmental Quality and Living Arrangements. New York: Garland STPM.

―――(1981) "Family networks of the rural aged," pp. 199-217 in R.T. Coward and W.M. Smith, Jr. (eds.) The Family in Rural Society. Boulder, CO: Westview.

Pratt, H. (1976) The Gray Lobby. Chicago: University of Chicago Press.

―――(1983) "National interest groups among the elderly: Consolidation and constraint," pp. 145-179 in W.P. Browne and L.K. Olson (eds.) Aging and Public Policy. Westport, CT: Greenwood.

Puglisi, J.T. (1983) "Self perceived age changes in sex role concept." International Journal of Aging and Human Development 16: 183-191.

―――and D.W. Jackson (1980-1981) "Sex role identity and self esteem in adulthood." International Journal of Aging and Human Development 12: 129-138.

Quinn, J. (1983) "Personal and family adjustment." Journal of Marriage and the Family 45, 1: 57-73.

Quint, J.C. (1965) "Institutionalized practices of information control." Psychiatry 28: 119-132.

Rabin, J. and B.R. Brown (1975) The Social Psychology of Bargaining and Negotiation. New York: Academic.

Rabins, P. (1983) "Ethical issues and the physician." Presented at the annual meeting of the Gerontological Society of America, San Francisco.

Rabkin, Judith G. and Elmer L. Struening (1976) "Life events, stress, and illness." Science 194: 1013-1020.

Rahe, Richard H., and Ransom J. Arthur (1978) "Life change and illness studies: Past history and future directions." Journal of Human Stress 4: 3-15.

Rahe, Richard H. and Evy Lind (1971) "Psychosocial factors and sudden cardiac death: A pilot study." Journal of Psychosomatic Research 15: 19-24.

Rahe, Richard H., Jack L. Mahan, and Ransom J. Arthur (1970) "Prediction of near-future health changges from subjects' preceding life changes." Journal of Psychosomatic Research 14: 401-406.

Rainwater, Lee (1974) What Money Buys: Inequality and the Social Meanings of Income. New York: Basic.

Red Horse, John G., et al. (1978) "Family behavior of urban American Indians." Social Casework 59: 67-72.

Reiss, Ira (1960) "Toward a sociology of heterosexual love relationships." Marriage and Family Living 22: 139-145.

―――(1980) Family Systems in America. New York: Holt, Rinehart & Winston.

Riley, M.W. (1979) Aging From Birth to Death. Boulder, CO: Westview.

―――and A. Foner (1968) Aging and Society: Volume One; An Inventory of Research Findings. New York: Russell Sage Foundation.

Rivlin, Alice (1977) "Allocation resources for policy research: How can experiments be more useful?" pp. 243-254 in W.B. Fairley and F. Mosteller (eds.) Statistics and Public Policy. Reading, MA: Addison-Wesley.

Roberts, R. and S. O'Keefe (1981) "Sex differences in depression reexamined." Journal of Health and Social Behavior 22: 394-400.

Roberts, W.L. (1979-1980) "Significant elements in the relationship of long-married couples." International Journal of Aging and Human Development 10: 265-272.

Robertson, ElDora K. and Richard M. Suinn (1968) "The determination of rate of progress of stroke patients through empathy measures of patient and family." Journal of Psychosomatic Research 12: 189-191.

Robins, Lee and Miroda Tomanec (1962) "Closeness to blood relatives outside the immediate family." Marriage and Family Living 24: 340-346.

Robinson, Betsy and Majda Thurnher (1979) "Taking care of aged parents: A family cycle transition." The Gerontologist 19: 586-593.

Rogers, Everett and E. Havens (1960) "Prestige rating and mate selection on a college campus." Marriage and Family Living 22: 55-59.

Rollins, B. and H. Feldman (1970) "Marital satisfaction over the family life cycle." Journal of Marriage and the Family 32: 20-27.

Rombout, M. K. (1975) Hospitals and the Elderly: Present and Future Trends. Ottawa: Staff Papers Long Range Health Planning.

Rose, A. M. (1962) "The subculture of the aging: A topic for sociological research." The Gerontologist 2: 123-127.

Rosenblatt, A. (1957) "Interest of older persons in volunteer activities." Social Work 2: 87-94.

Rosow, Irving (1967) Social Integration of the Aged. New York: Free Press.

———(1968) "Housing and local ties of the aged," pp. 382-389 in B. L. Neugarten (ed.) Middle Age and Aging. Chicago: University of Chicago Press.

———(1970) "Old people: Their friends and neighbors." American Behavioral Scientist 4, 1: 59-69 (special issue, Aging in Contemporary Society).

———(1974) Socialization to Old Age. Berkeley: University of California Press.

———(1976) "Status and role change through the life span," in R. H. Binstock and E. Shanas (eds.) Handbook of Aging and the Social Sciences. New York: Van Nostrand Reinhold.

Ross, Catherine E. and John Mirowsky, II (1979) "A comparison of life-event-weighting schemes: Change, undesirability, and effect-proportional indices." Journal of Health and Social Behavior 20: 166-177.

Rossi, Peter (1980) Why Families Move: A Study in the Social Psychology of Urban Residential Mobility. Glencoe, IL: Free Press.

———(1981) "Residential mobility," pp. 147-184 in K. L. Bradbury and A. Downs (eds.) Do Housing Allowances Work? Washington, DC: The Brookings Institution.

Roth, Julius A. (1963) Timetables. Indianapolis: Bobbs-Merrill.

Rubin, Zick (1973) Liking and Loving. New York: Holt, Rinehart & Winston.

Ruch, Libby O. (1977) "A multidimensional analysis of the concept of life change." Journal of Health and Social Behavior 18: 71-83.

Ryan, William (1971) Blaming the Victim. New York: Vintage.

Sanford, J. R. A. (1975) "Tolerance of debility of elderly dependents by supporters at home: Its significance for hospital practice." British Medical Journal 3: 471-473.

Sanier, Janet S. (1976) "The community cares: Older volunteers." Social Policy (November/December): 73-80.

———and Mary L. Zander (1971) Serve: Older Volunteers in Community Service. New York: Community Service Society of New York.

Santini, Rosemary and Katherine Barrett (1983) "The tragedy of Rita Hayworth." Ladies' Home Journal 100: 84-85, 139-142.

Sauer, William J. and Rex Warland (1982) "Morale and life satisfaction," pp. 195-240 in D. J. Mangen and W. A. Peterson (eds.) Research Instruments in Social Gerontology: Clinical and Social Psychology (Volume I). Minneapolis: University of Minnesota Press.

Schar, M., L. G. Reeder, and J. M. Dirken (1973) "Stress and cardiovascular health: An international cooperative study-II. The male population of a factory in Zurich." Social Science and Medicine 7: 585-603.

Schlesinger, A. (1944) "Biography of a nation of joiners." American Historical Review 50 (October): 1-25.

Schmidt, M. G. (1981) "Personal networks: Assessment, care and repair." Journal of Gerontological Social Work 3: 65-76.

Schutz, A. (1962) Collected Papers. The Hague: Martinus Nijhoff.

Schutz, Alfred and Thomas Luckmann (1974) The Structures of the Life-World. London: Heineman.

Schwartz, Leslie H., Robert Marcus, and Robert Condon (1978) "Multidisciplinary group therapy for rheumatoid arthritis." Psychosomatics 19: 289-293.

Secord, P. and C. Backman (1974) Social Psychology. New York: McGraw-Hill.

Seelback, W. and C. Hansen (1980) "Satisfaction with family relations among the elderly." Family Relations 29: 91-99.

Seligman, M. E. (1969) "Control group and conditioning: A comment on operationism." Psychological Review 76, 5: 484-491.

Seltzer, B. and I. Sherwin (1978) "Organic brain syndrome: An empirical study and critical review." American Journal of Psychiatry 135: 13-21.

Seyle, Hans (1956) The Stress of Life. New York: McGraw-Hill.

Shanas, Ethel (1962) The Health of Older People: A Social Survey. Cambridge, MA: Harvard University Press.

——— (1979a) "Social myth as hypothesis: The case of the family relations of old people." The Gerontologist 19, 1: 3-9.

——— (1979b) "The family as a social support system in old age." The Gerontologist 19, 2: 169-174.

——— (1980) "Older people and their families: The new pioneers." Journal of Marriage and the Family 42: 9-15.

——— with the assistance of Gloria D. Heinemann (1982) National Survey of the Aged. Department of Health and Human Services, Office of Human Development Services, Administration on Aging, DHHS Publication No. (OHDS) 83-20425 (December). Washington, DC: Government Printing Office.

Shanas, Ethel and George L. Maddox (1976) "Aging, health, and the organization of health resources," pp. 592-618 in R. Binstock and E. Shanas (eds.) Handbook of Aging and the Social Sciences. New York: Van Nostrand Reinhold.

Shanas, Ethel and Gordon F. Streib (1965) Social Structure and the Family: Generational Relations. Englewood Cliffs, NJ: Prentice-Hall.

Shanas, Ethel and Marvin B. Sussman (1977) Family, Bureaucracy, and the Elderly. Durham, NC: Duke University Press.

Shanas, Ethel, P. Townsend, D. Wedderburn, H. Friis, P. Milhoj, and J. Stehouwer (1968) Old People in Three Industrial Societies. New York: Atherton; London: Routledge and Kegan Paul.

Shearn, Martin A. and Bruce Fireman (1983) "Stress management and mutual support groups in rheumatoid arthritis (RA): A controlled study." Arthritis and Rheumatism 26 (Suppl.): S9 (abstract).

Sherman, Susan (1975) "Mutual assistance and support in retirement housing." Journal of Gerontology 30: 479-483.

Shulman, Norman (1975) "Life cycle variation in patterns of close relationships." Journal of Marriage and the Family 37: 813-822.

Silver, Susan (1981) "Evaluation of a hospice program: Effects on terminally ill patients and their families." Evaluation and the Health Professions 4: 3.

Silverman, C. (1968) The Epidemiology of Depression. Baltimore, MD: Johns Hopkins.

Simmel, George (1955) "The web of group-affiliation," pp. 127-195 in K. Wolff and R. Bendix (eds.) Conflict and the Web of Group-Affiliation. New York: Free Press. (originally published in 1922)

Sluss, T. K., E. M. Gruenberg, and M. Kramer (1981) "The use of longitudinal studies in the investigation of risk factors for senile Dementia-Alzheimer type," pp. 132-154 in J. Mortimer and L. Schuman (eds.) The Epidemiology of Dementia. New York: Oxford University Press.

Small, Albion and George Vincent (1894) An Introduction to the Study of Society. New York: American Book.

Smith, K. and V. F. Bengtson (1979) "Positive consequences of institutionalization: Solidarity between elderly parents and their children." The Gerontologist 19: 438-447.

Snow, Robert and Lawrence Crapo (1982) "Emotional bondedness, subjective well-being, and health in elderly medical patients." Journal of Gerontology 37: 609-615.

Solomon, Arthur P. (1974) Housing the Urban Poor: A Critical Evaluation of Federal Housing Policy. Cambridge, MA: MIT Press.
Sommer, R. (1970) "Small group ecology in institutions for the elderly," in L.A. Pastalan and D.H. Carson (eds.) Spatial Behavior of Older People. Ann Arbor, MI: University of Michigan-Wayne State University Institute of Gerontology.
Sorokin, Pitrim A. (1954) The Ways and Power of Love. Boston: Beacon.
Spanier, G. B., R. Lewis, and C. Cole (1975) "Marital adjustment over the family life cycle: The issue of curvilinearity." Journal of Marriage and Family 37: 263-275.
Spasoff, R. A., A. S. Kraus, E. J. Beattie, D. E. Holden, J. S. Lawson, M. Rodenburg, and G. M. Woodcock (1978) "A longitudinal study of elderly residents of long-stay institutions: 1. Early response to institutional care." The Gerontologist 18, 3: 281-292.
Spitz, Renee (1945) "Hospitalism: An inquiry into the genesis of psychiatric conditions in early childhood," pp. 53-74 in R. Spitz (ed.) The Psychoanalytic Study of the Child (Vol. I). New York: International University Press.
Sporakowski, M. J., and G. Hughston (1978) "Prescriptions for happy marriage: Adjustments and satisfactions of couples married for 50 or more years." The Family Coordinator 27: 321-327.
Spreitzer, Elmer and Eldon E. Snyder (1974) "Correlates of life satisfaction among the aged." Journal of Gerontology 29: 454-458.
Stahl, Sidney M., Clarence E. Grim, Cathy Donald, and Helen Jo Neikirk (1975) "A model for the social science and medicine: The case for hypertension." Social Science and Medicine 9: 31-38.
Stahl, Sidney M., Charles R. Kelley, Peggy J. Neill, Clarence E. Grim, and Joseph J. Mamlin (1984) "Effects of home blood pressure measurement on long-term BP control." American Journal of Public Health 74: 704-709.
Starr, Jerold M. (1982-1983) "Toward a social phenomenology of aging: Studying the self process in biographical work." International Journal of Aging and Human Development 16: 255-270.
Starr, Roger (1971) "Which of the poor shall live in public housing?" Public Interest 23: 116-124.
Steele, C. Hoy (1972) American Indians and Urban Life: A Community Study. Ph.D. Dissertation, University of Kansas.
Stone, Jerome H. (1982) "The self-help movement: Forming a national organization." Generations 7: 39-40.
Strain, Laurel A. and Neena L. Chappell (1982) "Confidants: Do they make a difference in quality of life?" Research on Aging 4, 4: 479-502.
Straus, Murray A. (1969) "Social class and farm-city differences in interaction with kin in relation to societal modernization." Rural Sociology 34: 476-495.
Strauss, A. L. (1975) Chronic Illness and the Quality of Life. St. Louis: C. V. Mosby.
——— (1979) "Chronic illness," pp. 97-113 in A.L. Strauss (ed.) Where Medicine Fails. New Brunswick, NJ: Transaction.
Strauss, Anselm (1978) Negotiations. San Francisco: Jossey-Bass.
Streib, G. F. (1979) "An alternative family form for older persons: Need and social context." The Family Coordinator 27: 413-420.
——— and C. Schneider (1971) Retirement in American Society: Impact and Process. Ithaca, NY: Cornell University Press.
Stroudemire, A. and T. L. Thompson, II (1981) "Recognizing and treating dementia." Geriatrics 36: 112-120.
Struyk, Raymond J. (1980) "Housing adjustments of relocating elderly households." The Gerontologist 20: 45-54.
——— and Marc Bendick Jr. [eds.] (1981) Housing Vouchers for the Poor: Lessons from a National Experiment. Washington, DC: The Urban Institute Press.
Stryker, Sheldon and Richard T. Serpe (1982) "Commitment, identity salience, and role behavior," pp. 119-218 in W. Ickes and E. S. Knowles (eds.) Personality, Roles, and Social Behavior. New York: Springer-Verlag.

Stueve, C. Ann and Kathleen Gerson (1977) "Personal relations across the life cycle," pp. 79-98 in C. S. Fischer et al. Networks and Places: Local Relations in the Urban Setting. New York: Free Press.

Stueve, Ann (1982) "The elderly as network members." Marriage and Family Review 5: 59-87.

———and Claude Fischer (1978) "Social networks and older women." Working Paper No. 292, Institute of Urban and Regional Development, University of California, Berkeley.

Suchman, Edward A. (1965) "Stages of illness and medical care." Journal of Health and Social Behavior.

Sudnow, D. (1967) Passing On. Englewood Cliffs, NJ: Prentice-Hall.

Sussman, Marvin (1955) "Activity patterns of post-parental couples and their relationship to family continuity." Marriage and Family Living 17: 338-341.

———(1959) "The isolated nuclear family: Fact or fiction." Social Problems 6: 333-340.

———(1965) "Relationships of adult children with their parents in the United States," pp. 62-92 in E. Shanas and G. F. Streib (eds.) Social Structure and the Family: Generational Relations. Englewood Cliffs, NJ: Prentice-Hall.

———(1976) "The family life of old people," In R. H. Binstock and E. Shanas (eds.) Handbook of Aging and the Social Sciences. New York: Van Nostrand Reinhold.

———and Lee Burchinal (1962) "Kin family network: Unheralded structure in current conceptualizations of family functioning." Marriage and Family Living 24: 231-240.

Svarstad, Bonnie L. (1976) "Physcan-patient communication and patient conformity with medical advice," pp. 220-238 in D. Mechanic (ed.) The Growth of Bureaucratic Medicine. New York: John Wiley.

Szasz, T. and M. Hollender (1956) "A contribution to the philosophy of medicine: The basic models of the doctor-patient relationship." Journal of the American Medical Association 97: 585-588.

Szinovacz, M. (1980) "Family retirement: Effects on spousal roles and marital adjustment." Journal of Family Issues 1: 423-440.

Tausig, Mark (1982) "Measuring life events." Journal of Health and Social Behavior 23: 52-64.

———and Henryk M. Wisniewski (1975) "Pathology and pathogenesis of dementia," pp. 135-145 in W. S. Fields (ed.) Neurological and Sensory Disorders in the Elderly. New York: Stratton.

Terry, Robert D. (1978) "Physical changes in the aging brain," pp. 205-220 in J. A. Behnke et al. (eds.) The Biology of Aging. New York: Plenum.

Thibaut, J. and H. Kelley (1959) The Social Psychology of Groups. New York: Wiley.

Thoits, Peggy A. (1981) "Undesirable life event and psychophysiological distress: A problem of operational confounding." American Sociological Review 46: 97-109.

———(1982) "Conceptual, methodological, and theoretical problems in studying social support as a buffer against life stress." Journal of Health and Social Behavior 23: 145-159.

———(1983) "Multiple identities and psychological well-being." American Sociological Review 48, 2: 174-187.

Thomas, W. I. and Florian Znaniecki (1927) The Polish Peasant in Europe and America. Chicago: University of Chicago Press.

Tilly, Charles and C. Harold Brown (1974) "On uprooting, kinship, and the auspices of migration," pp. 108-132 in C. Tilly (ed.) An Urban World. Boston: Little, Brown.

Tobin, S. S. and M. Lieberman (1976) Last Home for the Aged. San Francisco: Jossey-Bass.

Tolsdorf, Christopher C. (1976) "Social networks, support, and coping: An exploratory study." Family Process 15: 407-417.

Tomeh, Aida (1973) "Formal voluntary organizations: Participation, correlates, and interrelationships." Sociological Inquiry 43: 89-122.

Tomlinson, B. E. (1977) "Morphological changes and dementia in old age," pp. 25-56 in W. L. Smith and M. Kinsbourne (eds.) Aging and Dementia. New York: SP Books.

———G. Blessed, and M. Roth (1968) "Observations on the brains of non-demented old people." Journal of the Neurological Sciences 7: 331-356.

———(1970) "Observations on the brains of demented old people." Journal of the Neurological Sciences 11: 205-242.

Townsend, Peter (1957) The Family Life of Old People. London: Routledge & Kegan Paul.

———(1962) The Last Refuge: A Survey of Residential Institutions and Homes for the Aged in England and Wales. London: Routledge and Kegan Paul.
———(1978) "Isolation and loneliness in the aged." Cambridge: MIT Press.
Trapmann, Jane, Eleane Eckels, and Elaine Hatfield (1982) "Intimacy in older women's lives." Gerontologist 22: 493-498.
Trapmann, J. and E. Hatfield (1981) "Love and its effect on mental and physical health," in R. Fogel et al. (eds.) Aging: Stability and Change in the Family. New York: Academic.
Treas, J. (1976) "Social class and association membership: An analysis of age-graded and nonage-graded voluntary participation." Journal of Gerontology 31: 193-203.
———(1981) "Family support systems for the aged: Some social and demographic considerations," pp. 327-351 in C. S. Kart and B. B. Manard (eds.) Aging in America. New York: Sherman Oaks Publishing.
Treas, Judith and Anke VanHilst (1976) "Marriage and remarriage rates among older Americans." The Gerontologist 16: 132-135.
Trela, James E. and David J. Jackson (1979) "Family life and community participation in old age." Research on Aging 1, 2: 233-251.
Troll, Lillian E., Sheila J. Miller, and Robert C. Atchley (1979) Families in Later Life. Belmont, CA: Wadsworth.
Turner, Ralph (1970) Family Interaction. New York: John Wiley.
Turner, Victor (1977) "Process, system and symbol: A new anthropological synthesis." Daedelus 106: 122-140.
Udelman, Harold D. and Donna Lou Udelman (1977) "Team therapy in a rheumatology unit." Psychosomatics 18: 42-44.
Uhlenberg, P. and M. Myers (1981) "Divorce and the elderly." The Gerontologist 21, 3: 276-282.
U.S. Department of Commerce (1983) "Marital status and living arrangements: March, 1982." Current Population Reports, Bureau of Census, Series P-20, No. 380.
U.S. Department of Health and Human Services (1979) Policy Issues Concerning the Elderly Minorities. Washington, DC: Government Printing Office.
———(1981) Characteristics of Nursing Home Residents, Health Status, and Care Received: National Nursing Home Survey United States, May-December 1977. Washington, DC: Author.
U.S. Department of Housing and Urban Development (1980) Office of Policy Development and Research, Division of Policy Studies, Experimental Housing Allowance Program: Conclusions, The 1980 Report. Washington, DC: Government Printing Office.
U.S. Senate (1982) Developments in Aging: 1981. Washington, DC: Government Printing Office.
Van den Heuvel, W. J. A. (1976) "The meaning of dependency," in J. M. A. Munnichs and W. J. A. Van den Heuvel (eds.) Dependency or Interdependency in Old Age. The Hague: Martinus Nijhoff.
Verbrugge, Lois (1978) "Multiplexity in adult friendships." Social Forces 57: 1286-1309.
———(1983) "A research note on adult friendship contact: A dyadic perspective." Social Forces 62 (September): 78-83.
Veterans Administration (1982) Activities of Daily Living in Veterans Administration Nursing Home Patients: A Multivariate Model. Washington, DC: A Statistical Policy and Research Services, Office of Reports and Statistics.
Vinick, Barbara (1978) "Remarriage in old age." The Family Coordinator 27, 4: 359-363.
Vinyard, D. (1983) "Public policy and institutional policies," pp. 181-199 in W. P. Browne and L. K. Olson (eds.) Aging and Public Policy. Westport, CT: Greenwood.
Walker, Kenneth N., Arlene MacBride, and Mary L. S. Vachon (1977) "Social support networks and the crisis of bereavement." Social Science and Medicine 11: 35-41.
Wallace, James (1972) "A critique of federal income tax incentives in the development and operation of subsidized rental housing." Ph.D. dissertation, Department of Urban Studies and Planning, Massachusetts Institute of Technology, Cambridge.
Waller, Willard (1937) "The rating and dating complex." The American Sociological Review 2: 727-734.

Walsh, J. and N. Kiracofe (1980) "Change in significant other relationships and life satisfaction in the aged." International Journal of Aging and Human Development 10: 273-281.

Walster, E., G. Walster, and E. Berscheid (1978) Equity: Theory and Research. Boston: Allyn & Bacon.

Walter, Adrian Ruth (1983) "When I'm sixty-four: Social ties in the housing decisions of the elderly in the housing allowance experiment." Ph.D. dissertation, Department of Urban Studies and Planning, Massachusetts Institute of Technology, Cambridge.

Wan, Thomas T. H. (1982) Stressful Life Events, Social-Support Networks, and Gerontological Health. Lexington: Lexington Books.

——— and B. Odell (1983) "Major role losses and social participation of older males." Research on Aging 5, 2: 173-196.

Wan, Thomas T. H. and William G. Weissert (1981) "Social support networks, patient status, and institutionalization." Research on Aging 3: 240-256.

Ward, Russell A. (1978) "Limitations of the family as a supportive institution in the lives of the aged." The Family Coordinator 27: 365-373.

———(1979) "The never-married in later life." Journal of Gerontology 34: 862-869.

———(1984) The Aging Experience: An Introduction to Social Gerontology. New York: Harper and Row.

———M. LaGory, S. Sherman, and D. Traynor (1981) "Neighborhood age structure and support networks." Presented to the Gerontological Society of American/Canadian Association on Gerontology, Toronto, Ontario.

Ward, Russel A., S. R. Sherman, and M. LaGory (1984) "Subjective network assessments and subjective well-being." Journal of Gerontology 39: 93-101.

Warner, W. Lloyd, and J. O. Low (1947) The Social System of the Modern Factory. New Haven, CT: Yale University Press.

Warren, Carol A. B. (1983) "The psychological meaning of mental illness in the family to husbands and to wives." Journal of Family Issues 4, 4: 533-558.

Warren, R. L. (1978) The Community In America. Chicago: Rand McNally.

Watson, W. H. and R. T. Maxwell (1977) Human Aging and Dying: A Study in Socio-cultural Gerontology. New York: St. Martin's Press.

Weicher, John C. (1973) "The rationale for government intervention in housing," in U.S. Department of Housing and Urban Development, Housing in the Seventies, Volume 1, Working Papers.

Weisberg, Sanford (1980) Applied Linear Regression. New York: John Wiley.

Weiss, R. (1973) Loneliness: The Experience of Emotional and Social Isolation. Cambridge: MIT Press.

Weissert, W. G. (1977) "Adult day care programs in the United States: Current research projects and a survey of 10 centers." Public Health Reports 92: 49-56.

Welfeld, Irving and Raymond J. Struyk (1978) Housing Options for the Elderly. Washington, DC: U.S. Department of Housing and Urban Development, Office of Policy Development and Research, Occasional Papers in Housing and Community Affairs, Volume 3.

Wellman, Barry (1981) "Applying network analysis to the study of support," pp. 171-200 in B. Gottlieb (ed.) Social Networks and Social Support. Beverly Hills, CA: Sage.

———(1982) "Studying personal communities," pp. 61-80 in P. V. Marsden and N. Lin (eds.) Social Structure and Network Analysis. Beverly Hills, CA: Sage.

Wells, Charles E. (1978) "Chronic brain disease: An overview." American Journal of Psychiatry 135: 1-12.

———(1982) "Refinements in the diagnosis of dementia." American Journal of Psychiatry 139: 621-622.

Wells, Lillian and Grant Macdonald (1981) "Interpersonal networks and post-relocation adjustment of the institutionalized elderly." Gerontologist 21: 77-183.

Wetle, T. (1983) "Ethical issues in coordinating services for frail elderly." Presented at the annual meeting of the Gerontological Society of America, San Francisco.

White, Gregory (1980) "Physical attractiveness and courtship progress." Journal of Personality and Social Psychology 39: 600-668.

References

Wieder, D. Lawrence (1974) Language and Social Reality: The Case of Telling the Convice Code. The Hague: Moton.
Wilensky, Harold (1960) "Work, careers, and social integration." International Social Science Journal 12: 543-560.
Wilkening, E. A., S. Guerrero, and S. Ginsberg (1972) "Distance and intergenerational ties of farm families." Sociological Quarterly 13: 383-396.
Willemain, Thomas R. (1980) Statistical Methods for Planners. Cambridge, MA: MIT Press.
Williams, Gerry C. (1980) "Warriors no more: A study of the American Indian elderly," pp. 101-111 in C. L. Fry (ed.) Aging in Culture and Society. New York: Praeger.
Wills, T., R. Weiss, and G. Patterson (1974) "A behavioral analysis of the determinants of marital satisfaction." Journal of Consulting and Clinical Psychology 24: 464-469.
Winch, Robert F. (1977) Familial Organization: A Quest for Determinants. New York: Free Press.
——— and Scott Greer (1968) "Urbanism, ethnicity, and extended familism." Journal of Marriage and Family 30: 40-45.
Winsborough, H. H. (1979) "Changes in the transition to adulthood," in M. W. Riley (ed.) Aging From Birth to Death. Boulder, CO: Westview.
Wolfe, Marian F., William L. Hamilton, and M. G. Trend (1977) Jacksonville: Administering A Housing Allowance Program in a Difficult Environment. Cambridge, MA: Abt Associates.
Wood, V. and J. Robertson (1978) "Friendship and kinship interaction: Differential effect on the morale of the elderly." Journal of Marriage and the Family 40: 367-375.
Wood, Vivian, Mary L. Wylie, and Bradford Sheafor (1969) "An analysis of a short self-report measure of life satisfaction: Correlation with rater judgments." Journal of Gerontology 24: 464-469.
Worthy, Morgan, Albert Gary, and Gay Kahn (1969) "Self-disclosure as an exchange process." Journal of Personality and Social Psychology 13, 1: 59-63.
Wurster, Catherine Bauer (1966) "The dreary deadlock of public housing," pp. 245-251 in W. L. C. Wheaton et al. (eds.) Urban Housing. New York: Free Press.
Wyka, Cheryl A., Paul G. Levesque, Suzanne L. Ryan, and Edward J. Mattea (1980) "Group education for the hypertensive." Cardiovascular Nursing 16: 1-5.
Yarrow, Marian Radke, Charlotte Green Schwartz, Harriet S. Murphy, and Leila Calhoun Deasy (1955) "The psychological meaning of mental illness in the family." The Journal of Social Issues 11: 12-24.
York, Alan and Bernard Lazerwitz (1983) "Religious involvement as the main gateway to voluntary association activity." Ramat-Gan, Israel: Department of Sociology, Bar-Ilan University.
York, Jonathan L. and Robert J. Caslyn (1977) "Family involvement in nursing homes." Gerontologist 17: 500-505.
Young, Michael and Peter Willmott (1957) Family and Kinship in East London. London: Routledge and Kegan Paul.
Zarit, J. and S. Zarit, S. (1982) "Measuring burden and support in families with Alzheimer's disease elders." Presented at the annual meeting of the Gerontological Society of America, Boston.
Zarit, S. H., K. E. Reever, and J. Bach-Peterson (1980) "Relatives of the impaired elderly: Correlates of feelings of burden." Gerontologist 20: 649-655.
Zuckermann, I. G. (1979) "Pathology, adversity and nursing," pp. 159-166 in A. L. Strauss (ed.) Where Medicine Fails. New Brunswick, NJ: Transaction.